DOG TRAINING
THE HOLISTIC WAY

By Gianni Valesini

A Comprehensive Holistic Guide to Dog Training and Behaviour

The method that supports the physical, emotional,
and social wellbeing of your pet

Published by New Generation Publishing in 2025

Copyright © Giovanni Valesini 2025

The author asserts the moral right under the Copyright, Designs and Patents Act 1988 to be identified as the author of this work.

All Rights reserved. No part of this publication may be reproduced, stored in a retrieval system or transmitted, in any form or by any means without the prior consent of the author, nor be otherwise circulated in any form of binding or cover other than that which it is published and without a similar condition being imposed on the subsequent purchaser.

ISBN   9781835638576 – paperback
         9781835638583 – hardback
         9781835638590 - ebook

www.newgeneration-publishing.com

New Generation Publishing

This book is dedicated to my lifelong partner, Michele, whose unwavering support has shaped every step of this journey and to Ciuffo, our faithful companion for twelve unforgettable years. More than a pet, he was our teacher, our shadow, and the silent heart of our days. Though time has moved on, his spirit still walks beside us, guiding every word, every walk, and every lesson shared in these pages.

CONTENTS

PREFACE		1
1	EVOLUTION OF THE HUMAN-DOG RELATIONSHIP	4
2	A BRIEF HISTORY OF DOG TRAINING	31
3	HOW DO DOGS LEARN	42
4	THE PREY DRIVE INSTINCT	69
5	DOG TRAINING AND BASIC COMMANDS	79
6	HOW DOGS COMMUNICATE	120
7	THE HOLISTIC APPROACH	142
8	CHOOSING YOUR LIFETIME COMPANION	173
9	FINDING THE PUPPY THAT'S RIGHT FOR YOU	192
10	THE JOURNEY BEGINS: BRINGING YOUR NEW DOG HOME	229
11	THE HOLISTIC APPROACH TO BEHAVIOURAL ISSUES AND PHOBIAS	261
REFERENCES		356
APPENDIX A		363
APPENDIX B		372
ABOUT THE AUTHOR		373

PREFACE

My lifelong passion and fascination with dogs began in my childhood years. It is a passion that has helped to shape my character and personality, as well as my professional endeavours in the fields of pet care services, dog training, and behavioural modification treatments. This long-lasting love for dogs has served as a guiding force, fuelling my desire and dedication to understand their behaviour, their needs, and most importantly, their enduring relationships with humans. Although dogs were almost certainly the first animals to enter the lives of our primitive ancestors, and to this day continue to share their evolutionary journey with modern human societies, there is still so much we do not yet know about the canine species. Various archaeological discoveries have proven that since ancient times, dogs have served as indispensable companions to humans and have played crucial roles in their lives, ranging from assisting with hunting and guarding to, more recently, providing companionship and emotional support. Thus, it is fair to say that dogs have been by our side throughout the ages. In modern societies, dogs continue to enrich our lives in countless ways, serving as beloved pets, service animals, therapy dogs, and working partners. Their presence reflects the remarkable interspecies relationship that has evolved over tens of thousands of years, an evolutionary partnership shaped by mutual benefit, social bonding, and behavioural adaptability. On a personal level, my journey of discovery into the intricacies of their minds is ongoing and, with a humble sense of gratitude, I would like to think that, given my experience, I can contribute to the canine literature with a book that offers a fresh, novel approach to dog training practices, which I refer to as the holistic approach, that will ultimately help people to communicate more effectively with their beloved pets.

I certainly owe a great deal of gratitude to dogs. As a dog parent myself, I have experienced firsthand the invaluable companionship and unwavering loyalty they offer. Professionally, having navigated through various roles within the pet care service business, first as a professional dog trainer, then as a pet behavioural consultant, and now as the director of a dog walking company, I have witnessed their remarkable capacity for unconditional love, empathy, and the therapeutic support they are capable of offering their human companions. The aim of this book is to share with as many readers as possible the profound insights, experiences, and numerous invaluable lessons they have imparted to me over the course of my professional career.

My personal journey through various dog training methods mirrors the evolution of the field itself. I am not afraid to say that I began by using the dominance-based techniques that were extremely popular when I first started in the dog training world more than 30 years ago. However, over time, as I gained more knowledge and a deeper understanding of the dog's mind, I completely abandoned the military style approach and adopted more contemporary and modern methods based primarily on the concept of operant conditioning, most notably the use of positive reinforcement. The decision to fully embrace a more holistic approach, however, reflects my recognition of the interconnectedness between the physical, mental, and emotional well-being of both dogs and humans. This new approach goes beyond mere obedience commands: it encompasses a comprehensive understanding of the canine physiology, mind, body, and spirit; recognising that a well-trained dog not only responds to our instructions but also serves as a well-balanced and contented companion who seeks guidance and companionship from his or her human partner. To truly connect with our furry friends, we must strive to comprehend their psychology. What motivates them? How do they communicate? What are their needs? By deciphering the language of dogs, we can create a training environment that is not only effective but also respectful of their natural instincts. Moreover, holistic dog training takes into consideration the overall health of our canine companions. A physically fit dog is more likely to be mentally sound. Regular exercise, a balanced diet, and frequent mental stimulation play pivotal roles in shaping a well-rounded and happy dog. Whether you are a seasoned dog owner or a first-time puppy parent, I believe that the principles and techniques outlined in this book will equip you with the knowledge and tools needed to nurture a well-mannered, happy, and contented dog.

In these pages, you will not only discover information on the practical aspects of training but also acquire deeper insights into canine instincts and behaviours. From decoding the nuances of body language to understanding the psychology underpinning certain behaviours, each chapter is carefully crafted to guide you through various aspects of dog training practices ranging from basic commands to addressing behavioural challenges. Along the way, you will find anecdotes, tips, and real-life examples that bring the training concepts to life. Above all, it is important to bear in mind that training should be an enjoyable experience for both you and your dog, and this book strives to make the learning process engaging and rewarding. As we delve into the world of dog training, we also need to remember that every dog is unique in character and personality. What works wonders for one pet may require some tweaking and adjustments for another. Embrace the journey, celebrate the victories, and learn from the challenges. This book is designed to be your companion, providing guidance, encouragement, and a wealth of knowledge to enhance your relationship with our beloved furry friends. Let the journey begin!

Baloù

CHAPTER 1

EVOLUTION OF THE HUMAN-DOG RELATIONSHIP

The ability of dogs to form deep bonds with humans dates back to ancient times, making them one of the earliest, if not the first, domesticated animals. This remarkable bond has endured over millennia and has resulted in dogs living in perfect harmony alongside human societies. Together, we have managed to spread and thrive all over our planet. But how did this relationship start and how did it develop? What were the main factors that brought together two extremely diverse species? Evidence of the presence of humans and their dogs has been found in the remotest corners of our planet, from the icy expanses of the Arctic regions to the proximity of the highest peaks and the scorching heat of desert climates, and this widespread distribution underscores the adaptability and resilience of dogs as a species, as well as their profound impact on human societies. Whilst humans played a significant role in the domestication of dogs, I believe it was dogs' remarkable adaptability, intelligence, and understanding of human behaviour that truly cemented their place within our families and most definitely within our hearts. Their social structure, which is very similar to ours, along with their innate ability to read and nurture human emotions, respond to our needs, and provide unwavering loyalty and companionship, has endeared them to us in ways that transcend the mere process of domestication. Dogs' unique capacity for empathy, companionship, and unconditional love has allowed them to become cherished members of countless households worldwide, earning them the rightful title of "man's best friend".

In evolutionary terms, we can measure the success of any given species by quantifying the number of members it has, and the evolutionary journey of the canine species has, so far, been an incredible success story. In fact, it is estimated that the global population of canine species totals nearly one billion, of which 470 million are considered domesticated dogs, whilst the remainder include other canids such as wolves, foxes, wild dogs, and coyotes. Time-wise, traces of the existence of dogs living alongside humans can be found throughout history, with evidence of relationships dating back thousands of years. Recent archaeological discoveries, such as the cave wall paintings (also known as pictographs) uncovered in France in 1994 and carbon-dated back some 32,000 years, provide us with unequivocal evidence of the close relationship between humans and dogs. The presence of dogs in our culture is vividly reflected in legends and tales passed down through generations. These stories, often steeped in mythology and folklore, highlight the deep bond between humans and their canine companions. From ancient civilisations to modern times, dogs have been depicted as loyal protectors, faithful friends, and heroic figures. For example, Cerberus with his three heads is often seen as embodying the idea of guarding the boundary between life and death, making him a key figure not only in Greek mythology but also in Dante's *Inferno*. In Norse mythology, the god Odin was accompanied by two wolves, Geri and Freki, symbolising companionship and loyalty.

The god Odin enthroned and flanked by the wolves Geri and Freki and the ravens Huginn and Muninn, as illustrated by Carl Emil Doepler (1882)

Similarly, in the epic of Gilgamesh, one of the oldest known works of literature, the goddess Ishtar is often depicted with her faithful hounds. Some of the most ancient breeds were revered in ancient cultures and were often considered divine beings. Notable examples are the Saluki who originated in the Arabian Peninsula, the Mastiff used by the Romans during their belligerent campaigns, or the human-dog like figure of the god Anubis in Egypt who, like the Chihuahua in ancient Mexico, was entrusted to guide the souls of the deceased into the afterlife. References to dogs can also be found in mythological accounts, such as the myth according to which the nose of the Afghan hound is wet because the dog used it to plugged the hole formed in Noah's Ark, or the story of the Newfoundland who continued to swim around the area where the Titanic sunk in order to find and rescue his owner.

The preserved body of Barry, the most famous Saint Bernard, is on display at the Natural History Museum of Bern in Switzerland. It is said that during his illustrious career, Barry was credited with rescuing and saving the lives of more than forty people during their perilous journey through the alpine passes.

Barry's preserved body, which is currently on display at the Natural History Museum, Bern

The famous veterinarian turned distinguished writer, Ferdinand Mery, states the following in his book *The Life, History, and Magic of the Dog*: "In the beginning God created Man, but seeing him so feeble, he gave him a Dog". These stories have transcended time, embedding the image of dogs as integral figures into human life and culture. They are not merely pets but have been revered and celebrated in various forms of art, literature, and oral traditions. This enduring presence in cultural narratives further accentuates the significant role that dogs have played in human society, shaping and being shaped by our shared history. To this day, the origins of the relationship between humans and dogs remains a subject of debate and speculation. I believe that the challenge of reaching a definitive consensus on this relationship stems from the limitations of the available evidence. Although genetic studies, cave paintings, and anthropological analyses offer valuable insights, they only provide glimpses into the distant past, regrettably leaving many questions unanswered. Unlike written records, which can be passed down through generations and are able to provide more concrete proof, the evidence surrounding the early relationship between humans and dogs is more indirect and open to interpretation. One thing is certain though, the successful story of the domestication of dogs is a testament to the ingenuity and resourcefulness of our ancestors who, through a process of mutual cooperation followed by selective breeding, have forged a partnership that has endured for thousands of years. This remarkable feat required our primate ancestors to possess keen observation skills, an enormous amount of patience, and, most importantly, a deep understanding of animal behaviour which, coincidentally, is what I refer to as the holistic approach to dog training. By selectively breeding dogs with desirable traits and behaviours, our ancestors gradually transformed wild dogs into the loyal and diverse companions we know today. This serves as a testament to the power of human-animal relationships and the enduring bond between humans and dogs, a connection we must continue to nurture and preserve for the sake of future generations. It is therefore vital that we try to understand how the human-dog relationship and the consequent process of domestication have evolved, drawing on archaeological evidence and more recent scientific research carried out over the past few decades.

As an enthusiast and admirer of the canine species, I became completely immersed in the quest to find out more about this topic when I decided to share my life with a dog back in the 1990s. In those days, we did not have access to the vast amount of information, video tutorials, online courses, and other scientific based research and studies that can now be found and are readily accessible on the internet. The only way to gain and subsequently expand our knowledge on dog training and behaviour was through the literature available in bookstores and libraries, along with the concepts passed down through generations of scientists, dog trainers, and behaviourists. This traditional approach relied heavily on the wisdom and experience of seasoned canine ethologists and experts who meticulously documented their methods and observations. Books and written manuals served as the primary sources of information, capturing the collective knowledge and techniques that have been refined over centuries. These texts were often the culmination of years of practice and study, offering valuable insights into the intricacies of canine behaviour and effective training methods. Additionally, face-to-face mentorship and apprenticeships were crucial in enabling aspiring trainers to learn the craft. The hands-on guidance provided by experts in the field not only helped refine their practical skills but also fostered a deeper, more insightful understanding of canine behaviours. Furthermore, the exchange of knowledge and information took place through professional networks, seminars, and conferences, where trainers and behaviourists could share their experiences and discuss new ideas. This collaborative environment fostered a community dedicated to improving the welfare and training of dogs, even in the absence of modern technology. In essence, the foundations of dog training behaviour management and the origin of the human-dog relationship were built on a rich tradition of knowledge sharing, written documentation, and direct mentorship, laying the groundwork for the advanced understanding from which we now benefit. These days, sharing information happens mostly on social media and a variety of online platforms, where anyone can contribute regardless of their actual experience or understanding of dog behaviour. As a result, quantity has often taken precedence over quality. With so many voices offering conflicting advice, it is easy for dog owners to feel overwhelmed and unsure as to which methods or strategies are truly effective. This flood of information, although well-meaning, has unfortunately generated more confusion than clarity when it comes to training and behavioural guidance.

    The first opportunity to expand my knowledge and learn more about the development of the human-dog relationship presented itself years ago when, during one of my first trips to London, I visited the Mammals Gallery at the Natural History Museum in South Kensington. The exhibition was so well presented that I thought I would ask one of the curators if they could tell me more about how this relationship evolved. The curator, clearly a dog lover herself, was highly knowledgeable and very eager to assist in answering my questions. She generously took her time to explain at great length that the early scientific consensus suggested that at the end of the last ice age, wolves came scavenging around human farms to feed off the rubbish and leftovers. To gain better access, only wolves with a lower fear threshold were able to approach the human settlers, and did so in a humble and docile fashion. This habit was passed down among subsequent generations of wolves, hence creating "friendlier wolves" which allowed humans to take charge of their evolution through selective breeding, choosing those with desired traits and culling those who came up short. Although the conversation I had with the curator provided me with several new insights into the evolution of the human-dog relationship, ultimately it only confirmed what was already common knowledge among the canine community, which is the popular narrative that our dogs descended from the domestication of its ancestor, the grey wolf, with whom it shares 99.7% of its genetic code.

I often find that engaging in discussions with experts in different fields can lead to a deeper understanding and appreciation of the topics I am passionate about and further fuels my desire to expand my knowledge. For example, after speaking with the curator, I learnt that early evidence of the human-dog relationship was unearthed in the ancient village of Eynan ("Ain Mallaha" in Arabic) in modern-day Israel. Eynan-Ain Mallaha is one of the largest known Natufian settlements and was occupied, according to carbon dating estimates, between 14,500 and 11,700 BP. Hence, it is often described as one of the first villages of humankind. In this location, a burial site was unearthed and one of the 12 bodies found was that of a woman with her hand resting on a puppy, dated to around 12,000 years ago. At Hayonim Terrace, a man was found interred with two small dogs, and this was dated to approximately 13,000 years ago. These remarkable discoveries provide a poignant glimpse into the interconnected lives of humans and their canine companions during the transition from hunter-gatherers to settlers.

Perhaps the most compelling evidence on which the theory of domestication through selective breeding and its effects is based is provided by the renowned "Silver Fox Experiment" (Dugatkin, 2018) which was initiated by a team of Russian geneticists led by Lyudmila Trut. This experiment, which began in the 1960s and, as far as I am aware, still continues today, was the brainchild of Dmitri Belyaev, who embarked on a groundbreaking study to observe the domestication process in real time. His primary interest lay in understanding the process whereby wolves were domesticated into dogs. However, rather than using wolves as experimental subjects, he chose to use silver foxes, which are a colour variation of the red fox (*Vulpes vulpes*). I speculate that his choice was not a random one as silver foxes were already bred in captivity for their luxurious fur, which was highly prized in the fur industry at that time. By selecting these foxes, Belyaev could study the domestication processes while potentially benefiting from the commercial value of their fur. This dual purpose might well have facilitated funding and support for his research, merging scientific curiosity with practical economic interests. Belyaev observed that a large number of domesticated animals exhibited a suite of traits not commonly found in their wild counterparts. These characteristics included floppy ears, short and curly tails, and juvenile facial and body features. He also observed reduced levels of stress hormones, mottled fur, and extended reproductive seasons. By selectively breeding foxes that displayed the least fear of humans, Belyaev and his team successfully demonstrated how the process of domestication can engender profound changes in both behaviour and physical appearance, mirroring the traits observed in domesticated dogs. Today, this phenomenon is known as the "domestication syndrome". Although Belyaev's intuition was correct, he did not offer a plausible explanation as to how this phenomenon occurred and could only speculate that the process of domestication was, in part, the result of changes in gene expression patterns, that is, when genes "turn on" and "turn off" and how much protein material they produce.

However, recent support for Belyaev's theory comes from a study by Wang et al. (2018), which examined expression patterns at the genome level in both domesticated foxes and a second line of foxes selected for aggressive behaviour. This research reported that in the very early stages of a species' development, neural crest cells migrate from the neural crest to various locations, including glands in the endocrine system, bones, fur, cartilage, the brain, and other parts of a developing embryo. Neural crest cells are a vital component of the vertebrate's embryonic development, playing a critical role in the formation of various tissues and organs – thereby making them essential for the creation of numerous critical structures and systems in the body. The neural crest cell hypothesis for domestication syndrome proposes that selecting for tame behaviour reduces the number of migrating neural crest cells. This results in a variety of changes, such as alterations in fur coloration, facial structure, cartilage strength (manifesting as floppy ears and curly tails), hormone levels, and the length of the reproductive season. These findings corroborate Belyaev's observations and further elucidate the genetic and developmental mechanisms underpinning the domestication syndrome.

The theory of domestication, as illustrated by the silver fox experiment, thus offers a compelling explanation for the origins of the human-dog relationship. However, it cannot be the sole explanation, as it presupposes that this relationship began during the transition of humans from hunter-gatherers to settlers. Such an assumption overlooks the complexity and diversity of early human societies and their interactions with canines. The domestication process likely started much earlier, with wolves and humans forming mutually beneficial relationships. Early humans could have taken advantage of wolves' hunting abilities and keen senses, while wolves benefited from the food and protection offered by human groups. Furthermore, the domestication process was likely influenced by an array of factors, including environmental conditions, human cultural practices, and the specific characteristics of local wolf populations. Different human societies might have developed unique methods and reasons for domesticating wolves, leading to a multitude of different domestication pathways. Therefore, whilst the silver fox experiment sheds light on the mechanisms of domestication and the potential for selecting tame traits, it represents just one part of a broader and more intricate story. The beginning of the human-dog relationship was probably a multifaceted process that cannot be entirely captured by a single theory or experiment.

In fact, a few years ago, during yet another of my quests to delve deeper into the evolution of the human-dog relationship as part of the research for this book, I came across an extremely fascinating online article in The World Street Journal which, in my opinion, completely revolutionised the aforementioned theory about the beginning of the relationship with our canine companions and offered a valid alternative proposition as to the process underpinning the domestication of dogs. Specifically, the article unveiled the discovery of the caves in Chauvet (in the southwestern region of France), which I mentioned previously in this chapter. These caves house representational cave paintings dating back more than 30,000 years and depict, in their 400-plus images, humans with large grazing animals and the predators who hunted them. Remarkably, from these paintings we can discern that many wolf-dog-like animals accompanied humans during the hunting of large prey. The emergence of this new archaeological evidence, which was also supported by DNA analyses, challenges previous assumptions about the timeline of the human-dog interaction. Contrary to earlier archaeological studies that pointed to a transition from hunter-gatherer societies to settled farming communities around 12,000 years ago, these latest findings suggest a much earlier onset of the human-dog partnership, one dating back approximately 32,000 years. This discovery is highly significant as it pushes the timeline for the symbiotic relationship between humans and dogs back thousands of years, revealing a deeper and more longstanding connection than was previously thought. It is believed that this relationship was not based on subservience but rather on mutual respect for the different talents of each species. The most important principle established by the new theory is that wolves did not first interact with settled, agrarian human societies 12,000 or 14,000 years ago. Instead, the 30,000-year date means they would have first encountered and made contact with roaming bands of hunter-gatherer humans. It is possible to speculate that, over time, the two species would have started cooperating because of the similarities in their social structure and the size of wolf packs and early human clans, hence the compatibility of their hunting objectives and ranges. In addition, the ability to understand each other's moods and intentions would have greatly increased the likelihood of positive interaction and cooperation towards the achievement of a common goal; namely, a successful hunting strategy. As humans transitioned from hunter-gatherers to settlers, their newly found furry companions adapted alongside them. This transition coincided with the beginning of selective breeding, which ultimately led to the formation of the diverse array of canine breeds we know today.

Ultimately, I find the beginning of the human-dog relationship an extremely fascinating topic with several plausible theories in addition to those mentioned above. We can speculate that each one of these theories serves to shed light on different aspects of this ancient bond; hence we must take them into consideration when thinking about our relationship with our own dogs. The leading theories can be summarised as follows:

1. Self-Domestication Theory

- This theory suggests that wolves domesticated themselves by scavenging around human campsites. Wolves that were less fearful and more tolerant of humans would have had better access to food scraps. Over generations, these wolves became more accustomed to the presence of humans, eventually evolving into the first domesticated dogs.

2. Mutualism Theory

- The mutualism theory hypothesises that early humans and wolves formed a symbiotic relationship. Wolves assisted humans in hunting by tracking and cornering prey, while humans shared the spoils. This cooperation would have benefited both species and fostered a close relationship that led to domestication.

3. Adoption Theory

- According to this theory, humans adopted wolf pups and raised them as pets or companions. By taking in young wolves, humans could control their environment and socialisation, gradually selecting traits that made the wolves more compatible with human society.

4. Co-Evolution Theory

- This theory suggests that humans and wolves co-evolved to become more similar in behaviour and social structure. Both species are pack animals with complex social hierarchies and cooperative hunting strategies. Over time, these similarities may have created a natural bond between the two species, leading to domestication.

5. Protection Theory

- Protection theory posits that early humans may have kept wolves around their campsites as a form of protection against other predators and human intruders. Wolves' keen senses and protective behaviour would have made them valuable guards, eventually leading to domestication as humans bred them for their guarding abilities.

6. Cultural Theory

- This theory emphasises the role of human culture and societal practices in the domestication process. In various cultures, wolves may have been revered, symbolised in religious or spiritual beliefs, and integrated into human rituals. This cultural significance could have led to the intentional domestication of wolves.

7. Environmental Pressures Theory

- Changes in the environment, such as climatic shifts or resource scarcity, could have driven humans and wolves into closer proximity and cooperation. For example, during periods of glaciation, both species might have had to adapt to harsher conditions by relying on each other for survival, leading to domestication.

8. Taming Through Selective Breeding

- Similar to the silver fox experiment, this theory suggests that humans might have intentionally selected and bred wolves with desirable traits such as tameness and sociability. Over multiple generations, this selective breeding would have produced dogs with the characteristics we associate with domesticated canines.

However, it is perhaps another piece of information I found during my research for this book that can shed light on a highly interesting and more compelling theory, which in my opinion represents the most groundbreaking discovery based on a scientific research study. Professor Wayne N. Frankel (Columbia University Medical Center) is an evolutionary geneticist and the founding editor-in-chief of PLOS Genetics, a peer-reviewed open access scientific journal established in 2005 and published by the Public Library of Science. He led the first genetic studies based on genome analysis and was one of the 30 co-authors who debunked the old wolf-dog descent theories. His research analysed the entire genomes of modern-day dog and wolf populations and revealed that modern dogs are not actually the direct descendants of the grey wolf. Instead, the two species are "Sister Taxa". This is a term used in phylogeny, the science that studies the evolutionary history and relationships of a selected group of organisms, and demonstrates how organisms have evolved and to which species they are most closely related. Simply put, our domestic dogs and the grey wolf both descended from an unknown ancestor that has since become extinct. In other words, despite belonging to the same species, dogs and wolves are more closely related to each other than other canids such as foxes, coyotes, or jackals, in the same way that humans are more closely related to gorillas than baboons. I find these new studies to be extremely important as they unequivocally challenge previous theories based on old assumptions and speculations; more importantly, they highlight vast gaps in our understanding of domestic pets. The groundbreaking discoveries and assumptions stemming from these studies compel us to acknowledge that, despite belonging to the canids family, the evolutionary paths of the grey wolf (*Canis lupus*) and the domestic dog (*Canis familiaris*) diverged significantly at some point in their history. In light of these fresh insights, it becomes imperative to reassess and update our training methods, aligning them with evolving theories that recognise the distinct evolutionary trajectories of these closely related species. Professional dog trainers and dog owners alike should embrace these new perspectives because they can enrich our approach to understanding and interacting with our canine companions at a much deeper level. Each offers a different perspective on how the human-dog relationship might have begun. I consider it most likely that a combination of these factors contributed to the domestication of dogs, reflecting the complexity and variability of early human societies and their interactions with wild animals.

It is also worth noting that over the last few decades, a large number of canine breeders have shifted away from the well-established practice of breeding dogs for their traits, skills, and ability to complete specific tasks, including breeding for longevity and inherited health attributes. I often cite a powerful example from my school days – Homer's Odyssey –where Odysseus, also known by the Latin variant Ulysses, returns home after 20 years of wandering to find that his faithful dog, Argos, is still alive. Though old, frail, and neglected, Argos recognises his master instantly, wagging his tail one last time before quietly passing away. I find this moving scene to be more than a tale of loyalty; it is a testament to the longevity and resilience of dogs in ancient times. Argos must have been well over 20 years old, a rare feat by today's standards. By contrast, it is now uncommon to find dogs that live healthy, active lives beyond 15, perhaps 16, years. This change in life expectancy in our modern dogs raises important questions about modern breeding priorities. Nowadays, dogs are often bred for their looks according to current fashion trends, the hypoallergenic quality of their coats, and their supposedly tame nature. This shift is probably not what our ancestors envisioned for the future of the species! Once again, dogs are adapting to these new requirements, often at the cost of leading unfulfilled lifestyles and being unable to perform the tasks our ancestors so painstakingly nurtured in order to create a particular set of skills peculiar to each breed. Moreover, by purchasing these puppies, we encourage the perpetuation of genetically flawed physical attributes. For example, there has been a sharp increase in hip dysplasia among Labrador retrievers, golden retrievers, and German shepherds. Most people are aware of the condition known as Brachycephalic Obstructive Airway Syndrome (BOAS) in English bulldogs, pugs, and other short-muzzled breeds, which makes breathing a constant struggle. This worrying trend calls for a more responsible approach to breeding, one that prioritises the overall health and well-being of the dogs rather than promoting its superficial traits.

As the human-dog relationship shifted from a working partnership to more of a companionship-based interaction, it became increasingly evident that humans began favouring dogs which possess human-like physical features that are perceived as less threatening and more endearing. Thus, traits such as floppy ears, short muzzles, bigger and rounder head shapes, and fluffier coats became more desirable. This shift in preference influenced breeding practices, resulting in the prominence of breeds that exhibit these characteristics. Whilst these traits may make dogs appear more approachable and cuddlier, they can also come with significant health challenges, underscoring the importance of responsible breeding practices that prioritise the well-being of the animals. This irresponsible approach disregards the importance of maintaining genetic diversity, health, and temperament, leading to an increase in dogs displaying undesirable characteristics and behavioural issues. For example, when breeders prioritise aesthetic qualities or market trends over health and temperament, it not only affects the well-being of the dogs but also places a burden on owners and society. Dogs with severe behavioural issues can pose risks to themselves and others, and genetic health problems can result in significant veterinary expenses and reduced quality of life for both the dogs and their owners. Undesirable behavioural traits such as aggression, anxiety, or excessive nervousness may become more common if proper socialisation and temperament considerations are ignored when making breeding decisions. These behaviours can be particularly problematic and dangerous, especially in larger breeds where aggression can lead to serious life-threatening injuries. Unfortunately, as a direct consequence of this practice, I have come across numerous cases of dogs affected by inherited genetic disorders, including epilepsy, heart disease, and certain types of cancer, which have become more prevalent over the past few years due to the fact that some breeders do not conduct proper genetic screenings. These conditions not only shorten the lifespans of affected dogs but also place emotional and financial strain on their owners, who must cope with the challenges of managing chronic illnesses. More importantly, there are broader societal implications. Dogs with severe behavioural issues are more likely to be surrendered to shelters, exacerbating the problem of overpopulation and increasing euthanasia rates for otherwise healthy animals. The emotional toll on families who must give up their pets due to unmanageable behaviours or costly medical issues is profound.

During the course of my career working with dogs there have been multiple cases where I witnessed the application of these debatable practices, but I can cite one recent event in which I was directly involved, which is when my brother-in-law acquired a beautiful Czechoslovakian wolf-dog on the island of Tenerife where he lives. If the theory of our domesticated dogs descending exclusively from the wild wolf is true, then it should be straightforward to domesticate a wild wolf and turn it into a loyal and trusted pet companion, like our ancestors did, but that does not seem to be the case. It is common knowledge that all dogs share 99.7% of their DNA with wolves and that interbreeding is not only possible but probably happened at some point in their evolution, as evinced by the creation of wolf-dog hybrids (such as the Czechoslovakian wolf-dog) that are extremely popular in North America and Continental Europe. Because of their strong inherent instincts, these hybrid animals can exhibit any combination of wolf or dog traits such as maturation rates (in wolves, a period ranging from 1 to 4 years, and in dogs, a period of 6 to 18 months according to breed, size, etc.) and behavioural changes during their development, which makes their behaviour more inconsistent and therefore more difficult to predict. In fact, people who own hybrids find that in most cases, their pet's care and behaviours are more challenging to manage than those of an established domesticated breed. From the hormonal changes upon reaching sexual maturity, to food guarding, house training, social interactions and territorial marking, and basic commands training, everything that is so easy to control with any domesticated dog becomes a significant challenge for the owners of hybrids. In the US every year, large numbers of hybrids and pet wolves end up in rescue centres or are euthanised simply because people cannot cope with their inherent and unpredictable nature.

In my case, when I first went to see the breeder with my brother-in-law in order to choose a female puppy, I understood and appreciated the fascination and attraction that can lead some people to choose such a breed. The puppies were so cute, but compared to an established dog breed, that was where the similarities ended. The breeders kept the new born litter in a confined pen outdoors, without giving too much thought to the overnight drop in temperature given the warm climate the island enjoys all year around. So, after our first visit, we received a phone call from the breeder telling us that one of the puppies had suddenly disappeared. I was a bit baffled, but after careful consideration I came to the conclusion that the breeding couple must have eaten one of the puppies. In fact, for a few days after our visit, the otherwise mild seasonal overnight temperature had dropped significantly below average, causing the body temperature of one of the puppies, probably the weakest, to decrease as well. The mother must have thought that the puppy was ill due to the variation in its body temperature, so instead of wasting her energy and resources on raising what she perceived to be a sick puppy, she made the difficult but necessary decision, according to her strong inherited instinct, to eliminate the unfortunate animal. The next morning the puppy had simply vanished. Nevertheless, I assisted my brother-in-law in selecting a puppy by using the Volhard Aptitude Test in combination with the Campbell Test to evaluate the behavioural tendencies and, hopefully, the predicted temperament of the remaining puppies, aiming for the best outcome for the choice we made. Needless to say, the female puppy we chose grew into a beautiful-looking wolf-dog type, with most of her behavioural traits resembling those of a wild wolf. However, issues such as jumping up, pulling on the lead, resource guarding, digging, tendency to disperse, the need for high levels of social interaction, pack-like dependency, and other traits, quite easily managed in a pet dog, presented an extremely difficult challenge.

The more I delved into the topic by analysing the results from studies on the behaviour of wild wolves conducted by prominent scientists and animal ethologists, the more convinced I became that even with all the knowledge and information at our disposal, the theory of the evolution of the human-dog relationship cannot be based solely on the domestication of what was believed until recently to be our dogs' ancestor, the grey wolf. Reports from people who chose hybrids over dogs or have welcomed puppy wolves into their homes confirm the enormous challenges presented by raising these animals. In most cases, these animals live in an environment where their social and behavioural needs are not fulfilled and that, sadly, leads to an extremely poor quality of life, with the dogs forced to be on leads, chained, or kept in crates for most of the time.

The same concerns apply to the recent trend of crossbreeding poodles with other breeds to create so-called "designer dogs", often touted for their hypoallergenic qualities. Whilst the reason for creating these mixes, such as labradoodles, goldendoodles, cockapoos, even pyrendoodles and bernedoodles, is to produce dogs that shed less hair and are suitable for allergy sufferers, this practice has introduced a host of behavioural and health issues. In some cases, owners find out too late that managing the behaviours of these mixed breeds can be extremely challenging. These issues can range from aggressiveness and an uncontrollable prey drive to excessive anxiety and poor socialisation skills. For example, the high intelligence and energy levels of poodles combined with the working instincts of breeds like the Labrador retriever or the hunting drive of the cocker spaniel can result in a dog that requires more mental and physical stimulation than the average pet owner is prepared or is able to provide. I have also noticed some episodes of aggression in poodle crossbreeds that arise from poor breeding practices, lack of socialisation, and an unpredictable mix of genetic traits. Some inherit a strong prey drive or anxiety, leading to behaviours like chasing small animals, barking excessively, or fear-based aggression. Others may struggle socially, combining the poodle's aloofness with the sociability of breeds like the Labrador, resulting in dogs that behave unpredictably in social settings.

The popularity of designer breeds has also led to irresponsible breeding, prioritising profit over health and temperament. This increases the risk of both behavioural issues and inherited health problems such as hip dysplasia, epilepsy, and skin conditions. Moreover, the misconception that all poodle mixes will be hypoallergenic or low-shedding is not always accurate. The degree to which a dog sheds and produces allergens varies greatly, even within the same litter. This can lead to disappointment and potential rehoming when a dog does not meet its owner's expectations. Although the idea of creating hypoallergenic dogs through crossbreeding is appealing, I have first-hand experience of the fact that it can sometimes lead to significant behavioural and health challenges. Potential dog parents should thoroughly research and consider the implications of acquiring such a breed, including the possible need for extensive training, socialisation, and health care. Responsible breeding practices that prioritise the health and well-being of the dogs, rather than simply catering for market demands, are crucial for the sustainable and ethical development of these mixed breeds. By adhering to these principles, we can ensure that future generations of dogs are healthy, well-adjusted, and capable of living fulfilling lives, thus honouring the careful and thoughtful breeding practices of our ancestors.

As mentioned previously, there are significant differences between our domesticated dogs and what is believed to be its ancestor, the grey wolf. I am referring specifically to those domesticated dogs that live within human families, rather than feral or stray dogs that reside in the vicinity of human settlements and rely on whatever food, shelter, and breeding opportunities they can find. We should not depend solely on the results of behavioural studies conducted on grey wolves as a point of reference for training our domestic dogs, because most studies are based on observing animals raised and kept in captivity and therefore the results cannot be considered reliable. The social structures of wolf packs and our domestic dogs are indeed extremely similar in terms of the necessity for the presence of a leading couple (the so-called Alpha male and the Omega female) who direct and manage the activity of the pack in natural every-day situations. However, when it comes to our canine companions, the notion of a human "dominant pair" leading the pack is often misapplied and inconsistent, as the designated human leaders frequently struggle to meet the social and behavioural expectations that dogs would normally associate with confident leadership. For example, when our pets reach sexual maturity, their hormonal activities will provoke a sudden change in their priorities and, depending on its inherited demeanour, a male dog will either accept his position within the hierarchy structure of the human family or challenge for leadership of the "human pack". If the human leaders are capable of consistently maintaining their status and providing the rest of the family with the basic necessities to sustain the survival of the pack and, consequently, the species, such as food, water, shelter, social interaction, and physical activity, then the dogs might accept their position in the so-called "pecking order". This acceptance can lead to a balanced relationship based on trust and a deep understanding of each other's needs. The problem of a dog not fitting into a human "pack" arises when there is a lack of consistency within the leading couple in terms of providing and managing the basic resources for the rest of the pack. This inconsistency can inadvertently manifest itself during the prolonged absence of one of the human leaders due to a business trip, a work commitment, or a vacation. Additionally, the leader's inability to effectively establish a channel of communication with the dog due to a lack of training, mental stimulation, and physical exercise can further exacerbate the challenges of managing the dog's expectations and maintaining a balanced and harmonious relationship within the pack.

Among humans, it is considered natural for the young adult to "flee the nest" at some point in their lives and find their place in society, often forming their own family ties, thereby promoting the continuation of the human species. The same happens to other species in a natural setting. Upon reaching sexual maturity at around the age of 2 years, the young, wild male wolf has the chance to "disperse" which means that he has the choice to leave the pack and find a female with whom he can reproduce and form a pack. Alternatively, the young wolf may choose to return to the original pack and fit into the hierarchical order he left behind. This dispersal behaviour allows for the natural establishment of new packs and the continuation of the species. Our domestic dogs are born with the same inherent instincts, but unlike their counterparts in the wild, they are typically bound to us for the rest of their lives, whether they choose to do so or not. As a direct consequence, they must learn to adapt to a situation that does not quite align with any of the inherent behavioural responses that might have evolved naturally. In this case, the process of domestication has indeed altered the circumstances and challenges that dogs have to face. It necessitates a level of adaptation to the human environment and lifestyle for which our pets may not be inherently prepared. Domestic dogs are required to navigate and understand a human-centred world, posing unique challenges that contrast with their natural instincts and behaviours.

Thus, the holistic model of raising a dog in the context of our modern society should focus on understanding and addressing these challenges, which is crucial for fostering an harmonious and fulfilling relationship between us humans and our canine companions. If these challenges are not addressed promptly and dealt with through an empathic holistic approach, the relationship may be plagued by various behavioural issues. These can span from separation anxiety to fear, phobias, and aggression; they can also impact the overall well-being of the dog and the harmony of the human-dog relationship. To cope with the inability to choose their own paths, dogs may, in some cases, form a pack within the pack with whom they live, according to the circumstances. A common issue I have observed in some of our domesticated pet dogs, often requiring the intervention of a professional dog trainer/behaviourist, is the tendency to form an excessive attachment to a family member of the opposite gender. For instance, a female pet may become entirely disinterested in the female companion of the male owner, displaying an absence of the interaction or bonding that might otherwise be expected. Conversely, I have treated cases where the female client found it extremely challenging to manage her overly protective and aggressive male dog, especially in the park or during walks, when her human male partner was absent. The behaviour would manifest in the dog becoming more alert and defensive, displaying excessive vocalisation, and even showing signs of aggression towards other dogs or people. This behaviour is often rooted in the dog's natural instincts and their desire to establish a hierarchical order within their perceived "pack". In a domestic setting, the family becomes the dog's pack, and the dog may feel the need to protect or assert dominance over what it sees as its territory or favoured human. There are several factors that contribute to these issues and these can be summarised thus:

- 1. Lack of Socialisation – Dogs that have not been properly socialised, especially during the early stages of their physical and mental development, may struggle to interact appropriately with people and other animals. Socialisation helps dogs learn to share their space and understand their place within the family hierarchy.

- 2. Inconsistent Training - Without consistent training and clear boundaries, dogs may become confused about their role within the family. This can result in protective or aggressive behaviours as the dog attempts to assert control in the absence of a consistent leader within the family social structure.

- 3. Reinforcement of Aggressive Behaviour – If a dog's aggressive behaviour is inadvertently reinforced, for example by giving the dog attention or comfort when it acts out, the behaviour can become more pronounced and difficult to eradicate in future stages.

- 4. Breed Traits – Some breeds have stronger protective instincts and might be more prone to displaying aggression in these situations. Understanding breed-specific tendencies can assist in managing and mitigating these behaviours.

- 5. Hormonal Influences – Un-neutered dogs in particular may exhibit more territorial and protective behaviours due to hormonal influences.

Spaying or neutering can sometimes reduce these tendencies, although I recommend first considering all other non-surgical interventions.

As you will discover in the following chapters, the holistic approach to behavioural issues can differ according to each individual case. However, the core of treatment often involves a lifestyle overhaul for both the owner and the dog, and the introduction of a consistent training regimen that combines obedience work with behavioural modification techniques. This strategy helps establish the owner as a calm, trusted guide, reducing the dog's inherent impulse to protect or control. Reinforcing calm, non-aggressive responses, alongside gradual socialisation and exposure to new environments, can improve the dog's ability to behave appropriately. In more complex cases, guidance from a professional behaviourist may be beneficial. Though challenges like over-attachment or aggression towards a family member of the opposite sex can be difficult to treat, they can be successfully addressed with patience and a consistent holistic strategy. A chapter dedicated to this will follow, offering practical solutions for these behavioural problems.

As mentioned briefly in the paragraph above, hormonal influences can significantly impact a pet's behaviour, often leading to aggressive tendencies. Whilst neutering or spaying can sometimes help mitigate these behaviours, I firmly support exhausting all other non-surgical interventions before resorting to such irreversible procedures. In my professional experience over the past 20 years, I have noticed a sharp rise in the surgical sterilisation of dogs as a routine procedure in veterinary practices. The aim has been to address not only the problem of the overpopulation of pets with unwanted puppies and the potential health risks associated with cancer of the reproductive organs, but also the prevention and treatment of numerous undesirable behaviours in our dogs. It is true that the reduction of testosterone (known as chemical castration) or the complete absence of this extremely important hormone (through the physical removal of the gonad glands) in male dogs is extremely useful in tackling some of the most common behavioural issues. However, my personal opinion is that reproductive sterilisation through castration should not be considered a routine procedure. In fact, recent research (Hart et al., 2014) clearly demonstrates a direct association between the reproductive status of dogs (whether they have been spayed or neutered) and numerous long-term health complications. Because castration and spaying involve the removal of the gonads (ovaries or testes), the end result is also the removal of the hormones they secrete. Although the primary function of these gonadal hormones is reproduction, they are also important for hormonal, musculoskeletal, and behavioural health and may also play a role in protecting dogs from cancer. A growing body of research (e.g. Hoffman, Creevy & Promislow, 2013;

Zink et al., 2014) has revealed that any surgery (gonadectomy) that removes the testicles or ovaries (gonads) of our pet dogs causes a permanent change in hormonal production that affects the natural balance of the animal in multiple ways. In the intact dog after puberty, the hypothalamus secretes gonadotropin releasing hormone (GnRH), which stimulates the anterior pituitary to release luteinising hormone (LH), which in turn stimulates the synthesis of oestrogen in females and testosterone in males. The secretion of gonadal hormones sends negative feedback to the hypothalamus and anterior pituitary to decrease the secretion of GnRH and LH, respectively. Although LH is considered a reproductive hormone, there are dozens of non-reproductive tissues in dogs that contain receptors for LH, including immune system cells such as lymphocytes. Lymphoma is a common malignant cancer in dogs involving lymphocytes, and spayed/castrated dogs are reportedly 3-4 times more likely to develop lymphoma. Because there is no negative feedback in the castrated dog, LH will remain persistently elevated at levels greater than are normally found in the body of an intact dog (up to 30 times higher) for the remainder of the animal's life.

Other studies have also shown that high levels of LH circulating in the blood of a neutered dog can interact not only with lymphocytes (a type of white blood cell) but with other numerous non-reproductive tissues, such as the thyroid gland, adrenal glands, gastrointestinal tract, and cranial cruciate ligament. For example, LH receptors are found throughout the lower urinary tract in dogs. However, spayed female dogs with urinary incontinence have significantly more LH receptors here than intact females, indicating that LH concentrations may affect these tissues. Another finding supporting this conclusion is that urinary incontinence can often be successfully treated with hormones that decrease circulating LH concentrations. Serum thyroid hormone levels are significantly lower in dogs that have been spayed or neutered. There are numerous LH receptors in the thyroid gland and these are situated near thyroid stimulating hormone (TSH) receptors. Continuous stimulation of the thyroid gland LH receptors could interfere with the normal function of neighbouring TSH receptors, disrupting thyroid gland function and contributing to hypothyroidism. Neutered dogs have more lymphocytes (specifically, T cells) with LH receptors circulating in the blood stream than intact dogs. Cells in cancerous lymph nodes can also have LH receptors. Both processes explain how LH could influence lymphocytes and play a role in the development of lymphomas.

Most worryingly, one of the side effects of physical castration in male dogs is the increased risk of inter-species aggression with other un-neutered males. In a castrated male, the greater circulation of the hormones LH and FSH, which are responsible for the control of the oestrus in females, makes him smell like a female who is about to have her period. The confused un-neutered male cannot really understand that he is in the presence of another dog of the same sex, as he becomes aroused by the scent of a "female in season" and will therefore act as if he is in the presence of one. Like most mammals, our canine companions possess an additional olfactory organ known as the vomeronasal organ (VNO), also known as Jacobson's organ. The entrance leading through the nasopalatine duct into the VNO can be found in dogs just behind the line of the upper incisors (it is that little bump you see on the palate, right behind the front upper teeth). Nestled within the nasal cavity and connected to the roof of the mouth, this remarkable organ plays a crucial role in detecting chemical signals like pheromones, substances otherwise imperceptible to the human nose. Unlike the primary olfactory system, the VNO is wired directly to the part of the brain responsible for instinctive behaviours such as mating. Through this system, dogs can determine whether another dog is available for breeding. Helping to guide reproductive behaviour, its function begins early in life. In fact, newborn puppies rely on the VNO to identify their mother among other females and to locate her milk source. Adding another layer of biological precision, puppies also have heat sensors in their noses, enabling them to detect the warmth of their mother's body, thus giving them a survival advantage in their earliest days.

Although the VNO plays a well-documented role in a dog's sensory world, its function in humans remains a topic of ongoing scientific debate. There is clear anatomical evidence to suggest that a structure resembling the VNO exists in humans, as seen through endoscopy, dissection, CT and MRI scans, and even under electron microscopes. Yet, its significance and whether it plays any active role in adult human behaviour remain uncertain. Studies have identified the VNO in roughly one-third of adults worldwide (e.g. Stoyanov et al., 2018), with a higher occurrence on the left side. It appears to be more prominent in children and has been reported in up to two-thirds of young individuals, where it is often present on both sides of the septum. Some researchers even suggest that nearly all newborns have a bilaterally visible VNO. Despite this, it is frequently overlooked in clinical examinations, possibly due to its small size and the assumption that it is vestigial, a remnant from our evolutionary past. Whether functional or not, the human VNO continues to intrigue researchers. Although mainstream science often labels it as vestigial or non-functional, I personally believe that in some individuals, this organ retains a greater degree of functionality. This could explain why certain people seem to possess an unusually heightened sense of smell or a particular sensitivity to subtle chemical cues in their environment. Just as with other sensory abilities, the function of the VNO may vary from person to person, and we may only be scratching the surface in terms of understanding its true potential.

Nevertheless, the VNO in dogs plays an important role, as it communicates directly with the pituitary gland and triggers the courting behaviour that an aroused intact male simply finds impossible to control. A full male will start sniffing and licking various areas of the neutered male, such as the tip of his penis, his anal glands, and around the ears and neck, and will unknowingly attempt to copulate with the neutered dog. Whilst many people find this behaviour rather unappealing, a dog licking the urine of another dog and mixing it with its own saliva serves an essential biological purpose as the dog can push the sample up towards the opening that leads to the VNO. This allows for a more detailed analysis of the molecules contained in the urine, particularly LH, which provides crucial information about the reproductive status of the other dog. Within the repertoire of canine body behaviours, the act of mounting other males is perceived as an act of dominance and although some neutered males may accept the status quo and react neutrally to this behaviour, others may respond differently, especially those who were neutered because of their dominant demeanour. These dogs will not remain indifferent to the attention of other intact males and will first react by giving warning signals, like avoidance body postures and, eventually, growling sounds, but when these signals do not succeed in repelling the unwanted attention from the un-neutered male, the last resort is aggression. In most cases, this marks the beginning of a vicious cycle. The dog quickly learns to recognise the confident body posture of an approaching intact male, often from a considerable distance. Anticipating conflict or discomfort, the dog begins to bark and lunge in an attempt to create space between itself and the perceived threat. The owner's response, tightening the lead and offering reassuring phrases like "it's okay" or "don't worry", inadvertently reinforces the unwanted behaviour. Instead of calming the dog, this pattern validates its emotional response and strengthens the association between the presence of certain dogs and a need to react defensively.

The implications of this cycle can be far-reaching. I have witnessed numerous cases where a dog developed serious behavioural issues, particularly aggression, after being neutered. In some instances, the change was so profound that it led to ongoing tension and stress within the household, thus the pet ownership experience had become an unpleasant liability. Sadly, when the behaviour became too overwhelming, especially in homes with elderly family members or young children, some owners felt they had no choice but to relinquish their pets to a shelter. These situations highlight just how critical it is to approach such decisions with a full understanding of the potential behavioural consequences.

I recall the case of Blue, a magnificent Great Dane I used to see from afar during my walks in Richmond Park. Blue would bark at my group of dogs as soon as he could spot us from a distance. Prevention had become his way of keeping other dogs' unwanted attention at bay: he had a deep and huge barking sound that was enough of a deterrent for any dog who intended to get close to him and sadly to his owner, who had no option but to walk him on the lead and away from other dogs. The owner had sought help from professional dog trainers whose advice was to keep him away from other dogs, hence depriving Blue of a normal and fulfilling life. One day I decided to approach Blue's owner, who is probably one of the loveliest gentleman I have ever met, and asked him if he would be happy for the two of them to join our group walks. My request was initially met with words of warning about Blue's aggressive demeanour towards other dogs, regardless of their gender, but I reassured him and explained what I thought was the probable cause of Blue's behaviour. He was baffled by the fact that unlike other trainers who recommended him to stay clear of other dogs, I asked him to join my group. It is always advisable to have in place certain safety measures in order to guarantee the wellbeing of the dogs involved, therefore at the very beginning we put a muzzle on Blue and began our scheduled walks in the beautiful open spaces of Richmond Park. Our meetings in the park had become a daily routine and we would spend hours talking about dog behaviour and the correct approach to training in order to deal with behavioural issues. Our conversations were so deep and meaningful that they served as a distraction from worrying about Blue's behaviour towards the other dogs. Because the owner was more mentally and physically relaxed, he transferred this new state of mind to Blue, who adopted a completely different demeanour during our walks. For instance, he became so much more relaxed and even started showing signs of wanting to socialise with the other dogs. Consequently, the muzzle came off and after a few weeks he finally started to play with some of the dogs during our walks. During this period of therapy, we obviously avoided the approach of any un-neutered male showing some interest in our group and, over time, Blue completely recovered and his social skills improved so much that the owner felt comfortable walking him in the local park. Unfortunately, Blue passed away following gastro occlusion, which is typical of these large breeds, but he remains in my heart to this day with fond memories of our time spent together.

 I could mention numerous other cases that I have come across over the years, but the point is that it is not the dogs' fault that they cannot cope with a situation they could never possibly encounter in nature. Their natural evolution did not account for the practice of spaying or castration which we humans so widely use on our dogs in our modern society. Therefore, I strongly believe that we ought to consider every other possible option before taking such an important and life-changing decision on behalf of our pets who, by the way, have no say in this matter. There are other ways to sterilise our pets without the negative impacts of hormone loss as a consequence of neutering and castration. Hormone-sparing sterilisation procedures are now considered a new and different approach to neutering and spaying our pets.

I consider this a more holistic solution and a valid alternative to the removal of the gonads with surgical sterilisation. Hysterectomy (also called ovary-sparing spay) involves the removal of reproductive organs from the females, leaving the hormone-producing ovaries in place, and a vasectomy for male dogs, which consists of the same procedure that is performed on human males. Although studies are yet to be conclusive as they are still underway, we should perhaps ask ourselves whether these excessive LH levels could play a role in the adverse health effects associated with the practice of castration, and whether veterinarians and dog owners ought to discuss the possibility of side effects when deciding if or when to spay/neuter a dog. Over the last few years, there has been an increase in the number of spaying procedures following a technique called laparoscopy, which involves the removal of the ovaries as opposed to the alternative technique of hysterectomy which involves the removal of all female reproductive organs. Perhaps this is the reason why we see a growing number of our pets being diagnosed with all sort of cancers.

As explained previously, the distinctions between our domesticated dogs and their relatives within the canid species are so pronounced that we cannot simply use the behaviour of the grey wolf as a model when training or caring for our pets, despite what old-fashioned theories have led us to believe. All preceding studies on wolves primarily involved observations of subjects held in captivity, often in relatively small enclosures. This contrasts sharply with our current understanding of wolf behaviour, which reveals the expansive territories a single pack can traverse. Additionally, the composition of these captive packs was typically orchestrated by the scientists conducting the study, rather than occurring organically in a natural setting. In a more natural context, the formation of a wolf pack would involve the monogamous leading pair, referred to as the Alpha male and Omega female, meeting outside of captivity. This pair would then generate the first litter and subsequently expand their pack through natural processes, potentially reaching up to 30 members. The leading pair in a wolf pack would typically care for the entire pack in a manner akin to a couple of parents nurturing their offspring. They would allow the laws of nature, honed over thousands of years of evolution, to uphold the hierarchical balance within the pack. Each member would be viewed as a valuable contributor to the survival of the species, and physical force would not be utilised to maintain hierarchical order. In the chapter dedicated to training our pets, I will emphasise the distinctions between the social structure of the wild wolf and that of our dogs. I will explore how a holistic approach can assist in better comprehending our dogs' behaviour, supporting our endeavours to establish a healthy relationship with our pets and ensuring successful results during training sessions.

In our modern society, it is essential to acknowledge that we may be inadvertently responsible for a regression rather than an evolution in our relationship with our dogs. At times in my line of work, it seems as though we are unintentionally jeopardising the magical and unbreakable bond our ancestors painstakingly nurtured and cultivated with our canine companions over centuries. In modern times, we often require our dogs to adhere to certain behavioural norms and rules that meet the expectations of our social etiquette, but which contradict the natural evolutionary and domestication processes that have taken place over thousands of years. These expectations may have been acceptable until relatively recent times, perhaps until the last century, when our lifestyles and demands were markedly different from those of our ancestors. For example, dogs are inherently social animals, yet in our modern lifestyles, we often leave them alone at home for extended periods while we attend work or other commitments. We often assume that leaving our dogs alone in backyard or indoor enclosures equipped with the latest gadgets provides them with sufficient mental stimulation and distracts them from the need for social contact, but this assumption does not hold true. In fact, from my experience caring for my clients' pets, I have found that dogs become more tired and are more mentally balanced after spending a couple of hours interacting in the company of other dogs in the park, rather than going for a stroll around the block with their owners after they come home from work. It is commonplace nowadays to routinely separate puppies from their mothers and litter mates at the extremely young age of 8 weeks and expect them to seamlessly adapt to their new families and homes and behave impeccably, often overlooking the trauma they may have experienced as a result of this early separation. Additionally, throughout history, we have selectively bred and created dog breeds with specific skills and attributes tailored for tasks such as hunting, protection, cart pulling, livestock guarding, and herding, yet in our contemporary society, we sometimes perceive these inherited skills as behavioural issues rather than recognising and appreciating them for the valuable traits they represented for our predecessors.

As we age, a large number of us, when considering the acquisition of a new puppy, are often drawn to choosing the same breed we had when we were younger and in our prime. The familiarity and fond memories associated with that breed can be comforting and nostalgic. However, it is vital to recognise that our physical abilities and energy levels may no longer match those of our younger selves. The demands of raising and caring for a young, energetic puppy, especially one from a breed known for high activity levels, can be overwhelming for someone in their later years. This mismatch between the needs of a young, active dog and the capabilities of an older owner can create challenges in providing adequate exercise, training, and socialisation, leading to frustrations and complaints about behavioural issues. We need to thoughtfully consider whether our current lifestyle, energy levels, and physical health are well-suited to the demands of the breed we are considering. Sometimes, opting for an older dog or a breed with a more relaxed temperament might be a better match, ensuring a more harmonious and fulfilling companionship in our later years. With a holistic approach in mind, we ought to consider that in a natural pack setting, older members take on the crucial and respected roles of wise leaders, mediators, or caretakers of younger members, providing the pack with guidance and stability. Their experience and knowledge are invaluable in teaching younger dogs how to navigate the complexities of social interactions, hunting, and survival. The question we should ask ourselves in this context is whether, as we grow older, we can genuinely meet the demands of a young, energetic dog. Unlike younger pack members at the peak of their physical abilities, elderly dogs in a natural setting are invaluable as teachers and mentors, but are not expected to exert the same level of physical control or energy as their younger counterparts, and rightly so. In modern societies, our role is not allowed to shift from active leadership to that of providing guidance and stability only – we are required to retain the same physical capabilities in order to control our dogs in all situations, regardless of their age.

When we consider the course that the human-dog relationship has taken over the centuries, it becomes clear that this bond has undergone significant transitions and has evolved in response to changes in communication, lifestyles, and societal norms. Originally forged in the context of survival and utility, where dogs served as hunting partners, protectors, and working animals, this relationship has gradually shifted towards one of companionship and emotional support. As society has progressed and advanced, so too has the nature of our relationship with dogs. The roles they play in our lives have adapted to fit into modern lifestyles, where they are more often seen as family members rather than mere working animals. This evolution reflects broader changes in human society, such as shifts in how we live, communicate, and structure our daily routines. Yet, this process is far from complete. As our world continues to change, the relationship between humans and dogs will continue to evolve, adapting to new technologies, living conditions, and societal expectations. The pet service industry has increasingly become a target for large corporations eager to exploit its vast potential as a business opportunity. As a result, significant investments have been made in new research aimed at understanding and catering for this market. Notably, these studies have inadvertently led to remarkable discoveries about the heightened senses of dogs and their incredible abilities. Based on this new knowledge and understanding, the human-dog relationship has evolved far beyond its original roles of hunting, protection, and guarding. Dogs are now recognised for their capacity to perform more complex and sophisticated tasks, such as detecting cancer, aiding people with disabilities, providing therapeutic support as well as identifying drugs and explosives, participating in search and rescue operations during and after calamitous events, aiding in police work, supporting fire brigade operations, serving as therapy pets, guiding blind individuals as guide dogs, and assisting handicapped or mobility-restricted individuals, among other invaluable contributions.

They also contribute to our overall health. Numerous studies (e.g. Wisdom, Saedi & Green, 2009) have demonstrated that pet owners tend to have lower blood pressure and experience faster stress reduction following stressful events. Dog owners are renowned for living longer and healthier lives, as dogs enhance our immune systems and inspire us to exercise more regularly. Moreover, they play a significant role in enhancing our mental well-being by preventing loneliness, providing invaluable support during times of bereavement, offering companionship to elderly individuals, and reducing stress levels, ultimately contributing to increased happiness. These advancements have deepened our appreciation of dogs, highlighting their remarkable adaptability and further solidifying their place in modern society as indispensable partners in nurturing health, safety, and emotional well-being.

Ultimately, I can only hope that our relationship with this remarkable species continues to evolve and thrive. That said, it is imperative that we approach this relationship with respect and openness; more importantly, we need to embrace changes in our methods of training and day-to-day management of our pet dogs. The term "holistic", which I champion in this book to describe my training approach, encapsulates the endeavour to support the physical, emotional, social, and spiritual well-being of our cherished canine companions. Moreover, it seeks to establish a relationship founded on mutual benefit and respect. Thus, it is essential that we reevaluate the significance of dogs in our lives. Like any healthy relationship, a successful and gratifying partnership with our dogs requires active participation from both parties. Without this mutual commitment, I fear our bond with dogs may falter in the foreseeable future.

Ghost

CHAPTER 2

A BRIEF HISTORY OF DOG TRAINING

The origins of dog training can be traced back to the early domestication of dogs, which, as we have seen in the previous chapter, is believed to have occurred between 15,000 to 30,000 years ago. The exact timeline is still debated among researchers, but the domestication process was likely driven by a mutually beneficial relationship between early humans and the ancestors of modern dogs. We can speculate that these early interactions laid the foundation for training, as humans began to selectively breed dogs for specific roles. Initially, obedience training and canine psychology was not especially prevalent and the only reason people would own dogs was so that they could work and perform tasks, rather than serve as pets for companionship. If we analyse the historical development of dog training as an established practice among humans, we can define several key phases that have shaped its evolution:

Ancient Times: Evidence suggests that dog training began in ancient civilisations, where dogs were used for hunting, guarding, and herding (Krause, Ganslosser & Hohlfeld, 2023). As humans transitioned from nomadic hunter-gatherers to more settled agricultural societies, dogs played a vital role in what we can only imagine was a struggle for survival. Initially, this relationship was simply based on exploiting the mutual benefits each species could offer – dogs assisted in hunting and provided protection, while humans offered food and shelter. The earliest forms of dog training likely focused only on the basic commands that strengthened dogs' natural instincts. Various archaeological discoveries reveal that in the centuries since, the bond between humans and their dogs grew stronger, probably enhanced by dog training practices and interactions between the two species. In ancient Egypt, for example, dogs were not only trained for hunting and guarding but were also revered as divinity, while in ancient Greece and Rome, they were also trained for warfare and protection. Xenophon, a Greek military leader, philosopher, and historian, wrote one of the first dog training books, describing the characteristics and traits of the hound breed and giving detailed advice on training dogs for hunting small prey.

Middle Ages: During the Middle Ages, dog training became more specialised and structured, particularly among members of the nobility.

Hunting dogs were meticulously trained to assist in the hunt, while herding dogs became indispensable to agricultural life. The foundation of obedience training was laid during this period, although it was still primarily the preserve of the elite. It was around this time that members of the nobility and the elite began to keep dogs not only for their practical roles in hunting and guarding but also as symbols of status and companionship. For example, the Great Dane, with their imposing size and regal presence, were historically used to precede the carriages of noblemen. This practice was common among European aristocrats, particularly in Germany and other parts of central Europe, where these dogs were bred to be powerful and intimidating. Due to their size, strength, and fearless nature, their primary role was to protect the carriages from threats, whether this was from wild animals or potential assailants. As they walked ahead of the carriages, their presence would serve both as a deterrent to potential threats and as a status symbol for their noble owners. This period marked a shift in the relationship between humans and dogs, as they were increasingly seen as companions and symbols of wealth and prestige. Portrait art from this era vividly reflects this change. A multitude of paintings from the Middle Ages depict noblemen, women, and royalty with their dogs, showcasing these animals as prized possessions and loyal companions. These dogs were often small, elegant breeds, chosen specifically to complement the refinement of their owners, whereas large breeds would be purposely portrayed even larger to complement the stature and grandeur of the subject. The presence of dogs in these portraits symbolised loyalty, fidelity, and the high social standing of the individuals they accompanied.

Museum Del Prado Madrid - King Charles V with a Dog 1533. Oil on canvas.

Nineteenth Century: The modern approach to dog training began to emerge in the 1800s, particularly with the rise of organised dog shows in more advanced countries and the development of specific breeds. During this period, more structured training methods also flourished, with manuals and books being published on dog training and behaviour. The standardisation of breeds coincided with a greater emphasis on training dogs to meet specific criteria for certain behaviours and performance. Unfortunately, the nineteenth century and the beginning of the

Industrial Revolution marked not only a time of significant technological and social change for humans but also a period of widespread malpractice involving dogs. As urbanisation grew and traditional forms of entertainment declined, a darker side of human society emerged, where dogs were increasingly exploited for brutal and barbaric spectacles. During this era, dog fighting became a popular, albeit illegal, form of entertainment in many industrial cities. Consequently, dogs were bred and trained specifically for aggression, often pitted against each other in gruesome battles to the death. These fights were held in underground arenas, where spectators would place bets and cheer on the violence, oblivious to the suffering inflicted on the animals.

Beyond dog fighting, dogs were also used in other inhumane blood sports such as bull-baiting and bear-baiting. In these events, dogs were set upon these larger animals, forced to attack and engage in deadly combat. In London, the notoriously famous Westminster Pit, one of the most popular venues, was located on Duck Lane, Orchard Street (now renamed St. Matthew Street). The site was a legal enterprise at the time, and its activities were openly declared. The Westminster Pit reached the highest point of popularity between 1820 and 1830, and hosted such spectacles as dog-fighting, cock-fighting, bear-baiting, badger-baiting, monkey-baiting, and rat-baiting. These cruel spectacles were considered a form of entertainment for the masses, reflecting the darker aspects of society during that time. The rise of such practices during the Industrial Revolution highlights the complex and often contradictory relationship between humans and dogs. Although dogs had long been cherished as loyal companions and valuable workers, this period saw them also being exploited for the sake of human amusement, revealing a troubling aspect of our shared history. Thankfully, over time, societal attitudes began to shift, leading to the eventual banning of these cruel practices and a renewed focus on the welfare and ethical treatment of animals.

Twentieth Century: The 1900s saw significant advancements in the development of dog training techniques, particularly with the rise of military and police dog training during the two major world wars. In 1910, Max von Stephanitz, creator of the German shepherd breed, established the first formalised dog training school in Germany, laying the groundwork for several modern training techniques. Dog training had been a matter for the military since the early days of the nineteenth century, the methodology for which was based mainly on negative reinforcement and punishment. Regrettably, whereas before the 1914-1918 conflict, dogs had long been valued for their loyalty, intelligence, and utility in various roles, the extreme conditions of the war led humans to employ some tragic and ethically questionable practices. In fact, during both world wars, dogs were subjected to various forms of exploitation and mistreatment, reflecting the desperate and often inhumane circumstances of the time.

The first documented evidence of a large-scale dog training programme for military purposes is sadly associated with the creation of Anti-Tank Dog Units in Russia in the 1930s. After the use of dogs for military purposes was approved in 1924, the Soviet army started to organise a wide-scale programme encompassing tasks such as rescue, delivery of first aid, communication, tracking mines and people, assisting in combat, transporting food, medicine and injured soldiers on sleds, and destroying enemy targets. The programme ran until 1946 and during WWII, Russian military forces devised the particularly grim tactic of training dogs, mainly German shepherds, to deliver explosive devices under the tanks of the invading German army on the Eastern front. Initially, the intention was to train dogs to leave a timer-detonated bomb under the carriage of a tank and retreat, but after several failures this routine was replaced by an impact-detonation procedure which killed the dog in the process. The idea was that the dog would run under the tank with the explosive device and then pull a leather strap to release the device which would then detonate, causing significant damage to the enemy. Unfortunately, these dogs were often unable to distinguish between friendly and enemy tanks, either because they were initially trained using a static tank which made no engine noise or because the enemy started to shoot them before they could reach the target, aa result of which the dogs would run back to their starting point only to be shot by their own army. Needless to say, the programme failed miserably (not before the German and the American Forces tried the programme for themselves) and led to the inevitable deaths of thousands of dogs (mainly German shepherds), highlighting the desperation and moral complexities of wartime strategies.

There is plenty of material available online on this subject, including a movie called *Red Dog* (2017) which is described on the Internet Movie Database (IMDb) as "An action packed and heartwarming story of the friendship formed between a tank-destroyer dog of the Red Army during WWII and a group of soldiers". It never ceases to disgust me when I think of what the human species is capable of in regard to our relationship with the rest of the Animal Kingdom, but this should be the subject of another book.

During research into the various breeds I had the pleasure of working with, I came across a fascinating story concerning a breed very close to my heart, the Leonberger. The breed was created in the 1830s by the dog enthusiast and mayor of Leonberg, a city near Stuttgart in Germany. The mayor initially crossed a Pyrenean Mountain Dog with a San Bernard and later added the Newfoundland to the line, with the first dogs registered as Leonberger dating back to 1846. During the two world wars, Leonbergers were used to pull ammunition carts, a service to the breed's country that resulted in the near-destruction of these dogs. Karl Stadelmann and Otto Josenhans are credited as the breed's saviours, bringing them back from near extinction. Thus, the ancestry of modern-day Leonbergers can be traced back to the eight dogs that survived World War II and, although still used as herding dogs in some areas, Leonbergers have made names for themselves as search-and-rescue dogs, lifeguards, therapy dogs, and outstanding pet companions.

We are all familiar with the story of the horse named Joey in Steven Spielberg's (2011) *War Horse* movie, but large dog breeds, such as the Leonberger, were also exploited for their strength during the Great Wars. These dogs were used to pull carts loaded with ammunition, supplies, and sometimes even the wounded. Their powerful build made them valuable in this role, but it also meant they were often overworked, subjected to harsh conditions, and treated as little more than tools of war. Perhaps one of the most heartbreaking aspects of this period was the fact that, in times of extreme scarcity, dogs were sometimes killed and eaten by soldiers and civilians alike. With food supplies severely limited, especially in besieged areas or during prolonged campaigns, people were driven to desperate measures to survive. These examples illustrate the often tragic and utilitarian relationship between humans and dogs during times of conflict. Whilst dogs have served nobly in various capacities during wartime, such as messengers, sentries, and search-and-rescue animals, the wars also brought out some of the worst forms of exploitation. These practices stand in stark contrast to the deep bond that has historically existed between humans and dogs, and serve as a sombre reminder of the toll exacted by war on all living beings involved. The mid-twentieth century saw the beginning of the application of behavioural science to dog training, particularly the principles of classical and operant conditioning, which I will explore in more detail in subsequent chapters. Pioneers like B.F. Skinner influenced the move towards positive reinforcement training methods, which emphasised rewarding desired behaviours rather than punishing undesired ones.

Present Day: Today, dog training and behaviourism are well-established fields, employing an extensive range of methodologies and techniques. Contemporary dogs are trained not only for basic obedience commands, socialisation, and adaptation to the complexities of modern life but also for a wide variety of other roles, including service animals for people with disabilities, therapy dogs, search and rescue dogs, and even the detection of medical conditions like cancer or diabetes. As dogs have become more integrated into human families and societies, training has focused on ensuring that dogs can live harmoniously with humans in urban environments. The training methods themselves have become highly specialised to meet the specific needs of these diverse roles. For example, positive reinforcement, where good behaviour is rewarded rather than bad behaviour punished, has gained so much popularity that it has become the dominant approach among the dog training community. This reflects a broader societal trend towards more compassionate and ethical treatment of animals, which I refer to as Holistic Dog Training.

In conclusion, we can see how the historical development of dog training truly reflects a deepening understanding of the human-dog relationship, evolving from a basic survival partnership to a complex, multifaceted practice encompassing a wide range of techniques and goals. As our understanding of canine behaviour and cognition continues to grow, so too does the sophistication of dog training practices. Within this context we must ensure that dogs can fulfil their roles in society while simultaneously being allowed to lead healthy and happy lives.

I personally experienced a similar path at the very beginning of my journey into the dog training world when I started working with a Dobermann Pinscher I acquired from a friend. My first ever dog trainer instructor was, in fact, an ex-member of the canine unit in the military and, as far as I was concerned, that was the only effective dog training method I knew I could rely on, at least until I decided to begin my personal journey of discovery and research in order to find alternatives to these traditional methods. I still feel that the journey of learning and understanding is not over, as I sincerely believe there is still so much that we do not yet know about our canine companions. In those days, the main methods used to teach the various commands to dogs were based on negative reinforcement, punishment, and other aversive techniques. The main tools used were choke chains, prong or pinch collars, and, later, shock collars; the use of treats and positive reinforcement techniques were not even contemplated. For instance, to teach the basic command "Sit", an old-fashioned trainer would pull up on a choke collar to encourage the dog to sit, and when the dog complied, the trainer would release the pressure so that the discomfort created by the choke chain would go away. Thus, dogs would obey the command not because they understood what was required of them, but simply to avoid being subjected to physical discomfort or fear. Unfortunately, in some Western and other underdeveloped countries, this traditional method of training still thrives today. Coincidentally, in these countries there are very high rates of dog bites and attacks, resulting in the death or hospitalisation of the victims due to the serious injuries sustained.

In the 1960s and 1970s, wolf biologists and ethologists conducted various studies that profoundly influenced our understanding of canine behaviour, leading to the widespread adoption of the concept of the "Alpha Dog". This idea was rooted in the belief that because dogs share 99.7% of their genetic code with wolves, they must also share the same pack mentality. The thinking was that within a wolf pack, an Alpha male and Omega female dominate the hierarchy, maintaining control through physical confrontations and strict discipline. Thus, in order for humans to successfully train their dogs, they need to assert themselves as the "Alpha" and maintain a similar dominance-based hierarchy within the household.

Like many of my generation, I was initially taught that dominance-based training methods were the key to effective dog training. These methods operated on the assumption that dogs are constantly engaged in a battle for supremacy, continually challenging their human family members for control. Thus, if humans did not establish themselves as the ultimate autocrat leaders, the dog would assume the role, leading to behavioural problems and a lack of discipline. However, as I later discovered, this understanding of canine behaviour is deeply flawed. The concept of the "Alpha Wolf" in fact originated from a 1948 publication by Rudolph Schenkel, who studied captive wolves and described a rigid dominance hierarchy in which an alpha pair rose to the top through aggressive competition, securing exclusive mating rights. This idea was later popularised by American biologist David Mech in his 1970 book *The Wolf: Ecology and Behaviour of an Endangered Species*. However, both Schenkel's and Mech's early observations were based on wolves living in artificial, captive conditions where unrelated individuals were grouped together, leading to unnatural social dynamics. Mech himself publicly corrected this misconception in 1999, stating that the alpha theory does not accurately represent wild wolf behaviour.

Subsequent research and behavioural observations of wolves living in their natural habitats, such as that shared by the International Wolf Center (https://wolf.org) and other organisations supporting the reintroduction of wolves into various ecosystems, paints a very different picture. For instance, extensive research by the International Wolf Center has revealed that wild wolf packs function more like cohesive family units than dominance-based hierarchies. In these natural settings, the so-called "Alpha" wolves are simply the breeding pair, essentially the parents, guiding and nurturing their offspring in a cooperative and stable social structure. In the wild, therefore, the role of the wolf pack leader is more akin to that of human parents, which is to guide, teach, and care for their pack members. The parent-family model better describes wolf-wolf relationships than a competitive hierarchy model. This realisation led me to question the validity of applying the "Alpha Dog" concept to domestic dogs. If the behavioural traits observed in captive wolves were grossly misrepresented and do not accurately reflect the natural behaviour of wild wolves, then we must interpret these studies with caution. The behavioural patterns of wolves in the wild cannot be directly compared to those of our domestic dogs, who have been living alongside humans for thousands of years and have developed their own unique intra-species relationships and behavioural tendencies. Domestic dogs have complex relationships with their human families that are driven by a variety of factors, including breed type and genetics, early socialisation experiences, access to resources, levels of fear, conflicts, learning experiences, behavioural issues, and underlying health conditions. Their behaviour is not governed by a simple dominance hierarchy but rather by a combination of inherited traits, environmental influences, and their interactions with humans and other animals. Understanding this complexity is essential for developing effective, humane training methods that respect the true nature of dogs and their needs as social beings.

We have to go back to ancient Greece to find one of the first laudable examples of a dog training book. This was called *Cynegeticus*, usually translated as "On Hunting" or "Hunting with Dogs", and was written by Xenophon, a Greek philosopher and military leader. This book was an eye opener for me because in its various chapters, the philosopher Xenophon describes in minute detail every aspect of the hunt, including its benefit both for dogs and humans, its preparation, its description of suitable breeds for hunting dogs: he even provides a list of suitable names for hunting dogs. Moreover, at some point in Chapter 12, he discusses the health benefits of hunting, which he says improves sight and hearing as well as longevity and, most importantly, declares that hunting is the best way of training for war. This last sentence alone provided me with an answer to the behaviour I was constantly observing in my dogs while out in the park walking with them. I am sure this happens to every dog owner on a regular basis when their pets meet other dogs in the park – after the initial ritual of meeting, the dogs start to play the chasing game. If we observe carefully the behaviours they display, we soon realise that what we are witnessing is not simply a game of run and chase but, in reality, a re-enactment of the hunting scene. The dog who runs in front keeps his tail slightly bent downwards, a posture not to be misconstrued as a display of fear but as a necessity to avoid the predator grabbing its tail and pulling it down. The dog who is chased normally follows a zig-zag pattern as it runs as a prey would to escape from the predator. Occasionally, dogs switch roles so that they can both practise the roles of prey and predator. Moreover, the hunting scene is also re-enacted in accordance with the size and number of dogs participating. If more than two dogs are involved, you will notice one dog going for the back legs or trying to grab the tail of the prey (also known as a grab bite), while another aims at the prey's throat in order to suffocate and kill the prey (kill bite). If dogs of different sizes initiate the hunting scene, then you will probably notice that the bigger dog will pretend to grab the smaller one – acting as the prey – by the neck and simulate finishing it off by shaking it, as it would do in a natural setting with an hare or rabbit.

While all of this is happening, I often hear in the background the owners of the dogs screaming in horror and fearing for the safety of their pets. In fact, I forgot to mention that some dogs will vocalise out of excitement and to attract the attention of other predators in the vicinity in order to help in the hunt. This kind of behaviour is ingrained in dogs' minds, and is the result of thousands of years of evolutionary development. Although the domesticated dog is certain that he will receive his daily portion of food regularly as part of the daily routine, he needs to re-enact the hunting scenario in case circumstances change in the future. I cannot stress enough the important role that playing, as a form of interaction, has in the everyday life of our pet companions.

Similarly, for us humans, playing sports in particular is considered an extremely healthy activity and the opportunity to express a universal language that brings together people from different cultures and backgrounds. It is an effective way to enhance social relationships and build and reinforce bonds and friendships. Sports competitions provide an opportunity for individuals to communicate and interact with each other, promoting social cohesion and building bridges for collaboration and mutual understanding. Think about the role that major sport events represent in our modern society (The Olympic Games, the Football World Cup, Motorsport, etc.) and how they have assisted people in overcoming language barriers, cultural differences, and social disparities, allowing them to express themselves in various ways. According to a report published by UNESCO (2024), sports play a vital role in promoting tolerance, mutual respect, and social cooperation. Since the 1990s, The International Olympic Academy has been at the forefront of a programme known as Sport for Development and Peace (SDP). This primarily comprises initiatives run by non-governmental organisations (NGOs) that use sport as a purposeful tool to promote social development, peace-building, and positive social relations across the globe. Among the many initiatives I can cite the following: *UNDP Match Against Poverty*, regularly played by some of the world's top footballers, raises both funds and global awareness about the urgent need to eradicate poverty; *Segundo Tempo* in Brazil encourages school attendance among disadvantaged youth by combining after-school sports activities with free meals and extended educational opportunities; and *Play International* and *Open Fun Football Schools* offer structured sports programmes in Kosovo and the Balkans, designed to bring together children from different ethnic backgrounds to promote peace and reconciliation in post-conflict societies.

Humans and dogs share the same need to practise and reinforce this behaviour. By allowing our dogs to play and interact together on a regular basis, we give them the opportunity to improve their physical fitness and their flexibility, providing them with an activity that strengthens their muscles and enhances their cardiovascular and circulatory systems, thereby promoting overall health and helping reduce chronic diseases like obesity.

In the following chapter, I delve deeper into a variety of training and behaviour modification techniques that I have found effective over the years, exploring how they can be applied to support your dog's overall wellbeing and help build a stronger, more harmonious bond between you and your companion.

Barnaby

CHAPTER 3

HOW DO DOGS LEARN

Before delving into the intricacies of how dogs learn, which is probably the fundamental reason why individuals consult dog training literature, it is crucial to make a distinction between the concept of the learning process, which naturally occurs in any animal species, and the dog training activities undertaken by the majority of dog owners in order to establish a proper channel of communication with their pets. Understanding this distinction not only clarifies the objectives of dog training but also enhances the effectiveness of the methods employed. The learning process can be described as the innate and continuous way in which a species, in this case dogs, acquires new behaviours, skills, and understandings through experiences, interactions, and observations within their environment. It is an organic mechanism that shapes a dog's behaviour over time and is heavily influenced by its genetic heritage and personal experiences. Alternatively, dog training can be described as the structured, intentional process by which a human (trainer or owner) teaches a dog specific behaviours or skills. It involves using techniques based on learning principles to guide the dog towards desired behaviours. In essence, although the terms "learning" and "training" are closely related in the context of working with dogs, they refer to very different aspects of how dogs acquire behaviours, skills, and knowledge.

Before proceeding any further, I would like to talk about one extremely important aspect of any dog's behavioural development, often overlooked or even ignored, known as Imprinting. The imprinting period occurs in puppies during the early development phase. It is without doubt the most critical stage, as it is a period when puppies are highly receptive to learning from their environment and well-disposed to forming attachments. Thus, it plays a significant role in shaping the dog's future behaviour, social skills, and relationships with humans and other animals. Understanding the imprinting period is pivotal in enabling dog owners, breeders, and trainers to make sure their puppies develop into well-adjusted, confident adults. The imprinting period typically occurs between 3 to 24 weeks of age, depending on the dog's breed and their developmental rate. This phase can be further divided into specific sub-phases, the first of which is the Neonatal Period (0 to 2-3 weeks), when puppies are blind, deaf, and unable to relieve themselves (the mother will stimulate defecation and urination by licking their intimate parts). In this phase, the puppies are still developing basic senses and are primarily influenced by their mother and littermates. The Neonatal Period is followed by the Transition Period (lasting a further 2-4 weeks). In this phase, puppies begin to open their eyes and ears, becoming more aware of their surroundings, and start actively interacting with each other and the surrounding environment. The Socialisation Period (3-12 weeks) is considered the most critical phase as this is when puppies learn to interact with humans other than the ones they already know, other animals of the same or different species (cats and other pets), and – most importantly – their environment, which could be a noisy city with its cacophony of different sounds.

I can trace the origin of most of the behavioural issues I have encountered in my experience as behavioural consultant to the lack of early exposure and socialisation of dogs, especially during the imprinting period. If we want a clear example of what kind of damage a lack of socialisation or early exposure can do to a puppy or a young dog, we need look no further than the period during the COVID-19 pandemic when there was a dramatic surge in demand for puppies. Because millions of people worldwide were suddenly spending more time at home, many turned to pets, particularly dogs, for comfort and companionship. The loneliness and uncertainty of the pandemic made the idea of having a loyal, affectionate companion even more appealing. The increased demand led to a boom in both the adoption of shelter animals and the purchase of puppies from breeders. A large number of shelters reported a significant decrease in the number of available dogs as people rushed to adopt. However, this surge also had a dark side. Some breeders, eager to meet the high demand, resorted to unethical practices, leading to concerns about puppy mills, poor breeding standards, and the welfare of both puppies and their mothers. Moreover, the prices for puppies of any breed skyrocketed to unprecedented levels. The rush to acquire puppies also had long-term consequences for the dogs. Firstly, because training and socialisation classes were disrupted during the lockdowns, it was harder if not impossible for new dog owners to provide their puppies with the necessary guidance and social experiences. Most first-time dog owners, unprepared for the responsibilities of dog ownership, struggled with training, socialisation, and behavioural issues as their puppies grew. Secondly, to make matters even worse, as lockdowns ended and life began to return to normal, some people found it difficult to balance their new routines with the needs of their dogs, inevitably leading to an increase in dogs either being returned to shelters or re-homed. Furthermore, due to social distancing measures, puppies born and raised during the pandemic often missed out on the critical learning and socialisation experiences provided by the imprinting period, which resulted in an increase in behavioural issues such as anxiety, fearfulness, and aggression.

Returning to the distinction between learning and training, we can ascertain that although learning occurs naturally through the dog's inherited genetic heritage and personal experiences, training can be considered the specific application of learning. In essence, whilst all training involves learning, not all learning occurs through formal training. Understanding this distinction enables trainers and owners to recognise how dogs acquire behaviours both inside and outside of formal training sessions. I consider this the core aspect of what I describe as the holistic training method, where effective training harnesses and incorporates the inherited natural learning processes of dogs, using them symbiotically to teach our dogs desired behaviours in a structured way. To summarise, the key differences between learning and training can be discerned as follows:

1. Intentionality:
   - Learning: Can be both intentional and unintentional. A dog learns from exposure to its environment, personal experiences, and interactions, often without the direct involvement of its human companion.
   - Training: In this case the purpose is always intentional. Training is a deliberate process guided by a human to achieve specific behavioural outcomes.

2. Structure:
   - Learning: Occurs naturally, inadvertently, and continuously, with or without a structured plan on the part of the human companion.
   - Training: A structured and planned occurrence, usually involving a set of steps or routines to teach the dog specific behaviours.

3. Control:
   - Learning: This is influenced by the dog's experiences and environment, often outside of direct human control.
   - Training: Controlled by the trainer, who uses specific methods to achieve desired behaviours.

4. Outcome:
   - Learning: When dogs learn naturally, they acquire both desired and undesired behaviours, depending on what they experience.

- Training: Aimed at producing desired behaviours, with efforts to minimise or eliminate those considered undesirable by humans.

5. Examples:
   - Learning: A dog learns to be afraid of thunderstorms after being startled by one.
   - Training: A dog is trained to remain calm during thunderstorms through desensitisation and counter-conditioning.

Recognising the distinction between the natural learning process of dogs and the structured nature of training activities is paramount for effective dog training. Whilst the learning process provides the foundation, illustrating how dogs assimilate information and behaviours, dog training activities are the tools through which humans guide and mould this process towards positive outcomes. By appreciating and integrating both aspects through a holistic approach, trainers and dog owners alike will foster an environment that not only teaches dogs to perform desired behaviours which allow them to fully enjoy life in the settings of our modern societies, but also enriches the overall well-being and intelligence of both humans and their canine companions.

As explained previously, at the very beginning of the human-dog relationship, dog training and learning were not considered a high priority. In those early days, the needs of dog owners and trainers were basic, and the expectations placed on dogs were limited to simple tasks. Dogs were primarily valued for their ability to contribute to the survival of early human communities. Their roles were simple and utilitarian, such as hunting, guarding, and helping with basic herding duties. As human societies evolved and became more complex, so too did the roles of dogs. This gradual shift eventually led to a greater emphasis on training and learning, as dogs were expected to perform more specialised tasks such as herding specific livestock, retrieving game, or serving as companions to the nobility.

Fast forward to the end of the eighteenth century and we see the early development of the practice of training dogs as we know it today. This process of understanding how behaviours are acquired and modified through interactions with the environment continued and evolved until the early twentieth century, when the term "conditioning" was coined. It was during this time that psychologists began to systematically study and describe the mechanisms by which organisms learn from their environment. The concept of conditioning marked a significant evolution in psychology, moving the field towards a more scientific understanding of behaviour. Prior to the formalisation of these concepts, explanations for behaviour were often based on more abstract or philosophical ideas. Conditioning provided a more empirical and systematic way to study how behaviours could be learnt and modified, leading to practical applications in education, therapy, animal training, and beyond. It is through the work of Ivan Pavlov, a Russian physiologist, whose research is documented in numerous influential publications, including *Conditioned Reflexes* (1927) and *Lectures on Conditioned Reflexes* (1928), that the term "classical conditioning" became prevalent and can simply be described as the process of learning by association. While studying the dog's digestive system, Pavlov discovered that every time he rang a bell (termed a Neutral Stimulus) before they were fed, the subjects would salivate (termed a Conditioned Response), which is a natural reaction. The dogs soon developed a conditioned response to the sound of the bell (Neutral Stimulus), also known as a Pavlovian Response, so that any time they heard a bell, they salivated regardless of whether they were fed.

Pavlov also found that dogs actually formed a neurological connection with the sound that preceded the food. For example, Pavlov's assistant would enter the room with food and the assistant's footsteps (Neutral Stimulus) would cause the dogs to salivate (Conditioned Response). Another example of classical conditioning is a specific ring tone on your smartphone (Neutral Stimulus) being associated with a beloved person. When you hear it, you smile because you know your girlfriend is calling, or perhaps you grunt if it is your mother-in-law calling. After a while, classical conditioning takes over. You smile whenever you hear the ring tone, even if it is from someone else's phone. That smile is your Pavlovian conditioned response. With respect to animals, classical conditioning is the process whereby an animal learns to associate a stimulus with something it had not previously been associated with. For example, if you use an electric can opener in front of a dog who has never previously eaten anything out of a can, he or she may not respond to the sound in any way. But if you begin feeding the same dog canned food, the dog will soon learn to associate the sound of the electric opener with the advent of its dinner, and will begin to display great excitement whenever the electric can opener is turned on. Classical conditioning happens everywhere, all the time, with or without our help or knowledge. Most of us have dogs that get excited when they hear the jingle of keys. A set of keys, by itself, has no special meaning for dogs. But you will find that when those keys are linked with walks, they will trigger as much excitement as the walks themselves. Thus, you will notice the same exciting response whenever dogs hear the jingle of the keys, whether you go to the park or not. Classical conditioning is one of the most powerful and unfortunately often underutilised training tools available, and the alternative holistic method I have successfully used over the past few years, together with other more traditional methods, is based on this concept. Because classical conditioning occurs naturally, it allows the dog to spontaneously change its feelings about a given stimulus and consequently change its response in a more natural and unforced manner. Thus, in classical conditioning, the stimulus comes before the behaviour so that a relationship develops between the two.

Later, in 1937, American psychologist B.F. Skinner, while studying Pavlovian responses and reflex physiology, further developed the concept of classical conditioning and created a method known as "operant conditioning" that continues to be widespread and popular among the community of dog trainers. Operant conditioning, or instrumental conditioning, is a theory of learning which posits that behaviour is influenced by its consequences. Behaviour that is reinforced (rewarded) is likely to be repeated, whilst behaviour that is punished will occur less frequently. Skinner wanted to study the way certain learnt behaviours are acquired, modified, and eliminated by consistently reinforcing and punishing that behaviour. In this context, it is important to note that in dog training, when we refer to term Reinforcement (of a behaviour), our aim is for the dog to consistently repeat the behaviour we are trying to teach (in essence, all of the basic commands). Punishment, on the other hand, is not interpreted as the action of physically punishing our dogs, but rather refers to the practice of refrain them from performing certain unwanted behaviours (jumping up, pulling on the lead, excessive barking, etc.). Additionally, in the context of training, "positive" signifies adding something to the training process, whilst "negative" means subtracting something from the training.

There are four parameters of operant conditioning, each of which is explained below:

- Positive Reinforcement – This involves adding (Positive) a desirable stimulus (e.g. offering treats or your dog's favourite toy, letting your dog play, use of verbal praise) immediately after a behaviour occurs, with the intention of increasing the likelihood of that behaviour being repeated in the future. For example, giving a treat to a dog after it sits on command.

- Negative Reinforcement – This involves removing (subtracting) an aversive stimulus immediately after a behaviour occurs, with the intention of increasing the likelihood of that behaviour being repeated in the future. This reinforcement strengthens behaviour by removing or avoiding an undesirable consequence. An example is releasing tension on a leash (the leash pressure technique) when a dog stops pulling.

- Positive Punishment – This involves adding (Positive) an aversive stimulus (e.g. smacking the dog with a newspaper, spraying with a water bottle, screaming at your dog, the pinch of a prong collar) immediately after a behaviour occurs, with the intention of decreasing the likelihood of that behaviour being repeated again in the future. The punishment weakens the behaviour by adding an unpleasant consequence.

- Negative Punishment – This involves removing (Negative) a desirable stimulus immediately after a behaviour occurs, with the intention of decreasing the likelihood of that behaviour being repeated in the future. This punishment weakens behaviour by removing a positive consequence. An example is withdrawing attention by turning around when a dog jumps up on a person, or the use of the very popular time-out method.

To summarise, actions which result in desirable consequences will typically occur more frequently and actions resulting in undesirable consequences will typically happen less frequently (or not at all). Drawing on years of experience working closely with dogs and their owners, I find positive reinforcement and classical conditioning to be the two methods that best provide dogs with a stress-free environment in which they can learn and thrive – they also reflect the statement on the cover of this book. During my research on evaluating the effects of aversive-based and reward-based training methods, I came across an intriguing free article published on the National Library of Medicine website detailing research conducted by De Castro et al. (2020). In this extensive study, the authors compared the effects of negative reinforcement on 92 dogs taken from seven training schools, three of which used positive reinforcement and four relied on negative reinforcement. Levels of cortisol, the stress hormone, were tested in the dogs' saliva, and signs of stress and anxiety, such as lip-licking, panting, avoidance motion, and yawning, as well as postures indicating anxiety and tension, were noted. The authors found that dogs primarily trained with negative reinforcement displayed more signs of stress and tension. Moreover, they exhibited higher levels of cortisol and displayed pessimistic attitudes towards cognitive bias tests in comparison to dogs trained with positive reinforcement or a mix of the two.

Before I instigate the ire of some fellow trainers and colleagues, let me clarify: I'm fully aware that the topic of positive punishment is a controversial one in the dog training world and rightly so. It's a method that sparks strong opinions, and for good reason. Within the quadrant of the Operant Conditioning techniques, the use of Positive Punishment can be part of a trainer's toolkit, but it must be used with caution, expertise, and a clear ethical framework. This section of the book is not an endorsement for the use of outdated or harsh techniques. Nor is it a call to return to dominance-based training or punitive systems that ignore the emotional well-being of dogs. Quite the opposite. This issue is not whether positive punishment works; there is no question that the aversive control of behaviour is effective. The concern is whether the use of positive punishment is ethical, especially for animals, because they cannot consent. Moreover, the line between punishment and cruelty can be easily, and sometimes unintentionally crossed. Sadly, older dog-training literature is filled with harsh methods such as scruff shakes, alpha rolls, hanging, and other punitive tactics that have thankfully fallen out of favour.

Please bear with me and allow me expand further on this controversial topic. Positive Punishment involves adding an aversive stimulus immediately after an unwanted behaviour, with the goal of reducing or eliminating that behaviour altogether. If used correctly, the behaviour decreases in frequency. For instance, if an owner wants to stop a dog from jumping on the couch, they might shake a can filled with pebbles every time the dog attempts to climb up. The sudden, unpleasant noise startles the dog and, after a few repetitions, the dog learns that the best way to avoid that sound is to stay off the couch. Research shows that learning with positive punishment can be rapid and dramatic (Domjan, 2003). However, its effectiveness depends on several key factors:

- Intensity matters: A stronger and longer-lasting aversive stimulus is more likely to suppress behaviour than a mild one, which often results in only temporary change.
- Start strong: Beginning with high-intensity punishment is more effective than starting gently and building up. Low-intensity punishment can make the animal resistant over time.
- Contingency is key: Punishment that is clearly tied to a specific behaviour is more effective than random aversive experiences.
- Timing is everything: Immediate punishment is far more effective than delayed responses.
- Consistency counts: Punishing a behaviour every time it happens works better than doing it occasionally..
- Provide alternatives: If you punish a dog for lying on the couch, make sure they have a comfy bed elsewhere. Offering a rewarding alternative boosts the effectiveness of positive punishment.

That said, there is one caveat: dogs are very clever. If they only get punished for a behaviour when you're around, they'll simply avoid the behaviour when you're present. This is known as learning to discriminate based on the presence of a specific cue or discriminative stimulus. So if your dog only hears the pebble can when you're home, expect them to enjoy the couch freely when you're not. The holistic approach in this specific case would advocate that Positive Punishment is more effective when the animal is provided with other alternative solutions or appropriate activities for obtaining the reinforcement. For instance, a dog jumps on the couch for the reinforcement of a soft place to lie down. If the dog is provided with its own comfortable resting area, punishing the dog for getting on the couch is more likely to work than if the dog has no alternative for obtaining the reinforcement. Fortunately, today's trainers are better informed, and positive punishment is now used with more care, often only when absolutely necessary. Most modern professionals follow the "least aversive alternative" principle: the mildest effective method should always be the first choice. More often than not, there are gentler, more constructive ways to teach our dogs what we want from them, methods based on cooperation, not conflict.

In its simplest form, it is now believed that the majority of natural learning occurs through a combination of classical and operant conditioning. In my experience as a professional dog trainer, I have observed that some clients find it challenging to grasp the concepts of reward and punishment and therefore struggle to implement them effectively in training. For this reason alone, I cannot stress enough the importance of the notion that in operant conditioning, the positive and negative terms have the same meaning as in a mathematical equation – we either add or subtract a pleasant or unpleasant stimulus in order to modify the behaviour. Furthermore, the term punishment is not intended to inflict pain or discomfort during the training, but to stop the undesirable behaviour from occurring in the future. Conversely, the term reinforcement is used when our objective is for the behaviour to happen again. Although the concept of operant conditioning can be confusing, it is essential to understand how it works so that we can take full advantage of it when training our dogs. Unlike classical conditioning, where the stimulus comes before the behaviour, in operant conditioning the behaviour comes before the negative or positive reinforcement. In conclusion, we simply need to remember that if we are seeking to modify a particular behaviour, we can either increase its frequency (positive reinforcement), modify it by simply ignoring it (neutral reinforcement), or decrease or eliminate its frequency (negative reinforcement).

As a species, humans use both classical and operant conditioning extensively in different contexts such as business, marketing, and workplace settings in order to change the behaviour of consumers or employees. In the field of education, these techniques are used to change the behaviour of students or children in families. Governments also apply these concepts to change the behaviour of their citizens. Operant conditioning in business involves generating behavioural responses based on rewards or negative results, with a direct relationship between the two. For example, an employee may respond to a higher number of service calls to earn a bonus. A customer might eat at a certain restaurant more often because each visit earns a discount for the next meal. More often than not, however, there is the tendency to default to the quadrant of operant conditioning that involves punishment. Take, for instance, the issue of speeding while driving. In theory, we could implement a system that monitors vehicle speeds and rewards drivers who adhere to the limit, perhaps by offering a monetary bonus or petrol voucher as a form of positive reinforcement (adding a pleasant stimulus). At first glance, such a strategy might seem too expensive or impractical… but is it really? The Dutch city of Helmond, in the province of North Brabant, has implemented a remarkably creative solution known as the "speed-meter money box." The idea was developed by a behavioural researcher at Utrecht University, who sought a way to influence driver habits through positive motivation rather than punishment. Rather than issuing fines to speeders, this initiative rewards responsible drivers. Here's how it works: each car that passes a designated section of road while respecting the 30 km/h (19 mph) speed limit adds €0.10 to a community fund, up to €0.50 per car per day. The money accumulated goes toward local projects, such as improving parks or playgrounds, thus creating a direct link between individual behaviour and communal benefit. In one three-week trial, the initiative successfully reached its target of €500, which was then used to upgrade a nearby playing field. The device is mobile, fully customisable, and has been used across North Brabant throughout 2018 and 2019. Each municipality selects the project and fundraising target, effectively transforming road safety into a cooperative community effort.

Instead, the more common approach is to use positive punishment, that is, adding an aversive stimulus such as a fine or penalty points to discourage speeding. The problem with this method is that the behaviour often only changes in the presence of the punishment. Most drivers are conditioned to slow down only when they see a speed camera and then resume speeding once they've passed it. The behaviour is not truly modified; rather it is temporarily suppressed. The same principle applies to dog training. When behavioural modification relies solely on punishment, results are often superficial and short-lived. The dog may comply out of fear or avoidance when the punishing stimulus is present but reverts to the unwanted behaviour once that threat is removed. This creates a dynamic based on fear and submission rather than learning and understanding. Over time, it leads to inconsistent responses, heightened stress, and ultimately, a failure to achieve meaningful or lasting behavioural change.

When choosing a method of training using the holistic approach, you should begin by getting to know your dog's unique personality and communication style. You will need to observe and study your dog's body language, the use of vocalisations, and other signals (position of the ears, movement of the tail etc) which, when combined, provide a valuable insights into their emotions and needs. This is crucial for establishing an effective training plan and for building a strong bond. This new approach will help you better understand your dog's likes, dislikes, and individual quirks, enabling you to adapt your training sessions accordingly. Identifying your dog's personality traits and preferences will allow you to tailor your training methods to their individual needs. Some dogs may be more assertive and confident and you might choose to include one or more parameters of operant conditioning. Conversely, other dogs may be timid or shy, so you will want to opt for the gentler classical conditioning method. Recognising these traits allows you to adjust your training techniques so that they are appropriate and effective for your dog's personality, especially if you seek the help and advice of a professional dog trainer. I often hear negative or neutral feedback from clients after they have worked with professional dog trainers who have used or recommended a training method that did not match the personality of the client, the dog, or both. This mismatch can lead to unsuccessful experiences, leaving some clients hesitant to seek help elsewhere. Currently, there are a wide variety of dog training methods available, and each professional dog trainer employs one of these training models or a combination of several. Some of the more popular ones are detailed below:

- Balanced dog trainers who utilise all four quadrants of operant conditioning to train dogs and resolve behavioural issues. These trainers use a combination of primary reinforcers (typically treats or toys), secondary reinforcers (such as clickers or whistles), training collars (remote collars and prong collars), combined with systematic desensitisation and socialisation.

- Purely positive dog trainers nowadays are highly popular. Notable figures such as Karen Pryor, Jean Donaldson, and Ian Dunbar lead the way in this field. These trainers exclusively use positive reinforcement to train dogs and address behavioural issues. Their methods focus on rewarding desired behaviours to encourage their repetition, while minimising the use of aversive techniques.

- Dominance or "pack leader" trainers subscribe to the theory that dogs are similar to their wolf ancestors and need to be treated accordingly, often advocating a "strong pack leader" approach. However, these trainers often fail to recognise that our domestic dogs have not evolved from wolves (a theory that is still much debated, as discussed in other chapters of this book). The hierarchy and social dynamics observed in stray or feral dogs are distinct from the intricate social structure of wolf packs. Therefore, applying wolf pack dynamics directly to domestic dog training can be misguided and may not effectively address the complexities of canine behaviour in a modern context.

- "Behaviour Adjustment Training" (BAT) is a force-free method that relies on systematic desensitisation and careful observation of your dog's body language and reactions. The goal is to avoid overwhelming your dog or pushing them beyond their threshold. BAT utilises negative reinforcement, which involves removing or avoiding aversive stimuli, and sometimes incorporates clicker training to mark desirable behaviours. This approach emphasises empowering dogs to make choices and learn appropriate behaviours in various situations without the use of force or coercion.

- Science-based training, akin to a more balanced dog training method, aims to comprehend the interconnection among all four quadrants of operant conditioning, along with classical conditioning, sensitisation, and desensitisation versus flooding (prolonged exposure to a stimulus until the dog eventually stops reacting), and the alteration of psychological associations in dog training and their interaction with the canine psyche. This approach represents a relatively new school of thought that is continually evolving as scientific understanding expands through ongoing research projects and experiments.

- Mirror training, also known as "do as I do" training, involves a handler attempting to get their dog to mimic or mirror their actions or those of an already trained dog. Dogs are highly adept social learners, and whilst mirror training can be effective, it often works best when practised with others of the same species.

Let us consider for a moment how complex the processes of learning and training must be for dogs when they are placed in our households, an environment that is completely alien compared to the habitat they would find in a natural context. In nature, the learning process for dogs involves adapting to their environment and responding to stimuli based on both their genetically wired instincts and their personal experiences. These behaviours are often preprogrammed and shaped by evolutionary traits passed down through generations. However, when we ask dogs to perform specific tasks or follow commands that may not come naturally, we are challenging them to go beyond their instincts and learn new, sometimes complex, behaviours.

An apt analogy for the challenges humans face when learning to communicate with dogs can be drawn from our experiences when holidaying or living in a foreign country. Imagine moving to a new country where the language, customs, and social norms are entirely different from what you are used to. Even if you spend years in this new environment, as in the case of many ex-pats living abroad, the process of fully embracing and adapting to the new culture can be incredibly challenging. In such situations, people often tend to gravitate towards others who share their native language and culture. This provides a sense of comfort and familiarity in an otherwise foreign setting. Thus, despite being surrounded by a different culture and having ample opportunity to learn and integrate, the pull towards what is familiar can often lead to a kind of cultural insulation, where people find it difficult to fully immerse themselves in the new environment. Similarly, when we train dogs, we are essentially asking them to learn a new "language" and adapt to a different way of interacting with their environment, one that is often at odds with their natural instincts. It is as challenging for dogs to adapt to our human world, where expectations and behaviours can be vastly different from what their instincts dictate, as it is for us to fully integrate into a foreign culture. Moreover, just as humans may stick to familiar circles when abroad, dogs often rely on their ingrained behaviours and instincts, making it difficult for them to learn new commands or adapt to new environments.

This is precisely the reason why I always advise against acquiring puppies from the same litter. Whilst it may seem comforting and convenient to bring home two siblings, the reality is that these puppies will naturally gravitate towards each other, preferring the familiar and instinctual communication they share. In such cases, the puppies often focus more on each other than on learning the new, more complex language that humans use to communicate. Therefore, for a holistic approach to dog training to be effective, patience, empathy, and an understanding of the dog's natural inclinations are required, much like how one would need to approach learning a new culture with an open mind and willingness to adapt. In both cases, the key to success lies in a gradual, respectful approach to learning and integration, acknowledging the difficulties and working through them with understanding and perseverance.

Furthermore, training our dog the holistic way is not simply about issuing commands; it is about understanding canine behaviour, recognising their signals, and communicating in a way that makes sense to them. This task requires humans to develop a new, shared language that bridges the communication gap between species. Before acquiring a new puppy or dog, it is essential to take deliberate steps to ensure you and your new companion can enjoy a fulfilling and mutually beneficial relationship. Dog ownership should be a positive and enriching experience for both you and the dog, and proper preparation is key to achieving this goal. In essence, the holistic approach I promote with this book aims to encourage people to take simple but significant steps towards understanding the way dogs think and interact with other dogs and other humans, so that they are better prepared to be an integral part of our lives. The steps required to achieve our goals are not difficult to grasp, everyone has the capability and common sense to develop an effective way to communicate with their pets, but I would say that the three key points to take into consideration are as follows:

- Learn Canine Psychology: Understanding how dogs think and learn is crucial. This knowledge helps us create training methods that align with a dog's natural instincts and cognitive processes. Some of the basic concepts of canine psychology are included in this book, but with just a modest investment of your time, you will have the opportunity to expand on these ideas and deepen your knowledge, laying the groundwork for a more meaningful and informed relationship with your companion.

- Develop Clear Communication: Dogs do not understand human language as we do (unless a relation word-consequence is created): for them, our spoken words are a cacophony of sounds. They mostly rely on body language, tone, and consistency. Thus, humans must learn to use clear, consistent signals that dogs can easily interpret and relate to.

- Patience and Adaptation: Just as dogs must adapt to our expectations, we must adapt our training methods to suit the individual needs of each dog. Patience and flexibility are key, as what works for one dog may not work for another. No one knows your dog better than you do!

Although classical and operant conditioning are the cornerstones of most modern training methodologies, they do not encompass the full range of learning mechanisms available to our canine companions. Understanding the diverse ways in which dogs absorb, process, and apply information is essential when adopting a holistic approach to behaviour modification and training. Recognising these learning pathways not only enhances our effectiveness as trainers and caregivers but also deepens our empathy for the dogs in our care.

Amongst a variety of other learning mechanisms that our dogs have access and that are worth exploring, I can mention:

Habituation, which is one of the most fundamental ways dogs learn to navigate their environment. When a stimulus is perceived as neutral or non-threatening, the dog gradually learns to ignore it. A classic example is the puppy that initially reacts to the sound of a vacuum cleaner but, over time, learns that it poses no threat and no longer pays attention to it. This process is crucial for reducing unnecessary stress responses to everyday stimuli.

By contrast, Sensitisation occurs when a dog becomes more reactive to a stimulus over time, particularly when the stimulus is associated with discomfort or fear. For instance, if a dog feels anxious or frightened every time they hear fireworks, they may become increasingly sensitive to similar loud sounds up to a point where they develop a heighten and prolonged fear or phobia.

Social Learning, or observational learning, plays a significant role, particularly in puppies. Dogs can and do learn by watching others. A young dog might observe an older, more experienced dog performing certain tasks or reacting to specific triggers and then mimic the behaviour. Likewise, they watch and learn from humans simply by picking up on subtle cues, daily routines, and even emotional states.

Imprinting, as mentioned previously, takes place during a sensitive period in early development. It is a process that allows puppies to form strong, lasting associations with their caregivers, environments, and other animals. The quality of experiences during this critical window can significantly influence their future behaviour and social interactions.

Latent Learning refers to information that is acquired without immediate application but becomes relevant later. A dog may explore and observe an environment without any reinforcement, yet recall important details, like the location of food or an exit route, when needed.

Occasionally, we encounter moments of Insight Learning, where dogs appear to solve problems without relying on trial and error. This could be as simple as figuring out how to move an obstacle to retrieve a toy or opening a door latch after watching a person do it once.

Finally, there is a process known as Experiential Learning, which is learning through doing. This form of learning is often messy and involves mistakes, but it allows dogs to learn from their own outcomes – an essential element of behavioural development. The following table summarises the different types of learning that take place in dogs.

Learning Type	Description	Example
Classical Conditioning	Associating a neutral stimulus with a significant one.	A dog salivates when hearing a food bowl clink.
Operant Conditioning	Learning through consequences: reinforcement or punishment.	Sitting = treat (positive reinforcement). Jumping = no attention (negative punishment).
Social Learning	Learning by observing others (humans or dogs).	A puppy learns to use the dog door by watching an older dog.
Habituation	Becoming used to a stimulus after repeated exposure.	A dog no longer reacts to vacuum noise after hearing it frequently.
Sensitisation	Increased reactivity to a repeated stimulus.	A dog becomes more reactive to thunder after repeated storms.
Imprinting (in puppies)	Rapid learning during a critical early-life window, usually irreversible.	A puppy raised among cats may view them as social companions.
Latent Learning	Learning that occurs without obvious reinforcement and surfaces later.	A dog suddenly recalls a path through a park it previously explored.
Insight Learning	Problem-solving through understanding, not trial and error.	A dog pushes a box to reach a treat on a high counter.

Summary of various types of learning

By acknowledging that dogs learn in multiple ways, just like humans, we have the opportunity to expand our toolkit as trainers, behaviourists, and companions. I truly believe that a well-rounded training approach does not rely solely on repetition and reinforcement of the commands, but instead embraces all the avenues through which dogs naturally learn and adapt. In line with my personal beliefs, I strive to encompass the widest possible range of learning mechanisms during my training sessions, a philosophy I refer to as *the holistic way*. This approach goes beyond the traditional framework of classical and operant conditioning. It acknowledges that dogs, like humans, are capable of learning through a variety of channels such as observation, imitation, emotional association, social referencing, and environmental feedback. The holistic way means viewing the dog not just as a subject to be trained but as a thinking, feeling individual whose behaviours are shaped by genetics, past experiences, social context, and current emotional state. By recognising the full spectrum of how dogs learn about and process the world around them, we are able to tailor our methods more effectively, building a line of communication based on mutual understanding rather than asserting control. Ultimately, this approach allows for deeper connection, better results, and a more harmonious relationship between human and dog. It is not just about obedience; it is about trust, respect, and cooperation, and that is the foundation of the holistic way.

Aside from the natural learning that occurs through daily life, training regimens, and social interaction with other dogs, humans, and the environment, there are other specific and structured ways in which we can support a dog's development and learning experience, especially when we need to gently reshape certain behaviours. It is a fact that dogs are constantly learning, whether this is from the outcomes of their actions, the energy of their environment or new surroundings, or the way we respond to them. Have you ever noticed, for example, that when you take your dog somewhere unfamiliar, such as a new park, a friend's house, or even just a different walking route, they tend to stay closer to you than usual? Even something as simple as taking your dog to a new place, where they instinctively stay close to you, can become a learning opportunity. This is not simply about physical proximity; it is about trust. In moments of uncertainty, dogs instinctively seek the comfort and safety of their trusted human. You are their anchor, their point of reference in an unfamiliar world. When approached mindfully, these everyday experiences become powerful tools for behavioural change. By gently redirecting a dog's focus towards something new or unfamiliar, you open the door to change, not only in your dog's behaviour but also in its mindset. This shift in attention creates an opportunity for learning, for building confidence, and for rewriting old associations.

This is where behavioural modification comes in, using a variety of techniques that work *with* the dog's natural learning processes rather than against them. These methods do not rely on dominance or harsh corrections; instead, they are rooted in a holistic understanding of how dogs think, feel, and respond to their environment. Through patience, timing, and empathy, we can guide our dogs towards more balanced behaviours while nurturing the emotional connection we share with them. Some of the most widely used techniques include Habituation (helping a dog get used to something through repeated, neutral exposure), Extinction (removing whatever reward is keeping an unwanted behaviour alive), Desensitisation (gradually reducing a dog's sensitivity to triggers), Counter-conditioning (replacing negative associations with positive ones), Response Substitution (teaching a more appropriate behaviour in place of an undesirable one), and Shaping (reinforcing small steps toward a desired goal). In addition, there exists a technique known as Flooding, a method that involves overwhelming a dog with a feared stimulus (overwhelming traffic noise for example) in the hope that the reaction will eventually fade away spontaneously. However, this technique is rarely suitable as it can often heighten the dog's anxiety and damage the trust in its human companion. Most behavioural modification techniques are not complicated, they are grounded in common sense, empathy, and an understanding of how dogs learn. In fact, many can be used proactively to prevent issues before they take root. What they do require, however, is consistency, patience, and a willingness to invest time into building that bond. In the next section, I take a closer look at some of the core principles underpinning these techniques so that you can begin applying them with clarity and confidence in everyday life.

HABITUATION

As I previously stated, Habituation is one of the simplest and most natural ways dogs learn. It is the process by which a dog gradually stops reacting to something that is repeated over time, especially when it turns out to be harmless. There is no need for treats or praise, just repeated exposure in a safe and calm context will suffice.

For example, imagine a dog who hears the sound of a vacuum cleaner for the first time; it might bark, run away, or become tense. But if the sound is repeated regularly, nothing bad happens, and, perhaps most importantly, if the dog is not given extra attention or fussed over when reacting, he or she will likely stop reacting to it. This is the process of habituation at work. Over time, the stimulus loses its impact simply because it becomes part of the background – ordinary, unthreatening, and not worth reacting to. By not reinforcing the dog's behaviour with attention, or even well-meaning concern, we allow the dog to process and adapt on their own terms, building quiet confidence through repetition and neutrality.

It is important to be aware, however, that habituation is highly specific. A dog that learns to ignore the vacuum cleaner may still react to the blender or a new alarm sound. Imagine you move to a new home where airplanes occasionally fly overhead. In this case, because the sound repeats continuously without any negative consequences, the dog begins to relax and eventually learns to ignore it altogether. However, because the habituation process is specific to a particular place, a dog that gets used to the sound of airplanes in your new home will not necessarily continue to be unbothered if you take them to a hotel near an airport while travelling on holiday. On a positive note, because the dog has already undergone a similar learning experience, the adjustment period tends to be much shorter. New acoustics, vibrations, or the intensity of the noise might trigger a reaction, and here is the key point – if a stimulus is too intense or frightening, like an encounter with threatening dog, loud fireworks, or something that feels dangerous, habituation might not happen. In fact, the fear could worsen and even turn into phobia. Scientists believe that dogs are biologically wired not to become indifferent to potential threats; this is part of their survival instinct. Thus, although habituation can be a powerful tool, it has its limits and must be applied thoughtfully. This illustrates how dogs who are given the chance to fully share life's experiences by joining their owner in a variety of situations and environments can, over time, become more adaptable and resilient. When this exposure is paired with consistency, a sense of safety, and patient guidance, it serves to shape a well-rounded companion who learns to navigate the human world with confidence and trust. I now explain how we can use the process of habituation to help a dog with, for example, traffic reactivity by breaking down the technique step-by-step. This type of slow, steady exposure can be adapted to most other situations, such as dogs nervous around bicycles, vacuum cleaners, or unfamiliar sounds at home. Traffic reactivity is a common issue, especially in dogs who have not grown up around busy roads or had a negative experience with vehicles. Habituation can help, but it must be applied carefully and gradually. I can mention the case of Grady, the most beautiful and gentle golden retriever, who used to react with fear, stress, and agitation when exposed to the sound of traffic or the fast movement of vehicles. In these cases the initial reactions can include barking, freezing, lunging, or trying to escape in an attempt to distance themselves from what it is perceived as the trigger. Habituation works by allowing a dog to become gradually accustomed to a specific stimulus through repeated, non-threatening exposure. Over time, the novelty and emotional charge of that stimulus fades, and the dog no longer feels the need to react.

- Start at a Distance

    In Grady's case, I began by choosing a quiet spot near a road, far enough that cars could be seen and heard, but not so close that it would overwhelm him. The goal was to keep him just under his reactive threshold. At that distance he was able to notice the movement and sound of traffic without tipping into fear or reactivity. He remained alert but composed, which meant he was still in a state where learning could take place. This subtle exposure, paired with a calm presence and no added pressure, helped him feel safe and enabled him to begin the process of adjusting to something that had previously unsettled him.

- Let Them Observe Without Interference

    Simply stand or sit calmly with your dog. Avoid offering treats, talking to them, or soothing them if they seem a little unsure. The goal is for them to process the environment without added stimulation or unintended reinforcement of their nervous state. In our case, we found a bench in a quiet spot near a church where I sat and read a book while leaving Grady to get on with it.

- Keep It Short and Repeat Daily

    It is better to start with brief sessions of 5-10 minutes and repeat daily. Over the course of several days, perhaps a couple of weeks, I continued taking Grady to that same quiet spot. We would sit together, simply watching the world go by with no pressure, no commands, and no expectations. As the sounds and sights of passing cars became part of the background, I noticed a shift in him. His body relaxed, the tension in his shoulders eased, and he began to sniff the pavement or glance at me instead of locking onto every passing vehicle. That was my cue to take the next small step. As your dog becomes more comfortable, you will likely see them glance at the traffic and then go back to sniffing or relaxing. This is a good indicator that they are beginning to habituate.

- Gradually Decrease the Distance

    Gradually, I reduced the distance between us and the road, sometimes just a few metres at a time. If at any point Grady displayed signs of stress (like lip licking, freezing, shivering, or fixating), we would stop and go no further that day. The idea was not to push through his fear, but to give him space to adapt. Some days we moved forward, other days held our ground or even stepped back a bit if a novelty noise presented itself in the form of a vehicle backfiring or a huge waste-collector lorry. And that was perfectly fine.

- Avoid Reinforcing Fear

    Although it is natural for any human parent to want to reassure their dog when they are afraid, you must resist the urge to comfort or distract them during moments of tension. Calmly doing nothing is more powerful in helping them learn that there is truly nothing to fear, but you have to lead by example and show them there is nothing to be fearful about.

- Stay Well Below the Point of Overwhelming

    Remember to always stay below the overwhelming threshold throughout each subsequent step. This is because this whole process is not about tough love or flooding them with scary stimuli. In fact, overwhelming a fearful dog can worsen the problem. You want each exposure to feel safe, manageable, and even boring. Boredom is the friend of habituation.

Eventually, we were able to walk calmly on the pavement in the close proximity of traffic without any sign of reactivity. Grady had habituated to the once-stressful stimulus by being allowed to process it at his own pace. What for him was once a source of anxiety had become just another aspect of the environment, the sound had become a familiar, unthreatening, and easy to ignore occurrence. This approach not only changes a dog's behaviour but also contributes to building the resilience and confidence needed to tackle negatively perceived experiences in the future.

EXTINCTION

Extinction can be defined as the process of reducing or eliminating a behaviour by removing the reward that was perpetuating it and ultimately reinforcing it. One of the most common examples is a dog who jumps up at people for attention (not to be confused with the action of jumping up during greeting rituals). If, every time the dog jumps up, someone responds with petting, eye contact, or even reprimanding or scolding, the behaviour is being reinforced because attention itself acts as a reward. But if everyone consistently ignores the jumping, the dog eventually learns that the behaviour no longer "works" and the jumping up behaviour eventually fades away. However, extinction is not always immediate. In fact, when the reward disappears, the dog may initially try even harder, jumping more frequently or with greater intensity – this is called an *extinction burst*. If the owner gives in at that point, even once, it can reset the entire process and make the behaviour even more persistent. The more valuable or long-established the reward, the more determined the dog might be to keep trying.

And even without recent reinforcement, if the original reward was powerful enough, that behaviour might continue for a while. This is why consistency across everyone in the household is key: one moment of weakness can keep an unwanted habit alive.

A practical example where extinction works extremely well is to stop dogs begging at the dinner table. Imagine a dog who has learnt that staring, whining, or pawing at your leg during dinner earns a tasty scrap. Even if this only happens occasionally, the behaviour becomes deeply ingrained because the reward (a delicious piece of chicken from your plate!) is considered of high value. To apply the extinction method in this case, you must stop giving *any* food or attention during meals, and that means no eye contact, no speaking, and no scraps. Over time, the dog learns that begging no longer brings any benefit, and the behaviour eventually fades away. A word of warning though, before giving up, your dog may try even harder, as occurs in the habituation process. They might whine louder, paw more persistently, or add a dramatic sigh for effect. That is the "extinction burst" in action. If you hold firm and stay consistent, it will pass. But if anyone in the family gives in – "All right then! Just this once" – the dog learns that persistence pays off, and the begging may come back even stronger. Please be aware that extinction is not considered a method suitable for behaviours rooted in fear or anxiety. For example, a dog who barks or destroys furniture when left alone may instead be suffering from separation anxiety. If you try to ignore the behaviour, hoping that it will just go away, you could inadvertently make things worse. In fact, the distress behind the behaviour remains unaddressed, and without guidance or relief, the dog may escalate into more destructive behaviour like chewing through furniture and personal objects, injuring themselves, or becoming even more panicked. Thus, it is essential to recognise that behind such behaviours often lie much deeper emotional motives such as fear, insecurity, or past experiences of abandonment. That is why behavioural modification in these cases should never be about punishment or suppression, but about building security and trust. In these situations, techniques like desensitisation and counter-conditioning are far more effective and humane. They work by gradually shifting the dog's emotional response to being alone, anxious, or distressed to being calm and relaxed; helping them feel safe in their own space, even when you are not around.

RESPONSE SUBSTITUTION

Response substitution is one of my preferred methods for addressing some of the behavioural issues presented by dogs. It involves teaching our dog to swap an undesirable behaviour for a more appropriate one. For instance, instead of jumping up on guests, the dog learns to lie down or sit politely. The key here is to give them a clear, positive alternative that still gets them what they want, be this attention, interaction, or reassurance, but in a way that is more attuned to our social etiquette and works for everyone. Set the stage for success by starting in a predictable and comfortable setting for your dog. As soon as you enter the room or the dog approaches a visitor, give a clear and simple cue like "sit." The moment the dog responds and sits, reward this behaviour immediately with gentle praise or a treat. If the dog ignores the cue and jumps up instead, the most effective response is to withdraw your attention altogether. Turn away, avoid eye contact, and say nothing. This removes the reward (your attention), which helps the dog understand that jumping gets them nowhere. Once the dog calms down and offers the sit again, either on command or spontaneously reward it profusely. Over time, your dog will begin to associate sitting with more positive outcomes, while jumping is simply ignored. It is essential that everyone the dog interacts with follows this rule consistently. This means that family members, visitors, and even strangers should refrain from petting or speaking to the dog unless it is sitting. Repetition and consistency are key. With enough practice, your dog will learn that sitting politely gets the reward they want, your attention, while jumping up no longer brings the same satisfaction. This is response substitution in action: replacing an undesirable behaviour with one that is appropriate and positively reinforced. Once they have mastered the new, alternative behaviour you would like them to perform in that particular setting, you can gradually introduce more distractions to help generalise their response. In some cases, dogs may first need to be desensitised to the specific trigger before they are able to focus and reliably display the replacement behaviour. When implemented patiently and consistently, response substitution helps redirect energy in a constructive direction and builds good habits that stick in the long term. In this respect I would like to mention the Premack Principle, a powerful behavioural concept which essentially means that *"a more probable behaviour can reinforce a less probable one"*. In terms of dog training, it is the idea that something your dog really wants to do, like go outside or chase a ball, can be used as a reward for doing something they are less inclined to do, like sitting still or staying calm. For example, if a dog tends to bolt out the door the moment it opens, you can use this humane method to flip the situation. By teaching them to sit and wait patiently before being allowed outside, you are using the opportunity to go out (a high-value activity) as a reward for sitting (a lower-probability behaviour at that moment). Over time, the dog learns that good behaviour is the gateway to the fun stuff. I find that this principle works beautifully when we aim to reduce impulsive or unwanted behaviours not by punishing them, but by clearly showing the dog that good things happen when you make good choices.

SHAPING

Shaping is another highly powerful learning technique, and is especially useful when a dog has no idea what particular behaviour you are asking for. Rather than waiting for the perfect overall response, shaping initially rewards small steps – or successive approximations of the behaviour one intends to teach – that gradually lead towards the desired behaviour. For example, let us say you are teaching a puppy to sit. Initially, you might reward any action that even slightly resembles sitting, like a momentary squat or lowering of the hindquarters. As this behaviour becomes more consistent, you raise the criteria so that the reward now comes only when the squat gets deeper and, eventually, only when the pup plants their bottom fully on the ground. Step by step, you are building the behaviour from scratch, using positive reinforcement to guide them along the way. Shaping is like sculpting a masterpiece out of raw material, you start broad, then refine with patience and precision. It is particularly useful for teaching complex or unfamiliar actions in a fun, frustration-free way that encourages dogs to think and experiment.

The shaping method has proved to be so successful that it has become the go-to method for teaching complex or multi-step tasks, especially in professional settings like the film industry. Ever wondered how famous animal actors perform such clever tricks on cue? Think of Lassie navigating obstacles and performing tricks, or Jinx the cat flushing the toilet in the 2000 movie *Meet the Parents*. Those impressive stunts were not taught overnight but patiently using the shaping technique. Trainers break down these elaborate behaviours into small, manageable steps, rewarding each one until the animal naturally links them together into a fluid routine. For example, flushing a toilet might begin with simply looking at the handle, then touching it, then pawing it, and eventually using just the right pressure to make it flush. The shaping technique is often used in conjunction with the use of a device called the clicker, and is one of the most effective ways to apply this method in real time. The clicker is nothing more than a small device that makes a distinct "click" sound that acts as a marker that tells the dog, "***Yes! That's exactly what I wanted!***" The beauty of the clicker lies in the precise timing by which the wanted reward is marked. Simply put, it bridges the tiny gap between the desired behaviour and the tasty reward, enabling the dog to understand exactly which action has earned him or her the treat. When paired with shaping, the clicker becomes your communication superpower.

Imagine teaching a dog to crawl; you would not expect it to perform the full behaviour on day one. Instead, you might want to first click and treat when the dog lowers their chest. Next, when they take a small forward shuffle. Then a longer crawl. Each little step is marked and rewarded, gradually building towards the full movement which is then paired with the cue word, the command "Crawl". This process allows you to guide your dog through a learning journey, reinforcing each approximation with crystal-clear feedback. It is especially helpful for teaching complex, multi-step behaviours or working with dogs who are still trying to work out what you are asking. Instead of correcting mistakes, you are constantly saying "Yes, you're getting warmer!" One of the big advantages of clicker training is that because the click always predicts something good, it builds a positive emotional response to training. Dogs become more focused, motivated, and eager to offer behaviours, knowing they are playing a kind of "hot and cold" game with you where the click is the jackpot bell. Whether you are teaching a rescue dog how to navigate stairs for the first time, or building an elaborate routine for a film or demo, shaping with a clicker transforms training into an enjoyable, clear, and collaborative experience.

If using a clicker feels a bit tricky to manage, for instance if your hands are full with a leash, treats, or you are in a real-world setting where fumbling with a small device is just not practical, you can substitute the word "Yes" as your marker. The key will continue to be consistency and timing. Just like the clicker, the word "Yes" should be short, sharp, and always followed by a reward. It needs to become meaningful to your dog, signalling that they have just done the right thing and something good is coming. The main difference is that whilst a clicker delivers a mechanical, emotion-neutral sound, your voice can carry tone, so it is important to keep it consistent and not unintentionally signal disappointment or excitement. That said, owners often find using a verbal marker more intuitive and easier to integrate into everyday life, especially once their timing improves.

So, whether you are using a clicker or your voice, the goal remains the same – mark the exact moment your dog gets it right and then celebrate with a reward. Over time your dog becomes more confident, more responsive, and more in tune with you. By using shaping, trainers do not have to physically guide or force animals, they simply reinforce natural behaviours that move in the right direction. It is creative, empowering, and completely stress-free for the animal. In fact, most dogs enjoy shaping sessions because it gives them a chance to think, problem-solve, and earn praise and rewards just for trying.

FLOODING

Flooding is a behaviour modification technique that involves exposing a dog to a prolonged, intense exposure to the triggering stimulus until it stops reacting in its presence. It is the opposite of desensitisation, which works gradually and gently to change a dog's emotional response. I can say from personal experience that whilst it might seem logical in theory, flooding can be a highly distressing experience for a sensitive dog and is rarely appropriate in practice. The risk is that instead of adapting, the dog becomes even more fearful and phobic, or can even shut down emotionally. Think of it this way, you would not teach a child to swim by throwing them into the deep end of a pool, or force someone afraid of heights to stay on the edge of a cliff until they "get over it". In the same way, forcing a dog to face their greatest fear without escape or support does not build resilience; it breaks trust and can lead to lasting trauma. Because of its intensity and potential for harm, flooding should only ever be attempted by a qualified professional, and only when all other gentler methods have been tried and carefully ruled out. Even if used as a last resort, in a compassionate and holistic approach we must prioritise safety, trust, and emotional well-being, working with the dog not against them. Let me conclude by saying that behavioural modification techniques are essential tools that can effectively shape the dog's emotional responses and actions. Whether you are working on reactivity, fear, or undesirable habits, techniques like habituation, extinction, and shaping provide valuable pathways for change. But remember, the real magic lies in applying these techniques in a way that is patient, consistent, and sensitive to the dog's needs.

When it comes to more complex issues, especially those rooted in fear or anxiety, approaches such as Desensitisation and Counter-Conditioning are often key to long-term success in the rehabilitation of pets with behavioural issues. For a step-by-step guide on using these methods correctly, please refer to the final chapter of this book where they are discussed in full.

Having explored and described the process of learning in dogs, I would like to proceed with the next step which consists in planning a proper routine that incorporates structured training sessions with unstructured bonding interactions in order to maintain a healthy and happy relationship with your dog and ensure he or she can channel their biological needs (playing, hunting, socialising, exercising) in a context you can control. Whereas structured training sessions are important for reinforcing desired behaviours and improving communication, unstructured bonding time allows your dog to feel more relaxed and comfortable in your presence. Achieving this balance means your dog will view you not only as a trainer but also as a companion and friend, further strengthening the bond between you. However, before looking in detail at the various training methods and techniques, I would like to bring to your attention to another fundamental aspect of our pets' behaviour that is unique to all predators, one which is often overlooked but which is crucial to comprehend in order to fully understand how a dog's mind operates: the predatory behaviour or, more simply, the Prey Drive. This is an instinctual behaviour rooted deeply in a dog's genetic makeup, influencing everything from their way of playing to their response to training. By understanding the prey drive, we gain a further insight into why dogs behave the way they do, especially in situations that trigger their hunting instincts. This understanding is key to developing training strategies that work with, rather than against, a dog's natural tendencies.

Rocco

CHAPTER 4

THE PREY DRIVE INSTINCT

Predatory behaviour, or more simply the prey drive, is the natural instinct ingrained in all carnivores which motivates them to chase, capture, and kill a prey; in essence, it is all about acquiring food. Because this behaviour is instinctive, it does not need to be taught; it comes naturally to a dog and takes the form of a reflexive or automatic response triggered by something present in the environment. Our ancestors were able to observe and identify the entire prey drive sequence and, through domestication and selective breeding, managed not only to raise or lower the threshold of the behaviour occurring in some breeds (some dogs are described as having a low prey drive, others as having a high prey drive), but also to create breeds with particular skills uniquely associated with one of the stages of the predatory behaviour sequence, such as retrieving, herding, protecting, and guarding. The full prey drive sequence consists of eight distinctive stages: Orienting, Seeking, Stalking, Chasing, Grab Bite, Kill Bite, Dissecting, and Consuming. Other wild canids related to dogs, like wolves, foxes, coyotes, jackals, and so on will need to perform all of the stages mentioned above in order to hunt and to survive. Our domestic dogs no longer need to hunt for food, but that does not mean they will not give chase if the predatory behaviour is triggered.

Because the prey drive triggers the release of certain feel-good hormones, dogs do not necessarily have to complete the whole sequence to fulfil their needs; the act of chasing is its own reward and also self-reinforcing, creating a sort of natural high that makes a dog want to do it more and more. This explains why some of our dogs love chasing balls so obsessively. I will now analyse the eight stages one by one so that you can understand how important and relevant they are in relation to some of the behaviours displayed by our pet companions in everyday real-life situations, and how they could help you with the holistic training routines. Moreover, some of the behaviours triggered by the prey drive could potentially be extremely dangerous and occasionally even make the news, tragically for the wrong reasons. Therefore, please bear with me because what I am about to reveal could be extremely helpful in avoiding a life-threatening incident.

- <u>Orienting</u> – This is the very first stage of the predatory behaviour sequence. It is the stage where our dog, the predator, draws its attention towards the subject of his or her interest. This stage can be triggered by one of the dog's acute and well-developed senses such as scent, hear, sight or touch. You may have noticed that your dog's nose is always wet (if it is not, it means that he or she has a temperature and needs medical attention). One of the reasons for this is that a wet nose allows dogs to detect the direction of the wind (we stick our wet finger up in the air to do this) and if the wind is carrying the scent of the prey or anything else of interest (food, another dog etc.) they will redirect their attention in that particular direction. A quarry also possesses a formidable sense of smell and the same principles apply when it comes to detecting the presence of predators. In line with this, it's worth examining a behaviour that frequently puzzles and repels owners: a dog's tendency to roll in foul-smelling substances. Because predators cannot always choose the ideal position in relation to the wind, they camouflage their body odour by rolling in the smelliest thing they can find, like dead animals such as rodents, squirrels, and birds, excrement of all kind, cut grass, and more. I am positive that as dog owners, we have all experienced at some point the sight of our dogs rolling on some fox's excrement or a dead animal.

Our dogs' sense of hearing is also extremely well developed, more than their human companions as you must have realised observing your pets. They are able to hear a wider range of sound frequencies (how high or low the pitch is) between 65 and 45,000 Hz, whilst humans are limited to hear frequency between the range of 20 and 25,000 Hz. This means that dogs are able to hear sounds that are higher in pitch than humans, including ultrasounds of more than 20,000 Hz emitted from some silent whistles available on the market. Our dogs' ears are also better at determining the direction and distance of the sound. This is because their brain is able to compare the loudness of the sound between the two ears and how much the loudness falls as the noise travels from the source to their ears. Our little Chihuahua possesses a formidable sense of hearing, especially with high frequencies, because his proportionally enormous ears in comparison to his smaller head allows for greater amplification of the sound. When puppies are born they are unable to hear because their ear canals are completely closed, opening only after 12 to 14 days. When they start to interact with their siblings, they will use high frequency sounds to which they will become accustomed, and this is why later in life they regard our high-pitched verbal praise and baby talk as being very comforting and pleasant.

Finally, our dogs' sight has evolved so that it enables them to see when light is scarce. Like many other predators living on our planet, dogs have very few sweat glands and are unable to rely on sweating as a means of regulating their body temperature. For this reason, they tend to lay low during the hottest part of the day and prefer to hunt or move around during the coolest time, which is at dusk or dawn. The only sweat glands they have are located within their pads in their paws, on their cheeks, and under their chins where the whiskers are. If we think about it, this peculiarity of predators not being able to sweat provided humans with the great advantage of being able to move around whilst their predators were sheltering during the hottest times of the day. As a consequence, our dogs' sight has evolved and adapted according to their requirement to hunt at dusk and dawn, enabling them to see better in low light conditions as well as during daytime. Although they are unable to see the full spectrum of colours as they only possess two types of colour-sensing receptors (called cones) in their retinas – unlike humans who have three cones – they have more rods, which are the cells that help with night vision, and this allows them to detect even the smallest of movements at great distances. They also possess a unique structure in their eyes called the tapetum lucidum, a mirror-like membrane that enhances night vision by reflecting light back through the retina, allowing them to see in conditions up to six times dimmer than what the human eye can perceive. The tapetum, which some other animals such as cats and cattle also possess, sits behind the retina and reflects light back onto it, giving the receptors a second chance to gather more visual detail. This is also the reason why your pet's eyes glow in photos and in the dark. Our dogs see the world in shades of blue, yellow and grey, which are the only colours they can perceive. We can say that they are colour blind, as their vision is very similar to that of a human who has red-green colour blindness. To our dogs, the colour red may appear grey or dark brown, whilst yellow, orange, and green all look like varying shades of yellow, and violet appears to be just another shade of blue. Despite the fact that dogs cannot appreciate the entire spectrum of colour, they compensate for their lack of vision with their excellent sense of smell, so do not worry when sometimes they seem helpless at finding the ball during a game of fetch as eventually they will always find it, guided by their nose. Recent studies (e.g., Healy et al., 2013) conducted by scientists from Trinity College Dublin, including researchers from the University of Edinburgh and the University of St Andrews, have also identified something that was previously unknown, which is that the speed at which dogs can process the image of a moving object is 20% faster than that of humans, hence a dog's perception of a moving object can be described as slow motion in comparison to ours. No wonder they are so good at catching that ball!

- <u>Seeking</u> – Following orienting, the seeking stage involves actually eyeing up the subject of interest and determining what action is required – the dog will ponder whether is it worth pursuing the objective or ignoring it. In the context of dog training, the ability to spot and recognise this stage can be extremely useful in situations where you are training your dogs for recall or are trying to pre-empt them chasing other animals or even engaging with other dogs. At this stage your dog is not fully engaged with and committed to the predatory behaviour sequence, so it can still be stopped and redirected towards something you can control and manage.

- Stalking – I find this to be one of the most fascinating of the eight stages. It never ceases to amaze me to see a dog stalking its prey. I greatly enjoy watching people in the park stop and observe one of our dogs stalking a squirrel and the sound of disappointment when, after a few minutes of hard work and concentration, the squirrel manages to get away. But why do dogs perform and seem to enjoy the stalking stage so much? In reality, it is out of necessity. Let me clarify – all predators have their eyes positioned in front of their heads, which creates the depth of field that allows them to judge the distance relative to the position of their prey. However, this is only possible if the prey is in motion. For example, have you ever tried to clean up after your dog when it relieves itself far away from you? If you do not keep your eyes fixed on the spot where they have fouled, if you do not "stalk" the poop, it will be very difficult to find it once you reached the location. The same thing happens if you throw a ball in a field with high grass, it will simply blend in into the background; eventually the dog's nose will compensate for the lack of sight. If we think about it, the first line of defence for a prey that has spotted a predator is to freeze: if the predator does not keep his eyes on the prey by stalking it, then the image of the prey will blend in with the background and the predator will not be able to see it.

    I use this same principle when I exercise some of the most active dogs we regularly look after on behalf of our clients, and you could enhance your own dog walking experience as well by using a method called "blind retrieve". Instead of just throwing the ball for your dog, train them to come and sit on your left-hand side in a heel position and then give the command "Stay". Using your ball thrower, throw the ball a fair distance and wait until it stops, pause for a few seconds, and then give your dog the "Watch Me" command or gently move your dog's head away from the location where the ball has landed. The dog's eyes will have been hooked on the ball, following its trajectory until it lands (stalking), so he or she will have formed a memory association with its approximate location, but because you asked them to take their eyes off the ball with the "Watch Me" command, they will not be able to pinpoint its precise position. You can now release the dog with the command "Go Fetch" to find the ball and you will notice that they will soon put their nose down and start sniffing rather than looking for the ball; sometimes they even pass nearby without being able to see it. If you want to assist your dogs to start with, you could consider the direction of the wind, if any, and throw the ball downwind to make it easier for your dog to find it. This exercise not only provides a better outlet for your dog's endless reserve of energy, it helps strengthen your bond with them by creating an atmosphere of cooperation during an activity they perceive as hunting, giving you the chance to include and reinforce the basic commands in the routine. In addition, you will be able to refrain your dog from chasing squirrels or other wildlife which populate our national parks. Most importantly, it simulates the release of feel-good hormones which makes the dog want to engage more with you and pay less attention to other distractions. This is what I mean by holistic training.

- Chasing – This stage represents the start of the actual physical motion of the behaviour. Once dogs are engaged in chasing there is not much you can do to stop them. The only thing that would interrupt a predator during the chasing phase would be the immediate perception of a life-threatening situation occurring at the same time. Between the need to procure food and the need to preserve their life, the choice will always incline towards the latter, unless the predator is really desperate and is willing to risk their life to obtain food, such as after a long period of fasting. If chasing is an issue for a dog with a very strong predatory instinct, there are several strategies you can adopt to minimise the risks of the behaviour occurring uncontrollably. The first is to use a restrainer to stop the behaviour from happening in the first place, like a long line of 15 or 20 metres or so. You can then give your dog the choice of releasing the feel-good hormones and self-reinforcing their prey drive redirected towards an object you can control (their favourite real animal fur toy, for example) or the disappointment of not being able to chase the squirrels because they keep reaching the end of the line. I use this method profusely with Jack Russell, German shepherd, Belgian Malinois, and all other breeds with an exceptionally high prey drive. Alternatively, I prefer to teach our dogs the "Leave It" command which I use in association with a more assertive tone of voice in order to disrupt the behaviour. I immediately follow this with enthusiastic verbal praise and then engage in playtime and physical interaction.

One final consideration on this topic concerns a breed renowned for its strong prey drive, the Greyhound. If you happen to live with one, you'll know exactly what I mean. Their physical attributes and unique morphology make them nature's running machines. Greyhounds can reach the highest speeds of any canine breed and are able to change direction with remarkable agility, thanks in part to their long, balancing tails. Combined with their exceptional eyesight, these traits make them superb hunters. In my own observations, I've noticed that Greyhounds, being so fast, often bypass the stalking phase of the predatory sequence altogether, they simply don't need it. This makes modifying their prey-driven behaviour more challenging, as we have fewer moments of intervention available before the chase is already underway. And let's be honest, how frustrating must it be to have been selectively bred over thousands of years to chase and catch small prey, only to be told now not to do it?

- <u>Grab Bite</u> – As the phrase suggests, this stage consists of biting with the intent of grabbing and bringing down the prey. You can observe this behaviour happening all the time in the park during playtime interaction between dogs. As described in other chapters, dogs do not play just for the fun of it, they also practise their hunting skills by recreating the predatory behaviour. One dog will act like a predator and another will assume the role of the prey and, after displaying the initial stages of the prey drive, they will start running, with the dog being chased in front, keeping the tail slightly bent downwards, not to signal fear but to act as a real prey would. If the prey kept its tail high, swinging it side to side, it would be an easy target for the pursuing predator, so they keep it low while running. At some point the two dogs will swap roles and the chasing game starts again. If more than one dog is involved then there will be a change in the dynamics of the game as one dog will go for the grab bite and another will go straight for the kill bite, either aiming for the prey's throat and inflicting death by suffocation or aiming for its neck and inflicting death by shacking.

- <u>Kill Bite</u> – Have you ever heard the phrase, "When you welcome a dog into your home, you are living with a predator"? But what does that really mean? Those pet owners who prefer the company of cats will most likely have experienced them proudly bringing back home all sorts of small prey like birds, lizards, mice, and so on. I have seen some dogs in the park successfully complete the prey drive sequence and catch a squirrel or a little rabbit, but in the majority of cases, the dog ends up empty-handed. Although our domestic pets are fed regularly and consequently do not need to hunt, the instinct is still there and that is why it is extremely important to understand this often neglected aspect of their behaviour. The kill bite is the act of finishing off the prey once it has been brought down by another member of the pack following the grab bite. A single wolf would be unable to kill a large animal like a bison or a stag, but would certainly be capable of killing a rabbit or a hare with a single bite on the neck or by shacking it. Wolves prefer to work and operate in larger social groups or packs so that they can be more successful in catching larger prey. As such, they have developed a strategy and an understanding that imply an instinctive response to certain signals in the context of the hunting sequence. Let me explain – we must all have watched documentaries on wildlife and are aware of the screaming preys emanate when caught. However, there is a lot more to be learnt than just terror from the screaming of prey animals. In an article titled "Adaptation Unto Death: Function of Fear Screams" from the book *The American Naturalist* by Göran Högstedt, different theories are presented as to why a prey screams when caught. These range from the obvious, such as the need for the prey to vocalise the terror, fear, and pain of being ripped apart, to other fascinating propositions.

One theory is that prey animals are hard-wired to act for the good of the community in a selfless sacrifice to preserve their kind. According to this theory, prey animals react altruistically to warn other members of their species of danger, thus providing them the opportunity to escape while sacrificing their own lives, which makes a great deal of sense to me. The more interesting theory, however, is that animals possess a strong self-preservation instinct and this alone would require that they fight to the end in order to stay alive. As a last resort, according to this theory, it is possible that the distress screams are directed at other predators nearby who, in the hope of an easy meal, would join the hunt (see Curio, 1976, p. 98; Högstedt, 1983). Consequently, during the ensuing dispute between the predators, the prey would get a chance to escape. In fact, scientists have hypothesised that an animal's chances of escape increases when a second predator approaches and tries to steal the prey from the first predator. That said, predators know from experience that whenever they hear screaming, they assume that the physical wellbeing of the prey attempting to escape has been compromised, and they will not pass by the opportunity for an easy meal. Some adult predators will often capture and inflict minor injuries on a prey in order to allow youngsters to practise the prey drive sequence so that each time they hear the prey's screams, the association between these vocalisations and the potential for an easy meal is reinforced. In evolutionary terms those distress cries trigger a "dinner bell" response in predators. You might have witnessed a similar episode in your local park while walking with your own dog. If a group of dogs are playing and all of a sudden a fight breaks out, or perhaps one of the players is injured and starts screaming in pain, you will notice that other dogs nearby will run towards the injured animal and try to attack it. This can often manifest as an attempt to silence the injured dog by targeting the throat, mimicking what is indeed known in ethology as the "kill bite." This behaviour, rooted in a dog's ancestral predatory instincts, serves a critical purpose in the wild: silencing the prey quickly to avoid attracting the attention of competing predators. In essence, by applying the kill bite to the throat, a predator not only ends the struggle by suffocating the prey but also reduces the risk of drawing in others who may challenge them for the meal. Why is this behaviour so relevant to us humans? Because although our pet dogs live in domestic settings, these primal motor patterns can still re-surface under the right circumstances, especially in highly aroused or chaotic group dynamics. I strongly believe that in those dogs with an extremely high predatory behaviour, this instinct can also be triggered by the screams of humans, especially the high-pitched ones coming from infants and toddlers. Whilst I cannot scientifically prove this theory, I can't help but notice that the majority of fatal dog attacks are directed at the head and throat area of the victim. As I said, I can speculate that this pattern reflects a deeply ingrained predatory instinct, specifically, the drive to deliver a decisive bite that silences the prey, nevertheless, I urge you to consider it seriously and apply common sense: never, under any circumstances, leave an infant, toddler, or young child alone with a dog, no matter how trustworthy the dog may seem. Supervision is not a sign of mistrust, it is a necessary measure to protect both the child and the dog, and to prevent tragic outcomes. According to the Office of National Statistics, in 2023 alone there were 16 deadly dog attacks on people in the UK. This is just the tip of the iceberg, because although dog bites can result in serious and sometimes disfiguring injuries, most canine attacks are not deadly and are not reported to the authorities. Sadly, the majority of fatal attacks involve children and are perpetrated by dogs living in the same households or nearby neighbours. We only hear about them when they unfortunately make the news; yet apart from banning some dangerous breeds, no one ever seems to come up with a plausible explanation until the next incident occurs.

- Dissecting – Simply put, this stage involves tearing apart the prey after the killing. The dog's teeth are shaped so that they can rip through the flesh and literally crush the prey's bones.

- Consuming – This is the last and final stage. One comment I would like to make regarding this topic is that the speed at which some dogs consume their meals can be a concern for some pet owners. Dogs often eat quickly for various reasons. Firstly, they have a natural instinct to safeguard their prey and may eat rapidly to prevent it from being taken by others, even within their own group. Additionally, dogs may eat quickly to avoid sharing their food with other predators higher up the food chain. Furthermore, as opportunistic scavengers, dogs may encounter old carcasses that are still edible and eat them quickly to reduce the risk of infection from potential contaminants present in the carcass. With only a few taste buds, dogs rely heavily on their sense of smell to determine the edibility of food. Eating quickly and gulping down potentially contaminated food allows the acidity in their stomach to reduce the risk of infections from disease-carrying bacteria and viruses. Therefore, purchasing fancy slow feeder bowls may not be necessary for your dog, as eating quickly is a natural behaviour that forms part of their survival instincts. With respect to the point made above regarding the dog's primordial instinct of not wanting to share their meals with others, even with other members of the same group, it is important to note a significant difference from the behaviour observed in a pack of wolves. It all comes down to the fundamental difference in pack structure: dog packs tend to operate under a dictatorial hierarchy, whereas wolf packs are generally more egalitarian. In wolf packs, it's not uncommon for members to eat together peacefully. Even when a dominant wolf shows assertive or aggressive behaviour toward a subordinate, the lower-ranking animal often holds its ground and continues eating. In contrast, domestic dogs follow a stricter hierarchy. Subordinate dogs rarely eat at the same time as dominant ones and usually won't even attempt to access food until it's clearly their turn. I've witnessed this dynamic firsthand after group dog-walking sessions, when it's time to hydrate, each dog waits patiently, approaching the water one at a time, often in the same order day after day. It's a subtle but powerful display of social structure among domesticated dogs.

Understanding your dog's prey drive is essential when applying training techniques through a holistic lens. Every behaviour your dog displays in response to the environment, and during interactions with other animals and humans, is heavily influenced by this innate instinct. The key phases to focus on are orienting, seeking, stalking, and chasing, as these are the most relevant when it comes to shaping and managing the dog's behaviour.

If you want to improve your dog's recall, for example, it is important to intervene before or during the stalking phase begins. Once your dog has entered the chasing phase, there is very little you can do in that moment, unless you have already taught a strong and well-practised "Leave It" cue. It is important to avoid calling your dog when they are already chasing something, or when they are fully engaged in other activities such as playing, sniffing, eating, or drinking. Doing so will only teach them to ignore the recall cue over time. Similarly, when working with behavioural issues, especially reactivity, your goal should be to observe and recognise the early stages of the prey drive. By identifying and interrupting the sequence before it escalates, you will be able to redirect your dog away from triggers and reinforce more appropriate behaviours.

Having explored how this instinct functions in our dogs, we can now move forward and delve into the core principles that form the foundation of our training methods.

Pimm's

CHAPTER 5

DOG TRAINING AND BASIC COMMANDS

As discussed in previous chapters, dog training objectives and goals have changed greatly since the beginning of the human-dog relationship. Whereas in the past the majority of dogs were seen as mere tools in helping humans undertake different tasks, with a small minority kept purely as companions, this equation has now shifted drastically towards the latter. In the twenty-first century, we live in a unique period of human history where more people than ever live on their own. According to the last census held in 2021(ONS, 2024), people living alone account for nearly 30% of the households in London, slightly below the average of 31% for the rest of England and Wales, and in the USA we can find more or less similar statistics. Indeed, the roles and expectations we have for dogs in modern society have evolved significantly. Rather than relying on them for specific tasks like hunting, herding, or guarding, many people now seek companionship and social compatibility from their canine friends. As a result, the emphasis has shifted towards training dogs to behave appropriately in various social situations, such as when they are out in public. This shift reflects changes in human lifestyles and the unique bond that has developed between humans and dogs over time. Nowadays, dog training is about establishing a common language that allow us to communicate effectively with our pets and to help our dogs understand what is expected of them, keep them safe, and enable them to live harmoniously within the context of our modern society. There are an endless repertoire of commands that any pet can learn and I am always in favour of keeping our dogs engaged in short but frequent training sessions with the aim of expanding their vocabulary. However, our first priority should be to focus mainly on the most useful and basic of the commands so that anyone can manage to exert a certain degree of control over their dogs' behaviour, regardless of the circumstances.

The basic commands we should teach our dogs, in no particular order, can be noted down as:

- DOG'S NAME – We need to teach our dogs the difference between hearing their names as part of the recall and responding by redirecting their attention towards us, and hearing their names in all other different contexts (during a conversation with friends or family for example).

- WATCH ME – This command is used to get your dog to make eye contact with you and maintain it for the length of time required.
- COME – One of the most important of all commands, dogs must be able to recall reliably in any circumstances, with or without distractions.
- SIT – Some trainers believe this command is not strictly necessary as dogs tend to offer this behaviour spontaneously. I prefer to teach the "Sit command regardless, as it can be included in combination with other commands and also when dealing with behavioural issues.
- DOWN – Having a dog who lies down on cue is not only extremely helpful in everyday life situations, for example when we pop out for a coffee or visit a shop, but it can also be used as an off-switch signal for a highly active dog.
- STAY – This is another command that can be crucial in a real-life situation as it can enhance our dog's overall impulse control and the way we communicate with them.
- HEEL – Walking with your dog alongside you in a calm and controlled manner without pulling on the lead is a pleasant experience and every owner should invest time and effort in order to achieve a solid "Heel" command.
- LEAVE IT – This command can be used in situations where we need to pull the dog away from whatever object of attention they are focusing on and redirect their attention towards their human owner.

Besides the basic commands, there are several other very useful commands that you can teach your dog, not only to suit your individual requirements but also to better control your pets depending on their character and demeanour. For example, if your dogs have the tendency to vocalise excessively in certain situations (some breeds in particular are highly proficient at vocalising), then you should teach them the commands "Speak" and "Quiet", whereas if your dog rushes towards the door every time the doorbell rings, then "Settle Down" or "Place" can be particularly useful commands. If you wish to provide your dogs with physical exercise and mental stimulation during your walks in the park, commands like "Fetch", "Drop", "Find It", "Over", and "Under" (an obstacle) represent a great way to communicate and serve as a valuable addition to the basic commands they already know. There are so many other commands that can be taught to any dog for any reason you may think may come in handy depending on your individual circumstances, such as "Place", "Beg", "High

Five", "Play Dead", and "Roll Over". I will discuss these other commands in more detail later, but for now I would like focus primarily on the basic commands.

Whether you are preparing to welcome a new puppy or have recently acquired a pet, there are several essential items you will need to start your training sessions effectively. These include the following:

- Treats: I assume you will want to use a training method based mostly on positive reinforcement, given all of the advantages this method offers in comparison to other methods within the operant conditioning quadrant. Food is the quickest way to your dog's heart, so you will need to find some tasty, bite-sized treats to reward your dog for desired behaviours during training sessions. Choose treats that are small in size or can be broken down into smaller pieces, and that your dog finds highly motivating and easy to consume quickly. You do not want your dog to lose momentum chewing and tasting his or her treats between repetitions.

- Treats Pouch: Having a treats pouch that strikes the right balance between capacity and convenience is crucial for ensuring training sessions with your dog are successful. The pouch should be spacious enough to hold an adequate supply of treats for the entire session, ensuring you have enough rewards readily available to reinforce your dog's good behaviour consistently. Running out of treats mid-session can disrupt the flow of training and reduce its effectiveness. Look for a pouch that allows easy access to treats while keeping them securely contained. This enables you to quickly reward your dog for desired behaviours without fumbling or delays. Pouches with wide openings or magnetic closures can facilitate effortless treat retrieval. Opt for a pouch that is comfortable to wear and does not impede your movements during training. Adjustable straps or clips allow you to attach the pouch securely to your waist or clothing, keeping your hands free to handle the leash and provide your dog with cues. Choose a pouch made from durable materials that can withstand regular use and potential exposure to dirt or moisture. Additionally, select a design that is easy to clean or machine washable to maintain hygiene and freshness. Consider pouches with extra features such as multiple compartments for storing different types of treats, built-in waste bag dispensers, or additional pockets for carrying keys, clickers, or other small items.

- Leash and Collar/Harness: For exercises that involve walking or controlling your dog's movements, a leash and a properly fitting collar or harness are essential. Make sure the collar or harness is comfortable and secure for your dog. Choosing the right leash is essential for effective and safe dog training. Opt for a leash made of sturdy and durable material that can withstand regular use and provides reliable control over your dog. Common materials include nylon, leather, or cotton webbing. You should also select a material that feels comfortable in your hand and is easy to grip. The length of the leash depends on the type of training exercises you will be practising. For general obedience training, a leash with a length of at least 3 metres (approximately 10 feet) provides sufficient freedom of movement while maintaining control over your dog. Longer leashes may be preferred for specific exercises such as recall training. In addition, look for a leash with a comfortable and secure handle that allows you to maintain a firm grip during training sessions. Padded handles or ergonomic designs can reduce strain on your hands and provide added comfort, especially during longer training sessions. I would personally consider a leash with features that offer increased versatility and adaptability for various training scenarios. For example, some leashes come with multiple attachment points or adjustable lengths, allowing you to customise them according to your training needs. Choose a leash with high-visibility or reflective elements, especially if you will be training during low-light conditions or in areas with poor visibility. This will ensure you and your dog remain visible to others, reducing the risk of accidents or mishaps. You should also select a leash that is easy to clean and maintain, especially if you will be training outdoors or in muddy conditions. Machine washable or waterproof leashes are convenient options that can withstand dirt and moisture. Check for safety features such as sturdy hardware, reinforced stitching, and durable clips or clasps that securely attach to your dog's collar or harness. Avoid leashes with weak or flimsy components that could break or malfunction during training.

- Clicker (optional): A clicker can be a valuable tool for marking desired behaviours with a distinct sound, signalling to your dog that a reward is forthcoming (Positive Reinforcement Method). Whilst not necessary, trainers often find clickers helpful for precise communication during training. Alternatively, I substitute the clicker with the cue word "Yes", which I use as a marker with the same effect as the sound of a clicker. The clicker itself is one more item that you will have to hold in your hand, which means it can be lost, misplaced, or forgotten, and people sometimes find it difficult to use. In some cases, I have seen dogs having a bad reaction to the sound of the clicker and refusing to accept it as a training tool.

- Training Area: Select a quiet, distraction-free area for your training sessions, especially when starting out. A familiar environment can help your dog focus better on learning and reduce distractions.

- Clothing and Shoes: Wearing comfortable shoes and practical clothing during dog training sessions is also recommended and its importance should not be overlooked. Dog training often involves moving around, bending, kneeling, and sometimes running. Comfortable shoes with good support can help prevent fatigue and reduce the risk of injuries during these activities. Practical clothing that allows for ease of movement and flexibility can prevent accidents or injuries while working with dogs, especially during more active training sessions or outdoor activities. Depending on the training environment, you may encounter various weather conditions such as rain, mud, or snow. Practical clothing, including waterproof or insulated options, can keep you comfortable and protected from the elements. Avoiding the distractions caused by uncomfortable shoes or clothing will allow you to focus better on the training session and communicate more effectively with your dog.

- Patience and Positive Attitude: I cannot emphasise enough the fact that training takes time, consistency, and a positive mindset. You will need to approach each session with patience, encouragement, and a willingness to adapt to your dog's progress and needs. This is what holistic training is all about, fostering a strong bond with our pets built on understanding their individual characteristics, trust, and communication.

- Training Plan or Guide: Have a clear understanding of the behaviours you want to teach your dog and how you will accomplish them. A structured training plan or guide, such as the one provided in this book, can help you stay organised and focused on your training goals.

Before I delve into the essence of this chapter, which is to teach our dogs the basic commands, there is one final topic that needs to be addressed and that is the science behind the use of the reward (the reinforcer) applied during the Positive Reinforcement Method of training. For the reason I have highlighted in previous chapters, the best way to teach an animal (or a person) a new behaviour is to use positive reinforcement, where the subject is rewarded when the desired behaviour is performed. In our case, treats represent a highly motivating reward for our pets and have the advantage of generating an extremely quick response, especially with some particularly greedy breeds. Some of the most frequent questions I am asked before a training session begins concern the timing, the frequency, the duration, and ultimately the fading out of the dispensation of the treats. When a dog receives a treat each and every time it displays a behaviour, it is effectively receiving continuous reinforcement. This continuous reinforcement schedule is the quickest way to teach a behaviour, and is especially effective in training a new behaviour. Timing is also extremely important in this initial phase. We will be most successful if we present the reinforcer immediately after the dog displays the behaviour, so that they can make an association between the target behaviour (sitting, for example) and the consequence (getting a treat). Once a behaviour is trained, we then need to switch to another type of reinforcement schedule, called partial reinforcement. In partial reinforcement, also referred to as intermittent reinforcement, the dog does not receive a reward (the reinforcer) every time it performs the desired behaviour, but intermittently. The intermittent reinforcement schedule helps maintain the behaviour over the long term and prevents future dependence on treats for every action the dog performs. There are several different types of partial reinforcement schedules. These are described as either fixed or variable, and also either interval or ratio. Simply put:

- Fixed Ratio (FR) Schedule, refers to the number of responses between reinforcements, or the amount of time between reinforcements, which is set and unchanging. Let us apply the Fixed Ratio Schedule on a dog who is being trained to sit on command for example. According to this Reinforcement Schedule the trainer gives the dog a treat every 5 times the dog successfully sits on command.

So the reinforcement pattern looks like this:

- Sit → No treat
- Sit → No treat
- Sit → No treat
- Sit → No treat
- Sit → Treat!
  (then the cycle repeats)

This kind of schedule is useful when the behaviour is already learned but you're trying to increase the number of repetitions before reinforcement, which helps build persistence and a strong work ethic in training.

- Fixed Interval (FI) Schedule

  When using this method the dog gets a reward for the first correct behaviour after a set amount of time has passed. For example, you're teaching your dog to lie calmly on a mat (the "Place" command). With this Reinforcement Schedule the dog receives a treat only for the first correct behaviour that happens after a fixed time period, in this case, 30 seconds. In practice it looks as follows:

- You cue your dog to lie down on the mat.

- You start a timer for 30 seconds.
- If the dog is still calmly lying on the mat at the end of 30 seconds, success! Give a treat!
- If the dog breaks position before the 30 seconds are up no reward and restart the interval.
- Repeat the 30-second cycle.

    This type of Schedule of Reinforcement is used to build the duration of behaviours like staying in place or settling down. The dog begins to learn how long it has to maintain the behaviour in order to achieve the reward.

- Variable Ratio (VR) Schedule refers to the number of responses or amount of time between reinforcements, which varies or changes. Let's examine a scenario where you're teaching your dog to come when called. According to this Reinforcement Schedule, the dog is rewarded after an average of every 3 successful recalls, but not every third one exactly. The reward may come after 2, then 4, then 3 recalls, and so on.

    So the pattern might look like this:

- Come → No treat
- Come → Treat!
- Come → No treat
- Come → No treat
- Come → Treat!
- Come → Treat!
- Come → No treat
  (and continues unpredictably)

This unpredictability keeps the dog engaged and motivated, because it never knows exactly when the reward will come. It's the same principle behind why people keep playing slot machines, it builds a strong and resistant behaviour.

Variable Interval (VI) Schedule consists of rewarding the first correct response after a varying amount of time has passed. If you're training a dog to remain in a down-stay position, for instance, with this type of Reinforcement Schedule the dog gets a reward for staying down, but the reward becomes available after unpredictable time intervals, averaging around 30 seconds. Importantly, the behaviour must still be happening (the dog must still be in the down-stay) when the time interval ends in order to get the reward.

So the timeline might look like this:

- After 22 seconds → Dog still in down-stay → Treat!
- Next reward available after 35 seconds → Dog still in down-stay → Treat!
- Next reward available after 31 seconds → Dog got up before time → No treat
- Dog goes back into down-stay → New interval starts and so on.

This schedule rewards patience and duration. Since the dog doesn't know exactly when the next reward will come, it learns to maintain the behaviour for longer periods, ideal for things like calm settling, loose-leash walking, or staying in place during distractions.

The application of the above schedules in the different fields of dog training that are common nowadays, such as the use of dogs in the film industry, advertising, professional competitions, police and rescue dogs, agility, and so on, depends on various factors, including the complexity of the command or behaviour required to be taught, the dog's individual motivation and learning pace, and the effectiveness of the treats as rewards. However, for our dog training requirements, we can focus on just one of those schedules; namely, the *Variable Ratio (VR) Reinforcement Schedule*, where the number of responses needed for a reward varies. This is the most powerful partial reinforcement schedule and is considered the most difficult to extinguish once the reinforcer is no longer present.

In the context of human behaviour gambling is probably the easiest and most practical example of the application of the Variable Ratio Reinforcement Schedule, and given the number of people (me included) addicted to playing the national lottery or scratch cards etc., I can say that it works remarkably well, even our dogs are not immune to this addiction. In gambling, a variable reinforcement schedule is a key component of the addictive nature of certain games, such as slot machines, lottery tickets, or scratch cards. This schedule involves providing rewards to players at unpredictable intervals, which can lead to persistent and compulsive behaviour. When using this schedule, players receive rewards intermittently and unpredictably. Sometimes they win and sometimes they lose, but the uncertainty of when the next reward will come keeps them engaged and motivated to continue playing. Because the rewards in gambling can vary in magnitude, players may receive small wins frequently, larger wins occasionally, and jackpot prizes rarely. This variability in the size of rewards adds to the excitement and anticipation of playing. Slot machines in a casino, for example, are programmed to deliver payouts according to complex algorithms, ensuring wins are not too frequent or too rare. This pattern of payouts creates a sense of anticipation and excitement, as players hope for a big win with each spin. The psychological effects of the unpredictability of rewards in gambling activates the brain's reward system, releasing dopamine, a neurotransmitter associated with pleasure and reinforcement. Over time, individuals can become psychologically dependent on these intermittent rewards, leading to compulsive gambling behaviour. This guarantees the long-term engagement of the gambler in the game. In fact, research has demonstrated (e.g. Ramnerö et al., 2019) that variable reinforcement schedules are effective at maintaining long-term engagement with gambling activities. Even when players experience losses, the occasional wins and the anticipation of future rewards keep them coming back for more. Players are willing to accept losses in the hope of achieving a big win, and the uncertainty of outcomes adds an element of excitement to the experience.

Similarly, in dog training, a variable reinforcement schedule involves rewarding the dog's behaviour intermittently, rather than every single time. For example, when teaching a dog to sit on command, you might initially reward them with a treat every time they sit correctly. However, as the behaviour becomes more consistent, you can switch to a variable reinforcement schedule by rewarding them with a treat only sometimes. This variable schedule can be highly effective in maintaining the desired behaviour over the long term. Dogs learn that performing the desired behaviour may result in a reward, but are never quite sure when that reward will come. Consequently, they are more likely to continue displaying the behaviour, even when treats are not immediately forthcoming. By using a variable reinforcement schedule strategically, we ensure our dogs remain motivated and engaged in training sessions as this approach creates an environment of uncertainty and excitement that can keep them engaged over extended periods.

Finally, the transition from Continuous Reinforcement to Variable Ratio Reinforcement should be gradual – you know your dog better than anyone else and it is completely up to you to understand when your dog is ready to progress. Obviously, to keep your young puppy or dog motivated, you can use verbal praise (such as "Good boy/dog!") and also physical affection (such as petting, patting on shoulders, or gentle scratches) alongside treats as rewards during training sessions. One word of warning though, whilst treats are essential for positive reinforcement, it is crucial to factor in your dog's overall diet and calorie intake. Unfortunately, obesity has become an issue among pets as well as humans. As stated previously, use small, low-calorie treats or break larger treats into smaller pieces to prevent overfeeding during training sessions. In some cases you can also consider using your dog's regular kibble as training treats to avoid excessive calorie intake. As far as the frequency of sessions is concerned, I try to schedule several smaller weekly sessions rather than a singular long one over the weekend, as I believe it is imperative to continue reinforcing behaviours periodically so that they remain reliable over time.

DOG'S NAME

You might wonder why the dog's name has anything to do with the basic commands? The answer is that we need to make a distinction between calling our dog's name with the purpose of getting their full attention and mentioning their name when it comes up during an unrelated conversation or circumstances other than recall. Over the course of the day, during our normal conversations with family and friends, our dog's name comes up so many times that after a while our dog becomes accustomed to the fact that upon hearing its name, there is no connection or association with a command nor the need to redirect its attention towards its owner. If we take the recall for example, which I consider one of the first and most important commands we ought to teach our dogs, you can appreciate how it can easily be spoiled if we do not reinforce the response on the part of our pets when called. In this case we are inadvertently exposing our pets to the process known as habituation – a simple form of learning that involves decreased responsiveness to a particular stimulus after repeated exposure.

Within the context of the evolution of canine species, habituation is an essential adaptive mechanism as it allows our dogs to filter out irrelevant or non-threatening stimuli and focus on more important ones. However, it can also lead to desensitisation and a lack of responsiveness to important stimuli, as in the case of the recall. It is therefore essential to use a particular and unique tone of voice exclusively for the purpose of the recall in order to get the dog's full and undivided attention. I always recommend pronouncing the dog's name using a slightly higher pitch towards the end of their name and lengthening the sound during the recall so that the name "Daisy", for example, will sound like "Daaiiiissyyy". By doing this, you will create a sound pattern that will be interpreted by your dog as the action of running towards you and they will associate it with either a treat, enthusiastic verbal praise, or some unforgettable playtime – ultimately one of the best experiences your dog will share with you. Moreover, there is another reason for using a higher-pitched tone of voice for the name and recall. Dogs respond more positively to high-pitched tones because, from the earliest stages of their lives, they become used to hearing the high-pitched noise made by their siblings in the litter – a familiar and comfortable sound that remains such for the rest of their lives. You must have heard the same sound when you first went to see the breeder to choose your puppy. Conversely, a lower sound is associated more with a warning signal. When puppies or young dogs start to interact with other adult dogs, there may be occasions where the adult will growl at the youngster to warn him or her that they are pushing the boundaries too far and that they need to back off or stop whatever they are doing. If you are among that category of pet owners who live with more than one pet, I am sure you must have witnessed a similar situation when you welcomed a new puppy into your home.

Let me briefly expand on the topic of growling. Some of my clients have expressed concern about their dogs' use of the growling sound during their interactions with puppies and younger dogs or other pets in the park. When I say that training is about establishing a common language that allows us to communicate effectively with our pets, I also mean that as a more evolved species, we ought to learn and understand their language so that we can read and avoid unpleasant situations during the ritual of meeting. When dogs growl they are warning us that they are not comfortable with a particular event happening at a particular time in a particular environment, so we have the chance to modify any one of these parameters and allow the dogs to return to a normal and more balanced mindset. I often see owners discouraging their dogs from growling, especially in local parks and public places, as the behaviour is deemed embarrassing and socially unacceptable. Some dogs do stop growling after being told off several times by their owners, but in some cases I have witnessed these dogs completely avoiding the first steps of the normal ritual of meeting, like eyeing up the other dog, cautiously approaching it, sniffing each other's backsides, and, without using the warning sound of growling, reacting directly to a full physical confrontation with the other dog. I have also seen the same happening in households where a new puppy is being introduced to the existing resident dog. For the puppy, it is all part of the learning process and as with most juveniles interacting with older dogs, they will push the boundaries to access the resources they need and will sometimes compete with the older and more experienced dog. I find that it is always better not to interfere with these internal interactions and give the dogs the opportunity to sort it out among themselves. If you feel sorry when you see your puppy being growled at or denied their bone because your older dog has taken charge, please do not. If you intervene in the early stages of their interaction, you are simply postponing the inevitable and might inadvertently promote an escalation of the conflict that ends up in a more serious outcome.

When it comes to teaching the dogs their names and ensuring they respond by turning their heads and focusing on you, we can use different training methods. I prefer to associate a reward with any sound to which the puppy is initially attracted. For the purpose of this exercise, I use a smooching sound like "Mwah" (which resembles the sound of a kiss) to start with and then substitute the smooching sound with the dog's name, pronounced with the same unique tone of voice described above. This method can be applied not only to a new puppy but also to rescue dogs if you wish to change their names. To start with, prepare some treats and take the puppy to a familiar environment away from distractions. Execute the "Mwah" sound and wait for the puppy to turn their head in your direction. As soon as that happens, mark their behaviour with the positive marker "Yes" followed by the reward. Continue the session for a few minutes, or according to your puppy's attention span, and always finish the session with a game or some fun activities. Repeat these short sessions frequently throughout the day for a few days, or until the puppy reliably responds to the "Mwah" sound every time they hear it. When that happens, you are ready to proceed to the next step which consists of substituting the "Mwah" sound with the puppy's name. The whole routine will sound similar to the name "DaaaiiiiSSYYYY" being called first, followed by the mwah sound, and then the positive marker word "Yes". Repeat the short sessions again throughout the day or until the puppy turns their attention in your direction when they hear their name first. When that happens you can drop the "Mwah" sound and just call their names. If you wish to change your rescue dog's name you can use the same technique, only use their old name instead of the "Mwah" sound.

WATCH ME

Using this command to obtain your puppy's full attention with direct eye contact and then sustain their focus on you for a period of time can be highly productive during the first initial training sessions. If the puppy is looking at you, it is likely that he or she is also listening to you. The "Watch Me" command also helps the dog to focus on you in the presence of strong distractions when you transfer the training session outdoors. Additionally, it can be extremely valuable in real-life situations; for example, when, during a walk around the block, you prefer your dog to avoid eye contact with another reactive dog coming from the opposite direction. Staring directly into the eyes of a stranger dog is often perceived as an intended challenge by the other dog and can also be interpreted as threatening behaviour. By contrast, requesting eye contact should not be a difficult task for your dogs because researchers have shown that looking into their owner's eyes triggers the release of the love hormone, oxytocin. By encouraging mutual eye contact, you not only show your dog affection but also strengthen your bond with them. Teaching the "Watch Me" command is quite straightforward and should be done immediately after completing the dog's name exercise. Grab a tasty treat and put it right in front of your dog's nose, then gently move it towards your forehead and in between your eyes. Make sure your dog watches the treat and stares at your forehead throughout the action. Mark the behaviour with the positive marker "Yes" and then reward the dog by dispensing the treat with the other hand. After several repetitions, instead of starting the exercise by holding the treat in front of your dog's nose, simply rub your fingers with the treat (the scent should be enough to get their attention) and proceed by moving your fingers towards your eyes. When the dog makes eye contact, mark the behaviour and always reward with a treat coming from the other hand. You have now created the hand signal for the command and simply need to add the verbal cue "Watch Me" before moving your hand.

Repeat the exercise throughout the day, keeping the sessions short but interesting and fun for both of you. Once your dog reliably responds to the verbal cue, you are ready to proceed with the final step which involves allowing your dog to choose where to look in order to get the reward. Hold a treat in front of your dog's nose with the right hand and another treat in your left hand. Slowly extend your left arm on the side of your body and, without saying anything, wait for your dog's reaction. They will first follow and stare at the moving left hand, but when they realise that nothing happens, they will look back at you to see what's going on. As soon as they do so, mark and reward them for having made the correct choice and dispense the treat from the same left hand you moved away. Repeat this step until your dog reliably chooses to look at you instead of following the treat you are holding in your left hand; you can then use the verbal cue "Watch me" before you place the treat out to the side with your left hand. If your dog is not particularly motivated by food, use their favourite toy and exaggerate with verbal praise when they are successful. This exercise might take a little bit longer for your dog to understand, so do not be impatient as they will see that and perhaps will deliberately choose not to look at you at all. If this is the case, stop immediately and try again later.

THE RECALL "COME"

To be perfectly honest, I have rarely encountered a dog that had impeccable recall, which translates as having the ability to return to the owner promptly upon being called, irrespective of the presence of distractions and in any particular situation or environment. Even a professional trainer such as myself had to devise a back-up strategy to first interrupt whatever activity the dog is focused on by using the command "Leave It", which consequently allowed me to use the command "Come" and reward the dog by providing a similar or even better alternative to whatever was distracting them. To successfully achieve good and consistent recall, we need to create a positive and unforgettable experience for the dog each time they come back to us. The use of positive reinforcement, enthusiastic verbal praise, baby talk, and playtime will create such a pleasant outcome for your dog that they will want to come back to you every time you call them just to see what is in store. Conversely, we should never use the recall in association with a negative or unpleasant outcome, such as telling them off after a delayed response following your recall, going into isolation after they have come back to you, getting their nails clipped, or anything else your dog finds to be a negative experience. I often hear people in the park shouting the command "Come" followed by "Come here NOW" in a frustrated and unhappy tone of voice because the dog is not responding to the recall as they are having the time of their life playing with or sniffing another dogs, chasing a squirrel, or scavenging some delicious fast food left overs. As discussed in previous chapters, dogs are highly sensitive to the tone of voice (if you shout angrily they are less likely to want to be reunited with you) and more importantly they learn by association. If you reprimand them and put them on the lead when they do eventually come back, the next time you call them, they will think twice before coming back, fearing the worst. If you have done this already, do not worry as any mistake can always be fixed, but if that's the case I suggest you change the old verbal cue to something new and start the training all over again.

Before I go any further, it is also essential to point out that dogs are oblivious to the English language or any other language for that matter. Please refer to the next chapter dedicated to how dogs communicate. With training, we aim to shape the behaviour first and then associate that behaviour with a verbal cue (the "command") and that is the language they will understand. Based on this premise, the first step in teaching your puppy, young, or adult dog the recall consists of creating the physical motion of the dog walking towards you. You will need to start in a completely distraction-free environment, preferably in the comfort of your own home. You will also need to time the training session appropriately and preferably before mealtimes, so that food becomes a big motivator. Given that puppies requires at least four meals a day up until they reach the age of 3 months, you could set up four short training sessions before mealtimes – making sure you keep them short but fun and entertaining for both you and your puppy. One last thing to remember is to time the session when the puppy is fully awake, in good spirits, and physically and mentally active. It may sound obvious but not everyone is aware that there are specific times during the day where dogs are more active. As explained previously, they are unable to regulate their body temperatures by sweating and therefore have evolved so that they are more mobile during the coolest time of the day; namely, at dusk and dawn. Every dog owner is aware of those times during the day when their dogs seem to go mad and start running around the house jumping on and off furniture, barking, and zigzagging without apparent reason. These events occur at dusk and dawn, when it is a bit cooler, and rarely at midday when predators tend to rest (away from the scorching heat). Try to use this to your advantage and plan the training sessions for times when you will be more likely to get your puppy's full and undivided attention.

I can now proceed with the first steps to building up the whole sequence for the recall with the help of some useful exercises. If you have been working on the first two previous commands, "Dog's Name" and "Watch Me", it should now be quite easy to grab your dog's attention. This will be the starting point for the recall exercise, only this time you will hold the treat in front of your dog's nose and, while always keeping the treat level with your dog's nose and with your hand positioned in the centre between your knees, start walking backwards very slowly with the puppy happily following your hand holding the treat. There is no need to introduce the cue word "Come" at this point as our goal is to create the motion, shape the behaviour, and then add the command. Be extremely careful because two things can happen here: first, if you keep the hand holding the treat too high, you will inadvertently encourage your puppy to jump up, so keep it consistently at your dog's nose level throughout the motion. Secondly, if you keep the hand holding the treat on either side of your body and not in the centre between your knees, you will teach your dog to come and stand on either one of your sides, left or right. Always keep in mind that your objective during this first exercise is to teach your dog to come and sit right in front of you – no other position is desirable. Having walked backwards for a few steps with the puppy following you, mark the behaviour as usual with the positive marker "Yes" and reward profusely.

Initially, you do not need to walk great distances, just build up the distance steadily until the puppy is able to follow your hand until the end of the corridor or the opposite corner of the room. You can also practise this exercise with other family members or your friends too that the repetitions flow more smoothly and the puppy learns to respond to any person involved, not just the nominated handler. Repeat the exercise a few times throughout the day: remember, sessions should be short but frequent (according to your puppy's/dog's attention span) and always end with games and lots of verbal praises. When the motion is executed reliably, you can start adding the verbal cue after the dog's name. If your dog's name is Toby for example, you will call his name to grab his attention, "Toobbyyyy", followed immediately by the command "Come". At this stage it is also important to bear in mind that after using the special tone of voice dedicated exclusively to the recall, you only want to give the command "Come" once. If you repeat the command too many times after your dog's name, you will inadvertently train your dogs to come to you only the third or fourth time after they have heard the command. Repeat the exercise at will until you have achieved a consistent and reliable recall, ideally after the first time you have called your dog. If your dog fails to respond immediately, do not panic and fall into the trap of being tempted to repeat the command again, perhaps in a frustrated tone of voice. Instead, wait until your dog comes to you spontaneously, or eventually go back a couple of steps in the training process and start again. The final phase is to practise the same exercise, but with the added variation of choosing a starting point that is at an ever increasing distance from your dog. You can begin by calling your dog when it is positioned a couple of metres away from you, then start walking backwards – do not start the backwards motion until the dog has come close to you. With subsequent repetitions during short sessions throughout the day, your aim will be to increase the distance each time by one metre, making sure that the dog comes all the way to you. The last step consists of testing the whole recall exercise using the correct intonation, the right timing, and making sure your puppy is able to execute the command from any distance and from any room in your house, even when they are out of sight. If the recall works consistently 100% of the time and on the first attempt, then you can congratulate yourselves for having accomplished the first task. You may now reinforce the recall at home, exploiting every opportunity the dog has to experience a positive outcome after the recall – whether this is meal time, playtime, or potty time, the recall will become almost a muscle memory motion for your dog. One thing I forgot to mention is that some trainers prefer to integrate the final steps of the recall with the collar grabbing action, where you effectively train your dog to get used to being grabbed and held by the collar upon their return to you. They explain that by doing this, the dog will not be tempted to shoot off again immediately after they have received the reward and you can put them back on the lead more comfortably. I personally think that the collar grabbing action is unnecessary as I tend to complete the recall with the dog in a sit position. Moreover, I find it more useful to integrate other commands into the routine such as "Place", where the dog goes around my right-hand side and sits between my legs so that I can put the collar on, or the command "Heel", where the dog moves to my left-hand side and places himself in the heel position so that I can either put the lead on them or continue with my heel routine exercise. I leave it up to your preferences and requirements whether to integrate the collar grabbing motion into the exercise.

During these first few stages, if you have a puppy or a young dog and have been working successfully on the recall at home, do not be tempted to use the recall outdoors or in the park during the walks just yet. It is extremely easy to be tempted to call your dog, who is perhaps fully engaged with some strong distraction, and ruin all the hard work you have done in a matter of minutes. In the spirit of this book, you should always try to fulfil your dog's basic needs to exercise, socialise, play with other dogs, sniff, and, more importantly, bond with you when outside on walks. Our dogs clearly need to spend some time off the lead in order to do all of the above, but equally we feel responsible for their safety when they are off the lead and must be sure we have the means to get them back. There will be situations where you will need to intervene; for example, if the dog gets carried away playing too roughly with other dogs or is up to some mischievous behaviour. In these circumstances, you will want to prepare and set yourself for success before you let your dog off the lead, perhaps by leaving an old lead attached to their collar (the cheapest and lightest will do) so that you can step on it or grab it and regain control without having to use the recall. The time to make full use of the recall outdoors will come soon, but there is still some preparation work to do before you can confidently use the recall with your dog completely off the leash. In fact, in preparation for the first few outings with your puppy or young dog, this would be the best time to consider whether to incorporate into the recall routine a visual signal that can be used when your dog will be distant from you as well as the use of a whistle. I recommend integrating both these cues into the recall because they are very easy to teach and for your dog to comprehend. If you have chosen a particular breed or have opted to re-home a dog that requires a lot of mental and physical stimulation, then you should expect them to operate at a certain distance from you during your walks in the park. Sometimes the wind will work against you and your dogs will not be able to hear you calling them, but they will be able to see you and can easily pick up the higher frequency of a dog whistle. As far as the visual cue is concerned, I like to use what I call the scarecrow position, which involves spreading your arms sideways in conjunction with the verbal cue "Dog's Name" followed by the command "Come". You can try this at home for a few sessions and then see if your dog is able to respond to the visual cue alone and come back to you. The same goes for the whistle, all you need to do is to choose your own pattern of whistling (I tend to hoot three times at short intervals) and then whistle before every recall command is given. After a few repetitions, you can try to use just the whistle and observe your dog's response. If it does not work then you will need to go back one step and repeat the exercise a few more times.

So far you have been working on the recall command in the comfortable and familiar environment of your home – the puppy knows the routine and responds reliably every time it hears the command "Come". It is now time to put all your hard work into practice and introduce some distractions into your routine so that your dog will respond without hesitation and consistently, regardless of what is happening around them. It is imperative to choose carefully the location where you will start practising the recall outside. You certainly do not want to take your puppy into the local park where the presence of multiple strong distractions will present a challenge and make it more difficult for both you and the puppy to focus on each other. Don't get me wrong, it is vital that your puppy is exposed from a young age to all sorts of experiences, whether this is meeting different people and children, socialising with dogs of different sizes and breeds, or exposure to traffic noise, but training activities should take place in different circumstances away from the normal routine, at least at the beginning. If going to a completely new place is not an option, then choose an extremely quiet area of your local park with few or no distractions. If your puppy or young dog become more confident in the local park and you find yourself struggling with the recall, I recommend going for a walk to a new park as this will reset your dog's level of confidence and will make them more aware of the new surroundings, hence they will be more focused on you.

Let me expand further – I stated in previous chapters that the human-dog relationship is so intertwined that you can always find a dog wherever humans live, even in the remotest parts of our planet. I believe that to be true and it is reflected in the approach taken by humans and, consequently, by dogs when they were slowly but steadily moving and settling in all areas of the globe. Both species would share the same approach when it comes to expanding their territories. I can envisage the tribe with their canine friends, setting out from a familiar and secure environment and exploring a new adjacent territory, finding out whether the conditions were favourable enough to sustain life (food, water, and shelter), and eventually settling in the new territory or moving back to the familiar one. When treading in a new environment, there is the tendency to be more cautious and more focused on each other in case you encounter a dangerous situation. For example, when you walk your dog in a new park or take them somewhere new for the weekend for the first time, you will notice that in the majority of cases your dog will stay very close to you, and this is why I always recommend that pet parents take their dogs to a new place every so often, if convenient, so that their focus will be redirected exclusively onto their owners while practising and reinforcing the basic commands.

Once you have reached your chosen location, let your dog off the leash and give them the freedom to explore, sniff around, and familiarise themselves with the environment, but always keep an eye on them. At the beginning of your walk, you might notice your dog wandering quite far away from you. In fact, if the dog has not had the chance to relieve themselves, they will simply follow their instinct and distance themself as far as they possibly can so that they can defecate or pee. Even if your first reaction is to want them closer, there is no point in trying the recall at this particular moment because the dog will simply ignore you. Dogs are genetically wired to poo as far away as possible from where they live; they do that because if they defecated near their resting place, the smell of the faeces would attract predators and imperil the puppies or the younger adolescent dogs and give away the location of the den. Moreover, living in proximity of the excrement would favour the spread of various diseases among the pack. Once their toilet needs have been fulfilled you can start interacting with your dog, perhaps by playing some fun games or using their favourite toy. Every time they move towards you, use the recall the way you have been practising at home, using the same voice intonation and recall sequence of your dog's name and the command "Come". With no distractions around, you should be successful with each recall.

During the walk, there might be occasions where your dog redirects its focus on something else, such as a squirrel, pigeon, etc. You can easily spot that because your dog will initiate the prey drive behaviour – they will orient their attention towards the object of their interest, go into a seeking mode, and subsequently stalk. At this stage of the training process, these are the only chances you have to recall your dog. If the chasing starts then there is little chance your dog will listen to you. Do not be tempted to repeat the recall because, as I said before, your dog will learn to ignore the command and all your hard work will be wasted. If by any chance your dog turns their head towards you after you called them but does not actually move towards you, trigger their chasing instinct by running away from them. If that happens then make sure they have commenced the action of running in your direction, at which point you can stop, turn around, and recall them again.

What I refer to as "triggering the chasing instinct" is better described as allelomimetic behaviour – an instinctual and inherent behaviour that is hardwired in social animals with a strong social order and structure. This instinct drives them to follow and mimic the behaviour of other members within the same social group. For example, if you observe a flock of pigeons pecking away, you will notice that if just one gets startled and flies away, all the others will follow. Our canine friends, being such highly developed social animals, start showing allelomimetic behaviour from the young age of 5 weeks. I will revisit this topic in more detail in future chapters, when I explain how some of the most difficult behavioural problems can be treated by applying the allelomimetic behaviour technique.

Going back to the recall, if your dog looks at you even for a brief moment, you have options other than starting to run in the opposite direction. You could, for example, attract your dog's attention with their favourite stuffed toy, squeaky ball, frisbee, or whatever action-evoking activities your dog is into. As a last resort, and if the circumstances allow it, you can drop and lay down on the ground pretending to be injured or dead – this will surely cause your dog to run immediately towards you to investigate what has happened and upon their arrival you can praise and reward verbally or with treats. The amount of time your dog needs for physical activities will vary according to breed, age, and stamina. A working cocker spaniel requires more physical and mental stimulation than other non-working breeds and it is entirely up to you to structure the daily routine so that your dog's needs are fulfilled. I recommend following the initial recall training routine in a distraction-free environment until you reach a level of confidence that will allow you to gradually introduce stronger and more tempting distractions for your dog. Ultimately, you know your dog better than anybody else and if you are in any doubt about how successful your recall will be, then do not hesitate to use one of those long lines (you can find all sort of lengths available on the market up to a range of 20 metres) as a precautionary measure so that you do not risk the recall being totally ignored. A gentle pressure on the line is all you will need to distract them and ensure they refocus on you. The long line is a training tool and should only be used for this purpose. Once the recall is reliable, take the long line off and test the efficiency of the recall with different levels of distraction. If your dog does not respond at the first command, do not repeat the recall; instead, put them back on the long line and practice the previous steps for a little while longer. To make it a bit easier for you both and set you up for success, on the first few occasions you practise the recall off the leash, wait for the right moment to call. This means that whatever activity your dog is doing – sniffing, drinking, playing – there will always be a rather brief moment where they will pause and raise their head, perhaps checking where you are; this is the precise moment when you want to call your dog. The key to success is to build a wonderful relationship with your dog; he or she has to see you as the most exciting, loving, and funny experience they ever have every time they come back to you and, with time, their response to the recall will become almost a muscle memory reflex.

When you feel like you are more in control and no longer need to use the long line, you could leave a normal lead attached to your dog's collar as it will not affect their freedom of movement but will give you the opportunity to grab the lead and regain control if necessary. As your dog experiences more time off the leash, you will need to keep reinforcing the recall by having them randomly check in with you many times during the walk, for example while they are at play, especially with other dogs, or while they are busy sniffing or stalking a bird. Just call the dog to you, give them a treat, and then release them back to play. In this way, the recall "Come" is not associated with leaving or being leashed; instead, it will become a muscle memory motion that your dog will perform with great enthusiasm in expectation of the pleasure and positive outcome.

SIT

There are several reasons why "Sit" is considered a fundamental command in dog training. Firstly, it helps us to manage and control our exuberant dogs in various challenging situations such as jumping up on people familiar to the dog or even strangers, or other dogs in the park or on the street. It can also assist us in laying the groundwork for other, additional commands.

Including the "Sit" command in our pet's training regimen is vital and should be a key component of any effective obedience training programme. Moreover, in those situations where safety is a concern, "Sit" can be very useful in averting potential dangers like approaching busy roads. It is definitely a command that encourages your dog to concentrate on you and, consequently, enhances the effectiveness of training sessions and strengthens the bond between you. A dog that can reliably respond to the "Sit" command also tends to exhibit better manners in various social settings, allowing you to enjoy your dog's company in all kinds of diverse social environments like shops, bars, restaurants, and your friends and family's homes without causing disruptions. It is also one of the easiest commands to teach your dog and can be learnt extremely quickly because it involves the use of treats, which always creates a pleasant experience for your dog. The basic concept is that if you visualise the whole length of the dog's body like an axis, then whatever the dog's head does, the body moves in the opposite direction; that is to say, if the dog's head moves to the left, then the body will move to the right, if the dog's head moves upwards, then the body will move downwards.

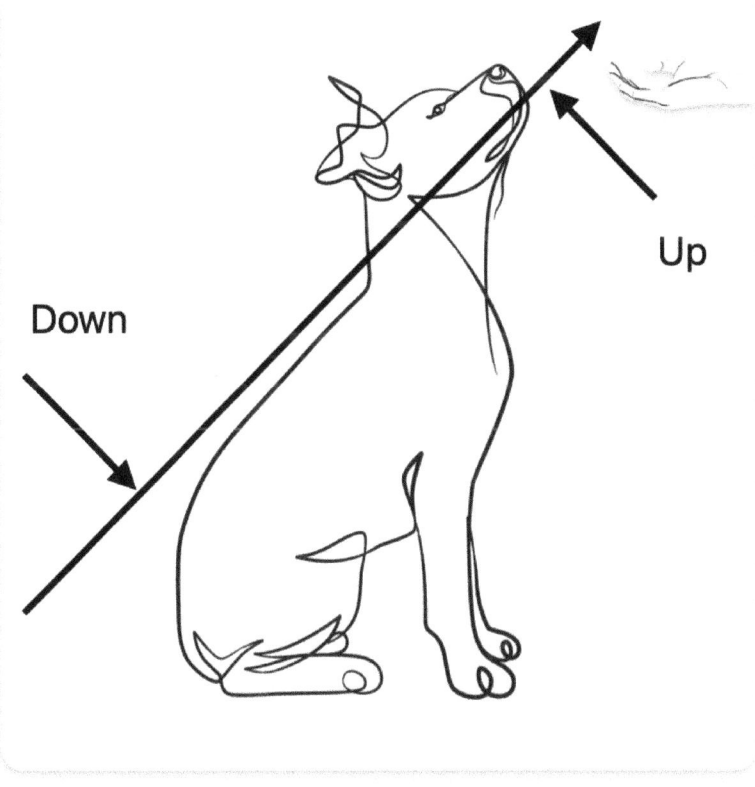

You can integrate the "Sit" command at the end of the recall exercise so that upon arrival, your dog will automatically go into the sitting position without the need for you to say the command. All you need to do is lure the dog into the sitting position by slowly raising your hand and then hold the treat once your dog has arrived and is standing in front of you in expectation of the treat. Your dog's head will move upwards to follow the slow upward movement of your hand holding the treat and their body will move downward. As soon as your dog's bottom makes contact with the floor, mark the behaviour with the positive marker (the word "Yes"). Once the behaviour is shaped after a few repetitions, start adding the command "Sit" before marking the behaviour with the magic word "Yes". Be aware that if you keep your hand holding the treat too high, the dog will tend to jump up to get the treat. Do not correct or punish your dog; instead, move a couple of steps backwards and call your dog again, this time while holding the treat at your dog's head level. Finally, as for all other commands, do not repeat "Sit", "Sit", "Sit"… Just say the command once and patiently give your dog the chance to process the information; after all, your dog is learning a new language and needs a bit of time to make all the connections between cause and effect.

As for the recall "Come", it is always a good idea to create a visual signal in connection with a command. In the case of the "Sit" command, the hand signal will be represented by the action of raising your cup-shaped hand, as if it is holding a treat, just above your dog's head. After a few repetitions, try and make the gesture only without speaking the word and see if your dog is able to understand the action they are required to perform. For working dogs or highly active ones that like to wander off a bit further away during walks, it is worth considering the addition of an extra visual cue paired with the sound of the whistle. The visual cue would be your arm raised high as much as possible paired with a single but longer blow of the whistle (let's say a couple of seconds). To begin with, choose a quiet place with no distractions like the garden in your house, your living room if you do not have a garden, or the familiar place where you normally train your dog. Start the exercise by standing right in front of your dog, raise your hand high, blow the whistle, and then give the command "Sit" which your dog already knows. Repeat until the response is consistent, but more importantly, do not move away from your dog as you practise the exercise. It is essential to first build up the time and achieve some consistency, then gradually increase the distance between you and your dog with each repetition. After a few sessions your dog will become so efficient in performing the exercise that they will sit when you raise your hand and whistle even before you have had the chance to give the verbal cue "Sit". When that happens, you can simply stop using the verbal cue altogether. You will then need to transfer the training sessions outdoors, choosing again a quiet place in your local park where there are no or very few distractions and practise what you have been doing at home. Have fun and make every training session a memorable experience for both you and your beloved pet. Among all the advantages described above, the sitting command can be extremely helpful in solving one of the unwanted behaviours that most bother pet owners, which is a dog that jumps up on every other person they meet and greet. I have dedicated a whole chapter to this and other behavioural issues which you can refer to if you are experiencing the same problem with your pet.

DOWN

Like the "Sit" command, teaching your dog to lie down on command offers numerous benefits (which I will analyse separately) and can be instrumental in managing your dog's behaviour in various real-life situations. However, because our dogs assume the same position lying down as when they are sleeping, it is much easier and less stressful for them to maintain that position over a longer period of time than the sitting position, and therefore the use of this command is preferred to "Sit". I highlight some of the other advantages below:

- Control and Calmness: The "Down" command helps us gain more control over our dogs, especially in situations where they need to remain calm and composed. It is an extremely useful tool for preventing unwanted behaviours or excessive excitement.

- Basic Obedience: Similar to "Sit", "Down" is a fundamental command that contributes to basic obedience training. It establishes a foundation for further commands and helps create a well-behaved and responsive dog.

- Safety: In situations where a dog needs to be under control, such as near busy roads or crowded areas, the "Down" command can ensure your dog stays in a safe and secure position.

- Greeting People: Teaching your dog to lie down can be an alternative behaviour when greeting people, especially if your dog is particularly exuberant and has the tendency to jump up. It is a polite and controlled way for your dog to interact with others.

- Vet Visits and Examinations: The "Down" command is especially beneficial during veterinary visit routines. It can keep your dog calm and relaxed during the examinations, allowing veterinarians to perform necessary procedures without stress.

- Mealtime Manners: Training your dog to lie down before meals promotes good manners. It prevents them from rushing to their food and teaches patience, reinforcing the idea that good behaviour is rewarded.

- <u>Settling in Various Environments</u>: The ability to lie down on command is useful in various environments, such as at home, in public places, bars and restaurants, or when visiting friends. It helps your dog settle comfortably and adapt to different situations.

- <u>Stress Reduction</u>: The "Down" command can be a cue for your dog to relax and alleviate stress. It is particularly useful in situations where your dog may feel anxious or uncomfortable.

To teach the "Down" command to any puppy or young dog, I have successfully used the same luring technique for many years and rarely it has taken more than one session to achieve a reliable and consistent result. Because treats are involved, dogs switch very quickly into that training mode they enjoy so much because they learn to perceive the training sessions as the time when they receive full undivided attention from their owners and plenty of rewards and fun. The "Down" command is much easier to teach with the dog sitting because they are already halfway in the position required.

To begin the exercise, you will need to hold a treat in your hand and show it to your dog, making sure it catches the scent of the treat, then position your hand right under the dog's chin. This action will make the dog want to lower their head while following your hand holding the treat. With a slow but consistent action, start lowering your hand further under the dog's chin and observe their reaction. They will probably stop halfway through the motion as they might think that they have performed the "Sit" command as requested and remain a bit puzzled by the lack of cause and effect they have been used to in previous exercises. If your dog stops their downward movement of the head, you must also stop and wait until the movement resumes; as soon as that happens, slowly lower your hand further down and continue the motion until you have reached the floor. If the dog finds it difficult to execute the whole movement all the way to the floor, you can deconstruct the exercise and reward each incremental improvement. For example, if your dog moves only one paw forward, mark that action and reward it. Your dog might subsequently move the other paw forward, so mark again the movement and reward it. Repeat the exercise again, but this time wait until the dog moves both paws even further than before, mark the behaviour and reward, and then continue until your dog slides with both paws down and goes into the down position, at which point "Bingoo!!!" You then praise your dog profusely and reward it enthusiastically for having successfully assumed the sphinx position.

If your dog is not responding to the conventional method just described, you could try to get more creative and find an alternative way to encourage your dog to lower its head and go into a lying down position. For example, you could ask your dog to sit first and then sit on the floor with them, remaining perpendicular to their position. While your dog is sitting, extend both your legs and create a bridge, then insert your hand inside the bridge so that it emerges on the side where your dog is sitting, right in front of them. Your dog will lower its head to sniff the treat and will put its head under the bridge to reach the hand holding the treat. Because this method combines the power of positive reinforcement (using treats) with a physical cue, the result is a multi-sensory experience that can capture the dog's attention and encourage the desired behaviour. It is essential to be patient and consistent with this technique, rewarding the dog each time it successfully lowers its head or tries to get under your legs. For obvious reasons, this method can only be used if your dog's size allows it; if you have a larger breed which cannot physically get under your legs, then you will have to find another item that serves the same purpose, like a piece of furniture, a chair, or a coffee table.

Another method you can use to successfully teach the "Down" command would be to capture the behaviour when your dog naturally exhibits it. Let's say, for example, that you are in the kitchen making yourself a cup of tea and your dog has followed you, hoping that at some point you will reach the cabinet where you keep the treats. You will notice that even if you are not paying any attention to your dog, it will spontaneously offer all the behaviours it already knows in the hope of triggering the marker and the reward as if it was a normal training session. If you keep ignoring your dog's attempts to get your attention, it will at some point spontaneously lie down near you – that is the precise moment at which you can quickly reward and praise the behaviour. If you continue to reward the behaviour, your dog will perform it spontaneously and consistently, at which point you introduce the verbal cue "Down". After the behaviour is shaped and the complete motion terminates with your dog lying down in the sphinx position, you should minimise the need to continuously bend forward during the exercise. The final goal is to create the visual cue, which consists of lowering just your hand, and then associate the cue with the desired action, allowing you to use it without bending over. Your dog's acute observation of your body language and posture will allow it to spot even a subtle change in your cue and that can affect its response; it is therefore important to check that your hand movement remains consistent throughout the exercise. Once your dog reliably responds to the hand lowering gesture, gradually reduce the frequency of the treat rewards. To reinforce the execution of the command using only the verbal cue, you will have to clearly use the word "Down" and after a brief moment use the actual hand gesture. In future sessions, the occasional rewards will help maintain the newly learnt behaviour, but at the first signs of confusion or regression, temporarily reintroduce treats to reinforce the behaviour.

STAY

The "Stay" command involves teaching our dogs to maintain a certain position for any length of time and can be used effectively in association with other commands in the building of more complex behaviours. Depending on the order in which we have planned our training programme, it can be a bit challenging to grasp for some of our more sensitive pets. If taught after the recall command "Come" for example, it can be confusing for some dogs to learn to remain seated or in the "lie down" position when we walk away from them. You know your dog better than anyone else and if your dog has formed an extremely powerful bond and follows you everywhere constantly, you may want to introduce the "Stay" command after the commands "Sit" or "Down". The hand signal associated with the "Stay" command is your right or left hand positioned in front of your dog's face with your fingers spread wide and your body slightly leaning forward (please do not use the finger point gesture). Because your dogs are likely to be baffled by this new word, they will maintain the position for a second or so, in which case mark their behaviour with the Positive Marker "Yes" and release the treat with the other hand. If that is not the case and your dogs are unable to maintain the position, you will need to anticipate the hand gesture and drastically reduce the time between the "Sit" or "Down" commands and the "Stay" command. It will sound more like "Sit-Stay" or "Down-Stay" rather than having a brief interval between the commands. Once that is achieved, you can then start building up the time in which your dogs can maintain the position without moving towards you by counting in your mind for up to 45 seconds or a minute. At the same time, slowly assume a more upright position so that you only need to use your extended arm and the hand signal positioned in front of your dogs to signal them to stay.

Once you have successfully completed the first phase and your dog can reliably hold the position for the length of time you have been practising for (perhaps using the reinforcement schedules previously mentioned above), you can proceed with the second phase which consists of walking away from your dog. You have a couple of options to choose from depending on your dog's reaction upon seeing you walking away. The first is to just walk backwards for a couple of metres or so after giving the command and check that the dog is not moving. If you detect even the slightest movement, correct with the negative marker (AAHH!!! or NO!!! in the lowest tone possible) and then repeat and reinforce the command "Stay". With the following repetition, try to turn around and walk away, showing your back to your dog. After a few metres, stop and turn around to face your dog, wait a few seconds, and then walk backwards to your dog and stand in front of him/her. If the position is maintained throughout the exercise, use the positive marker "Yes" with exaggerated emphasis and enthusiasm and praise your dog.

With future repetitions, once you have arrived back to face your dog, you could include the motion of going around his/her left-hand side and stop so that your dog is positioned on your left. You can then reward and release your dog or progress with the routine; for example, you could commence the heeling exercise starting from the "Sit-Stay" position. If your dog tends to follow you and cannot really understand that the exercise requires them to maintain the position, you will have to adopt a different approach and avoid walking away as the start of the exercise. To do this, lure your dog to your left-hand side and ask it to sit, followed by the new command "Stay". Instead of walking away in front of the dog and triggering the desire to follow, you will have to take one lateral step to your right while keeping your left leg still. If the dog holds the position, move the right leg back and praise them profusely. Practise a few times until your dog is able to maintain the position when you complete a full step, moving both legs to your right and return. At this point you can proceed to the next step which consists of moving diagonally away in front of your dog, following exactly the same procedure as described above, one leg at a time. Finally, you can move in front of your dog and turn around. If you have followed the instructions correctly, your dog should be able to maintain the same position and stay still. Now that you have achieved this stage of the exercise, you can start building up the time and then moving farther away, following the same steps described above.

The final step is to practise the exercise by introducing some distractions, starting from the least attractive to the most valuable and desirable for your dog (you know which is which). It is also worth noting that some people prefer to use the word "Wait" instead of "Stay", which is okay but I think should be used in different circumstances. I would use the "Stay" command to tell our dogs that it might take considerably longer before they can be released, whereas "Wait" could be used when we need to keep our dogs still for a shorter period of time; for example, before jumping in or out of a vehicle, in and out of the main door, etc. It is also imperative to prevent the dogs from releasing themselves after the "Stay" command. I recommend using a release word such as "Okay" or "Break" after the "Stay" command to signal to the dogs that the task has been completed and they are free to go. Always work at your dog's pace, do not rush and walk away expecting them to hold the position straight away – you might get frustrated and it might take longer for the dog to understand what it is required. Once our pets fully understand and can reliably perform the "Stay" command, it can help them keep safe in different real-life situations as well as act as an impulse-control exercise for the most enthusiastic and boisterous dogs. As always, make training sessions an enjoyable and fun experience for both yourselves and your dogs and always end on a positive note because that will be the long-lasting memory they associate with the sessions.

HEEL

A dog pulling on the lead is probably one of the most common problems reported by dog owners who seek the professional advice of a professional dog trainer. For any dog, wearing a collar and being on the lead is something they have simply not evolved to do; on the contrary, having their movements restricted and being denied the freedom to choose the correct response when faced with a particular stimulus can be a cause of distress. In addition, it can unwittingly create behavioural issues that can be extremely challenging to address and solve once they become embedded into their behaviour. That is why it is crucial to start training a puppy or a young dog to walk at your own pace in the heel position without pulling in the very early stages of any training plan. In some cases, these problems can start as early as the first few weeks of a puppy's life, when we first introduce them to the collar or harness. This introduction must be conducted gradually and without any force or restriction of movement for the dog and, most importantly, must be perceived as a positive experience from the outset. Most dog owners are tempted to put a collar and lead on their puppies, take them out for the first few walks, and expect them to behave impeccably regardless of the discomfort they may experience when wearing a novelty item like a collar. Without proper preparation, guidance, and training, puppies cannot possibly understand what is required of them when on the lead. The most likely scenarios are puppies who reluctantly follow the owner and end up being dragged on the pavement or carried back home, puppies who sit and refuse to walk any further, puppies who pull in every direction to try and free themselves because they find the collar and lead uncomfortable to wear, or, in some cases, puppies who cry and scream in total distress. Once the damage is done it can be exceptionally difficult and time-consuming to reverse this negative experience.

One of the most relevant issues to which some owners pay little attention is the weight and material of the new collar or harness that they buy. Because a collar or harness are considered foreign objects by the young puppy, it is advisable to buy something light and simple that puppies can wear without having any burden to carry around their neck or feeling constricted in their movements. A simple plain cloth puppy collar is best to start with and ought to be preferred to the heavier and uncomfortable designer leather material. Moreover, because puppies grow extremely quickly, it will be easier to adjust a harness to fit your puppy's neck or body. As a rule of thumb, you should be able to pass two fingers between the collar and your puppy's neck in order to obtain a snug but not constricting fit. In addition, although we need to make sure the collar is comfortable enough, we also need to think about safety, so we must make sure that the puppy cannot slip out of it when you are both out and about. Depending on your puppy's tolerance level, you can try and fit a collar and harness and leave it on for a short period of time to start with, preferably before any pleasant activities like playing, eating, or cuddling so that the excitement of the game or the pleasantness of a cuddle will distract the puppy from the novelty of the apparel. You will notice that at the very beginning, the puppy will start to shaking their head, scratching, and even attempt to bite the collar, but after frequent repetitions throughout the day, during which you will gradually increase the time the collar or harness are worn, your puppy should become accustomed to and comfortable with it.

However, some puppies or young dogs display an extremely low tolerance threshold towards such devices and therefore a different approach should be considered. If this is the case, you will need to prepare your puppies beforehand by creating a positive association with the collar or harness before you even attempt to put it on them. To do this, hold the harness in the proximity of your puppies and give them a tasty treat, make a loop with the collar or harness and invite the puppies to get the treat by putting their head through the loop, then release the treats and praise them enthusiastically with each repetition. Once the puppies are comfortable with smelling, touching, and seeing the harness, you can put it on and then leave it on a few minutes at a time, gradually increasing the amount of time until they are completely at ease with wearing it. When you are completely confident that your puppy is happy wearing its collar or harness, the heel work can start.

When it comes to selecting which training method to use, you have the option of choosing between different methods or even a combination of them, depending on your dog's individual nature and predisposition. If you choose to use the classical conditioning technique, all you have to do is to take advantage of the fact that your puppies will tend to follow you everywhere and simply reward them each time they display the behaviour you want to shape and then name the behaviour with the command "Heel". To use this method, have your puppy follow you in a quiet and distraction-free area so that it can focus exclusively on you. Walk around calmly and observe your puppy's behaviour. As soon as the puppy positions themselves to your left (or right if preferred), praise them and give them a treat. After this first interaction, begin walking again in a straight line or follow an imaginary circle, paying attention to walking counterclockwise if you prefer your dog to walk on your left-hand side, or clockwise if you intend to walk them on your right-hand side. Your dog will soon realise that each time it walks on your side it gets rewarded and will continue to do so in order to get a treat. At this point, name the behaviour "Heel" and practise the exercise by following a more random walking pattern that includes a mixture of sudden changes of direction, left or right turns, straight lines, circles, and so on.

The other methods available are based on using one of the quadrants of operant conditioning. Within the four different quadrants, I prefer to use positive reinforcement which involves using treats or a high valuable toy to lure the puppy into the position required, shaping and marking the behaviour with the word "Yes", and then rewarding the puppy with a treat to encourage them to repeat the behaviour. Start by calling your dog and have them sit in front of you, as you would normally do when practising the complete recall sequence, only this time, instead of praising your dog for offering the presentation position, keep luring them further so that they move to your left hand side and sit. To achieve this, keep holding on to the treat in your hand and extend your left arm forwards and towards your dog's nose. When your hand gets close enough to their nose, so that they catch the scent of the treat, start moving your hand with a slow but flowing gesture in a counterclockwise motion. Imagine drawing a circle starting from the dog's nose and ending with your hand touching your left thigh. This circular motion allows you to guide your dog towards the desired heel position and encourages it to follow your hand closely, so that it can complete the exercise by sitting on your left-hand side. This will represent the starting point for the "Heel" work routine.

With the dog on your left-hand side, you can both start moving forward and begin with the first few steps of the "Heel" training routine. Because you have created a visual association with other commands so that your dog understands to sit if you raise your hand, or to come if you spread out your arms, you can also create a visual clue for the dog to commence walking in the heel position. If, each time you give the command "Heel", you start walking moving forward, putting your left leg first, at some point your dog will learn that visual clue and act accordingly. You can do the same when you stop by always using the same left leg to come to a halt, perhaps associating it with the different command "Stop" or "Halt". The following series of various routines have as their main aim teaching your dog to be aware of your body position; hence, following you and not being followed walking at your pace and not pulling on the lead, walking at the side of your choice and not ahead or behind you, and walking close to you and focusing on you at all times. I will now describe these heel-work exercises in more detail.

Holding the lead correctly

The Random Pattern

The objective of this first exercise is to teach your dog to be conscious of your body position and keep them focused on you at all times. It consists of walking with your dog on the lead on your left-hand side, following a completely random pattern so that your dog needs to maintain its focus on you in order to guess your next change of direction. The idea is to slowly build up the exercise, starting with just a couple of steps while keeping your dog completely focused on you and then increasing the number of steps with each random change of direction. The leash should be always slack with no tension whatsoever until you come to a halt. With your dog in the sitting position on your left-hand side, place your right thumb in the looped end of the lead and hold it with the right hand (as shown in the picture above) and keep your left hand free so that you can hold a treat, your dog's favourite toy, or whatever motivates your dog to be willing to work for it. Next, show the stimulus to your dog and start moving forward with the left leg. Again, it is crucial to notice that as for other commands, it is always a good idea to associate a visual cue with the verbal command. You can raise your hand without saying "Sit" and your dog will comply because it associated the verbal command with your hand movement as you were practising; you can then lower your hand and the dog will lie down, etc. Equally, if you always start the heel work exercise by moving your left leg forward first, your dog will associate that visual clue with the beginning of the heel work and will stop and perhaps sit as you come to a halt with your left leg. Commence the exercise by saying "Heel" and move forward for two or more steps. If your dog keeps up with and is totally focused on you, stop and mark the behaviour with the word "Yes", followed by a reward.

Please bear in mind that leash walking is a new concept for dogs and they might need a bit of time to adapt and learn this new exercise. If you find that your dog continued to walk ahead of you when you stopped, this is probably because it was not fully engaged with you to start with or that it lost focus during the exercise, which can be considered a mistake on our part as handlers. We need to be patient and proceed a few steps at a time so that your dog has the opportunity to understand what is required of them when walking on the leash. You know your dog's temperament and attitude towards training better than anyone else and therefore might want to introduce other training methods like classical conditioning or one of the different parameters of operant conditioning such as the leash pressure technique, where you keep the tension on the leash for whatever time is needed until the dog stops pulling and the leash is slackened and relaxed. To regain your dog's attention during the exercise, use the command "Watch Me" and when your dog's focused is redirected towards you, start walking again.

Having managed to increase the number of steps with each repetition, you will then need to continuously change direction and gradually increase the number of steps still further. Always observe your dog's behaviour during the exercise and every time the correct behaviour is displayed, which means that your dog is happily walking, holding its head up at the level of your knee, mark the behaviour with the magic word "Yes" and reward your dog as described above. Continue practising this routine with brief yet regular sessions throughout the day, ensuring the exercises remain engaging and enjoyable for both you and your dog. Incorporate direction changes and continue to increase the number of steps, making each variation a fun and rewarding experience. The goal is to make these training sessions feel like a game for your dog, reinforcing positive behaviour and establishing walking by your side as a natural habit, one that is almost like second nature. With patience and consistency, your dog will develop the desired behaviour while enjoying the training process. With regular practice, it should progress to walking consistently by your side for extended periods, while remaining attentive to your movements and changes in direction. Each session builds upon the previous one, reinforcing the desired behaviour and enhancing your dog's ability to follow your lead seamlessly. As your dog becomes more proficient, you will notice an increased understanding of your cues and commands, resulting in smoother and more synchronised walks. Celebrate these milestones along the way, and continue to reinforce positive behaviour to solidify the training outcomes. With dedication and patience, you and your dog will achieve a mutual understanding and harmony in your walks and be able to enjoy a multitude of happy adventures together, both on walks and in all aspects of everyday life situations.

The Circle Pattern

This exercise is really a follow up to the previous one, but with variation in the walking pattern, which will be random but in a circle. It should be considered a refinement of the previous heel work exercise and is crucial for achieving more advanced leash walking skills. Like the previous exercise, it aims to teach your dog to walk very closely beside you on your left-hand side at the level of your left leg while continuously maintaining eye contact, the difference being that you are doing it with your dog off the leash. Walking off-leash adds an extra level of challenge and freedom and requires a strong foundation of trust and obedience between you and your dog.

Begin by practising in a secure environment with minimal distractions. A fenced yard or quiet park can provide the space needed. The starting position for this exercise is similar to other heel work exercises, with your dog on the lead and sitting on your left-hand side, fully focused on you. Place your right thumb through the looped end of the leash and grasp the leash firmly with your entire hand. If you are left-handed and prefer your dog to walk on your right side, simply reverse these instructions. For this exercise, you will need to establish a central focal point which will represent the centre of your imaginary circle; you can use any object to mark this point (a tree, your backpack, a jumper, or even a partner who could film you while practising for review later). You will use this point as a reference for you and your dog to practise the "Heel" command while walking in an imaginary circle counterclockwise. Give your dog the command "Heel" and simultaneously start moving forward with your left leg. Keep your dog engaged and focused on you by using verbal cues, hand signals, and maintaining eye contact. Use a cheerful tone of voice to reinforce the desired behaviour. You can use a special treat, such as your dog's favourite toy or a ball, to motivate them and redirect their attention towards you in case they stray away from your side. Because you are both walking in a counterclockwise motion, your dog will naturally position itself with its head and shoulder in close contact with your leg, keeping its head held high and focusing on you in expectation of a reward. When you notice that your dog can walk even for a few steps in the required position (as described above), immediately mark the behaviour and reward it with great enthusiasm using a treat, a ball, or their favourite toy. Ask your dog to return to the heel position and repeat the exercise again, following your imaginary circle, only this time try and complete more than a few steps, then stop and reward profusely.

From this point on, you will need to gradually increase the number of steps and the duration of your dog's focus on you as it becomes more comfortable with the exercise, and continue rewarding your dog as it progresses. Mark and reward further successful improvements as they occur.

Remember that training should be fun and rewarding for both you and your dog, therefore you should celebrate your dog's successes with enormous enthusiasm and be extremely patient with the inevitable setbacks. Every dog is different and learns at his or her own pace, so I recommend avoiding pushing your dog too far while progressing with the exercise and actually go back a few steps if you notice they are struggling to maintain the required position or their focus. Refer to your dogs' body language (as explained in Chapter 6) and the different signals they display in order to understand when you have exceeded their attention span, in which case you will have to stop promptly. Yawning during a training session, for example, is a sign of distress when displayed and it means your dog's attention span is completely depleted. In this case, pause the session and engage in a more enjoyable activity with your dog like a game or a gentle stroll. When you are ready and feel confident that your dog has mastered walking closely beside you on-leash in a circular counterclockwise motion, you can try and add a few steps, walking in a straight line in between the usual circling patterns. Start with just a couple of steps and slowly build up until your dog is able to walk in a straight line for as long as you desire, adding some circling patterns every so often to reinforce the command.

In addition to the introduction of walking in a straight line, you could also practise a few of the exercises that your dog already knows, like walking in random patterns, or left or right. Also include a few complete recalls within the heel work routine as this will reinforce your dog's responsiveness and ensure they return and position themselves to your left-hand side when called in preparation for when they will be left totally off the leash. As your dog becomes more proficient at walking at heel on the leash, you could gradually introduce distractions such as other dogs, people, or enticing scents and also practise in different environments to generalise the behaviour and build up your dog's confidence in different settings, especially if you live in a big city.

You are now both ready to progress with the most challenging part of the exercise which involves teaching your dog to repeat all of the above, but this time completely off the leash. What we aim to achieve in this next phase is for you to have complete confidence that your dog will fully follow your instructions regardless of the presence of any temptations or distractions, and maintain their focus on you throughout the duration of the exercise until you feel it is safe and appropriate to release them again, as you would do in a real life situation. However, it is essential to bear in mind that if your dog is not entirely ready and struggles with off-leash walking in certain situations, you should revert to on-leash training until he/she is ready to progress. Having total control over your dog in off-leash situations is extremely important because it will enable you and your dog to share and enjoy precious moments in every different context of your life.

Even if you are confident that you and your dog have both mastered the heel-work routine, it is always advisable to set up the training session so that typical mistakes are avoided. You will need to choose a distraction-free location to start with, in order to avoid your dog becoming distracted and wandering off and socialising with other pets or people in the area. Moreover, you will need to prep the leash in a slightly different way from usual, so that in the beginning your dog will be under the impression that they are still on the leash when effectively they are not. You can use your normal leash, provided its length will allow you to slip its loose end between your dog's collar and neck during the exercise. You then hold the leash in the right hand in the usual manner while holding the other loose end of the leash in the left hand together with the hanging part of the leash. You are now ready to proceed with the normal heel-work routine as previously described. To make it easier for your dog, start walking by following a pattern that your dog is very confident with, like the circling pattern for example, and when your dog is fully engaged and focused on you, slowly release the loose end of the leash you are holding in your left hand and let it gently slip through your dog's collar. Your dog should be still fully engaged with you, without entirely realising they are actually walking off the leash. Praise profusely and reward by making a big fuss of them. Gradually build up the exercise as you did at the beginning of the heel-work routine on the leash and slowly introduce different walking patterns to make it more challenging for your dog to keep the momentum going.

The Square Pattern

The square or quadrant pattern exercise for heeling in dog training is a more complex routine, as it involves sharp left-hand and right-hand turns while your dog keeps walking in a precise heel position in relation to your body movements. As always when teaching new exercises, begin in a spacious area with your dog on a leash. Start with your dog in a sitting position on your left side, ready to walk. Begin walking forward with your left foot first, leading your dog to follow with the command "Heel". At this point of your training plan, you should be able to keep your dog close to your left leg, ideally with their shoulder aligned with your leg and completely focused on you. After a few steps, make a sharp right turn by pivoting with your left leg. Your dog should turn with you, maintaining its position at your left side. If the turn is successful, praise and reward. Continue walking in a straight line for a few more steps, ensuring your dog remains in the heel position with its shoulder aligned with your leg and motivated. When you are ready, make another sharp right turn by pivoting with the left leg. Again, your dog should turn with you and maintain their position. Repeat the sequence and continuously make sharp right turns to form a square or quadrant pattern as you walk. Each turn reinforces the heel position and helps your dog learn to stay in sync with your movements. Throughout the exercise, be sure to reward your dog for maintaining the proper heel position and following your cues. Use treats, praise, baby talk, or whatever motivates your dog to reinforce the desired behaviour. At the same time, keep them engaged and remember that it is all about fun and building an even stronger bond with your dog. As you both progress with the exercise, gradually introduce left sharp turns, always making sure to point and pivot on your left leg before executing the turn. Practise the quadrant or square pattern exercise regularly to help your dog master the heel position and become more responsive to your movements. With time and repetition, heel work will become almost a muscle memory movement for your dog as it learns to walk reliably at your side in a variety of situations. This exercise helps build focus, coordination, and responsiveness in your dog while reinforcing the heel position. Moreover, it is imperative to start slowly and gradually increase the difficulty as your dog becomes more proficient and in the event of a regression, just step back and start again. Have fun!!!

The About Turn

The about turn is one of the most visually striking moves among all the other heel work manoeuvres and is also extremely funny and enjoyable to perform for both the dog and the handler. It should be regularly included in all heel work drills as it allows the handler to make a complete U-turn while the dog maintains a perfect heel position on the left-hand side and is totally focused on the handler. Although the movement appears extremely natural and fluid when observed in dogs that have fully mastered the technique, it can be quite challenging for those dog owners that lack some of the necessary coordination skills. The exercise involves walking in a straight line with a dog in a perfect heel position and then executing a 180 degree U-turn manoeuvre with the handler turning towards their left and the dog turning on the right and around the body of the handler to rejoin the handler's left-hand side.

To lure the dog into the required position, it is necessary to hold a piece of tasty treat in both hands; therefore, I recommend you start working on this routine only when you are confident your dog can consistently perform the heel-work routines off-leash. Also, given the complexity of the movement, which can be confusing for the dog, especially in the initial stages of the exercise, I advise breaking the behaviour down into smaller steps so that it will be easier for you to check on the improvements your dog makes and then adjust the speed with which to progress to the next stages according to their requirements. For instance, give the command "Heel" and start moving forward with the left leg, following a straight line. Hold a piece of treat in both hands and fully engage with your dog, maintaining eye contact as it walks alongside you, its head held high. Move your right hand to your left and position it right in front of your dog's nose, making sure that it picks up the scent of the tasty treat. Allow your dog to follow your right hand which you will slowly move back to your right-hand side and behind your back while simultaneously turning to your left with a sharp 180 degree U-turn. As you do this, you should have your arm right behind your back with the dog hopefully following the treat in your right hand. At this point, bring your left hand in front of your dog's nose while simultaneously lifting your right hand so that you can lure your dog back onto your left-hand side in the heel position (please refer to the photo sequence on the next page for a step-by-step description of the motion). As I advised previously, if the whole routine appears too complicated to perform in one go, feel free to break down the exercise into smaller and more manageable steps until you are able to coordinate the movements effectively in order to maintain the correct position throughout the turn. Remember to always approach each session with patience, encouragement, and a willingness to adapt to your dog's learning pace and ability, as this will allow you to create a memorable experience for both you and your loyal companion.

The tricky "About Turn"

The V Pattern

This last training exercise shares similarities with the preceding heel work drills I discussed. However, it offers an additional benefit by effectively addressing a prevalent issue faced by many dog owners – leash pulling. If you have followed and successfully executed a carefully planned training regimen, you should not experience any issues with your dog pulling on the leash. In most cases, however, people find themselves dealing with the problem of leash pulling through no fault of their own because they have acquired an untrained pet from friends or relatives, adopted a dog from a rescue centre, or because of inherent behavioural traits that make dogs more susceptible to anxiety while on a leash. Because each dog is different, it is essential to identify the root cause of the problem so that a tailored solution can be adopted to address the issue effectively. The set-up for this exercise is exactly the same as for the other routines you have been practising and with which your dog is already familiar, the only difference being the pattern you need to follow in order to create a physical obstacle when your dog starts pulling ahead of you. In fact, as your dog starts applying tension on the lead, even before it has the chance to move ahead of you, you will need to position your left leg right in front of your dog's chest and perform a sharp move to the left, again pivoting on the left leg while simultaneously getting your dog's attention. The move to the left will effectively be an 180 degree U-turn and will look like a V shape. Repeat the sequence, alternating between right and left turns to form a V pattern as you walk. Each turn reinforces the heel position and helps your dog learn to stay in sync with your movements.

LEAVE IT

There are occasions when we need to communicate to our dogs that they need to step away from whatever they are doing and refocus their attention on us. For example, we might want to stop them from picking up leftovers left on the pavement during a walk, or we might need to stop them from chasing or engage with other pets. If we teach our dog to "Leave It" on command we can also prevent them from ingesting harmful items, such as toxic substances or foreign objects, which could lead to serious health issues or even emergency medical situations. Dogs have a natural curiosity to explore and investigate their environment, whether at home or outdoors, which can sometimes lead them to pick up and chew on items that are not intended for them. In this case, using the "Leave It" command, we can effectively manage our dog's behaviour at home and prevent them from damaging furniture, shoes, or other valuable belongings. We might need to stop them from wanting to chase a football during a game involving our children in the park.

We can also use the "Leave It" command to address certain behavioural issues. Dogs that have not been trained to "Leave" objects may exhibit possessive or aggressive behaviours when confronted with situations where they are asked to relinquish an item. Teaching the "Leave It" command can help promote positive social interactions with other dogs and people by preventing resource guarding or conflicts over possessions. We can all appreciate that having a dog who understands the "Leave It" command is invaluable in such situations. It not only helps prevent unwanted behaviours but also reinforces our dog's responsiveness to our commands and therefore contributes to strengthening our bond with them. By teaching our dog to "Leave It", we are essentially providing them with an alternative behaviour to engage in when faced with tempting or potentially dangerous situations. This command empowers us to redirect our dog's attention away from the undesirable behaviour and towards us, thereby promoting safety and preventing escalation of the situation. Moreover, by using positive reinforcement techniques to teach the "Leave It" command, we ensure they learn to associate compliance with a positive outcome, such as treats, praise, or play. This makes the command more reliable and reinforces our dog's willingness to respond promptly in various environments and contexts, regardless of the presence of any distraction.

The behaviour we intend to shape with the "Leave It" command is for our dogs to actually move back and disengage from whatever activity they are involved in and then turn their heads to redirect their attention back to us. The way I start shaping this behaviour is by triggering the natural instinct of any dog to investigate a new object or, alternatively, using food as a means to promptly redirect their attention towards me. In the first case, using the natural instincts of dogs can be highly effective in teaching them to respond to the command. It involves introducing a novel object or an item that our dog may be curious about – this could be a toy, a household item, or something new that you have placed on the ground. In order to have better control during the initial trials, keep your dog on the leash and then allow them to approach the object and show interest in it. Dogs naturally investigate new things with their senses, so they will likely sniff, paw at, or examine the object. Just as your dog approaches the area where the object lies and is showing interest in it, let them get to the end of the leash and then stop. Use the "Leave It" command in a calm and firm tone of voice and wait patiently for your dog's reaction. As soon as your dog turns its head towards you and makes eye contact, mark the behaviour emphatically with the magic word "Yes" and reward using a high-value treat or a favourite toy. Repeat the exercise over and over, remembering to allow for short but frequent sessions throughout the day. At some point you should be able to set your dog up by purposely leaving an object on the floor and then walking by the object with your dog in the heel position, asking it to "Leave It" as you approach the object. If everything goes according to plan, your dog should lift its head towards you in expectation of the tasty treat. As your dog progresses with the command, practise the exercise regularly in different environments and with various objects, or even food, to generalise the behaviour. As your dog becomes more familiar with the command, gradually increase the level of distraction and difficulty. From then on, use the "Leave It" command exclusively for all those instances that require the dog to leave or disengage from objects or situations.

The method I mentioned above involves using a tasty treat or food instead of the novelty object to attract the dog's attention. In my experience, this method is equally effective in triggering almost immediately the desired response and, because food is involved, can be easily learnt by any dog. To start, choose a quiet and distraction-free environment, perhaps somewhere in the house your dog is comfortable and familiar with. Grab a tasty piece of treat and hold it in a closed fist in your hand. Sit comfortably with your elbow resting on your knee, allowing your forearm to stick out. This position creates a clear visual cue for your dog and allows it to sniff your hand. Keep a close eye on your dog's reaction, which should consist of starting to lick, tap, or mouth your hand to get you to release the treat. As with the method previously described, use the "Leave It" command in a calm and firm tone of voice and wait patiently for your dog to move its head backwards and away from your fist. As soon as that happens, promptly and emphatically mark the behaviour with the magic word "Yes" and proceed with the reward using a high-value treat which you will give the dog using the other free hand (do not give the same treat you were holding in your fist). With repetitions and practice, your dog should respond promptly to the cue "Leave It" and even voluntarily offer an alternative behaviour, like sitting or lying down at your feet, to get you to release the treat. That would be ideal because you will have obtained an even better response which will allow you to have your dog in a more relaxed state of mind and in a body position ready to respond to the next command. As your dog becomes more proficient in performing the exercise, you can push temptation further and repeat the same routine, but this time with the palm of your hand completely open. Your dog should be able to ignore the treat in your hand and remain completely focused on you. Gradually start lowering your hand until you are able to leave the treat on the floor and, as in the previous exercise, try walking with your dog on the lead and heeling on your left-hand side and pass very close to the treat, giving the command "Leave It" if necessary. If your dog completely ignores the treat and remains focused on you despite being offered the opportunity to grab the treat lying on the floor, than you can celebrate yet another success and progress further with your training plan.

Toby

CHAPTER 6

HOW DOGS COMMUNICATE

The evolutionary journey shared by humans and dogs over a period of time that we now know to be over 30,000 years has profoundly shaped the way both species communicate with one another. During the process of domestication, which led to the close cohabitation and cooperation between the two species, humans have learnt to interpret and shape the canine language and developed methods of communication with their canine companions through the implementation of training techniques and clinical observations of their behaviour. Simultaneously, dogs have managed to expand their vocabulary with a rich repertoire of communicative signals, ranging from body postures and facial expressions to vocalisations, that have allowed them to express their emotions and intentions and engage meaningfully with their human counterparts in ways not found in other Canidae species. If we compare our dog's use of vocalisation to that of their counterparts still living in the wild, we can clearly see how our canine companions have impressively adapted their communication repertoire to better suit life alongside humans. With the notable exception of breeds like the Basenji, known for their inability to bark in the typical sense, most domestic dogs have become prolific vocalisers. We can understand how this feature likely played a role in why early humans, shifting from nomadic to settled lifestyles, found them such valuable companions. Over generations, dogs have developed an impressively nuanced vocal range, using barks, howls, whines, grumbles, and other sounds to communicate everything from excitement to distress, curiosity to warning. In fact, their vocal expressions have become so sophisticated that most pet owners can readily distinguish the difference between a "play with me" bark, a "someone's at the door" bark, or a "please feed me" whine.

However, in the wild, barking is actually one of the least preferred forms of communication among their relatives. Excessive noise, in fact, could jeopardise the safety of the pack by revealing their location to predators or scaring off potential prey during hunting. Vocalisations are typically reserved for moments of real importance such as alerting the group, coordinating movement, expressing discomfort, or establishing social boundaries. Howling is used to recall and reunite the pack, growling as a warning to rivals or potential threats, and whining, especially in puppies, as a way to seek attention or care from the mother. In essence, the vocal repertoire of canines in the wild is both complex and sophisticated, but most notably, is used only sparingly. By contrast, our domestic dogs, who live in an environment where such risks are largely absent, have expanded their use of vocalisation dramatically. They have adapted these sounds into a rich, often exaggerated language tailored to human interaction, where barking, whining, and even play-growling serve to express a wide range of needs, emotions, and intentions. In addition, we must recognise that dogs are also unique individuals whose communication skills are shaped not only by past experiences and interactions with their human companions, but are also heavily influenced by the exposure to different environments. As a consequence, some dogs, like people, are naturally more expressive and skilled at communicating than others. You only have to take a quick glance at social media content to see this in action. Platforms are overflowing with hilarious videos of dogs doing what they do best, expressing themselves with an endless range of goofy sounds, dramatic facial expressions, and award-worthy body postures. From the husky having a full-blown argument with its owner to the golden retriever who can produce a side-eye performance worthy of an Oscar, we can all agree that dogs are absolute masters of non-verbal communication. No wonder they rack up millions of views, the whole world can't get enough of their natural talent for saying a thousand things without uttering a single human word.

But beyond the laughs and viral fame, these moments reveal something much deeper about our dogs, in that they are constantly evolving and developing new ways to communicate with us and with each other, we just have to learn to pay attention and most of us dog parents do. In fact, just as dogs have adjusted their vocal repertoire to communicate more effectively with us, humans have also evolved an impressive sensitivity to their canine companions' vocal and behavioural cues. I am sure I speak for many when I say that most dog owners, often without any formal training, can instinctively tell when their dog is excited, anxious, in pain, or simply bored. I firmly believe that this responsiveness is not just a casual occurrence but a reflection of a deep, co-evolved emotional resonance with our pets. It is fascinating to think that over thousands of years, humans and dogs have shaped each other's behaviour in a unique feedback loop, fine-tuning their interactions to form a kind of shared language. We have learnt, often subconsciously, to respond to different tones of bark, the pacing of footsteps, or the subtle shift in a dog's body posture. A whining dog may elicit concern and nurturing, a bark at the window prompts us to investigate, even a gentle sigh as they settle beside us on the sofa can trigger a reassuring pat or kind word. This mutual sensitivity shows that communication between our two species is not just about words or signals, rather it is about the sharing of emotional state of minds. It is a dance of give-and-take, refined over millennia, that continues to deepen the bond between us to this day.

Unfortunately, in modern households, these natural vocalisations are frequently misunderstood or even actively discouraged. A dog that howls might be seen as disruptive, a growl mistaken for aggression, or a whine dismissed as attention-seeking. Yet these sounds are essential components of a dog's communication system, so suppressing them can lead to frustration, confusion, and in some cases, more problematic behaviours. For instance, punishing a growling sound removes a critical warning signal, leaving the dog with fewer ways to express discomfort, which increases the risk of a sudden bite without warning. Similarly, constant reprimands for barking or whining may not address the underlying emotional or physical need the dog is trying to express. Rather than silencing these signals, a more empathetic approach is to understand the context surrounding them. From a holistic perspective, instead of punishing barking, we should seek to channel it productively for our own benefit by teaching our dogs to bark on cue with the command "Speak" and then introducing a "Quiet" or "Shush" command. This respects their need to express themselves while giving us the tools to manage their vocal behaviour in a positive and cooperative way. If anything, shouting or screaming in an attempt to silence our dogs can often backfire. Rather than discouraging the barking, it may inadvertently validate it, your dog might think, *"Great, my human is barking with me!"* This kind of response can reinforce the very behaviour we are trying to stop.

So, what exactly is communication, and why does it play such a vital role across all species? Communication is described as the transmission of information from one individual to another in a way that influences the behaviour of the recipient of the message and in some cases the behaviour of the sender. In biological terms, this exchange of information between individuals of the same species includes signals that can be visual, auditory, chemical, or tactile, and it plays a fundamental role in maintaining the social cohesion of the group, coordinating its movement in relation to the environment, establishing and reinforcing social hierarchies, avoiding unnecessary conflict, and promoting cooperation among its members. Moreover, it allows individuals to share important information about the presence of food or predators, their emotional state, their intentions, or reproductive status. We have already established that for dogs, effective communication helps prevent aggression, supports group bonding, and enables smoother interactions between individuals, much like many other species that live in social groups and form dominance hierarchies. In certain species, communication is so advanced that it plays a critical role in the survival of the group.

Take the case of the vervet monkeys, for example (Seyfarth & Cheney, 1990). These monkeys have developed a highly sophisticated alarm call system that allows them to warn other members of the colony not only about the presence of a predator but also the specific type of predator. For instance, when a vervet monkey spots an aerial predator like an eagle, it emits a distinct "cough" call. The other monkeys understand this signal and respond by seeking cover among the vegetation on the ground. If a terrestrial predator like a leopard were nearby, a different call would be used, prompting the monkeys to climb trees for safety. This sophisticated system of communication enables vervet monkeys to make rapid and informed decisions based on the nature of the threat and that greatly increases their chances of survival.

Similarly, I consider our dogs to be amongst the most socially attuned domestic animals on the planet, and the unique communication system they use to exchange information with us humans is both rich and adaptable. As in the case of the vervet monkeys, where the signals were originally developed to facilitate social interactions within their own species, our domesticated dogs had to adapt and learn, as well as interpret and respond to, human signals with remarkable accuracy, often better than any other non-human species. This level of connection reveals that dogs have not only evolved to understand us cognitively but also to bond with us emotionally, often reading signals we are barely conscious of ourselves. After thousands of years of cohabitation, they have become such experts at navigating our moods, rhythms, and social expectations that they have created a form of interspecies communication that is as sophisticated as it is extraordinary. And I would bet that most dog parents would agree with me when I say that this connection works both ways. We can often sense exactly what our dog is feeling just by the way they look at us. It is a deeply emotional exchange, one that is hard to put into words, especially when talking to someone who has never shared their life with a dog.

Intriguingly, among the numerous behaviours that form the foundation of communication within species that live in social groups, one stands out as particularly relevant to all dog lovers and yet is often overlooked. I am referring to the *allelomimetic behaviour* – which, as noted previously, is defined as the tendency of individuals to mimic the actions of others in their group. Just like the prey drive and other instinctual patterns that our ancestors observed and harnessed during the domestication of dogs, allelomimetic behaviour holds significant potential, particularly because humans, as a species, also display this type of behaviour. This shared tendency to mimic the actions of others is probably one of the reasons why our two species get along so well together as it creates a unique bridge when it comes to interspecies communication. Whether it is a mother pretending to eat her baby's food to encourage feeding or a person yawning and triggering yawns in others, these forms of social mirroring show how deeply ingrained and universal allelomimetic behaviour truly is.

Dogs do not just observe and respond to the behaviour of other dogs, they are remarkably attuned to human actions as well. This ability is no accident. The process of domestication selected for specific cognitive skills that enhanced dogs' capacity to interact with people. Over the past few decades, researchers have extensively studied these canine adaptations, revealing that dogs can both perceive and imitate human behaviour with surprising sophistication. In our relationship with dogs, this mutual responsiveness can be a powerful tool, not only in training but also in reinforcing emotional bonds, establishing trust, and enhancing daily interactions through synchrony and shared experiences. It can be applied in various contexts such as training, behavioural therapy, and the day-to-day management of our dogs, offering a powerful and natural way – the holistic way – to influence and guide their behaviour. In training, allelomimetic behaviour can be harnessed by using social learning and modelling. For example, when working with a group of dogs, a well-trained individual can act as a role model. This model can be especially useful when reinforcing desirable behaviours in puppies or newly adopted dogs, as they naturally observe and imitate more experienced dogs or even their human caregivers. Less experienced dogs, in fact, will often begin to mimic the calm or obedient behaviour of a trained dog, whether it is responding to a recall, settling on a mat, or walking calmly on lead. Allelomimetic behaviour can also be used by the owners themselves. When teaching a reliable recall, they might leverage allelomimetic behaviour by creating movement that encourages their dog to follow, like running away playfully while giving the recall command "Come" with enthusiasm, or perhaps having other dogs recalled first. These actions can all trigger the same copying reflex.

One other well-documented example of allelomimetic application is the "Do as I Do" training method, in which dogs learn to replicate human-demonstrated actions such as spinning or jumping over obstacles. What is even more impressive is their ability to generalise: once trained, most dogs can copy completely new behaviours they haven't been specifically taught, like opening a door or moving an object, simply by watching a person do it. In the context of treating behavioural issues, by pretending to investigate or enjoy something (like food or a toy), owners can prompt their dogs to follow suit. Further research also shows that dogs are able to mirror their humans in social settings. When owners are friendly to a stranger, their dogs are more likely to approach; when the owner is wary, the dogs hang back. Dogs are highly sensitive to subtle human cues, they follow pointing gestures, gaze direction, and even head turns. They can read our facial expressions and body language, and adapt their behaviour based on our apparent emotional state. This mimicking tendency is deeply ingrained in the dog's behavioural repertoire and can create an intuitive and playful communication loop that strengthens the dog-human bond and improves the dog's responsiveness without any coercion.

The holistic approach means that by understanding and applying these principles, we can shift from a mindset of command-and-control to one of communication and cooperation. Training becomes less about imposing behaviours and more about inviting participation, building a relationship founded on trust, shared experience, and mutual understanding. Furthermore, allelomimetic behaviour plays a key role in group synchrony during daily routines. Dogs often adjust levels of activity like resting, eating, or playing based on the rhythm of their human or other canine companions. Recognising and intentionally guiding these moments of synchrony can create a much more harmonious relationship in multi-dog household settings as well as deepen the understanding between dogs and humans. Our little Chihuahua is a perfect example of interspecies synchrony. He is remarkably attuned to our daily rhythms, from the moment we wake up in the morning to the quiet cuddling time we share on the sofa in the evening. His ability to mirror our routines and emotional states speaks volumes about the depth of connection that is possible between humans and dogs. It is a living demonstration of how allelomimetic behaviour transcends species boundaries, creating harmony, mutual understanding, and a shared way of life.

Perhaps one of the most compelling illustration of interspecies communication can be found in therapy dogs. These animals are trained to provide emotional comfort and support to humans, often in demanding settings like hospitals, schools, care homes, or disaster zones. Scientific studies (e.g. Zenithson et al., 2014) have shown that therapy dogs can sense changes in human cortisol levels, pick up on subtle shifts in body language, and react empathetically to emotional cues. What is really striking is how therapy dogs appear to understand not just mere commands but the emotional moods of their human. I have witnessed in person the fantastic support that therapy dogs can offer to patients. They may approach someone who is anxious or grieving, lean gently into them, offer sustained eye contact, or even place the head or a paw on their lap. These are not random gestures, they are targeted, emotionally attuned actions that seem to reflect a genuine attempt to connect and comfort the patient. What is more, other scientific research supports the idea that therapy dogs can help to reduce stress, lower blood pressure, and even promote the release of oxytocin, the so-called "bonding hormone", in both the dog and the human. In a study by Galvany-López et al. (2024), it was found that children with autism spectrum disorder who interacted regularly with therapy dogs demonstrated improved emotional regulation and social engagement. In yet another study, veterans with PTSD reported a significant reduction in anxiety symptoms when partnered with a trained support dog.

Another great example of the emotional depth and communicative ability of our domesticated dogs comes from an unlikely place: the prison system (Smith et al., 2023). Across several countries, innovative rehabilitation programmes have introduced dogs into correctional facilities, not only to help prepare the animals for adoption or service work but also to offer inmates a rare and transformative opportunity for emotional growth. I have heard that these programmes typically pair incarcerated individuals with dogs who may have come from shelters, challenging backgrounds, or are being trained as service animals. Over the course of several weeks or months, the inmates are responsible for the dogs' care, training, and emotional development. For many of these men and women, who perhaps have been through some bad ordeals in life, caring for a dog is their first experience of unconditional love and nonjudgmental companionship. In return, the dogs, who are often anxious or poorly socialised themselves, learn to trust, listen, and thrive under the patient attention of someone who, like them, has known confinement and struggle. I think it is an extremely good programme, and studies have shown that participants reported reduced levels of stress, aggression, and anxiety. The daily routines and training sessions give structure to their lives. A large number of inmates described the experience as life-changing, helping them rediscover parts of themselves they thought were long lost.

On a highly personal note, I think that in today's society, we do not always need to give dogs the formal title of "therapy providers" to acknowledge the unique role they play in our daily lives. The truth is that they offer therapeutic support every single day, whether they are sitting quietly beside someone in a hospital, walking through the halls of a care home, comforting an inmate in a prison, or simply curling up next to their human in the living room after a long and stressful day at work. Life brings emotionally charged moments for all of us in the form of grief, anxiety, stress, and loneliness, but those who live with dogs often find in them a silent companion who listens without judgment, offers comfort without words, and seems to understand our emotional landscape better than we do at times. I would like to think that their presence is healing, not because they have been trained for it, but because it is simply who they are.

The way each species has developed its own communication system is the result of thousands of years of evolution and adaptation to specific environmental pressures, all aimed at ensuring the survival and reproduction of the species. In this respect, our dogs are no exception as their communication skills are deeply embedded in their DNA. For instance, the submissive behaviours we notice in some of our pets, such as lowered body posture, avoiding eye contact, licking the muzzle of another dog, or even rolling onto their back, all serve the purpose of appeasing more dominant individuals and reducing the likelihood of conflicts. Similarly, more confident dogs may display calming signals to prevent escalation and therefore maintain social harmony. Just as wild animals use contact calls to coordinate movement and stay connected, dogs use vocalisations like barking, whining, or howling to keep in touch with group members, humans included, especially when out of sight or separated. Although dogs can adapt these behaviours to our human environments, they remain fundamentally rooted in their evolutionary history. So, next time our dogs try to communicate with us, let's open our hearts and listen, it's the least we can do for them.

As noted earlier, *listening* to a dog means *observing*. Unlike humans, who rely heavily on verbal language, dogs communicate primarily through body language, posture, facial expression, and subtle shifts in the energy we project. One particularly embedded behaviour that humans and dogs species share, and yet again is often overlooked, is known to ethologists as *Social Referencing*. This behaviour, well documented in human infants and their mothers, occurs when an individual looks to a trusted figure for cues on how to interpret a new or ambiguous situation. Dogs exhibit exactly this same tendency. When faced with something unfamiliar or uncertain, they often glance at their owner, not just for comfort but for information. They are reading our facial expressions, body language, and even tone of voice to decide how to respond. In doing so, they are actively seeking guidance on whether something is safe, exciting, or potentially threatening. We can see this clearly when we take our dogs for walks in new environments, when we move into a new home, or when we face unexpected events, such as a loud noise, an encounter with an unfamiliar object, or a sudden change in the daily routine. In these moments, dogs tend to stay physically close and will often glance at their owner in a referential manner. If we appear calm, relaxed, and confident, they are more likely to mirror that emotional state and move forward without fear, or they will approach an unfamiliar dog or object confidently. But if we appear tense, alarmed, or hesitant, they may interpret the situation as threatening and respond with avoidance, barking, or defensive behaviour in order to avoid the object altogether.

Understanding social referencing offers an exceptionally powerful insight into how we can become more effective communicators with our dogs, the holistic way. Furthermore, as dog parents and lovers, we can harness this behaviour to shape positive associations. For example, when socialising our new puppies, if we remain upbeat and relaxed while exposing them to new experiences, such as walking on different surfaces, meeting new people, or hearing loud sounds, we can help them build the resilience they need to face our modern world. In this context, social referencing is not just a fascinating aspect of interspecies communication, it becomes a key tool for effective behaviour modification.

In addition to their keen senses, dogs, like most other carnivores, rely heavily on chemical communication to exchange information with other dogs and interact with the environment through the use of chemical compounds like pheromones and glandular secretions. One of the most significant of these chemical signals is the secretion produced by their anal sac glands (ASGs). These tiny glands produce a cocktail of scent molecules that essentially function as a canine calling card. Each dog's scent is unique, serving as a kind of chemical fingerprint that reveals not just the identity of one individual, but potentially its gender, emotional state, reproductive status, and even its social rank. In the wild, similar secretions are used by wolves and hyenas to mark territory, signal alarm, or identify members of their group. If you've ever taken your dog for a walk and felt mildly embarrassed as they zeroed in on another dog's rear end, you can rest assured that there is more going on than meets the eye. What might seem like an awkward habit is actually a deeply ingrained and highly sophisticated form of communication among the canine species. For our domesticated dogs, the intense sniffing of another dog's behind is part of what I like to describe as the ritual of meeting, it is their way of saying, "Nice to meet you, who are you, really?", and while most of us have learned to politely shake hands or nod hello, dogs prefer a more direct and very nose-driven approach. Interestingly, this ritual it is not just reserved for first meetings, but it continues daily among familiar pack members. Look at it as their way of checking in, reaffirming bonds, and maintaining group harmony.

Sometimes, in moments of intense fear or stress, dogs can involuntarily release the entire contents of their anal sacs, producing a sharp and offensive odour (very pungent and fishy smell). It is believed that this act may have evolved as a defensive mechanism, a kind of biological alarm bell, much like a skunk's spray, that warns others of danger and potentially deters would-be threats. Dogs may also release these secretions while defecating to act as lubricant, but most importantly, dogs can use them to mark their territory, much like their wild relatives. Despite how central this behaviour is to canine life, scientific research into the molecular makeup of these scent signals has been surprisingly limited. What we do know, however, is that this form of chemical communication plays a critical role in how dogs experience and understand their social world. So, next time your dog lingers a little too long during a sniffing session with a fellow dog, try not to rush them. What looks like an odd or comical moment to us is, in fact, a vital part of their daily ritual, a way of saying hello, gathering news, and confirming that all is well in their world.

I previously mentioned that when two different species like dogs and humans find themselves cohabiting in close contact, communication becomes essential for their mutual harmony. This requires both species to find a common ground, a shared language that allows them to understand each other's signals and intentions. I view dog training, particularly through a holistic behavioural approach, as the very bridge that we must build to develop that common language. It is not merely about teaching them commands or correcting their behaviour so that they can adapt and integrate harmoniously within our society, it is about deepening our understanding of another species' way of perceiving and interacting with the world. It is essential to remember that, despite domestication, dogs are still born with a rich set of innate communication skills that enable them to interact effectively with both their environment and other dogs. However, when dog owners interfere with or unintentionally suppress these natural behaviours, they may inadvertently create confusion or force maladaptive responses. This can lead to behavioural issues, as the dog struggles to communicate in a way that aligns with their instincts while simultaneously trying to adapt to human expectations. In recent years, because we have selectively bred dogs based only on their appearance (designer dogs), failed to implement consistent training regimens in our dogs' daily routines, or inadvertently rewarded inappropriate behaviours, we have disrupted the way our dogs can signal intent, de-escalate conflict, or maintain social harmony. As a result, modern dogs often struggle to read or respond appropriately to other dogs' body language. This breakdown in communication often manifests as increased reactivity, including excessive barking, lunging, posturing, and, in some cases, full-blown attacks. It is truly baffling that we expect dogs to understand and respond to our language and gestures, when in reality, it is us who need to adapt to theirs. We often forget that dogs are wired to communicate in a completely different way, using body language, vocalisations, and subtle cues that we might not immediately notice or understand. The key is recognising that they do not inherently speak "human", and expecting them to do so is a bit like asking us to suddenly become fluent in a language we have never been taught. It is our responsibility to put the effort in to learn their language and adjust our communication style accordingly, so we can foster a deeper, more meaningful bond with them. Among the most common mistakes made when deciphering our dogs' language, I now highlight those that can lead to a breakdown in communication:

1. Tightening the leash when meeting other dogs

When a dog encounters another dog while on a leash, it may feel nervous, defensive, or excited, and instinctively rely on its body language to communicate. However, if the owner tightens the leash when this happens, it can make the dog feel trapped and unable to retreat or defend itself. This increases stress, which may trigger reactive behaviours such as barking, growling, or lunging. Over time, the dog learns that being around other dogs is stressful, and it may become more reactive or fearful in future interactions, creating long-term issues with leash reactivity. Instead, the owner should leave a slacked leash and leave the pet free to engage in the ritual of meeting.

2. Pulling the dog away from social interactions

This is another typical scenario I unfortunately see happening all too often. When a dog is trying to interact with another dog or a human, and the owner pulls the dog away or prevents the interaction, the dog can feel frustrated and confused. This can lead to a sense of isolation and prevent the dog from learning how to properly communicate and engage with other dogs. If this happens regularly, the dog may begin to associate other dogs with negative experiences or tension, leading to fear, anxiety, or aggression towards unfamiliar dogs.

3. Inadvertently reinforcing a dog's reactivity

When a dog reacts to a stimulus (such as another dog, a loud noise, or a person) by barking, lunging, or growling, some owners may inadvertently reinforce this behaviour by comforting the dog, speaking in soothing tones, or giving the dog attention. Although this is done out of concern, it can reinforce the dog's fear or anxiety, teaching the dog that these reactions result in attention or relief. This increases the likelihood that the dog will repeat the behaviour, causing an escalation in reactivity over time. Prevention and leading by example are the best options in these situations.

4. Ignore the fight-or-flight response

Dogs are naturally inclined to react to perceived threats using the fight-or-flight response. If a dog is constantly restrained or prevented from escaping from a stressful situation (such as being pulled on the leash towards a threatening or overwhelming stimulus), the dog may feel forced to either fight (become aggressive) or shut down emotionally (become withdrawn). If the dog's natural response is suppressed, it can create long-term emotional issues, like heightened anxiety or aggression, as the dog is not allowed to express its discomfort or fear appropriately.

5. Unnecessary punishment after the dog has submitted

When a dog offers a submissive posture, such as lowering its body, turning away, or exposing its belly, this is a form of communication meant to show deference and reduce potential conflict. However, if an owner punishes the dog for offering these signals (e.g. by scolding or reprimanding the dog further), the dog may learn to suppress its natural responses, leading to confusion about appropriate behaviour. Over time, this may result in increased anxiety or aggression because the dog has learnt that its attempt to diffuse conflict (submissiveness) is met with punishment instead of reassurance.

6. Direct eye contact

In the canine world, direct eye contact can be perceived as a challenge or threat, particularly from a dog that is unsure of the interaction. If a human maintains direct eye contact with a dog in a tense situation, it may escalate the dog's anxiety or defensiveness, especially if it is already feeling threatened. Some dogs may respond to this perceived challenge with aggression, fear, or avoidance. If humans do not recognise the significance of body language and eye contact, it can worsen the situation and create long-term issues with a dog's trust in its owner.

7. Patting a strange dog on the top of the head

Another example of miscommunication between humans and dogs is the common habit of patting a dog on the top of the head, especially if they do not know the dog. Many humans do this unconsciously, often as a way to show affection or perhaps assert control, but from the dog's perspective, it can feel quite an intrusive or threatening gesture. This can lead to fear-based reactions, such as cowering, snapping, or avoiding the person. When this type of interaction is repeated, it can contribute to a lack of trust and even aggression in the dog, making future positive interactions difficult to establish. I actually think that this gesture is the result of our subconscious desire to assert our dominance over the Animal Kingdom, our superiority over other species. In human culture for example, especially when directed towards children, this gesture may be perceived as affectionate or paternal. However, when done to another adult, it often carries a connotation of condescension or dominance, and can even be seen as humiliating. Subconsciously, when we do this to dogs, we may be communicating, *"I'm in charge here"*, a message that dogs may not receive the way we intend. Instead, dogs prefer physical interactions that better align with their own species-specific preferences. For example, they are far more comfortable being scratched gently on the side of the face or under the chin, which are the areas where the scent glands are located, as this allows for a calming exchange of scent between the species. Dogs also enjoy being patted or stroked on the shoulders or chest, much like the contact they initiate during friendly play with other dogs. Understanding these preferences not only improves our bond with dogs in general, by showing a knowledge of their own language, but also demonstrates respect for their communication style, rather than forcing our own human-centric communication style upon them.

So, what can we do to enhance our communication skills with our pets? And what tools are available to help us translate our dog's language? Unlike humans, who are primarily listeners and use complex verbal language to share highly specific information, dogs are essentially watchers and sniffers, and communicate more general emotional states through the use of body language and scent. Simply put, visual cues and scents are much more important to canine communication than vocalisations. These signals express feelings such as fear, excitement, or uncertainty, but they do not always reveal specific intentions or planned actions. Their messages are honest, raw, and instinctive, but more importantly, unlike humans they are unable to lie or hide their emotions. To communicate effectively with our dogs, we have to *watch* more than *listen*. Another key aspect is that the exchange of information between dogs and people does not happen through a structured and tangible "language". In fact, between different species, the messages that are conveyed are often approximate and can be easily missed or misinterpreted. That is why it is important to always read a dog's body language *as a whole,* as one signal alone might not be telling the full story. To get the clearest picture, we need to simultaneously look at a dog's posture, face, tail, and movement, as often a wagging tail alone does not always mean a happy dog. For dog owners who want to better understand their canine companions, learning how to recognise and interpret these signals, especially body language, is crucial, because that is where the real conversation is taking place. Of course, vocalisations like barks, growls, whines, and yips add an extra layer of information, but always remind yourself that dogs are primarily watchers and not talkers. Dogs do not waste time with articulate sentences and complicated words; they show us how they feel through movement, expression, and energy. If we could only make an effort to become better "watchers" instead of just "listeners", we would be able to open up a whole new world of understanding when it comes to our dogs' communication skills, one where trust, empathy, and connection can really thrive.

Having explored the fundamental forms of communication rooted in our dogs' innate behaviours, we can now turn our attention to some of the more visible and expressive tools in their repertoire. As we now know, dogs are masters at using their body language to communicate to other dogs and to us their emotional states, intentions, and reactions to various stimuli. Their reactions are expressed primarily through posture, facial expressions, tail carriage, ear position, and a variety of vocalisations. Understanding these subtle (and sometimes not-so-subtle) signals is essential for interpreting what our dogs are trying to tell us. From the confident stance of an alert dog to the appeasement gestures of one trying to de-escalate tension, every movement carries a specific meaning. In the following section, I explore how posture, vocal tones, tail and ear positions as well as vocalisations all work together to form a rich, nuanced language, one that, when observed carefully, gives us remarkable insight into our dogs' inner world.

A dog's posture is a powerful indicator of their emotional state. A relaxed dog, for example, will display loose and balanced movements, a gently wagging tail, and a soft, open mouth. By contrast, a fearful or uncertain dog may lower their body, tuck their tail, avert their gaze, or freeze entirely. An alert or reactive stance might include a forward-leaning posture, a stiff tail, raised hackles, or intense staring – all are signs worth paying close attention to in order to avoid escalation. The phenomenon of raised hackles, commonly referred to as "Piloerection", is another visible trait that our dogs use to communicate when interacting with other dogs, humans, or during other challenging exchanges. It occurs when the hair along a dog's back stands on end, much like goosebumps in humans. I am often asked what it means and how it can help us predict our dog's behaviour, as people frequently assume that a raised hackles are a sign of aggression and they can become very concerned when this happens. The truth is that piloerection does not automatically signal aggression, it simply indicates that the dog is going through a phase of emotional arousal. There are three main patterns worth noting which can give an indication of the dog's intentions. The first is a full-length raising of the hair, from the neck all the way to the base of the tail. This typically reflects boldness and high confidence and may suggest the dog is gearing up for assertive or aggressive action. The second pattern is more localised, with hair raised only over the areas of the shoulders and neck. This can indicate low confidence, fear, uncertainty, or alertness – the dog is assessing the situation and has not yet decided whether it poses a threat. The third and most subtle pattern is when hackles are raised over the shoulders and base of the tail, but with the middle of the back left flat. This rear-focused piloerection often appears in defensive or ambivalent dogs, signalling vulnerability or the desire to create space. Dogs displaying this pattern are highly unpredictable and mitigating action is necessary to defuse the situation. I cannot stress enough the notion that piloerection signals arousal, not necessarily aggression. Dogs may raise their hackles out of fear, excitement, surprise, or conflict. Some of these states can lead to reactive behaviour, but not always. The key lies in reading the dog's entire body language and context, including the environment.

Let us now take a look at the different dog's body postures and what they typically communicate. Each of these displays is part of a complex, rich visual language that dogs use naturally and effectively when interacting with both humans and other animals.

1. ***Relaxed and Happy***

Posture: Loose body, weight evenly distributed, soft muscles.

Tail: Neutral or wagging gently.

Ears: Natural position (varies by breed).

Eyes: Soft, blinking or relaxed gaze.

Mouth: Slightly open, relaxed, may be panting.

Meaning: The dog is comfortable, content, and not feeling threatened.

2. ***Alert and Curious***

Posture: Standing tall, weight forward.

Tail: Horizontal or slightly raised, may be still or wagging slowly.

Ears: Upright or directed toward the stimulus.

Eyes: Focused, wide open.

Mouth: Closed.

Meaning: The dog is interested in something and gathering information, not necessarily anxious or aggressive.

3. *Fearful or Submissive*

Posture: Crouched body, lowered head, weight shifted back.

Tail: Tucked tightly under body.

Ears: Flattened back against the head.

Eyes: May avoid eye contact, whites of eyes ("whale eye") visible.

Mouth: Closed or tight-lipped, may lick lips or yawn.

Meaning: The dog is unsure or frightened. If cornered or pushed, fear can turn into defensive aggression.

4. *Defensive Aggression, Threatened*

Posture: Stiff body, weight shifted backward.

Tail: Low but may be stiffly wagging.

Ears: Pinned back.

Eyes: Narrowed or hard stare.

Mouth: Lips pulled back, may growl or snarl.

Meaning: The dog is warning you; they are scared but willing to defend themselves if necessary.

5. *Offensive, Confident Aggression*

Posture: Tall, rigid stance, body leaning forward.

Tail: High, rigid, may be bristled.

Ears: Upright and forward.

Eyes: Hard stare, intense focus.

Mouth: May show teeth, lips curled.

Meaning: The dog is asserting dominance or feels in control of a perceived threat. This posture is often a response to a challenge or territorial issue.

6. *Playful*

Posture: Play bow (front legs stretched forward, rear end up).

Tail: High and wagging quickly.

Ears: Up and alert or flopping playfully.

Eyes: Bright, excited.

Mouth: Open, panting, may bark in high-pitched tone.

Meaning: Invitation to play! It is exaggerated and bouncy to signal fun and no threat.

As we have seen, dogs use a combination of body posture, tail position, ear orientation, and vocalisations to express how they feel and respond to their environment. This multi-layered communication system allows them to send clear signals to other dogs, animals, and humans. However, to truly understand what a dog is trying to convey, it is also essential to observe each of these elements individually. Each component, whether it is a high tail carriage, pinned-back ears, or a low growl, offers specific insight into the dog's emotional state. By learning to read these signals not just in combination but also in isolation, we gain a deeper, more nuanced understanding of canine communication. For example, whilst many people associate tail wagging with happiness, the reality is a bit more complicated.

Tail Language

- A high, stiffly wagging tail often signals alertness, arousal, or even agitation. This is not always a friendly display; in some cases, it can be a sign of warning.
- A tail held high and gently wagging is usually a sign of confidence and interest, especially during social interactions.
- A mid-level wagging tail, relaxed and sweeping side to side, typically suggests a calm, friendly, and content dog.
- A low or tucked tail indicates fear, submission, or uncertainty, especially when combined with other appeasement gestures like crouching or avoiding eye contact.
- A stiff, straight-out tail, whether wagging slowly or not at all, can signal that the dog is tense and evaluating a situation carefully.

Ear Language

- Ears pricked forward show that the dog is alert, interested, or sometimes assertive, especially when accompanied by a forward-leaning posture.
- Ears pinned back against the head may indicate fear, submission, or anxiety, particularly if the dog is also showing a lowered posture or avoidance behaviours.
- Ears turned outward or to the side can suggest confusion or indecision, as the dog processes an unfamiliar stimuli.
- Relaxed ears in their natural position generally indicate a calm, non-confrontational state of mind.

It is important to consider the position of the tail and ears in relation to the rest of the dog's body language, environment, as well as breed traits. For example, a naturally curled or upright tail (as in a husky, Shiba-Inu, or Akita) does not always signal dominance or arousal, it is just how the dog is built. Similarly, floppy-eared dogs like Labradors or golden retrievers may use more subtle movements, like slight ear shifts or muscle tension, to convey the same messages.

Barking is one of our dogs primary vocal forms of communication: it is a rich and varied collection of tones and patterns, but we need to be aware that not all barks mean the same thing. Each type of bark, in fact, can carry a different emotional tone and purpose, depending on the context, pitch, repetition, and intensity. Here is a breakdown of some common types of barking and what they typically indicate:

Alert Barking

Tone: Sharp, short, and repetitive

Purpose: To let you (or the pack) know something unusual is happening

Example: A dog hears the doorbell or sees someone walking past the window

Message: "Something's out there, go check it out!"

Alarm or Defensive Barking

Tone: Louder, more intense, sometimes lower in pitch

Purpose: To warn or scare off a potential threat

Example: A stranger approaches too closely or enters the dog's territory

Message: "Back off, keep your distance, this is my space!"

Demand Barking

Tone: High-pitched, persistent, often rhythmic

Purpose: To get attention or ask for something

Example: The dog wants to play, eat, go outside, or get your attention

Message: "Hey! Look at me! Let's do something!"

Frustration Barking

Tone: Repetitive and strained, sometimes escalating in volume

Purpose: To express dissatisfaction at being unable to access something

Example: A dog on leash sees another dog and wants to greet it but cannot

Message: "Let me at it! This isn't fair!"

Fearful or Anxious Barking

Tone: High-pitched, sometimes mixed with whimpering or growling

Purpose: To signal distress or fear

Example: A dog left alone or reacting to loud noises

Message: "I'm scared! Please help me!"

Play Barking

Tone: Short bursts, medium pitch, often paired with a playful bow or bouncy movement

Purpose: To invite play or express joy

Example: A dog barking during a chase or tug game

Message: "This is fun! Let's keep going!"

Compulsive or Habitual Barking

Tone: Repetitive, rhythmic, often without an obvious trigger

Purpose: Often stems from boredom, stress, or lack of stimulation

Example: A dog left alone for long periods in the yard

Message: "I am bored, I've got nothing else to do…"

Each bark type can be decoded more accurately when combined with body language and context. Even if at times barking can be considered annoying and a nuisance, it is essential to understand that it serves a purpose for our dogs. To resolve the issue of excessive barking, the key is not to stop the barking altogether but to understand what your dog is trying to say and address the underlying need or emotion behind it.

Whilst tail position, ear movement, and overall posture are key components of canine communication, dogs also rely on a range of more subtle signals to express how they are feeling. These calming behaviours are often overlooked, but they play a vital role in helping dogs manage stress, avoid conflict, and communicate discomfort or confusion, especially in emotionally charged situations like training or social encounters with other dogs or humans.

Let us take a closer look at three of the most common of these calming behaviours:

Yawning

Contrary to what we might assume, a yawn does not always mean that our dog is tired. In the context of training or unfamiliar environments, yawning often signals frustration, confusion, or emotional overload. It is the dog's way of trying to self-soothe or release tension. The best course of action in these situations is to stop immediately or engage in some other stress-free activities.

Lip Licking

Dogs may lick their lips quickly and repeatedly when they are feeling anxious or uncertain. This is a common sign of stress, especially if no food or treats are present. If you notice this during a walk, interaction, or training session, it is a cue to slow down and assess what might be making your dog uncomfortable.

Paw Lifting

A lifted paw, particularly in a stationary position, can be a sign of hesitation or uncertainty. It is often seen when a dog encounters something unfamiliar, such as a new object, sound, or person. In some cases, it may also be a gentle appeasement signal to indicate the dog means no harm.

Among the wide variety of communication skills our domesticated dogs have developed, particularly when interacting with their human companions, perhaps the most hilarious one that many dog owners fall for, and I include myself here, is the classic "guilty dog" act! And it is easy to see why. You come home to find your precious Jimmy Choo shoes or your Ray-Ban sunglasses chewed to bits, and suddenly, your dog's head is down, eyes averted, tail tucked between their legs, looking like they have just committed a crime. But let's burst that guilty myth bubble, shall we? When your dog looks guilty what you are seeing is not actual guilt in the way humans experience it. Instead, your dog is likely displaying submissive or appeasement behaviours, which are often misunderstood as signs of guilt. These behaviours, such as cowering, avoiding eye contact, or rolling over onto their back, are instinctive responses to human body language or past experiences with punishment. Essentially, the dog is not apologising for a specific action, but rather attempting to communicate "Please don't hurt me". This behaviour is quite similar to how humans might react when they want to diffuse conflict. When we argue with someone, we may feel sorry, perhaps try to apologise, or offer a kind gesture like giving flowers to make the situation better. However, the apology might not always mean we understand the underlying reason for the disagreement. It could just be an attempt to reduce the tension or threat, much like how your dog is reacting. The key point here is that dogs do not have a moral compass like humans. They do not understand that chewing shoes is "wrong"; they respond to your body language and posture upon finding the damaged shoes as well as the emotional environment around them, which is why they act "guilty" when scolded. It is more about de-escalating the tension in the moment rather than an admission of fault. Instead of seeing this as a sign of guilt, it is more accurate to view it as a dog trying to avoid negative attention by showing submissiveness and seeking reassurance.

 Another important communication tool that dogs use is facial expression. Interestingly, dogs are the only non-primate species known to exhibit a left-gaze bias, a tendency to look first at the right side of a human face. This mirrors how humans typically assess emotional expression in others, by focusing on the right side of the face (from the observer's point of view), which is often more expressive. Dogs seem to have picked up on this cue. Research has shown that while they do not exhibit this same behaviour when looking at other animals, they consistently fixate on the right side of human faces. This suggests an evolved sensitivity to human emotion, likely developed through domestication. I recall watching a BBC documentary a few years ago that beautifully illustrated this point. In the program, scientists took photographic portraits of various individuals and split each one down the middle. They then created two new mirrored images: one using the left half of the face reflected on itself, and one using the right. Remarkably, the portraits made from the right side consistently appeared happier and more emotionally expressive, supporting the idea that this is the side of the face dogs (and humans) are most drawn to when trying to read emotion. This subtle visual bias is just one example of the deep interspecies connection we've developed with dogs, and how attuned they have become to our emotional world.

 It's important to emphasise however, that when compared to wolves, domestic dogs still come up short in this particular area. In fact, wolves possess a far more elaborate and refined system of facial expressions which combined with a richer displays of body language, allows for smoother and more precise communication within their social groups. Wolves are capable of producing up to sixty distinct facial expressions, giving them a remarkably abundant facial repertoire that plays a key role in intra-species communication. This nuanced expressiveness allows wolves to convey subtle emotional states, intentions, and social signals within the pack. In domestic dogs, this facial expressiveness has been significantly compromised. Due to human intervention through selective breeding, primarily for aesthetics rather than functionality, the facial morphology of many modern dog breeds has changed dramatically. As a result, the effectiveness of this essential communication tool has been diminished. Dogs with flattened faces, excessive skin folds, or exaggerated features often struggle to convey or interpret facial signals clearly, especially when interacting with breeds of vastly different appearances. This reduction in facial expressions contributes to social communication challenges among dogs. It's not just the face, body postures in dogs are generally less numerous, less differentiated, and more limited in amplitude and clarity compared to those of their wild relatives. This lack of subtlety can lead to misunderstandings, tension, or even conflict during dog-to-dog interactions. It's no surprise, then, that I often hear people say, "My dog just doesn't like that particular breed." In many cases, the issue may not be about personal dislike, but rather a breakdown in communication rooted in the physical traits we've selected for.

Ultimately, when it comes to expressing their emotional side, we have to admit that dogs are brilliant at sharing their state of mind with their human companions. But reading a dog's emotions goes beyond physical signs, it is deeply personal, often based on the trust and connection between the dog and their caring person. The better the relationship, the clearer and more honest the communication becomes. It is like tuning into a private frequency only you and your dog can hear, and once you start noticing the signs, you will wonder how you ever missed them before. Our little Chihuahua, for example, has not just mastered the art of communication, he seems to have developed his own multilingual approach, adjusting his signals depending on who, within our family, he is interacting with. The connection we share with him is so profound that we are able to understand nearly all his cues and messages. Through his body language and facial expressions, he communicates a wide range of needs and emotional states, such as when we have missed feeding time, when he wants to play, go for a walk, or take a toilet break, or even when it is time to visit friends or relatives. But his communication goes far beyond these everyday needs. He intuitively senses when a family member is about to go away on a trip, or when someone is unwell or emotionally drained. His ability to express such subtle, empathetic messages is a true testament to the bond we have nurtured since early puppyhood. His actions speak volumes, and we have learnt, with open hearts, to truly listen.

Trudy

CHAPTER 7

THE HOLISTIC APPROACH

My extensive experience working with dogs and their owners over the past 30 years has given me invaluable insights into the evolving needs of dogs within the context of our modern society. From my humble beginnings as a dedicated pet parent in Italy, attending dog training classes and various courses, I embarked on a journey that, in 1997, led me to London, where I founded my own Pet Care Service company. As a professional dog trainer, I have worn multiple hats – running puppy classes, providing dog walking services and behavioural consultations – and I consider myself extremely fortunate to have achieved my goals in one of the most exciting and dog-friendly capital cities in the world. Throughout my career, I have witnessed the profound changes that have taken place in our society, largely driven by technological advances. These have inevitably impacted the way we interact with and care for our dogs. As our lives become ever more fast-paced and digitally focused, it is essential to recognise that our dogs' lifestyles and needs have struggled to keep pace with this transition; after all, their priorities have remained extremely basic and do not always fit with our own needs.

The idea of reassessing and adapting dog training methods to meet these evolving needs has been central to my work, leading me to refine my professional approach to dog training and behavioural consultations. Ultimately, I have come to an important realisation: to truly embrace a holistic approach to our relationship with dogs, we must first look inward, both as individuals and as a species. My own personal journey has emphasised the importance of fully embracing, or at least incorporating, certain elements of my own holistic lifestyle into my working principles. By doing so, I have been able to enhance not only my ability to assist our clients but also to promote a much healthier and more balanced relationship between people and their dogs. Adopting a holistic lifestyle that humans can share with dogs requires the creation of a balanced, healthy, and nurturing environment that benefits both species. It is a lifestyle that emphasises the interconnectedness of physical, mental, and emotional well-being, and recognises that the health and happiness of humans are deeply intertwined with the lifestyle and mindset of their pet companions. I understand that making lifestyle changes can be challenging, and it has never been my intention to impose a particular way of living on anyone. On the contrary, I want to emphasise that even small adjustments can have a significant impact on both our lives and those of our pets. Sometimes it is the little changes, like switching off our mobile phones and instead spending a few extra minutes playing with our dog, choosing a healthier treat, or taking a moment to enjoy a quiet walk together, that can bring about meaningful improvements in well-being. These are not drastic lifestyle overhauls, but rather small steps that can contribute to a healthier and happier life for both you and your furry companion. By gradually incorporating these positive habits into your daily life, you may find that they not only enhance your dog's life but also bring unexpected joy and fulfilment into your own. It is all about finding what works for you and your dog and making choices that feel right for both of you. Let me now suggest how you can incorporate small changes into your lifestyle that you and your dog can share:

- Balanced Diet and Nutrition

For Humans: Eating whole, natural, and minimally processed foods, with an emphasis on a balanced diet rich in fruits, vegetables, lean proteins, and healthy fats.

For Dogs: Providing a diet that includes high-quality, species-appropriate foods, whether this is high-grade commercial dog food, raw food diets, or home-cooked meals. Avoid artificial additives and focus on nutrition that supports your dog's overall health.

- Regular Exercise and Outdoor Activities

For Humans: Engaging in regular physical activity or sport, whether this is walking, running, yoga, or any other form of exercise that keeps you active and fit.

For Dogs: Ensuring your dog gets plenty of exercise appropriate for their breed, age, and health. Activities such as daily walks, playtime, agility training, and hikes not only keep them physically fit but also provide mental stimulation and help strengthen their bond with you and your family members.

- Mental Stimulation and Learning

For Humans: Continuously learning new things, challenging your mind, and staying mentally active through reading, playing a musical instrument, puzzles, or learning new skills.

For Dogs: Providing your dog with mental stimulation through training, interactive toys, puzzle games, and new experiences. Teaching them new tricks or commands keeps their mind sharp and prevents boredom.

- Mindfulness and Stress Reduction

For Humans: Practising mindfulness techniques such as meditation, deep breathing, or yoga to manage stress and maintain mental clarity.

For Dogs: Creating a calm and stable environment for your dog. Use techniques like massage, aromatherapy (with dog-safe essential oils), pheromone diffusers, or just some quiet time together to help your dog relax and reduce anxiety.

- Socialisation and Companionship

For Humans: Maintaining social connections with friends, family, and community for emotional support and well-being.

For Dogs: Ensuring your dog regularly interacts with other dogs and people. Socialisation helps them develop good manners, reduces fear or aggression, and strengthens their bond with you.

- Environmental Consciousness

For Humans: Living in a way that minimises your environmental impact, such as recycling, reducing waste, and using eco-friendly products.

For Dogs: Using natural and eco-friendly grooming products, toys, and accessories. Choosing products that are safe for your dog and the environment.

- Holistic Health Care

For Humans: Taking a proactive approach to health through regular check-ups, alternative therapies like acupuncture or chiropractic care, and preventive measures. I always say that we do not need more hospitals but fewer patients. Most modern diseases are very much preventable and are caused by our own lifestyle choices.

For Dogs: We should regularly check our dogs for any signs of underlying issues and, where necessary, seek the advice of a holistic veterinarian who may recommend holistic treatments such as acupuncture, herbal remedies, and alternative therapies to maintain their health and address issues naturally.

- Spiritual Connection and Quality Time

For Humans: Finding spiritual fulfilment through practices that resonate with you, whether this is through religion if you believe in a higher power, meditation, or spending time in nature.

For Dogs: Strengthening your bond with your dog through quality time, whether this is quiet moments of affection, shared adventures in nature, or simply being present and supportive for each other.

- Balanced Lifestyle

For Humans: Striving for a balance between work, play, and rest. Ensuring you have time for family, friends, hobbies, relaxation, and personal fulfilment.

For Dogs: Creating a routine that balances your dog's need for activity, play, training, and rest. Dogs like a consistent schedule that helps them feel secure and content.

- Sustainable Living

For Humans: Supporting sustainable practices like buying locally produced goods, reducing your carbon footprint, and conserving resources.

For Dogs: Choosing sustainable pet products, such as biodegradable poop bags, organic dog food, and eco-friendly toys. Supporting brands that prioritise the environment and animal welfare.

Personally, I have found that by integrating these key elements into my own lifestyle, I have achieved a mindset that has led me to a healthier, happier, and more harmonious life with my pet companions and people in general. I often try to put myself in the shoes of our dogs and imagine what kind of picture they might have of our modern world. From their perspective, it must seem a strange and rapidly shifting place. Although dogs still rely on instincts honed over thousands of years, they now find themselves navigating an environment filled with loud noises, flashing screens, and the constant hum of technology, things far removed from the natural world they and our ancestors knew. In this modern context, their human companions are often distracted, spending hours staring at devices rather than engaging directly. Social interactions are less frequent, with more time spent indoors, whilst walks in nature are sometimes reduced to quick trips around the block. The routine that dogs once depended on for stability is now constantly in flux, as their humans' schedules are dictated by the demands of a fast-paced, technology-driven society. I can only imagine the confusion they might feel as they try to make sense of this world. The smells, sounds, and sights they encounter daily are foreign and sometimes overwhelming. Despite these changes, they continue to look to us for guidance, comfort, and companionship, adapting as best as they can to an environment that has transformed dramatically in just a few generations. Yet, at their core, dogs remain the same loyal and loving creatures they have always been. They seek out the familiar – the scent of their human, the comfort of a warm bed, and the joy of a play session with their owner. Understanding this contrast between their ancient instincts and the demands of our modern world can help us empathise with them and strive to create a balance that meets their needs, ensuring they feel secure and loved even in a world that is constantly evolving.

Therefore, we must recognise that although our lifestyle has shifted towards a world increasingly driven by technology and media, the fundamental needs of our dogs have remained constant. While we navigate a rapidly changing landscape where communication, relationships, and daily routines are influenced by modern advancements, our dogs continue to rely on the same basic essentials and needs: physical exercise and mental stimulation, food, water, shelter, companionship and social interaction, and sex, all in the context of a nurturing environment. These needs are timeless and universal, unaffected by the technological changes shaping our lives. In fact, as our world becomes more fast-paced and digital, it becomes even more crucial to take into consideration the enduring requirements of our canine companions. Let me briefly analyse in turn each of their basic requirements.

Physical Exercise and Mental Stimulation

Like humans, regular physical exercise and mental stimulation have a plethora of health benefits and are essential for any dog's overall health and well-being, regardless of breed and size. Holistic training incorporates various activities such as walks, runs, and hikes to provide outlets for energy and stimulate their minds. However, physical exercise is crucial not only for maintaining their physical health but also for allowing our dogs the opportunity to practise their inherited hunting skills through interactive play sessions with other dogs. Contrary to the beliefs of many dog owners, dogs do not play solely for enjoyment; they also engage in playing to practise important skills, particularly hunting, through the role-playing game of predator and prey. During play sessions, dogs alternately take on the roles of both prey and predator, allowing them to refine their hunting instincts and behaviours. If you observe two or more dogs playing, you will notice that they will follow the whole prey-drive sequence, including the chasing phase. During the latter, one dog assumes the role of the prey, typically by running ahead of the other dog while keeping the tail slightly bent downwards. The "prey" dog displays this specific behaviour to signal its role and to maintain the dynamics of the game as close as possible to a real hunting scenario. This tail posture is not a signal of fear but rather a strategic position to prevent the "predator" dog from easily grabbing (grab bite) their tail and ending the chase prematurely. We can also notice that the "prey" dog will run by following a zigzag pattern which involves moving in a series of diagonal lines, alternating between left and right or back and forth directions. Because this movement pattern is characterised by unpredictability, it is used in this context to resemble the evasive manoeuvres of a prey in a real-life scenario and makes it more engaging and challenging for the "predator" dog. If the "predator" dog is successful in his endeavour, it will then proceed by enacting the kill bite, usually around the throat area, to finish the prey by means of suffocation. At this point the "prey" dog gives the appropriate signal of submission and the game comes to an end.

To an observer, this game may seem too risky or even aggressive, given the display of loud vocalisations, growling sounds, assertive body postures, and so on, leading some dog owners to discourage their dogs from engaging in it, especially in public parks or areas where other people and pets are present, although we do not call the park police or threaten to sue the owner of the other dog. Yet ironically, when we attend a football match or any other sporting event, we are often exposed to an environment that can be even more threatening or dangerous. The fact is that humans as a species also need to play sports in order to satisfy most of the same psychological needs we find in warfare, as the psychological and social effects of sport activities are similar to those of war. From childhood onwards, we learn that playing sports or games with our peers provides a sense of belonging and unity. Fans of soccer, baseball, or basketball teams, for example, feel a powerful sense of allegiance. Once they have formed an attachment to a team (usually during childhood) they "support" it loyally through thick and thin. The team forms part of their identity; they feel bonded to it and display a strong sense of allegiance to other supporters, a tribal sense of unity similar to that I see in, for example, rugby matches. Sport also enables the expression of "higher" human qualities which often lie dormant in ordinary life. It provides a context for heroism, a sense of urgency and drama where team members can display courage, daring, loyalty, and skill. There is clear evidence (e.g. Lombardo, 2012) to suggest that basketball, football, and rugby, to name but a few sports, have all descended from long forgotten games used to prepare warriors for combat. In addition, various Olympic sporting events, such as the marathon and javelin throw, were moulded from events that took place during ancient battles.

In the context of providing a nurturing environment through the holistic education of our pets, I firmly believe that our domesticated animals, whose social structures closely resemble our own, possess a similar need for an outlet where they can hone their skills and engage in social interactions with each other. Thus far, I have clearly established the importance for both ourselves and our furry companions of a consistent physical activity regimen and social interaction through playing. It is certainly impossible to overlook the fact that a lack of consistent physical activity and social interaction can lead to various issues for both humans and their pets. Indeed, certain breeds of pets, particularly those selectively bred for specific tasks such as working, hunting, or rescue missions, possess a genetic predisposition towards high levels of energy and stamina, as they are required to perform consistently for longer periods of time. These breeds are often more suited to living with owners who can provide them with the physical and mental stimulation they require to thrive. However, in today's society, the need of humans for exercise translates quite differently with respect to the inherent needs of our domestic dogs. The evolutionary journey of our dogs is closely intertwined with ours, and that has enabled dogs and humans to thrive in the most diverse environments and to coexist successfully together for such a long period of time, and we will continue to do so for the foreseeable future. This close relationship, however, is also the cause of a particularly worrying trend, which is the emergence in both species of what are commonly known as "lifestyle diseases" such as obesity, heart disease, Type 2 diabetes, and cancer. Consider this, the first humans emerged around 200,000 years ago and, unsurprisingly, their lives looked very different from ours. We now know that humans and dogs started to coexist around 32,000 years ago as they shared a similar social structure and hunting patterns. Nowadays, we complain if the lift breaks down and instead we have to use the stairs, but we forget that our ancestors were running from predators and hunting for prey for most of their lives. In fact, as humans, we have spent 95% of our evolutionary history, as you can clearly see in the graph below, living as nomadic hunter-gatherers and have managed to survive through hunting and gathering practices. Therefore, our bodies and behaviours are adapted to this lifestyle, and so too are the bodies and behaviours of our domesticated dogs.

As hunter-gatherers, our ancestors' main advantage was endurance. We were certainly not the strongest or fastest of the animals out there, so our survival was heavily dependent on our ability to outrun our predators and prey. In evolutionary terms, we are endurance athletes, adapted for consistent, long bouts of physical activity, but at the same time we are also adapted for inactivity and energy conservation whenever possible. If we think again about how successful the hunter-gatherer lifestyle was, it is because our ancestors were constantly trying to maintain a correct energy balance; food intake vs. energy expenditure. It made sense to exercise only when necessary for survival, and conserve our precious energy as much as possible. In today's society, this biological tendency no longer serves us, as our environment has been engineered for an extremely positive energy balance; excess food, available 24/7, and little energy expenditure due to the use of motor transport. To maintain good health, we must go against our biological tendencies and make an effort when deciding whether to exercise, even when our body is telling us not to. This is not the case for the majority of our domesticated dogs and that is why it is so important that our holistic training incorporates activities such as walks, runs, hikes, and interactive play sessions to provide outlets for energy, stimulate the mind, and promote relaxation.

The amount of exercise required for an adult dog can vary depending on factors such as breed, age, size, overall health, and the climate. However, as a general guideline, most adult dogs benefit from at least 45 minutes to 1 hour of physical activity each day. For high-energy breeds or working dogs, such as border collies, Australian shepherds, and retrievers, more exercise may be required to keep them mentally and physically stimulated. These breeds may benefit from 1 to 2 hours of exercise per day, which can include activities like brisk walks, jogging, hiking, agility training, or interactive search and retrieve, as well as play sessions. Puppies and elderly dogs do not need a great amount of physical activity in their daily routine for obvious reasons, and it is crucial to balance exercise with appropriate rest periods, especially for young puppies whose joints and bones are still developing. However, every breed is different and every puppy can possess lower or higher levels of stamina and energy; therefore, we need to take these factor into consideration when planning our puppy's daily routine. Working breeds, such as cocker spaniels, border collies, Australian shepherds, and Labrador retrievers, are often bred for specific tasks that require high energy levels, intelligence, and stamina. As a result, they typically have higher exercise needs compared to other breeds, even from a young age. Nonetheless, when it comes to dog ownership, embracing a holistic lifestyle involves considering the amount of time we can dedicate to our dogs before choosing a breed.

Researching the exercise needs, temperament, grooming requirements, and overall characteristics of different breeds is crucial to finding a good match for your lifestyle. For example, if you lead an active lifestyle with plenty of time for outdoor activities such as hiking, running, or playing fetch, you might consider a high-energy breed that thrives on exercise and outdoor adventures, such as a Labrador retriever, a Dalmatian, a Vizsla, or a border collie. On the other hand, if you have a more laid-back lifestyle or live in an apartment with limited outdoor space, you might prefer a smaller or less active breed that requires less exercise, such as a cavalier King Charles spaniel or a Chihuahua. It is essential to choose a breed that aligns with your activity level, living situation, and preferences in order to develop a harmonious relationship and prevent potential issues arising related to mismatched energy levels or exercise needs. You might also consider adopting a dog from a shelter or rescue organisation instead of a pure bred puppy. This could represent a great option, as many mixed-breed dogs offer a combination of traits that may suit your lifestyle perfectly. Regardless of the breed or mix, providing proper exercise, mental stimulation, and socialisation is essential for any dog's overall health and well-being. Unfortunately, most of my referrals for behavioural consultations indicate the lack of a proper physical exercise regimen in the pet's daily routine. Recently, I read an article published in National Geographic magazine (National Geographic, n.d.) which stated that since 1995, wolves have been reintroduced in Yellowstone National Park and the EU has now commissioned a study to evaluate the impact on farmers of the presence of wolves and other large predators (Linnell & Cretois, 2018). Scientists have finally come to the realisation that wolves are an important element within the natural food chain and the overall ecosystem. Some of these wolves have been fitted with trackers to monitor their movements and to study their migratory patterns. I was amazed to learn that they can cover distances of up to 100 kilometres per day. Our domesticated pet and their distant relatives of the canid species are genetically wired to roam great distances. This forms an important part of their evolutionary history, thus it is of the utmost importance to ensure we are able to satisfy one of their fundamental and basic needs.

 Another factor to consider when planning our dogs' daily physical activities is the time of day. As noted previously, dogs, like some other predators, do not possess a large number of sweat glands and find it very difficult to regulate their body temperature through sweating. The only sweat glands are used mainly as scent markers (hence they prefer to be scratched on their cheeks so that they get some of their scent on us, rather than being tapped on their heads which is perceived as a sign of forced submission). Moreover, their normal body temperature ranges between 38.5 and 39.2 degrees Celsius, so do not be surprised to see your Labrador taking a dip in the pond's cold water in winter! Ironically, the human's ability to sweat profusely, along with other physiological and cognitive adaptations, likely played a significant role in our ancestors' ability to thrive in different environments. In fact, by being able to regulate body temperature effectively, early humans could engage in activities such as hunting, gathering, and traveling during the hottest parts of the day when potential predators might have been less active or sought a spot in a shade. This adaptation provided a competitive advantage, allowing humans to expand into new territories and adapt to diverse climates. Similarly, our dogs prefer to exercise in the early or late hours of the day, especially on those hot summer days. Ever wondered why your puppy all of a sudden goes crazy and starts running around acting like he or she is possessed? Such behaviour can be explained as the result of the natural evolution of the canine species as they are genetically wired to be more energetic during hours usually dedicated to hunting. If you cannot avoid exercising your dog in the middle of the day, you will need to carry plenty of fresh water with you or risk your dog taking a dip in the local pond or, worse, in a nice dirty and muddy paddle. Conversely, during winter months the problem does not arise, although I have been asked on multiple occasions if it is okay to walk our dogs barefoot on snow or icy surfaces, either on the pavement or in the park after a snowfall.

Remarkably, mother nature has provided all canids with a solution to this problem which could limit their opportunities for hunting. This fascinating anatomical adaptation is also known as the counter-current heat exchange system and it is located in their legs and paws. I am sure you must have seen several documentaries on wolves living in the northern hemisphere or the arctic fox, happily moving around and hunting in the snow. A brilliant Japanese physiologist, Dr Hiroyoshi Ninomiya, a professor at Yamazaki Gakuen University in Tokyo, discovered that the secret lies in how the blood of dogs circulates to prevent cold surfaces from chilling the rest of their bodies (Ninomiya et al., 2011). Because of the closer proximity of the arteries and veins carrying the blood, in a dog's legs and paws, the circulatory system acts like an internal central heating system. This system uses warm, oxygenated blood to heat the cold blood that has been in contact with a cold surface before returning it to the dog's heart and central circulation. Dr Ninomiya explained that "Dogs exchange heat at the end of their legs. Arterial blood flows to the end of their legs and then heats up venous blood before returning it to the heart. In other words, they have a heat exchange system in their feet". Moreover, the counter-current heat exchange system in a dog's paws plays a dual role in thermoregulation. In cold weather, it helps prevent frostbite by conserving core body heat, ensuring that while the paws are cooled, the blood returning to the body is warmed, thus protecting vital organs from temperature drops. In hot weather, although less prominent than mechanisms like panting and sweating through the paw pads, this same system can assist in dissipating excess heat, particularly when the dog places its paws on cooler surfaces.

This may also explain a common summertime behaviour: dogs often enjoy placing their paws in water bowls or puddles. It's not just play, rather it's an instinctive way to cool themselves by transferring heat through their paws. While not as efficient as evaporative cooling through panting and breathing, this behaviour demonstrates how dogs intuitively use all available mechanisms, given the opportunity, to maintain thermal balance in changing environments. Humans' interference with some breeds, however, has caused a change in the morphology of the legs and paws with the result that many varieties of dogs are no longer able to stand the cold.

To sum up, a proper physical exercise regimen is crucial for ensuring the well-being and balanced life of our dogs. Regular exercise serves to maintain their physical health by promoting cardiovascular fitness, muscle strength, and joint flexibility. Additionally, exercise provides mental stimulation, which is essential for preventing boredom, anxiety, and destructive behaviours. Engaging in activities such as walks, runs, hikes, or interactive play sessions not only helps to fulfil dogs' innate need for physical activity but also allows them to practise their natural behaviours, such as exploring their environment, chasing, fetching, and socialising with other dogs and people. Furthermore, regular exercise strengthens the bond between dogs and their owners, as it provides opportunities for quality time together and reinforces positive interactions.

Food

Proper nutrition plays a vital role in a dog's health and behaviour. Holistic dog training emphasises feeding dogs high-quality, balanced diets that meet their nutritional needs. Good nutrition supports overall health, including digestion, immune function, and energy levels, which can also impact behaviour. In our modern society we tend to project our own dietary preferences and needs on to our pets, but dogs have evolved with different nutritional requirements shaped by their evolutionary history. Primarily carnivores, they are also scavengers by nature and are capable of digesting a variety of foods. Their digestive systems have adapted to efficiently process animal-based proteins and fats. Unlike humans, dogs have a limited ability to digest and derive nutrients from plant-based foods. Whilst they can consume some fruits, vegetables, and grains, these should be provided in moderation and ideally as part of a balanced diet. Furthermore, dogs require certain essential nutrients that may not be present in sufficient quantities in a solely plant-based diet. These include amino acids like taurine and arginine, as well as vitamins and minerals that are abundant in animal tissues. Many years ago I came across a book from a vet turned author named Ian Billinghurst titled *Give your dog a bone* (1993). This book is a fascinating and extremely interesting read; it is packed with valuable nutritional information and is based on the concept that a natural, raw food-based diet is the best choice for our dogs. After finishing the book I was very tempted to switch my own dog's premium-quality kibble diet to a fully raw diet, but I found handling and preparing raw meat to indeed be extremely inconvenient. It required careful storage, handling, and cleanliness of the raw meat in order to minimise the risk of bacterial contamination for both myself and my pet. Additionally, the preparation of a balanced raw diet that met all of our dog's nutritional needs was quite challenging and required additional research and planning, which was scarcely available back then. In those days, the concept of a BARF (Biologically Appropriate Raw Food) diet was not even contemplated by the pet food industry; on the contrary, the big corporations responsible for producing the main pet food brands mounted a negative marketing campaign to highlight all the cons associated with the BARF diet, while failing to mention all its advantages. Nowadays, the three major corporations who own almost all of the UK's best known pet food brands are as follows:

Mars - Pedigree, Cesar, Chappi, Frolic, Kitekat, Pal, Nutro, Greenies, James Wellbeloved, Royal Canin, Sheba, Whiskas.

Nestle - Bakers, Beneful, Beta, Bonio, Felix, Friskies, Just Right, ProPlan, Purina One, Purina Veterinary Diets, Winalot.

Colgate-Palmolive - Hills Science Plan, Hills Prescription Diets.

These major producers have not come to control almost the entire pet food market based solely on the quality of their products, they are the only companies rich enough to have TV advertising and the only ones that can afford the terms imposed by supermarkets. Moreover, by buying out the most successful independent brands and effectively inventing veterinary diets, these major corporations have even taken a large bite of the pet shop and veterinary market. It is true to say that 9 out of 10 of vets now recommend foods from one of the big three. The corporations have long understood the importance of veterinary recommendations and have spent millions on securing their positions as vets' diet of choice with "sponsored" nutritional modules at veterinary college and substantial monitory incentives for veterinary practices. In the USA, Mars also teaches nutrition directly to veterinary students and offers accredited continuing education programmes for vets, creating a built-in bias instead of an objective understanding of all forms of nutrition. But that is not the only place in which Mars has focused their investments – they have also been buying up independent veterinary practices. By mid-2018, Mars Inc had more than 50,000 veterinary professionals working for them. The acquisition of The Mark Morris Institute and Hills Science Diet by Colgate-Palmolive in 1988 marked a significant development in the pet food industry. With its focus on research, development, and education in pet nutrition, MMI brought a wealth of expertise and resources to Colgate-Palmolive. Following the acquisition, Colgate-Palmolive strategically targeted veterinary departments at US universities as part of its marketing and promotional efforts. By offering financial donations, product placement, distribution of nutrition information, discounted food, and even teaching opportunities, Colgate-Palmolive sought to establish strong relationships with these institutions and gain endorsements from veterinary professionals. As a result of these efforts, links to Hill's sponsorship can be found on numerous university veterinary department websites, highlighting the influence of Colgate-Palmolive's marketing strategies within the academic and veterinary community. This approach enabled the company to leverage the credibility and authority of academic institutions to promote its pet food products and further establish its presence in the market. Ultimately, I think that, as pet owners, we should feel empowered to discuss nutrition with our veterinarians and seek advice tailored to our pets' specific needs and health concerns. It is vital to have open and informed conversations with veterinary professionals to make the best decisions for your pet's well-being. Understanding and meeting a dog's nutritional needs based on their evolutionary biology is crucial for their overall health. This includes providing them with a diet rich in high-quality animal proteins, fats, and essential nutrients, while minimising the intake of unnecessary fillers and additives commonly found in commercial pet foods. Nowadays, the availability of information on pet nutrition has increased significantly with the rise of the internet and the emergence of small independent pet food companies focused on the well-being of pets rather than profits. These companies often prioritise using high-quality ingredients, minimising additives and fillers, and being transparent about sourcing and manufacturing processes. Since the year 2008, I have become an advocate of the BARF diet as I have personally experienced its numerous benefits for my own dogs over the course of their lifespan, as well as the positive impact on the pets owned by most of my clients who have embraced it.

Notably, the morphology of our dogs' digestive system is entirely different from ours. If we analyse their mouths, we can immediately spot the differences in the shape of their teeth, each of which is designed to perform different and precise functions. Fang teeth are used to catch and kill prey and to tear off meat. The front teeth are mainly used to scrape meat off bones and the small incisors to grab and hold. You will also notice large incisors that work like scissors to cut sinews and muscles. Located at the back are molars to crush bones. Unlike humans, none of these teeth are capable of grinding food. Indeed, if you gently try to move a dog's jaw from side to side (necessary for grinding and chewing) you will find that it is impossible.

A dog's jaw can only move vertically up and down. In comparison to humans, the dog's digestive process starts in its stomach. This differs dramatically from ours, in fact their stomach acid is more concentrated and can reach a pH level of 1 or even lower during digestion. By contrast, human gastric acid typically has a pH between 1.5 and 2.0. This higher acidity can also contribute to a dog's ability to digest certain foods that humans might not be able to tolerate. Moreover, dogs produce significantly more acid in their stomachs than humans, potentially up to 100 times more. Simply put, if you touched the natural acids in a dog's stomach, you would burn your fingers. This guarantees that any potentially harmful pathogen is almost always killed. The acid can even digest most bones, a feature that evolved to support their scavenging lifestyle.

I am often asked why dogs eat so quickly and what type of slow feeder I would recommend for such dogs. In response, I explain that dogs possess very few taste buds and that they rely more on their sense of smell when it comes to deciding whether the food is edible or not. Indeed, sometimes they eat things we humans find utterly disgusting like vomit, rotten meat, or leftovers, even the excrement of other animals: if it smells good then it is edible. Dogs also tend to gulp down their food, not only to get rid of potentially harmful substances but also because they do not like to share their meals with other animals. There is no need to worry if our dogs tend to eat extremely quickly as this feature is the result of an evolutionary process that has lasted thousands of years. Most surprisingly, most people are not aware that a dog's stomach can also store food. In humans, most food spends between 40 and 120 minutes in the stomach before moving on to the small intestine. Not so for dogs. The canine stomach is more of a "storage area" where food can be held for as long as 12 hours and released into the intestines as needed (depending upon a dog's activity level) where it is absorbed to provide energy. This is also the result of the evolutionary process as our dogs used to behave more like predators and scavengers before we started feeding them. It permitted them to comfortably endure longer times in between meals. For this reason, I often recommend feeding our pets the BARF diet once a day and not, according our own feeding schedule, three times a day. Another noticeable difference is that we use our teeth not only to grind our food but also to moisten it with our saliva, which contains digestive enzymes so that the digestive process is well in hand by the time we swallow. Dogs, on the other hand, do not have any digestive enzymes in their saliva and even if they did they would be useless because they cannot grind their food due to having jaws that only open and close. Instead, as we have often seen, they gulp their food with a view to getting it to where the action takes place (the stomach) as quickly as possible.

The digestive system of dogs serves multiple purposes, including digesting food, absorbing nutrients from food, eliminating waste from the body, and maintaining the balance of fluid and electrolytes. It also affects other critical systems within the body. For example, our dog's gastrointestinal tract contains about 70% of their immune system. If a dog's body does not receive the nutrients it needs, its ability to fight off invading infections and diseases is considerably reduced. It is also no secret that dogs' brains, like ours, are linked to their gut health. In fact, the gut and brain are in constant communication, and there is substantial scientific evidence to suggest that dogs' gut microbiomes affect their mood and behaviour, including aggression and anxiety (e.g. Kiełbik & Witkowska-Piłaszewicz, 2024). When comparing both the commercial and BARF diets, important differences can be identified in terms of richness, diversity, and differentially enriched bacteria. In fact, the microbiome of dogs fed the BARF diet is characterised by higher richness and diversity compared with the commercial diet. By feeding our dogs a commercial diet, we prevent them from acquiring all the necessary bacteria that contribute to building a strong immune system. Moreover, the majority of commercial dog food manufacturers have substituted expensive, high quality protein with inexpensive, low quality carbohydrates, most notably in the form of grains, which they use to bulk up their food and bolster their bottom lines; namely, profits. Some dry dog biscuits are said to contain up to 75% of bad carbohydrates. It is my belief that there is nothing wrong with adding carbohydrates to our dog food provided they are complex carbohydrates – as found in fresh, good quality fruit, and vegetables – because these ingredients supply our dog's diet not only with energy but also valuable nutrients. The natural order according to which our dogs use their body's energy resources must be maintained, so fats represent the first call for an energy supply, whilst complex carbohydrates can provide a slow-release energy supply and proteins which are responsible for short- and long-term body maintenance and repair.

Over the past two decades, I have noticed a sharp increase in cancer patients among our pet population and this goes hand in hand with the plethora of cases within the human population. Surely something must have gone wrong with our lifestyle choices, our nutritional habits, and the ever increasing environmental pollution. It has been estimated that there are approximately 65 million dogs and 32 million cats in the USA. Crude estimates of cancer incidence indicate that there are roughly 6 million new cancer diagnoses made for dogs and a similar number made for cats each year. Although billions of dollars have been spent on research, it is appalling to learn that most of this is focused on the treatment of cancer, not the cause. We know that cancer cells cannot obtain their energy from fat, they need sugar as they use the process of fermentation to grow. By reducing the amount of bad carbohydrates which are subsequently metabolised into sugar, we deny cancer cells their preferred fuel source for energy; as a consequence, they dramatically lose their ability to grow and metastasise. In addition, I found the BARF diet to have a positive outcome regarding the house training of young puppies. Because water is the main component of raw food, young puppies tend to drink much less water in comparison with a kibble based diet, drastically reducing the need to relieve themselves throughout the day and crucially overnight. My other observation concerns the ready provision of the energy content, as well as the timing of when this energy becomes available in commercial diets. The latter often contain high levels of carbohydrates and other ingredients that can rapidly provide energy to dogs. This can lead to fluctuations in energy levels and may contribute to behavioural issues, similar to how the consumption of junk food in humans can result in energy spikes and crashes. For dogs, excessive energy intake without sufficient physical and mental stimulation can manifest in various ways, including hyperactivity, restlessness, destructive behaviour, and attention-seeking behaviours. Additionally, dogs may develop issues such as anxiety and aggression if their energy needs are not adequately met or if they experience disruptions in their energy balance.

Another advantage of feeding our dogs a BARF-based diet lies in the consistency, quality, and quantity of the stool produced. It might sound a laughable matter, but because most of the ingredients in the raw diet are digested in almost their entirety, there is very little left for the dog to defecate. Some people have issues when it comes to handling dog faeces and this certainly does encourage these people to clean up after their pets. Moreover, because the stools produced as a result of the BARF diet are solid-hard and extremely condensed, the passing of the stool during defecation naturally helps the expression (squeezing) of both the anal glands located at either side of the dog's anus, near the rectum, and therefore contributes to the prevention of long-term medical issues. These issues may include: i) Anal gland impaction: this occurs when the glands become blocked and can cause pain, discomfort, and scooting (when your dog is dragging the bottom along the ground), ii) Anal gland infection: blocked glands can become infected, leading to swelling, redness, and discharge, and ii) Anal gland abscess: if an infection is not treated, it can develop into an abscess, requiring veterinary intervention. I appreciate that switching to a BARF diet can result in a sharp increase in the cost of feeding our pets and that not everyone can budget for (or has the physical space for) the purchase of a bigger fridge freezer to store the frozen food, or the time to prepare the meals, but in the long term these costs are most often offset by the hefty vet bills, the expenditures for training/behavioural consultations, and the damage to valuable household items.

Water

Water is essential for dogs, just as it is for humans and all living beings. It plays a critical role in various bodily functions and is vital for maintaining overall health and well-being. There are multiple reasons why water is important for dogs, but for our purposes the most relevant are as follows:

1. Hydration: Adequate water intake is necessary to prevent dehydration, which can lead to serious health issues and even death if left untreated. Dogs lose water through urination, defecation, panting, and sweating from their paw pads, so they need to replenish their fluids regularly.

2. Regulation of body temperature: Water helps regulate a dog's body temperature, especially during hot weather or periods of physical activity. Panting is the primary way dogs cool themselves down, but they also rely on evaporative cooling through moisture on their tongues and respiratory tract. Sufficient hydration is crucial to support these cooling mechanisms and prevent heatstroke.

3. Digestion and nutrient absorption: Water is essential for the proper digestion of food and the absorption of nutrients in the digestive tract. It helps soften food, break it down into smaller particles, and facilitate the movement of nutrients into the bloodstream.

4. Lubrication of joints and tissues: Adequate hydration helps maintain the lubrication of joints and tissues, promoting mobility and preventing conditions like arthritis and stiffness.

5. Waste elimination: Water is necessary for the formation of urine and the elimination of waste products from the body through urination. It also supports the normal functioning of the kidneys and urinary tract.

6. Overall health and well-being: Proper hydration supports various physiological functions in the body, including circulation, cellular function, and organ health. It helps keep organs functioning optimally and promotes overall health and vitality.

In summary, water is crucial for dogs to stay healthy and thrive. As responsible pet owners, we should make sure our dogs have access to clean and fresh water at all times, especially during hot weather, periods of physical activity, illness, or pregnancy. Monitoring our dog's water intake and ensuring they stay adequately hydrated is essential for their overall health and well-being. Yet, like most dog owners, I have watched in dismay as some of our dogs walk right past a clean bowl of water, instead opting with great enthusiasm for a muddy puddle. Perhaps I am not alone in wondering about this! The truth is that yes, dogs can absolutely smell the chlorine and other additives in tap water. Their sense of smell is tens of thousands of times more powerful than ours, so even tiny traces of chemicals or minerals are highly noticeable to them. To us, the water might seem neutral or even fresh-tasting, but to a dog, it might have a sharp or unnatural scent, especially if it has been sitting in a plastic bottle or bowl. By contrast, puddles of water, despite being muddy, might smell more like the outdoors, with earthy, organic scents that probably align better with their natural instincts. Of course, that does not mean it is safe to let them drink from those spots, as standing water can contain bacteria, parasites, or pollutants. But from a dog's point of view, that puddle might just smell more alive and appealing than our "sterile" offerings.

If your dog consistently snubs tap water, but you need to keep them hydrated, there are a few things you might try. For example, you can use filtered or spring water in a stainless steel or ceramic bowl, or try adding a bit of bone broth or a splash of tuna water to further encourage hydration (especially on hot days). Avoiding plastic containers, which can retain smells, also helps, and perhaps try to offer water in different temperatures – some dogs prefer cool water, some like their water at room temperature. I would argue that, as humans, we are not all that different. How many of us opt for bottled water over tap, especially in light of recent concerns about water quality from utility companies? We like to believe we are making a choice that is "purer", even if science sometimes tells us to believe otherwise. Although tap water in developed countries generally meets safety standards for human consumption, it can contain various contaminants, some of which may pose health risks to both humans and pets. To name just some of these contaminants, the E. coli bacteria is commonly found in the intestines of animals and humans. Whilst most strains are harmless, some can cause illness if ingested, leading to symptoms like diarrhoea, abdominal pain, and fever. Lead is another contaminant that can be found in drinking water and typically occurs due to old plumbing systems or lead pipes. Ingesting lead can result in various health issues, especially in children and pets, including neurological damage, developmental delays, and organ damage. Fluoride is commonly added to tap water in many countries to help prevent tooth decay. However, excessive fluoride intake can lead to dental fluorosis, skeletal fluorosis, and other health problems. Chlorine is often used to disinfect tap water and kill harmful bacteria and pathogens. Although it is generally safe in small amounts, some pets may be sensitive to chlorine, and high levels can irritate the eyes, nose, and respiratory tract. Giardia is a microscopic parasite that can cause gastrointestinal illness in both humans and animals if ingested through contaminated water. Symptoms include diarrhoea, stomach cramps, and nausea. One final thought about hard water – it contains elevated levels of minerals such as calcium and magnesium. Whilst these minerals are generally not harmful to us or our dogs, they can lead to limescale buildup over time, both in plumbing and in our pet's water bowl. To ensure our dog stays healthy and hydrated, it is important to regularly clean their water bowl and refill it with fresh water. Stagnant or unclean water can become a breeding ground for bacteria, especially if the bowl is exposed to sunlight or outdoor elements. A simple daily rinse and weekly deep clean can go a long way towards maintaining good hygiene and encouraging our dog to drink regularly.

Shelter

The concept of shelter has evolved significantly throughout human history. In ancient times, shelter was primarily about protection from the elements and predators. Early humans sought refuge in caves, rock shelters, or rudimentary structures made from natural materials like branches, leaves, and animal hides. As societies progressed and settled into agricultural lifestyles, the idea of shelter expanded to include more permanent dwellings. Simple structures made of wood, mud, or stone were constructed to provide a more stable and comfortable living environment. Over time, architecture became more sophisticated, leading to the development of villages, towns, and eventually cities with diverse housing options ranging from modest homes to grand estates. Today, shelter encompasses a wide range of housing types, from traditional single-family homes to apartments, condominiums, and even innovative eco-friendly dwellings. Modern shelters not only offer protection from the elements but also provide amenities for comfort and convenience, such as heating, air conditioning, electricity, and plumbing. In essence, shelter continues to be a fundamental aspect of human existence, serving not only as a place of physical protection but also as a reflection of cultural identity, social status, and personal expression. However, what matters most to our pets is that their basic needs for safety, comfort, and security are fulfilled. Whether they live in a grand mansion or under a tent with their homeless human companion, as long as their fundamental requirements for food, water, shelter, social interaction, and healthcare are provided, pets can thrive and lead fulfilling lives. Most people are led to believe that pets need a big garden or constant access to the outdoors, when in reality they cherish simple pleasures in life like spending time with their human companions, exploring their environment, and enjoying moments of relaxation.

The holistic approach I am advocating should indeed consider that the fundamental needs of our dogs for a suitable shelter are very simple, as has always been the case since ancient times – a shelter must simply provide protection from the elements and predators. Their expectations are extremely modest and, contrary to our beliefs, a great effort is required for our domesticated pets to meet our expectations when we welcome them into our modern and sophisticated types of dwelling. Not only do pets need to adjust to living in an environment vastly different from what they would encounter in nature, but they must also learn to navigate and manage the numerous potentially hazardous elements present in our modern homes. Some of these hazards include toxic substances like household cleaners, chemicals, certain plants, as well as some human medications that can be toxic if ingested. Another hidden hazard is electricity, as pets may chew on electrical cords, leading to electrocution or electrical burns. Pets may also ingest small objects such as coins, buttons, or toys, leading to choking or intestinal blockages. I have also seen pets getting injured by jumping or climbing on furniture, leading to falls or broken bones. For example, I once witnessed a little Jack Russell falling out of open an window from a multi-story building. Another hazard is household appliances; pets may become trapped inside appliances such as washing machines or dryers if they crawl inside. They can also suffer traumas caused by the noise emitted by appliances such as vacuum cleaners, blenders, and so on. Pets may accidentally get locked in closets, cabinets, or other tightly sealed areas and develop phobias and other behavioural issues. Human foods such as chocolate, grapes, onions, and xylitol (found in sugar-free gum) can be toxic to pets. Finally, candles may be knocked over by our most vivacious pets or they can get too close to open flames, leading to burns or fires. To put it in a nutshell, our beloved pets must face a unique set of challenges in our modern world, from adapting to indoor living to navigating hazards within our homes. As responsible pet owners, it is crucial for us to understand and address their needs to protect their well-being and prevent behavioural issues and other more serious problems from occurring like injuries and related traumas.

In terms of shelter, whilst some dogs may be content with a basic shelter that provides protection from the elements, others may have different requirements based on factors like breed, size, coat type, and individual preferences. For instance, breeds that originated in colder climates may appreciate a cozy, insulated shelter during chilly weather, but they might find it difficult to adapt to living indoors in our modern over-heated dwellings – let us not forget that our dog's normal body temperature ranges between 38.3 and 39.2 Celsius and that our homes are far too warm for some breeds. Conversely, those with thick coats may seek shade and ventilation in warmer climates and this factor should not be overlooked when choosing a double coated breed if, for example, you live in the Canary Islands. Additionally, factors like age, health conditions, and behavioural traits should also be taken into account when determining the most suitable shelter for a dog. When we take a young puppy or a new dog home, we ought to remember that in evolutionary terms, the fundamental purpose of a shelter has remained consistent: to shield them from extreme temperatures, predators, and various environmental dangers. From a puppy's perspective, the entire house may not be perceived as the whole shelter in the same way it is viewed by humans. On the contrary, an oversized den is much more difficult to protect against potential attacks from predators, more difficult to maintain at an adequate and comfortable temperature for puppies, and definitely much more difficult to guarantee it remains hazard-free.

When it comes to house training for example, puppies living in a big house may think it is okay to relieve themselves away from the den – the room where they eat, socialise, play or sleep – although this space is still somewhere indoors. The correct approach would be to teach them that certain areas, such as outdoors or a designated potty area indoors, are appropriate places for elimination, but it takes time for them to understand what is required. Another challenge our pets must navigate when living indoors is the inclination of some dog owners (including myself) to maintain impeccably clean homes that include pristine furniture. Some house-proud owners have, in fact, inquired whether their dogs can be trained to refrain from jumping onto their expensive, designer, and often neutral-coloured furniture. As dog parents of two dogs ourselves, we established a rule that they are permitted on the sofa only when it is protected by its dedicated cover. However, training our pets to comply with this rule can sometimes be challenging because their noses are capable of another remarkable ability: the capacity to detect weak thermal radiation. Like most mammals, our domesticated dogs have a naked, smooth skin on the tips of their noses around the nostrils. This area is called the Rhinarium, but it may be also known as the "truffle", "wet snout", or "wet nose" because its surface is always moist, enabling dogs to detect the direction of the wind and trap volatile molecules to aid their sense of smell. The Rhinarium is also colder than the ambient temperature and richly endowed with nerves, which a recent study (Bálint et al., 2020) has suggested gives our dogs the ability to detect heat. I must say that before I came across this article in a medical journal (Scientific Reports), I unconsciously used this ability to educate our dogs to use the sofa's cover over the years. In fact, during our relaxing time, we put the cover on the sofa and sat with our dogs. When we got up, they always moved to our warmer spot and seemed to enjoy the heat as well as our scents. When there was no cover on the sofa, we consistently asked them to get off and after a few trials they got the gist of the exercise and refrained from jumping on the sofa again.

Companionship and Social Interaction

Socialisation and companionship are fundamental aspects of life for both humans and dogs, playing a crucial role in our mutual well-being and overall happiness. In the context of dogs, socialisation is more than just an opportunity to interact with other dogs; it is a vital process that shapes their future behaviour, builds their self-confidence, and enables them to adapt to various environments. I often compare the opportunity for puppies to socialise and play during their developmental stages with that of their siblings and other young dogs, much like the process of sending our children to school. Just as school serves as a microcosm of society for children, exposing them to a variety of situations, rules, and social norms, interacting with other puppies and young dogs provides crucial learning experiences for the young puppy and will shape their ability to navigate the broader world once they reach physical and mental maturity. Providing the proper environment through attendance at puppy classes, interactive playing sessions, and allowing them to interact and socialise in a controlled environment with other puppies in every daily-life situations enables them to learn essential social skills, such as how to communicate effectively with other dogs, understand boundaries, and interpret body language. These interactions teach them about hierarchy, cooperation, and play, all of which contribute to their emotional and social development. Similarly, when children attend school, they are exposed to diverse perspectives, personalities, and challenges. They learn to interact with peers, follow rules, and develop the social etiquette necessary for navigating various aspects of life. Both puppies and children benefit enormously from these formative experiences as they prepare them for the complexities of adulthood, ensuring they can thrive in their respective social environments.

This phase of socialisation has a relatively narrow window in dogs as their physical and mental development occurs at a much faster rate than that of human children. Depending on the dog's breed, it can last from to 4 to 8 months after the Transition Period and helps puppies grow into well-adjusted adult dogs capable of responding appropriately to different social cues and environments. The lack or complete absence of exposure to diverse social interactions during their formative periods can have dire consequences for young puppies, as poorly socialised dogs are more prone to developing behavioural problems such as fear, anxiety, and even aggression. For humans, the companionship of a dog offers not only emotional support as studies (News in Health, 2018) have shown that dog owners tend to have lower levels of stress, a reduced risk of heart disease, and an increasing sense of purpose and connection. The act of caring for a dog also fosters a routine and gives individuals a sense of responsibility and purpose, which is particularly beneficial for those who live alone or are experiencing emotional challenges. I would like to point out, however, that the process of socialisation should not be considered a one-time event limited to the developmental period of a puppy, but an ongoing process that continues throughout his/her life as an adult dog. Dogs are pack animals by nature, and they thrive in environments where they feel connected to a group, whether that group consists of other dogs, humans, or a mix of both. Adult dogs also require regular interaction with others in order to maintain their social skills, emotional well-being, and develop a sense of security, belonging, and purpose. Without regular companionship, dogs can become lonely, anxious, and depressed, leading to a decline in their overall health and behaviour.

Sex

When it comes to sexual behaviour, the evolutionary journey of our domesticated dogs has diverged significantly from that of their wild counterparts. Living in close proximity to humans and other dogs, often in densely populated urban environments, dogs have had to adapt to a lifestyle where natural mating behaviours are no longer left entirely to instinct. With the ever-growing dog population, humans have found it necessary to intervene and manage reproductive behaviours through methods such as neutering, spaying, and controlled breeding. As you will see, this shift reflects not just a practical solution, but a major evolutionary and social turning point in the life of our domesticated modern dog.

Managing the sexual needs of dogs holistically involves considering their physical, emotional, and mental well-being. Instead of relying solely on surgical or medical interventions, a holistic approach addresses a variety of factors in order to maintain the dog's hormonal balance and overall health. Because sexual behaviour in dogs is a natural part of their development and plays a particularly crucial role in their social interactions, we might need to consider changing our attitude towards this subject and perhaps try to understand the role of sex in dogs, from mating behaviours to the impact of the influence of hormones, and find a way to manage their natural sexual needs rather than resorting to neutering and spaying as a first approach or quick fix, especially if behavioural issues arise. Nevertheless, choosing not to sterilise your dog is a decision that should be made with careful consideration and a realistic understanding of what it entails. Owners must be prepared to take full responsibility for the potential challenges that come with keeping an intact pet. Ask yourself the following questions: Will I be consistent and committed to a regular training regimen if behavioural issues arise, particularly with an un-neutered male? Can I confidently manage my dog in all environments and situations, including around other dogs? Am I equipped to maintain harmony within my human pack without relying on neutering as a behavioural management tool? Only by answering these questions honestly can a responsible pet owner make an informed and unbiased choice that truly supports the wellbeing of both the dog and their household. Ultimately, the decision to sterilise a dog should also take into account the environment in which both humans and their dogs live. In densely populated urban areas, where people and pets are exposed to a wide range of unpredictable situations and challenges, sterilisation is often the more practical and responsible choice. In such environments, where off-lead encounters, crowded parks, and overstimulating settings are common, having a neutered or spayed dog can greatly reduce the risks associated with territorial behaviour, mating instincts, and conflicts with other animals. Among its numerous advantages, sterilisation can help minimise hormone-driven behaviours, lower the likelihood of certain health issues, and contribute to a calmer, more manageable companion.

You will find additional information on this topic in the dedicated chapter, but for now I analyse the key aspects I consider essential and which should be common knowledge for responsible pet ownership and management.

Dog Behaviour and Sex

When female dogs enter puberty, they go through a reproductive cycle known as the Oestrus Cycle, more commonly known as "coming into heat" or "coming into season". The Oestrus Cycle typically occurs twice a year but can vary by breed and individual. Although I will not go into exhaustive detail by describing the entire cycle, I will provide a concise overview of the key phases and explain why it is so important to understand how the cycle occurs in order to address any potential behavioural concerns. The Oestrous cycle consists of four distinct stages: Pro-Oestrus, Oestrus, Diestrus, and Anestrus.

Pro-Oestrus typically lasts 7-10 days and represents the beginning of the cycle. It is marked by a surge in the production of the hormone oestrogen, which is responsible for major changes in the female's body in preparation for potential mating. Physical signs include the presence of bloody vaginal discharge and swelling of the vulva (or external genitalia). During this phase, even though the female is attracting male dogs, she will often respond to their advances with clear signals of rejection. This can range from growling and snapping to outright aggressive behaviour. The aggressive response is a natural defence mechanism, as the female dog is not yet in the receptive Oestrus phase. I have experienced several cases of behavioural issues directly related to this topic. These episodes of aggression can be distressing for owners, particularly if they are unfamiliar with the perfectly natural behavioural changes that accompany the Oestrous cycle. Witnessing their usually calm and friendly pet suddenly become aggressive can really shake the owner's confidence. This can exacerbate the problem as dogs often pick up on their owners' anxiety or uncertainty, which can create a vicious circle and ultimately lead to an escalation in undesirable behaviours. Addressing aggression related to the Oestrous cycle is complex because it requires a multi-faceted approach. The challenge lies not only in managing the dog's behaviour but also in reversing the owner's altered attitude and confidence towards their pet.

The Oestrus phase follows Pro-Oestrus and begins when the female shows signs of being receptive to breeding. It usually lasts 5 to 9 days but may vary between 1 and 21 days. Oestrus generally starts with a surge in the production of Luteinising Hormone (LH) and a decrease in the production of oestrogen together with an increase in the presence of progesterone. These hormonal changes influence the female's receptivity to breeding and can cause increased restlessness, irritability, and changes in appetite. The vaginal discharge may become straw-coloured, although numerous variations exist between individuals. Diestrus begins when the female no longer shows signs of Oestrus, such as standing and flagging her tail to the side to be mounted. It is characterised by an elevation in progesterone, which peaks 2-3 weeks after ovulation and then plateaus at that elevated level for 1-2 weeks before slowly decreasing over 10-30 days. Progesterone (the pregnancy maintenance hormone) will increase during this stage, regardless of whether a dog is pregnant. Diestrus usually lasts about 60-90 days if the dog is not pregnant and ends when progesterone concentrations return to baseline levels. During this stage, female dogs will no longer be attractive to males, nor will they allow mating. The body either begins to return to its normal state or proceeds with pregnancy. The swelling of the vulva decreases and the discharge stops. Aggression may persist if the female experiences a "false pregnancy" (pseudopregnancy), leading to protective behaviours over toys or areas of the house as if preparing for puppies. This can also lead to increased anxiety and mood swings. The external genitalia is indistinguishable between Diestrus and the final stage, the Anestrus. The latter is the stage where the female either enters the end of her heat cycle or occurs after having a litter. Progesterone levels remain low throughout this stage.

There is a period postpartum, or after a regular heat cycle, where the uterus must undergo a process called involution. This process repairs the uterus to prepare for repeating the Oestrous cycle once again and takes about four months to complete. Knowing when a female dog is in the Pro-Oestrus or Oestrus phase allows owners to anticipate and manage potential behavioural issues such as aggression or anxiety. For example, during these phases, it might be wise to avoid dog parks and limit interactions with other dogs to prevent incidents and conflicts.

Male dogs, like certain human bachelors, tend to adopt a "straight to the point" approach when it comes to sex. No cycles, no drama, just an unfiltered enthusiasm for sniffing butts and chasing romance wherever it may wander. Their instincts run like clockwork: spot a lady, switch on the charm (or what passes for it), and give it a go, whether she is interested or not. Simpler, yes. Smarter? Well, that's up for debate. This simplicity, however, does not necessarily equate to a lack of complexity in their needs and behaviours. Male dogs are sexually active all year-round and thanks to the highly functional VNO (Vomeronasal Organ), they can sense the scent of pheromones when a female is in heat from miles away, often becoming more agitated, persistent, and focused on finding a mate. Testosterone is the hormone that influences their sexual behaviour and is responsible for their desire to mate along with other natural behaviours such as marking territory, roaming, and mounting. Contrary to common beliefs, the sexual needs of male dogs can be managed with a holistic approach. I consider myself one of those advocates who believe that dogs should be allowed to develop naturally, which includes experiencing the hormonal changes that come with puberty. Key hormones such as oxytocin, vasopressin, and testosterone are central to understanding your dog's emotional and behavioural patterns. Furthermore, these hormones play a crucial role in the physical and psychological development of a dog, influencing everything from bone growth to social behaviour. There is ongoing debate about the long-term health effects of early castration and spaying in dogs. Some studies (Moxon et al., 2023) suggest that early neutering may be linked to an increased risk of certain cancers, joint disorders, and other health issues. Therefore, the holistic approach ought to be crucial in prioritising these health concerns, advocating for a case-by-case evaluation rather than a one-size-fits-all solution. Although castration can reduce behaviours like roaming, marking, and intra-dog aggression in some dogs, it should not be considered a universal solution. I can draw from my personal experience when I say that behavioural issues often have multiple causes, including genetics, environment, lack of training, irresponsible ownership, and socialisation. Addressing these factors holistically can be more effective than relying solely on surgery.

However, there are two main currents of thought that champion surgery intervention and challenge the adoption of a holistic approach. One is proposed by veterinary practices who recommend early castration as a standard procedure, often citing the prevention of unwanted litters, the reduction of certain cancers, and the management of behavioural issues. This recommendation is widely accepted and practised, making the holistic approach less common. The other current of thought is represented by the strong societal belief that castration is a responsible choice for dog owners. This belief is reinforced by animal shelters, rescue organisations, and some dog owners who emphasise the benefits of neutering, most probably because of their personal experiences with their own dogs. Again, owners who choose a holistic approach may face criticism or pressure to conform to these norms. For those who prefer a holistic approach, it is essential to be well-informed and to work closely with a veterinarian who respects and understands this perspective. As responsible dog parents, we can take the following steps to make sure that male dogs live balanced and fulfilling lives without the stress and frustration that can come from unfulfilled sexual needs:

- Exercise and Mental Stimulation: Providing plenty of physical exercise and mental stimulation can help manage a male dog's sexual drive by redirecting his energy into more productive and satisfying activities. Regular walks, playtime, and training sessions focused on reinforcing the basic commands and attention can be beneficial.

- Behavioural Training: Training can help a male dog understand boundaries and reduce unwanted behaviours associated with his sexual drive. Positive reinforcement can be used to teach him appropriate behaviour when he is around female dogs, or when he becomes overly excited.

- Managing Exposure to Females in Heat: If a male dog is not neutered, managing his exposure to females in heat is crucial. Keeping him on the lead in areas where we know there has been a female in season, or perhaps using a long line in order to prevent marking and roaming, can help prevent behavioural issues. I appreciate that some owners of females in Oestrus might be unaware of the sexual state of their pets and hence take them to the park at peak times where they might encounter an intact male dog, but I appeal to the common sense of every owner and urge them to try and help each other out.

- Natural Calming Aids: Some owners use natural calming aids such as pheromone diffusers, herbal supplements, or essential oils to manage their dog's sexual drive and reduce stress. These should be used under the guidance of a veterinarian.

- Chemical Castration: Chemical castration in dogs is a non-surgical method of sterilisation that temporarily suppresses a dog's reproductive hormones. Unlike traditional surgical castration, which involves removing the testes, chemical castration uses injectable drugs or implants to achieve similar effects without permanent alteration. One of the main benefits of chemical castration is that it is reversible. If the owner decides they want to restore the dog's fertility or natural hormone levels, the treatment can be discontinued and the dog's reproductive system will return to normal over time. The two main methods of chemical castration come in the form of injectable hormones; Deslorelin Implants and Medroxyprogesterone Acetate (MPA). Deslorelin is a gonadotropin-releasing hormone (GnRH) agonist which suppresses the production of sex hormones like testosterone. The implant is typically placed under the skin, where it slowly releases the drug over a period of several months to a year. This method is reversible, as normal hormone production resumes once the implant is removed or its effects wear off. MPA is another injectable drug which contains a type of progestin that can also suppress testosterone production. However, its use is less common due to potential side effects.

- Vasectomy as a Last Resort: Whilst neutering is often recommended to manage sexual behaviour, the alternative procedure known as vasectomy could be considered part of a holistic approach. A vasectomy in dogs is a surgical procedure in which the vas deferens or sperm ducts, the tubes that carry sperm from the testes to the urethra, are cut off or sealed. This procedure renders the dog sterile while preserving his testicles and the production of male hormones such as testosterone. Unlike castration (neutering), which removes the testicles entirely, a vasectomy only prevents the dog from fathering puppies; it does not alter his hormone-driven behaviours or physical traits.

There are several other precautions one can take to manage the behaviour of intact males. One of the most important, I believe, is to discourage excessive marking, particularly around the home and surrounding areas. When taking a dog for a stroll around the block, it is advisable to allow him a couple of opportunities to fully relieve himself and empty his bladder. However, it is equally important to discourage excessive marking along the way. Although a few targeted pees are normal and often part of a dog's natural communication, persistent marking on every tree, lamppost, or neighbour's gate can become problematic. Not only can it reinforce territorial or over-excitable behaviour, but may also create tension with other local dogs or residents. Teaching your dog to walk with focus and composure, rather than stopping every few steps to lift a leg, will make outings more enjoyable for both of you, and for the neighbourhood too. Other key precautions and strategies you can take to manage the behaviour of intact male dogs include the following:

Controlled Socialisation

When introducing your dog to new environments or unfamiliar dogs, particularly other intact males, it is important to proceed gradually and with confidence. As the leader of your team, your energy sets the tone, so you should always take the lead by calmly approaching other owners and their dogs first. Intact males are often more susceptible to posturing or displaying assertive behaviour, especially when they sense competition. By facilitating early, positive, and well-managed social interactions, you can build your dog's confidence and reduce the likelihood of reactivity or tension in future encounters.

Mental and Physical Stimulation

A well-exercised dog, both mentally and physically, is far less likely to develop unwanted behaviours. Engaging your dog in activities such as scent work, puzzle toys, obedience training, or structured play like fetch or tug not only channels their energy productively but also satisfies their natural drives. By establishing a consistent training routine and offering controlled play sessions, you are reinforcing your role as the decision-maker. The dog learns to follow your lead and adopts a more cooperative mindset, naturally strengthening your position as a calm, confident leader in their eyes.

Structured Training and Boundaries

Teaching reliable cues such as "Leave It", "Come", and "Heel" is essential for maintaining control, especially in high-distraction or high-stakes situations. Due to hormonal influences, intact males in particular can be more prone to arousal and distraction when in the presence of other males, so routine and consistency become even more important. Structured training helps redirect your dog's focus, allowing you to shift him from an excited or overstimulated state of mind to a more cooperative, training-oriented mindset, one that your dog already associates with fun, clear communication, and positive reinforcement. This strategy not only enhances control but also deepens your bond as the trusted guide and leader.

Scent Management at Home and Outside

One key strategy for managing an intact male's behaviour is controlling where and how often he marks. Try to discourage marking indoors or directly outside your front door, especially if this is the canine equivalent of a busy high street with lots of other dogs passing by and leaving their own scent signatures. Over time, this kind of territorial messaging can stir up tension and even trigger unwanted guarding behaviours. If other dogs are regular visitors to your patch, a pet-safe scent-neutralising spray can help tone down the invisible conversation. After all, as much as we might want to "speak their language", it is probably best to avoid trying to out-mark other dogs ourselves, unless you are prepared to stroll around the neighbourhood armed with a bottle spray of your own urine (not exactly a crowd-pleaser).

Promote Calmness at Home

Creating a peaceful, low-arousal home environment at all times is also crucial, especially for intact males who can be more prone to excitement fuelled antics such as marking, mounting, or excessive vocalising. You should keep greeting rituals as calm as possible when returning home. No need to throw a welcome parade every time you walk through the door. In fact, it would a good idea not to make a fuss over your dog at all in those moments. If you greet your spouse, partner, housemates, or even the goldfish (if you have one) first, your dog will surely take note of your behaviour. This subtle act reinforces your role as the one who sets the social tone in the house. After all, if you throw your arms around the dog first whenever you return back home, do not be surprised if he starts acting like the centre of the universe. Keep it cool, and he will follow your lead.

If you are feeling unsure about whether you can consistently provide the structure, leadership, and emotional balance that an intact dog may require, either due to lifestyle, environment, or group dynamics within your household, do not be hard on yourself in these circumstances as opting for sterilisation can be a responsible and compassionate choice. A truly holistic approach also means recognising when a different path may lead to greater peace and wellbeing for everyone involved. Sterilisation is not a failure, it can be an act of love, a choice made to support a calmer, more manageable life together, especially in a busy household or urban environment. After all, what matters most is to recognise our limitations and choose the path that best supports long-term harmony and wellbeing for both the dog and the human pack, the bond you nurture, and the life you share together.

Rebus

CHAPTER 8

CHOOSING YOUR LIFETIME COMPANION

I often refer to my work as being more of a passion or vocation than a job in the traditional sense. It is something that goes beyond the usual nine-to-five routine as it represents a profound commitment that brings me immense joy and fulfilment. Most definitely, one of the greatest pleasures and most exciting experiences in my line of work is when I am asked to search for a new puppy and follow up with behavioural consultations and training during their developmental stages, or when I am invited to visit an animal shelter to help a potential owner choose a suitable dog to adopt. The process of finding the right puppy or a new dog for a client is not simply about matching a breed to a preference; it is more about finding a new family member whose temperament, needs, and potential will align harmoniously with the requirements of the household. The satisfaction I get from seeing a dog grow into a well-adjusted, happy member of the family is indescribable, and it is amongst other things what keeps me motivated every day. The reasons why people decide to acquire a new dog, whether this is a puppy from a breeder or a rescue dog from a shelter, are as varied and personal as the individuals themselves.

When considering where to get a dog, potential owners usually have two options: they can choose to go through a breeder, or adopt a dog either from a shelter or family and friends, as happened in my case with my first dog, a Dobermann Pinscher. Thinking at my own journey, I cannot deny that the initial motivation for getting a dog was primarily for security and protection, as when I worked as a travelling salesman back in Italy, my car was targeted multiple times by thieves. I therefore hoped to prevent further break-ins. I think this must be one of the most common reasons why people consider getting a dog, as they do provide a strong sense of security and can act as an effective deterrent against potential threats. However, what I later discovered was that the benefits of dog ownership extended far beyond my expectations for safety. In fact, as I got to spent more time with my dog, the relationship evolved into something more meaningful, truly enriching various other aspects of my life. Thus, each choice comes with its own set of considerations, but regardless of the source, the positive impact a dog can have on a person's life remains significant. Each person's motivation is unique, shaped by their life experiences, family dynamics, and emotional needs. Nonetheless, rather than delving too deeply into these motivations, I would like to focus on the undeniable benefits a dog's companionship brings to their human counterpart. Dogs are known for unwavering loyalty without asking for too much in return and this kind of unconditional love can be a rare find in human relationships, where emotions and expectations often complicate interactions. Dogs provide emotional support without judgment and can be a constant source of comfort, especially during difficult times. When we humans face challenges, such as loneliness, stress, or personal loss, our dogs remain a constant source of comfort. They do not need to understand the complexities of our emotions and their presence alone can provide solace.

I have had the privilege of meeting many people who, like me, had a harsh upbringing, whilst others have experienced a difficult break-up in their relationships or suffered the loss of their lifetime partners. For these people, the bond with a dog has served as a form of emotional healing, providing a sense of stability and acceptance that can be deeply therapeutic. Another reason why people choose to share their lives with a dog is that it often encourages a more active lifestyle. Regular walks, playtime, and outdoor activities like jogging, hiking, and swimming all lead to increased physical exercise, which can improve cardiovascular health, reduce stress, and help maintain a healthy weight. Several studies (e.g. Thelwell, 2019) have shown that the presence of a dog contributes to reducing symptoms of anxiety, depression, and loneliness. The routine and responsibility of caring for a dog can bring structure and purpose to a person's life, which is particularly beneficial for those struggling with mental health issues. It is not by chance that dogs are now increasingly used in therapy for their calming effects on people with PTSD, autism, and other conditions. Their ability to detect human emotions and provide comfort makes their presence invaluable in therapeutic settings like hospitals, especially in children's wards and residential homes.

From the first day I became a pet parent, I discovered that dog ownership is one of the easiest way to meet new people as they can act as social catalysts. Whether it is has been through my dog-walking business venture in the park, attending or teaching dog training and puppy classes, or participating in various pet-friendly events, dogs are capable of providing opportunities for social interactions and friendships. They have this incredible ability to connect us. I remember one instance where, during our holidays in Egypt, we were sitting in a vehicle in the company of two other couples on our way to visit Mount Sinai and experiencing the stunning sunrise. We spent the first few minutes in complete silence, waiting for someone to break the ice and start a conversation. Eventually, we introduced ourselves and started talking about our two dogs, which we had left behind back home, and what started as an uncomfortable silence quickly transformed into a warm and engaging exchange, all because of our shared love for dogs. The fact that after a few minutes everyone eagerly pulled out their phones to share pictures and stories of our pets shows just how much joy and pride our dogs bring us, and how much we enjoy sharing that joy with others. I find it amazing how dogs give us stories to tell, memories to share, and reasons to smile, even with people we have just met.

While interacting with my clients and other dog owners in the park, I have also noticed that caring for a dog often gives people a sense of responsibility and purpose. The daily routines of feeding, grooming, and exercising a dog require commitment and dedication, which can be particularly fulfilling for those seeking meaning or structure in their lives. For families in particular, a dog can be a unifying presence. Children often form strong bonds with pets, learning valuable lessons about empathy, responsibility, and compassion. Dogs can also strengthen the family unit, providing a shared focus of love and attention. Choosing to bring a dog into your life, whether from a breeder or a shelter, is a decision that most definitely comes with numerous benefits and should be a positive and enriching experience for both you and the dog. That said, this is a long-term commitment that requires careful consideration of the responsibilities involved and therefore it is essential to take deliberate steps to ensure you and your new companion can enjoy a fulfilling and mutually beneficial relationship which will last a lifetime. For those ready to take on the challenge, the good news is that you can rest assured that the rewards of dog ownership are immeasurable and that the benefits will certainly outweigh the drawbacks.

Before acquiring a new puppy or dog, there are some important steps to consider, which I jokingly refer to as the Ten Commandments. These are as follows:

1. Assess Your Lifestyle and Environment

Time Commitment: Dogs require time for exercise, training, socialisation, and companionship. Consider your daily schedule and whether you and/or your family have enough time to devote to a new dog. Consider hiring the service of a reliable dog walking company.

Living Space: Evaluate whether your home is suitable for a dog. Consider factors like space for the dog to move around; a Great Dane or a Saint Bernard will easily enjoy your company, even in a small flat, but they can be like a bull in a China shop. Also consider access to a back garden or a yard, and whether your home environment is dog-friendly and free from potential hazards.

Energy Level: Different breeds have different energy levels. Contrary to most common beliefs, big dogs (Leonbergers, Newfoundlands, and Saint Bernards) may have less energy in comparison to smaller breeds (Jack Russell, spaniels, Patterdales, etc.) who were bred to carry out tasks requiring high levels of energy and stamina. Make sure your lifestyle aligns with the energy needs of the breed you are considering.

2. Research the Right Breed

Breed Characteristics: Research breeds that match your lifestyle, living situation, and experience level. Consider factors like size, temperament, exercise needs, grooming requirements, and potential health issues.

Purpose of Ownership: Determine your primary reason for getting a dog, whether for companionship, working, or specific activities like hiking, agility, running, or therapy work. Choose a breed that fits that purpose.

3. Prepare Your Home

Dog-Proofing: Make sure your home is safe by removing hazards like toxic plants, chemicals, or small objects that could be swallowed. Secure rubbish bins and make sure any electrical cords are out of reach, especially if you are welcoming a new puppy home.

Designated Areas: Set up designated areas for your dog, such as a sleeping area, feeding spot, and a safe space where they can retreat and feel secure away from children and other interfering elements. If you are getting a new puppy you will need to prepare an area suitable for toilet training.

4. Gather Necessary Supplies

Basic Needs: Before bringing your dog home, have all the necessary supplies ready, such as a bed, food and water bowls, high-quality dog food, toys, a leash, a collar with an ID tag, and grooming tools. Do not forget to arrange for health insurance which can come in very handy if you are acquiring a puppy or a young dog.

Training Aids: Invest in basic training tools, like a crate for house training to get your dog used to feeling comfortable in a confined space in case of travel, treats for positive reinforcement, a clicker if you plan to use clicker training, a basic collar and lead, a long line for practising recall, and other items described in the chapter dedicated to training.

5. Establish a Routine

Feeding Schedule: Plan a consistent feeding schedule that aligns with the dog's age and dietary needs. This should also fit your lifestyle and routine. Please bear in mind that in a natural setting, dogs will eat when they find food and their stomach acts as a deposit which can hold the food for up to 12 hours so that they can use it as needed. Consequently, if your schedule only allows you to feed them once a day, schedule a feeding routine accordingly and do not feel sorry for them.

Exercise Routine: Determine how you will meet the dog's exercise requirements. Regular walks, playtime, socialisation with other humans and dogs, as well as mental stimulation are crucial for a dog's well-being.

Training Time: Set aside regular times for training and reinforcing good behaviour. Consistency is key to successful training. I always recommend trying to schedule a couple of short but daily frequent training sessions rather than a two-hour long session once a week.

6. Plan for Veterinary Care

Vet Selection: Find a reputable veterinarian in your area and schedule an initial check-up shortly after bringing your dog home. Sometimes puppies or dogs may suffer from underlying health issues undetectable to the eyes of a neophyte, but that can cause behavioural problems as the dogs grow.

Vaccinations and Preventatives: Make sure you are aware of the necessary vaccinations, flea, tick, and heart worm preventatives your dog will need.

7. Consider Socialisation

Early Socialisation: Expose your puppy to various environments, people, noises and other animals from an early age to help them develop into a well-adjusted adult dog. Please take into consideration the importance of the imprinting period, as described in the previous chapter.

Puppy Classes: Consider enrolling your puppy in a socialisation or basic obedience class to help with their development and training.

8. Prepare for the Long-Term Commitment

Lifespan Consideration: We are all familiar with the famous phrase "A dog is for life and not just for Christmas" (or "Lockdown" I may add). Remember that owning a dog is a long-term commitment that can last 10-15 years or more depending on the breed chosen. Consider how your life might change during that time and whether you can provide for the dog's needs throughout their life.

9. Financial Preparedness

Budgeting: In the context of living in our modern society, dogs can be expensive to care for, with costs for food, vet visits, grooming, training, dog walking and overnight boarding services, and unexpected medical expenses. Ensure you are financially prepared for these costs.

10. Understand the Responsibility

Emotional Commitment: Owning a dog primarily requires emotional rather than financial and material commitment. Be prepared to provide love, attention, and care throughout all stages of your dog's life.

There are also some vital ethical considerations to keep in mind. If you are thinking about bringing a new dog into your life, consider adopting from a shelter or rescue organisation where many dogs are in need of loving homes. These places are filled with dogs of all ages, sizes, and breeds, each one hoping for a second chance. Among them, there is likely to be one whose heart is waiting to meet yours, one whose path is meant to cross yours and is ready to bring joy, companionship, and unconditional love into your home for years to come. In choosing adoption, you not only save a life, you invite grace, gratitude, and an unspoken bond into your home.

Now that I have explored the essential steps to consider before deciding to acquire a dog, I will move on to consider the differences between the over 400 purebred dogs currently available in the world. Some 360 of these breeds are officially registered with the canine association responsible for compiling the Stud Book of Dogs – usually known as the Fédération Cynologique Internationale (FCI) or the international canine organisation. The FCI currently classifies all dog breeds into seven main dog groups based on their particular uses, purposes, and characteristics. The exact number of recognised breeds can vary slightly depending on the organisation, as some kennel clubs may recognise certain breeds that others do not (the American Kennel Club [AKC], for example, recognises around 200 out of the 360 breeds recognised by the FCI). The process of registering a breed with one of these canine associations is quite lengthy and complex and some established breeds do not belong to any of the seven main groups. In America, for example, the parent club of a breed initially asks to be accepted by the AKC. Once accepted, the breed is placed in the Miscellaneous Breed group. This classification allows the breed to compete in AKC obedience trials and earn obedience titles. The breed may also compete at conformation shows but is only allowed to compete in the miscellaneous class. At this point, the breed is not eligible to earn championship points. Once the AKC Board of Directors is satisfied that there is adequate interest in continuing the breed and the parent club is devoted to expanding it, it is admitted for registration in the AKC Stud Book. The breed is then placed in the appropriate group class and is allowed to compete in regular dog shows and events.

Regardless of what the process of classification entails, it is essential to understand that each dog breed was previously selected and carefully bred by our ancestors to fulfil specific traits and requirements that were crucial in those times. These traits were not only physical characteristics but also skills and behaviours that were necessary for tasks such as hunting, herding, guarding, or companionship. These skills are deeply ingrained in a breed's DNA, meaning that the instincts and behaviours associated with these traits are naturally present in the dog, even if they are not actively trained or utilised in our modern society. For example, a border collie, bred for herding sheep, will often display an instinct to herd, even in a domestic environment. Similarly, a golden retriever might have a natural inclination to fetch and carry objects. Understanding these differences is crucial for making a well-informed decision that aligns with your lifestyle, preferences, and expectations. What follows is an overview of the main breed groups and the key factors like characteristics, temperament, and aspects to consider when choosing a new dog:

1. Sporting Group

Characteristics: This group includes breeds such as retrievers, spaniels, setters, and pointers. These dogs were originally bred for hunting and retrieving game, particularly in water and forests. On a funny note, I must mention that on countless occasions I have been asked to teach a golden retriever or a Labrador to keep out of muddy paddles or water. Holistically speaking, I am morally compelled to explain that the breed's characteristics would make the task extremely challenging to achieve and would be unethical and unfair to the dog.

Temperament: Sporting dogs are generally active, friendly, and good with families. They have a high energy level and require regular exercise.

Considerations: These breeds need ample physical activity and mental stimulation. If you enjoy outdoor activities like hiking, running, or hunting, a sporting dog might be a good fit for your lifestyle.

2. Hound Group

Characteristics: Originally bred for hunting, dogs in the Hound Group have a powerful sense of smell that also makes them ideal for law enforcement applications. This group is divided into Sighthounds (like greyhounds and Whippets) and Scenthounds (like beagles and bloodhounds). Sighthounds hunt by sight and speed, whilst Scenthounds rely on their strong sense of smell.

Temperament: Hounds are often independent, determined, and can be quite vocal, especially Scenthounds. They may be more challenging to train due to their strong hunting instincts.

Considerations: Hounds need space to run and an experienced handler or someone willing to seriously commit to training: they may also require a securely fenced garden. They can be good family pets but may have a strong prey drive instinct. They may not be reliable when responding to basic commands when out and about during walks as they can easily be tempted to follow a scent rather than listen to the owner.

3. Working Group

Characteristics: This group includes Siberian huskies, boxers, Leonbergers, Pyrenean mountain dogs, Saint Bernards, Neapolitan Mastiffs, Portuguese water dogs, German pinschers, giant schnauzers, greater Swiss mountain dogs, Newfoundlands, Samoyeds, bullmastiffs, Bernese mountain dogs, and Rottweilers. They were bred to perform jobs such as guarding, pulling sleds, and rescuing.

Temperament: Working dogs are strong, intelligent, and protective. They are often loyal and bond closely with their owners. Due to their powerful and sometimes independent personalities, they require firm but gentle handling during training.

Considerations: These dogs require training and socialisation from an early age. They need both physical and mental exercise. Unlike some breeds in the Sporting or Hound Groups, which might be more easy-going or forgiving of training inconsistencies, dogs in the Working Group can be less tolerant of unclear or inconsistent leadership. They often thrive under a confident, consistent, and compassionate handler who can establish boundaries while building a strong, trust-based relationship. The key to successfully training these breeds lies in balancing firmness with gentleness. Harsh training methods can lead to resistance or behavioural issues, while too lenient an approach might result in the dog trying to take on a leadership role. Positive reinforcement, clear communication, and setting consistent expectations are essential strategies for ensuring dogs in the Working Group reach their full potential as reliable, well-behaved companions. They are best suited for experienced dog owners who can provide a good and regular training regimen as well as a firm and consistent presence.

4. Terrier Group

Characteristics: Terriers were originally bred to hunt and kill vermin. Specific breeds include the Jack Russell terrier, bull terrier, Yorkshire terrier, and Scottish terrier.

Temperament: Terriers are energetic, feisty, and sometimes stubborn. They are brave and can be quite tenacious.

Considerations: Terriers often need plenty of exercise and mental stimulation. They may not get along well with other small animals due to their strong prey drive. They require consistent training and may have a tendency to dig or chase. People who enjoy outdoor activities, like hiking, running, or even just long walks, or prospective owners who enjoy engaging their dogs in activities like puzzle toys, obedience training, or agility exercises, will find a good match in a terrier.

5. Toy Group

Characteristics: Toy breeds include dogs like the Chihuahua, Pomeranian, and cavalier King Charles spaniel. They were bred primarily for companionship.

Temperament: These dogs are small, affectionate, and usually very good with families. They are often easier to manage physically due to their size, making them a good choice for older adults or those with limited mobility. They tend to be adaptable and enjoy being close to their owners.

Considerations: Toy breeds are ideal for apartment living and may not require as much exercise as larger breeds. However, they can be fragile and may not be the best choice for families with extremely young children. Because they are small and delicate, they may not be the best choice for homes with toddlers or young children who may not understand how to interact gently with a small dog and rough handling by small children can lead to injuries. Being the proud companion of two Chihuahuas (one acquired from such a home), I can confirm that my two little ones are exceptionally eager to please and have formed a strong bond with us. They are also extremely intelligent and training sessions are easy and entertaining for all parties involved. The other advantage for you to consider is that due to their small size, toy breeds are also easier to travel with, whether in a car or on a plane. We have travelled extensively with our Chihuahuas as they fit into small carriers and are more readily accepted on commercial flights (usually airlines allow a pet to travel in the cabin provided the combined weight of pet and carrier does not exceed 8 kilos in total), in hotels, and other forms of accommodation, making them a great addition for people who travel frequently. Potential owners should also be aware of the fact that some toy breeds can be quite vocal, often barking to alert their owners, get their attention, or express their feelings.

6. Herding Group

Characteristics: This group includes breeds like the border collie, German shepherd, and Australian shepherd. They were originally bred to herd livestock.

Temperament: Herding dogs are intelligent, energetic, and highly trainable. They often excel in obedience, agility, and other new sports involving dogs such as flyball, dog surfing, heeling to music, and canine freestyle.

Considerations: These dogs need a lot of exercise and mental stimulation. They may try to herd people or other pets, which can be a challenge if not properly trained. They are best suited for active individuals or families with children.

7. **Non-Sporting Group**

Characteristics: This is a diverse and unique group because it does not classify dogs by a particular purpose or size; instead, it is more of a catch-all group for dogs that do not fit into other groups. Consequently, dogs from the Non-Sporting Group run the gamut in terms of physical and personality traits, but all are ready candidates for a loving pet and would make ideal companions for all sort of personal circumstances, such as families, couples, or people who are single. Having said that, I have met several proud dog owners whose dogs have been included in such a category and have achieved great success in diversified sporting fields, ranging from all the activities mentioned in the groups above to new sporting categories such as Dog Agility, Flyball Disc, Obedience, Lure Coursing, Canicross, Canine Freestyle, Heel-work to Music, Tracking, Sled dog Racing, Dog Surfing, Scent Work, and Dog Diving. Examples of breeds in the Non-Sporting Group include Dalmatians, Chow Chows, Finnish Spitz, American Bulldogs, poodles, Boston Terriers, Lhasa-Apso, Shiba-Inu, French Bulldogs, Schipperkes, and American Eskimo Dogs.

Temperament: Because the group is so diverse, temperaments can vary widely. Some may be more active, whereas others are more laid-back.

Considerations: When considering a dog from the Non-Sporting Group, it is essential to research each breed to understand its unique characteristics and temperament. This diverse group includes all types of dogs, including both active and less active breeds, making it crucial to select a breed that aligns with your requirements and needs. Once you have found a breed you think may be right for you, I recommend that you conduct extensive research online and perhaps contact a few breeders and other dog owners to find out if it suits your lifestyle better than another. If it can be of any additional help, I have included a section dedicated to explaining how to carry out the temperament test for puppies (Campbell Test) in the next chapter, where you can find some advice on how to choose the best possible puppy to match your circumstances, energy level, and expectations, even among those breeds whose characteristics, traits, and temperament are less well known.

There is another unofficial group of dogs, the Miscellaneous Group, that includes breeds not yet fully recognised by the mainstream kennel clubs like the AKC, the FCI, or the Kennel Club in the UK, but are in the process of being considered or recognised. Examples include well-established breeds, some new types of dogs including those created by mixing poodles, or emerging breeds that are still relatively unknown because they originated in a foreign country where they were bred for a specific purpose that might not be necessary in your own country. Temperaments can vary widely depending on whether you are considering acquiring an unknown but well established breed or are opting for one of those new mixed breeds.

Mixed breeds like the puggle (a mix between a pug and a beagle) or cockapoo (a mix between a cocker spaniel and a poodle), to name but two, can give rise to several disadvantages due to the unpredictability of temperament, appearance, and health. Unlike purebred dogs, where centuries of careful breeding have honed specific traits and temperaments, mixed breeds resulting from the pursuit of recent trends often lack the stability that comes from a long process of selective breeding. In fact, it is difficult to predict which traits from each parent breed will dominate. For example, a puggle might inherit the beagle's strong hunting instinct and high energy, or the pug's laid-back nature and stubbornness. Similarly, a cockapoo might inherit the cocker spaniel's sensitivity and high energy, or the poodle's intelligence and aloofness. I can name several examples of these types of breeds owned by some of our clients and other people we meet during our regular walks, and I can assure you that in some cases, the nature of their unpredictability can often lead to frustration for owners who were expecting a specific type of temperament and demeanour and instead ended up with something completely different.

Finally, I would like to spend a few words talking about another option that it is worth considering when thinking about getting a new dog, and that is adopting a dog from a shelter. Adopting a rescue dog is a rewarding and compassionate choice that can bring immense joy and fulfilment. Working with numerous clients who adopted their dogs, either by helping them with some behavioural issues or simply taking care of them as part of our services, I have come realise that whilst there are certainly some challenges, particularly in relation to the unpredictability of temperament and unknown aspects of the dog's history, the rewards far often outweigh these difficulties. Mixed breed rescue dogs are often resilient, loving, and loyal, and with patience, understanding, and proper care, can become treasured members of your family. From an ethical perspective, by adopting from a shelter, you are giving a dog a second chance at life. Most shelter dogs are there through no fault of their own, and giving a dog a loving home helps reduce the number of dogs euthanised each year. Another great advantage of adopting from a shelter is that mixed breed dogs often benefit from "hybrid vigour" or "heterosis", which in the context of breeding refers to the occurrence of a superior offspring being born as a result of mixing the genetic contributions of its parents. This can lead to fewer inherited health problems compared to purebred dogs, whose gene pools are more restricted.

You might wonder why some scientists conduct lengthy and expensive studies of this kind. The reason could be that they are trying to improve some of the characteristics of breeds employed in specialised fields, like guide dogs for visually impaired people or those with limited mobility. A study of actual hybrid vigour between Labradors and golden retrievers by Ennik et al. (2006) found that the offspring of this heterosis trial had a 12.4% greater chance of graduating as a guide dog. Mixed breed dogs also tend to have unique combinations of traits and characteristics, making them truly one-of-a-kind. This uniqueness can be appealing to owners who want a dog with a distinct personality and novel appearance. Shelters often have adult dogs available for adoption, which can be a good option for those who do not want to deal with the challenges of raising a puppy, such as housebreaking and teething, as they typically have more established personalities so you have a better idea of what you are getting in terms of temperament and behaviour.

This was one of the main reasons why we decided to adopt our first dog, an adult one-and-a-half year-old Dobermann Pinscher, rather than a puppy. With an eye on the financial side, adopting from a shelter is generally less expensive than buying from a breeder. Shelters often include vaccinations, spaying or neutering, and microchipping in the adoption fee. They also offer resources and support after adoption, such as training classes or behavioural consultations, which can help new owners adjust to life with their new dog. Adopting a mixed breed rescue dog from a shelter can be one of the most fulfilling decisions you will ever make and can be considered a holistic choice that aligns with principles of compassion, environmental responsibility, and the overall well-being of both the adopter and the dog. A holistic approach to adoption considers not just the act of bringing a pet into your home but also the broader impact on society, the environment, and your own physical and emotional health.

When choosing a dog breed, it is also vital to consider the type of coat the dog has, as this can significantly influence their ability to cope with different climates and environments. If we consider the structure of the canine coat as a whole, then we include both the skin component as well as the hair or fur. Both have their own individual functions, and both are crucial to your dog's ability to thrive in different climates. The skin of a dog plays a crucial role in maintaining its overall health and well-being. In fact, not only does the structure of the skin prevent water and electrolyte loss to help maintain body homeostasis and avert dehydration, it also forms a protective barrier which helps protect against infections, parasites, and the elements. The hair sprouting from the follicles in the dog's skin is also known as fur. Fur is a term generally used to describe a double coat as opposed to the term Hair which is used in reference to single coats – although both protect our pets against harsh weathers, temperatures, and ultraviolet light damage. Dogs may grow primary and/or secondary hairs. Primary hairs are just single hairs that grow from the follicle in the skin. Secondary hairs, if present, grow from the same follicle but in much larger quantities. As a matter of fact, you can have anywhere from 3-15 of secondary hairs existing alongside a primary hair from the same follicle. Primary hairs are often referred to as the outer coat and secondary hairs as the undercoat. Double-coated breeds like the German shepherd, Alaskan Malamute, Husky, and Akita have both primary and secondary hairs, whereas single-coated breeds, like the Poodle or Bichon Frisé, simply have primary hairs. In double-coated breeds, hair growth and the thickness of the undercoat are strongly susceptible to environmental conditions. During cold months, double-coated dogs grow a thick undercoat which traps the air right next to the outer layer of the skin. Think of it like the wetsuit of a scuba diver. The way a wetsuit works is by trapping a thin layer of water between your body and the suit. This layer of water is then warmed by your body and water has the excellent physical property of retaining heat, hence keeping you warm. The same happens to our double- coated dogs during the winter months. At the other end of this scale, warm months call for a thinner undercoat that must be maintained, well-brushed, and not matted. This allows air to circulate, drawing cool air over the skin. A regular issue found in double-coated breeds occurs when the secondary hairs become matted and the air is unable to circulate, meaning it gets trapped and warms up from the heat of the body. The issue is further aggravated when the dog takes a dip in the pond; if the coat gets damp because of the rain, or if you wet your dogs, thinking you are doing them a favour by cooling them down, your dog's skin health can be compromised.

    As is the case for humans, the dog's skin also plays a more fundamental role as its very composition provides an immunological and microbial barrier because of its bacterial community, also known as its microbiome. The skin microbiome includes a range of bacteria, fungi, and viruses that, in normal circumstances, function symbiotically in that helpful microorganisms keep potentially harmful microorganisms in check. An issue arises, however, when there is an unbalanced alteration in the number of microorganisms forming the microbiome. Essentially, when dogs and humans are suffering with red and itchy skin, this suggests alterations have occurred in the skin microbiome in that some bacteria have grown in numbers and others have reduced. Because all bacteria have their own specific needs in order to survive, which encompass food, water, and the correct environment (including a specific temperature favourable to them), the types of bacteria also vary depending on the site of the body on which they are located. For example, the type of bacteria found between the toe digits will be different to that found in the groin area. Some bacteria will thrive in cooler temperatures, some prefer warmer climates. This is the main reason why we need to pay attention to the coat condition of double-coated breeds, as they will have their own community of bacteria on their skin. If not properly cared for, some bacteria will outnumber others and the type of bacteria that thrives will largely depend on your dog's lifestyle, including their nutrition.

I hope I have not overwhelmed you with an excessive amount of detail about the composition of a dog's coat. Nevertheless, I believe this topic is quite pertinent when selecting a new puppy or considering adopting a dog from a shelter. The type of coat and its maintenance should be a significant consideration if you prefer not to engage in regular brushing or are not prepared to invest in professional grooming sessions. Additionally, I believe this information could be useful if you live in a region with extreme temperatures, whether hot or cold, or near bodies of water such as lakes or rivers, in which case grooming becomes even more crucial. Regular brushing is possibly the most important thing you can do to ensure the skin and coat of your dog remains healthy and balanced. Not only does brushing remove unwanted knots, matts, and dead hair, the very motion encourages blood flow and stimulates the dog's lymphatic system. This system is crucial in assisting the movement of toxins out of the body and the transportation of a fluid containing infection-fighting white blood cells. In addition, a matted undercoat is detrimental to temperature regulation, so it needs to be well maintained and cared for. If your dog spends a significant amount of time swimming in the water, damp during poor weather conditions, or is in the process of drying off, I suggest you consider investing in a professional hair dryer or blaster-dryer. I worked for almost a year in a grooming parlour when I first moved to the UK and having witnessed firsthand how practical and efficient they are, I realised it was worth the investment. Blaster-dryers work wonderfully well, especially when it comes to double-coated breeds. They are much more powerful than a standard hairdryer and often run at a lower temperature, hence are much better tolerated by dogs. If your dog has never been exposed to one at a groomer's parlour, start by allowing it to sniff and investigate the novelty object at their own pace and then introduce the dryer by switching it on and running it at its lowest setting and from a distance, so that your dog accepts it and realises it poses no threat. Brush the coat out with a slicker brush as you are drying to achieve even coverage. Finally, consider how often you bathe your dog and what type of shampoo you use.

The dog's skin is made up of three layers:

Subcutis, which is the innermost layer separating the skin from internal organs and muscles.

Dermis, which is the middle layer of the skin and is filled with nerves, blood vessels, hair follicles, and other structures important for overall skin health and function.

Epidermis, which is the outermost layer of skin. This is the layer that protects the body from most foreign substances and pathogens.

The dermis and epidermis host thousands of oil glands which are responsible for secreting a greasy substance called sebum. The sebum is vital for maintaining the dog's skin and coat in good health. This substance covers the hairs to keep them shiny and resilient and the skin moist and flexible. However, the sebum's most important function is to act as a potent antibiotic that can destroy most pathogens that come into contact with it.

In essence, when we over-bathe our dogs, there are three major issues that may arise that can interfere directly with skin health. The first obvious issue is that we wash away the sebum, that valuable greasy oil that keeps our dog's coat glossy and shiny and their skin resilient. With enough over-bathing, skin and fur become brittle and bad bacteria can move into the cracks appearing in the epidermis. Moreover, without sufficient sebum and its antibiotic properties, the growth of harmful bacteria goes out of control, and the dog becomes more vulnerable to skin diseases and infections. The second problem is that the constant rubbing and scrubbing of the skin induces faster production of keratinocyte cells. This results in thicker skin across the entire body, rather than being localised to areas like the elbows and foot pads where it is needed most. Thicker skin is generally less flexible, contains fewer oil glands, and is more prone to cracking. This lack of natural oils and flexibility can create an environment where bacteria thrive, increasing the likelihood of skin infections and other health issues. Last but not least, frequently over-bathing your dog using a regular dog shampoo, thinking you are implementing a good hygiene regimen, is also not recommended as it washes away all of the bacteria, including the good bacteria that help protect the skin. In fact, the same shampoo you are using to wash away the bad bacteria, odour, and dirt from your dog's coat will also modify the microbiome on your dog's skin. It takes quite some time for the body to re-establish a balanced microbiome, and while this is happening, your dog is at risk of infection and pathogen overpopulation.

As responsible dog parents, there are three simple steps we can take to help our pets maintain healthy and resilient skin. The first is to feed our dogs a good quality fresh or raw high-protein diet (BARF). A diet consisting of real meat and the occasional oily fish will supply all the protein and fat your dog's skin and coat needs to thrive. As a matter of fact, about 35% of the protein your dog eats is used to maintain skin and coat health. Skin problems are usually the first sign that your dog is not getting enough quality protein in their diet. Secondly, try to avoid bathing your dog using shampoos, instead opt for a simple water bath. I understand that for some dog parents it is difficult not to give their dogs a bath after a walk on a rainy day, especially if their dogs belong to one of those water loving breeds or cannot keep themselves out of muddy paddles. Nevertheless, by simply using warm water and massaging your dog's coat to get rid of dirt and debris, you will not interfere with the natural microbiome on your dog's skin. Finally, stay clear of medicated shampoo and antibiotics which are extremely damaging to the skin as they wash away the good as well as the bad bacteria. The way I see it is that although both medicated shampoos and antibiotics may provide some temporary relief from itching and infection, the problem is only likely to get worse in the long run. The reality is that these products also reduce the skin's ability to heal itself, and when more pathogens find their way onto your dog's skin, and believe me they will, there will be nothing to stop them from exacerbating the issues and causing more problems. Ironically, this situation often leads to a cycle of bathing to eradicate problems caused by over-bathing.

Lastly, I would like to point out another interesting feature that can help determine the type of dog we might choose. It is a morphological characteristic pertinent to certain breeds of dogs which is often overlooked but equally important during the selection process. The feature I am referring to is the shape of a dog's head, which can tell us a great deal not only about its breed but also about its temperament and social tendencies. Intriguingly, the rounded skull shape seen in many popular companion breeds does more than give them a non-threatening, approachable appearance. It is also believed to be linked to enhanced social behaviour. A more rounded cranial structure allows greater space in the frontal part of the brain, which coincidentally corresponds to the region responsible for processing social interactions. As a result, these dogs often appear more friendly, expressive, and easier to connect with. Conversely, breeds with a flatter frontal skull, common in many traditional working or guarding breeds, tend to have a more focused, independent, and sometimes aloof disposition. These structural differences may explain why certain dogs naturally excel as companions, while others are better suited to protective or sentinel roles.

We have all heard the phrase "You can't judge a book by its cover", but when it comes to dogs, that might not be entirely true. According to a large-scale study conducted by Holly Stone and her team at the University of Sydney (Georgevsky et al., 2014), a dog's size and head shape can offer valuable clues about its personality and behavioural tendencies. As mentioned previously in the book, this makes sense when you consider how deeply we have shaped dogs through selective breeding. Over thousands of years, we have created breeds to serve specific roles, herders, hunters, guardians, and companions. In the process, we have influenced not only how dogs look but also how they think and behave.

The study in question involved applying a standardised behavioural assessment known as the Dog Mentality Assessment Test to more than 67,000 dogs from 45 different breeds and took place over eight years in Sweden. It measured traits such as aggression, sociability, curiosity, fearfulness, and playfulness. The researchers then compared the results with physical measurements like height, weight, and the cephalic index, a numerical way to classify head shape. The cephalic index is the ratio between the width and length of a dog's skull. The dog's head shape can be classified as follows:

- Dolichocephalic (long-headed) dogs like greyhounds and Afghans
- Mesocephalic (medium-headed) dogs like golden retrievers and beagles
- Brachycephalic (short-headed) dogs like pugs and French bulldogs

And here is where things get interesting. What the research found is that shorter dogs were more aggressive, while taller dogs displayed greater affection, cooperation, and playfulness. Moreover, heavier dogs were generally bolder and more attentive, whereas lighter dogs leaned towards being more cautious and fearful. The head shape also predicted key personality traits in that brachycephalic dogs (those with short, rounded skulls) engaged more with their humans and enjoyed human-directed play, but were also more defensive in unfamiliar or ambiguous situations, whilst dolichocephalic dogs were less playful with strangers but tended to be less reactive and recovered more quickly from unexpected events. These findings do not suggest that one shape or size is "better" than another, but they do offer an insight into why certain breeds may be more suited to companionship, protection, or specific working roles. As Freud once said, "Physiology is destiny", and in the canine world, it seems he had a point. In my own experience, both as a dog trainer and through the research carried out for this book, understanding the link between a dog's physical build and its behaviour has proven invaluable. Whether you are selecting a breed for your lifestyle or trying to decode your own dog's temperament, these insights can help you make better choices and develop a more empathetic, tailored approach to training.

Ultimately, when it comes to choosing a companion dog, there are a great number of points to take into consideration. It is essential to consider factors such as the breed's temperament, energy level, size, and, as I have discussed, the type of coat they have. Each aspect will affect how well the dog fits into your lifestyle, whether it is grooming needs, exercise requirements, or how they interact with other pets or children. It is easy to become overwhelmed with so many details, but taking the time to understand these elements will ensure that you make an informed decision and lead you to choose a pet that will thrive in your environment and fit into your lifestyle. I sincerely hope that with the information I have provided, I have been able to assist you in making such a life-changing decision.

Mario

CHAPTER 9

FINDING THE PUPPY THAT'S RIGHT FOR YOU

Now that you have set your heart on a particular breed, or perhaps opened it up to a rescue pup from a shelter, it is time to focus on choosing the right individual who will become part of your family and accompany you for the rest of your lives. Whether you are picking up a puppy from a litter or meeting a group of hopeful shelter companions, this is a moment filled with excitement, curiosity, and, understandably, a bit of uncertainty. In this section, I will explore what to look for in a puppy or young dog, how to read their personality, and which steps can help guide you towards making a confident, informed, and heartfelt decision. After all, this marks the beginning of a lifelong bond, one built on mutual trust and understanding. It is also a crucial moment, as your choice will shape your life and theirs for years to come. Making the right match ensures that your new family member will blend naturally into your home, creating a relationship that feels like it was always meant to be.

Depending on the breed, puppies are considered ready to leave their mothers and littermates after a period that varies between 8 to 12 weeks of age. There are other circumstances where puppies are required to spend more time with the breeder, for example in cases when their place of origin is a foreign country and hence they need a full course of the rabies vaccine, tape-worm treatment, and other documents like a Pet Passport in order to enter the country of residence of the new owner. I have found that in this and other circumstances, if puppies have the opportunity to spend more time with their mothers and littermates, they grow into better balanced young dogs because during this extended period spent with their own family, they learn important behaviours that have lifelong implications. From a holistic perspective, there are 5 different stages in the development process of a puppy and we need to make sure their needs are met during each phase. You will notice numerous behavioural changes during each life stages, so knowing how to handle your puppy throughout each developmental stage will help shape them into a well-adjusted lifelong family member.

Puppy Developmental Stages

The first stage is called the Neonatal Stage (0 to 2 weeks of age) and begins immediately after birth. At this age, puppies are completely blind and deaf: they can only count on their sense of smell, which helps them root about the nest to find their mother's scent-marked breasts, along with the senses of taste and touch, and they rely totally on their mother's support for their survival. Newborn puppies are also unable to regulate their body temperature; in fact, they depend on their mother and littermates to keep warm, huddling in cozy piles to conserve body temperature. If a puppy is separated from this warm furry nest, it can quickly die from hypothermia (low body temperature) and therefore will cry loudly to alert mum to their predicament. At this stage, puppies are unable to urinate or defecate on their own, so their mother will lick them all over their bellies and intimate parts to stimulate them to defecate and urinate. She will then eat their excrement to keep them and the nest clean and free from harmful diseases. Another reason why mothers eat their puppies' faeces is because the scent of the excrement could potentially attract predators. During the first two weeks of life, puppies usually sleep nearly 90 percent of the time, spending the rest of their time awake nursing. The first milk the mother produces is called colostrum and is extremely rich in nutrients and antibodies which provide passive immunity and protect the puppies from disease during these early weeks of life. All of their energy is funnelled into growing, and in the first week their birth weight doubles. Newborn puppies are not yet able to support their weight, and will crawl about using their front legs as paddles. This limited locomotion provides the first physical exercise that helps the puppies develop muscle mass and coordination, and, within a couple of weeks, the puppies are already able to crawl all over each other and their mother.

 The second stage is called the Transitional Stage (2 to 4 weeks of age). Because the developmental rate of dogs is so fast, it brings great changes for the puppy. The puppy's ears and eyes, which were completely sealed since birth, begin to open; the ears at about 2 weeks and the eyelids between 10 to 16 days. This gives the puppies a new sense of their world as they learn for the first time what their mother and other dogs look and sound like. Simultaneously, they begin to expand their own vocabulary, going from the initial grunts and mews to proper yelps, whines, and barks. Puppies are generally able to stand by day 15 and can take their first wobbly steps by day 21, very fast indeed in comparison with humans. This stage represents a time of rapid physical and sensory development for the puppy, during which they go from being totally dependent on their mother to experiencing a bit of their own independence. They begin to play with their littermates, start getting familiar with the environment and learning about their newly formed canine society (much like our children at the beginning of their schooling), and begin sampling food from mummy's bowl. Puppy teeth will begin to erupt painfully until all the baby teeth are out by about 5 to 6 weeks of age. At this stage, puppies are able to control their need to potty, and will naturally begin to move away from where they eat and sleep to relieve themselves, keeping the den clean by doing so, and avoid attracting potential predators. Some responsible breeders also take this opportunity to potty train young puppies at this age, so as to facilitate the task on behalf of their future owners.

The Transitional Stage is immediately followed by what I consider the most important stage of them all, the Socialisation Period (4 to 12 weeks of age). This stage is crucial because it also happens to coincide with the beginning of the process called Imprinting, which is generally considered to be between 3 to 16 weeks of age, although, depending on the breed, some elements of imprinting can continue beyond this timeframe.

In ethology, imprinting is described as the process by which an animal forms a strong attachment and, subsequently, a solid association with a figure or an object as a result of an early exposure to the same figure or object. In animal behaviour, imprinting is a concept that was first observed in domestic chickens by a fascinating British historical figure, Sir Thomas More. On countless occasions I have passed by the commemorative statue of Sir Thomas More located on Cheyne Walk on the Chelsea Embankment in London, and my curiosity led me to find out more about him. Sir Thomas More was not only a prominent English lawyer but also a judge, social philosopher, author, statesman, and amateur theologian. He served under King Henry VIII as Lord High Chancellor of England from October 1529 to May 1532 and because he opposed the annulment of Henry VIII's marriage to Catherine of Aragon and the separation from the Catholic Church, was swiftly tried for treason and executed. In the year 2000, Pope John Paul II made him patron saint of statesmen and politicians. Although he is not directly connected to the field of ethology or that of animal behaviour, More's legacy as a thinker, particularly through his work *Utopia*, compels us to consider the complexities of human society, its morality, and its governance. In *Utopia*, More explores the idea that a well-functioning society requires order and discipline, sometimes at the expense of individual liberty. This notion parallels the way social structures operate in both human and animal communities. For example, in a wolf pack, strict hierarchies and social rules guarantee the group's survival, similar to how human societies create laws and norms to maintain order.

I find it highly fascinating to note how the work of a philosopher, written more than 450 years ago, continues to be so relevant and still resonates across various fields, including the study of human and animal behaviour. More's vision of a society where the common good is prioritised over individual wealth aligns with the idea that social cohesion is essential for group survival. In dogs and many other animal species, behaviours that promote group welfare, such as cooperative hunting, protection of the territory, or shared childcare, are crucial for the survival of the group. Similarly, in human societies, the promotion of the common good through social policies and cooperative behaviours can lead to greater stability and the long-term well-being of its members. As described in previous chapters, this could have been one of the reasons why humans' and dogs' paths crossed during their evolutionary process, and why the shared principles for societal structure and cooperation made them such a successful combination that still endures today. However, over the past few decades, as modern societies began to put much greater emphasis on individualism and entrepreneurship, often at the expense of communal values and collective well-being, dogs have continued to adhere to the social structures and communal instincts that have been part of the characteristics of their species for thousands of years, reflecting several of the concepts developed by Thomas More. This shift has far-reaching implications, not only for how people interact with each other, and I may add that we are gradually suffering the consequences, but also for how they relate to their dogs and other pets. For example, dogs may be left alone for long periods of time due to their owners' busy lifestyles and this can lead to behavioural issues, stress, and frustration, or they might be trained with methods that prioritise control over understanding, leading to a breakdown in the human-animal bond.

In the spirit of the holistic approach I wish to promote with this book, we need to bear in mind the fact that our dogs (and our ancestors) have evolved to live in groups, whether as part of a pack or a human family. Their behaviours, such as loyalty, cooperation, and the desire to form strong social bonds, are deeply ingrained and reflect a communal, rather than individualistic, mindset. If we think about it, throughout history, great civilisations like the Ancient Egypt, the Roman Empire, the Islamic Golden Age, and the Inca achieved remarkable success by adhering to principles of mutual cooperation, shared benefits, and collective responsibility. These societies often thrived because they recognised that the well-being of the community as a whole was crucial to their prosperity and stability. Conversely, when these civilisations began to prioritise the interests of a select few over the needs of the majority, they often experienced decline and eventual collapse. Nowadays, it would appear that history is repeating itself as the contrast between the declining Western civilisation and the emerging Asian societies, particularly China, can indeed be seen as a reflection of different values, including those that align with the communal concepts expressed by Thomas More. In this context, the Chinese model of governance and societal organisation (with all its flaws) highlights a focus on collective well-being and social order which has contributed to their increasing global political, military, and economic power. Conversely,

Western societies, with their emphasis on individualism and personal freedom, are experiencing growing economic disparities, social fragmentation, and widespread financial insecurity.

As conscious dog parents, we must realise that if we base the relationship with our dogs exclusively on values that promote individualism (e.g. I do not appreciate my dogs socialising with other dogs, I cannot be bothered with walking or training sessions) and entrepreneurship (my lifestyle is too busy with family commitments, work, travelling, holidays, etc) these values often will clash with the communal and social instincts of our dogs. As part of the dog walking service we provide for our clients in the beautiful setting of Hyde Park or Kensington Gardens in London, I often allow our group of dogs to meet, socialise, and play with other dogs we encounter. During these chance meetings, I often observe, after the usual rituals of meetings, how the social interactions among dogs starkly contrast with those of their human companions. Unlike humans, dogs generally do not have a strong sense of possession and are often quite willing to share toys, treats, water, and even cuddles. In essence, as social animals, dogs are more focused on the dynamics of the pack and maintaining harmony within their group. Their interactions are still driven by instincts of cooperation and mutual benefit rather than competition or ownership. Thomas More's ideas about the importance of social order, discipline, and the common good resonate strongly with the natural behaviours of dogs, who thrive in environments that value a consistent structure, cooperation, and social bonds. Recognising and respecting these instincts can lead to more fulfilling and balanced relationships with our pets, ensuring both humans and dogs coexist happily in a modern world that often pulls them in different directions. I apologise for having taken a little detour on the main subject, but I think it is important to acknowledge the crucial role imprinting plays in our puppies' early development.

Remarkably, some 350 years later, following Sir Thomas More's manuscript, another British biologist and animal behaviourist, Douglas Spalding, reprised the concept of animal imprinting, paving the way for further studies conducted later in the nineteenth century by the German ethologist Oskar Heinroth. However, it was one of Oskar Heinroth's followers, the famous Austrian zoologist and ethologist Konrad Lorenz, who extensively studied and popularised the concept of imprinting. His groundbreaking work in the mid-twentieth century, particularly with geese and ducks, significantly advanced our understanding of imprinting and its importance in the development of social animals. In a series of experiments, he observed that young birds, particularly goslings and ducklings, would follow the first moving object they encountered immediately after hatching. This phenomenon, which he precisely termed "imprinting", demonstrated how young animals rapidly learn to identify their parent or another significant figure during a critical period shortly after birth. In one of his most significant experiments, detailed in his influential publication *Der Kumpan*, published in 1935 (Birkhead & Schulze-Hagen, 2024), Lorenz famously split a group of goose eggs into two groups. One group was allowed to hatch naturally in the presence of their mother, while the other group hatched in an incubator where Lorenz was the first moving object the goslings saw. The goslings in the first group followed their biological mother, while those in the second group followed Lorenz as if he were their parent. This experiment highlighted that imprinting is not a learnt behaviour in the traditional sense but rather a natural, instinctual process that occurs during a specific time window early in life. In dogs, this time window occurs between 3/4 weeks and 4/6 months. I cannot stress enough the importance of imprinting in our dogs. Puppies exposed to a variety of sights, sounds, and social experiences during this period are less likely to develop fears or phobias later in life. Moreover, early exposure to different environments, such as homes, parks, and urban areas, helps puppies adapt to the variety of settings they will encounter as adults.

Studies (e.g. Dietz et al., 2018) have demonstrated that the various experiences puppies have during the imprinting phase have a long-lasting impact on their behaviour and temperament. Positive and enriching experiences lead to confident, well-socialised dogs, while negative experiences or lack of exposure to different stimuli can result in fearfulness, aggression, or anxiety. The other crucial aspect of imprinting is that it is irreversible and is considered a rapid and permanent process. Once the bond is formed, it is difficult to reverse. For instance, the goslings that imprinted on Lorenz continued to follow him even when their biological mother was present. Because of the irreversible nature of the process, traumatic events sustained during this stage of a puppy or a young dog's development are extremely difficult to treat, as I have often experienced in my line of work. Therapy for these traumas often requires a significant investment of time, money, and effort on the part of the owners, as they typically involve desensitisation, which is a rather lengthy treatment based on gradual exposure of the subject to the feared object or situation in a controlled and positive manner, and/or counterconditioning, where the dog is taught to associate the previously traumatic stimuli with positive experiences (I will explain these and other procedures at length in a dedicated chapter). This therapeutic approach is not a quick fix and may take months or even years of consistent and patient work. Holistically speaking, it is also essential to approach such cases with compassion and understanding, recognising that the dog's responses are deeply rooted in their early experiences and have perhaps been inadvertently reinforced by the owners. On a positive note, with the right approach it is possible to help a dog overcome the impact of early trauma, but it requires a thoughtful, individualised plan, often with the guidance of a professional dog trainer or behaviourist. In recognition of his contributions to the understanding of animal behaviour, Konrad Lorenz was awarded the Nobel Prize in Physiology or Medicine in 1973, alongside fellow ethologists Karl von Frisch and Nikolaas Tinbergen.

The Socialisation Stage is immediately followed by the Juvenile Stage (12 to 24 weeks of age), which is another crucial period for the puppy's growth and socialisation. I like to refer to this stage as the Rebellious Stage, as it is when puppies start to exhibit a greater sense of independence and may test boundaries more frequently. They also become more aware of their social status and may start to assert themselves, challenging their owners to assess who is in charge, which can sometimes lead to dominance-related issues. All of a sudden these young pups seem to "forget" any training they have learnt up to that point and act like rebellious teenagers. If you recognise your puppy as fitting the description above, fear not as what is often described as delinquent behaviour is actually influenced by the spurt in physical growth and hormone production, their coordination skills, energy levels, and the teething phase. Unlike many other species, a male puppy's testosterone level from age 4-to-10 months has been found to be up to five times higher than that of an adult dog. This has been purposely orchestrated by mother nature, so that adult canines recognise they are facing a juvenile who needs a bit of canine "schooling" the dog's way, which is normal and usually sounds scarier than it actually is, including growling, barking, and even assertively scolding a younger dog into submission. Some unexperienced or overly concerned dog parents fearing for their young dog's safety tend to interrupt or avoid these types of noisy interaction and inadvertently prevent their dogs from working out where they stand as regards the hierarchy of the group. Some squabbling and play fighting is expected. It is a dog rule that older animals teach the pup their limits, status, and place within a group of dogs during socialisation.

Because the jaw and palate of a puppy is too small to accommodate permanent teeth, puppies start growing baby teeth from the age of 2 weeks through a process called teething. The teething phase will last until he or she reaches the age of 6 months. As happens with humans, teething can be an extremely uncomfortable and painfully experience for puppies, but the canine species has excogitated a strategy to help young puppies as, through the action of chewing, puppies naturally produce a hormone that soothes the pain caused by the inflamed gums. Given the fact that this is also a period of heightened curiosity, where puppies explore their environment more thoroughly, they will tend to chew whatever they can find around the house, so keep your Jimmy Choo shoes, Ray-Ban sun glasses, and coveted collection of Birkin bags out of reach; instead, run to your local pet shop and order some deer antlers, Kong rubber toys with holes you can fill with peanut butter, or wet an old towel in some chicken broth and put it in the freezer to help your puppy through this phase. To summarise, this is probably one of the most important phases in the development of your puppies. Even if you have done everything right and invested time and effort in educating your little mischief-makers, they will inevitably go through some drastic physical, mental, and hormonal changes which will test your patience and call into question your abilities as dog parents. All you have to do is to clench your teeth, keep your puppies under control, possibly on the lead or on the long line, and continue providing them with love, consistent guidance, and holistic training, telling yourself, "He's testing me, it'll get better". Because eventually it will.

If you have managed to successfully survive the testing time of the Juvenile phase, you will have reached the final stage of your young dog's development – the Adolescence Stage (from 6 to 12/18 months). Dogs generally go through adolescence much earlier than people; for small breeds, it can start as early as 6 months of age, while larger breeds start at 9 or 10 months of age. Adolescence in larger breed dogs continues until they are 18 to 24 months, whilst smaller breeds usually reach maturity at about 18 months. Typically, the larger the dog, the slower the development. During this period, the young dog will continue to grow and reach their full height for the breed's standard and will also gain muscle mass and body weight; the level of testosterone in a male dog's body will still be extremely high, five to seven times more than that of an adult dog, and this can lead to new behaviours, such as humping, territory marking, an escalated tendency to roam, and also an increased interest in other dogs. Females might go into season for the first time, which can also bring about behavioural changes and the potential for pregnancy. If they have their first period at 8 or 9 months of age, they will more likely have two seasons every year, if they go into season after 12 months of age, they will probably have one season every year. In both sexes, the adult coat will replace the puppy coat and you might notice a change in its colour.

Like adolescent humans, young dogs often exhibit a stronger yearning for independence, as well as the desire to test boundaries, and sometimes they are more determined to maintain a certain attitude towards a task or a command – what we humans call stubbornness. Behaviours that were well-managed in the puppy stage, such as obedience to commands, might regress as the dog tries to assert its independence. The drive to explore and investigate is so strong during adolescence that it can sometimes lead to trouble, such as digging, chewing, or attempting to escape from the garden. As in the previous Juvenile stage, without proper training and structure, this period can also lead to the development of behavioural issues such as fearfulness, anxiety, aggression, or excessive barking. Dog parents who have chosen to focus on a more holistic approach to raising their puppies should bear in mind that during this period dogs can be more emotionally sensitive – they can experience mood swings and may react strongly to changes in their environment or routine. Moreover, a large number of behaviours in our young dogs that we, as a society, consider undesirable or problematic, such as jumping up, biting, chasing, hunting, barking, or even rolling in faeces, are, in fact, perfectly normal and natural for a growing young dog, especially during their adolescence. These behaviours are deeply rooted in their instincts and are essential for their development and need to coexist in the context of a pack. With proper guidance, training, and socialisation, we can assist our dogs to navigate this stage successfully, leading to a well-adjusted and well-behaved adult dog that will be able to cope in every situation life throws at them.

The final stage in the developmental process of dogs is the Maturity Stage. This is the period when a dog transitions from adolescence into adulthood, typically between 1.5 to 3 years of age depending on the breed. During this stage, a dog's physical and mental characteristics stabilise, and they reach their full size and strength. This period is marked by several key changes that are often welcomed by the majority of dog parents. Their physical growth is accompanied by a stability in their energy levels and they usually become more predictable and less erratic compared with the adolescence phase. Although they retain their unique personality traits and attitude towards training and working, dogs develop a more settled and calmer demeanour; most noticeably, the impulsive and unpredictable behaviours tend to subside. During this period, they also understand their place in the family hierarchy and routine training regimens become easier as dogs are more focused and less distracted. Social relationships with humans and other animals are reinforced and solidified, and their temperament will become more apparent and consistent. Some dog owners notice huge improvements in the behaviour of their dogs and tend to transition into a more relaxed approach towards the everyday management of their routines, but I always recommend that they should continue to provide mental and physical stimulation to prevent boredom and guarantee a well-balanced temperament.

In essence, the maturity stage is a significant period in a dog's life, as it sets the foundation for their behaviour and health for the rest of their adult years.

Breeder Search

At this point, I assume that any new prospective pet parent has carefully evaluated their lifestyle and the commitments that pet ownership entails, and have researched extensively the breed they would like to acquire. They should now be ready to begin the search for a reputable breeder. The starting point for the search of a new puppy is often the websites of various canine associations like the AKC or the FCI, which are present in every modern developed country. In the UK for example, The Kennel Club (KC) provides a puppy search platform where breeders and prospective owners can meet and exchange information about the various breeds, information on when new litters are due as well as the number of puppies available, the genders of the puppies, and details about the lineage of the parents of the litter - in other words, their pedigrees. The majority of breeders I have met through this channel have been extremely responsible people, highly professional, and extremely knowledgeable about their chosen breed, but I have also come across a few unpleasant people. Although they were a minority, I always advise our clients to be extremely cautious when researching the breeder, as they may acquire a puppy of dubious origins, sometimes of a different breed from what was originally declared, and some have even carried serious genetic diseases or worse.

I remember a few years ago in 2008 when the controversy surrounding pedigree dogs came to public attention. The BBC aired an investigative programme called Pedigree Dogs Exposed which looked into the health and welfare issues facing pedigree dogs in the UK. The programme specifically investigated the case of a King Charles cavalier who had won Crufts, the world's most prestigious dog show, despite carrying life-changing genetic diseases. The dog was later used as a stud for numerous litters, passing on these hereditary conditions to numerous puppies. I had the unfortunate experience of meeting just two of these cases and it was excruciatingly painful to witness the suffering of both the dogs and their owners who ultimately had to take the drastic decision to euthanise them, despite the emotional attachment they and their families, children included, had already established with their dogs. The KC, the body governing pedigree dogs in the UK which runs Crufts, was heavily criticised for allowing breed standards, judging standards, and breeding practices to compromise the health of pedigree dogs. As a result of the investigation, the BBC lost its exclusive contract to air the prestigious dog show, but I believe the exposure of these issues was crucial in preventing further suffering of dogs.

Another convenient and efficient way to find the right dog for your home is through specialised websites where breeders can advertise the puppies they have available for sale. You should look for websites where only certified breeders who follow ethical breeding practices are allowed to post. Reputable breeders who advertise on these sites often provide detailed information about the puppy's pedigree, including the health history of the parents and any genetic testing that has been done. I have used some of these sites myself in the past and have found that they often have forums or community sections where you can connect with other owners of the breed, get advice, and share experiences. Ultimately, by combining this method with your own personal research and possibly visiting the breeder in person before even considering leaving a deposit, you will ensure you are making a responsible and informed decision.

Curiously, my recent personal experience in finding a new puppy led me to reflect on the idea of fatalism, the belief that certain events are predetermined and out of our control. A couple of months before the world was hit by the COVID-19 pandemic, my partner and I lost our little long-haired Chihuahua due to heart failure. We were aware of the problem because after collecting the puppy from the breeder, we took him to our vet for a routine check-up and were told that, like several other small breeds, our puppy had a heart murmur. Most heart disease in dogs is caused by the weakening or slow deformity of heart valves to the extent that they no longer close tightly. As a consequence, blood then leaks back around these weakened valves, straining the heart. Pets with heart valve disease (sometimes called mitral valve disease) are often diagnosed with a heart murmur and, depending on the severity of the disease and timing of the diagnosis, need to be under medication and tested every year to monitor the status of the condition. In our case, the heart valve disease was diagnosed quite early, and the vet said that although the medication could have helped slow the progress of the disease, we should expect our puppy to live only another two to three years. From that moment on, we did our utmost to provide our little puppy with the best possible lifestyle and diet and I think that we were blessed, because those two to three years became twelve. Nowadays, there have been huge advancements in veterinary treatments for this particular disease and thanks to Dr Masami Uechi, a Japanese Veterinary Surgeon who created the first mitral valve repair (MVR) surgical procedure, most dogs have the chance to live healthy and happy lives. Recently, the procedure has also been performed in London by Dr. Daniel Brockman, who was trained by Dr. Uechi, at the Royal Veterinary College (RVC), but the waiting list is long and the procedure itself prohibitively expensive (£20,000 last time I checked). Anyway, upon the passing of our dog, we decided to scatter his ashes in the place he loved most and while the wind was blowing his ashes away, I made the wish to have another chance in life to experience the act of giving and receive pure love as only a dog can do. A few months later, browsing through various ads of dogs in need of a new home, we unexpectedly found another young dog who was the spitting image of the dog we lost. As if the resemblance was not enough, he was coincidentally born on the same day our dog passed away and had the same name as my partner. If that was not a clear manifestation of fatalism, then I don't know what else to call it.

I am pretty certain that, like me, countless other dog owners must have experienced the same process when choosing a new puppy. I am convinced that certain events like this resonate with the idea of fatalism. Sometimes, it has happened that despite our best efforts to find the "perfect" match, after carefully planning every single detail and perhaps lingering over the decision of a lifetime, the dog that enters our lives can feel like it was meant to be, as if fate played a hand in bringing us together. Numerous dog owners have told me stories of how they "just knew" a particular dog was meant for them, often in unexpected or serendipitous circumstances. To me, these moments can feel like a reminder that not everything in life can be planned, and sometimes the best things come when we least expect them. Often, it is not just about finding a dog that fits your criteria, but about the emotional connection that forms when you meet a puppy. This bond can override any preconceived notions you had, making you feel like the choice was guided by something beyond logic, perhaps even fate. It certainly reminds us that whilst we can prepare and plan events that we consider extremely important, sometimes life has other ideas, and those unexpected turns can lead to some of the most rewarding experiences. I might dare to define this experience as Love.

A Boy or a Girl?

Another important consideration to make when choosing a puppy concerns their gender, as there are notable differences in behaviour, temperament, and physical traits between the two. Moreover, recent studies have shown that male and female dogs respond differently to men and women. Understanding these differences can help you make a more informed decision that better aligns with your lifestyle and preferences. Male dogs are generally larger, heavier, and more muscular than females of the same breed. This can be a key factor if you are looking for a dog that may need to perform tasks requiring strength or endurance. Conversely, female dogs tend to be slightly smaller, lighter, and less physically imposing. This can be advantageous if you prefer a dog that is easier to handle or manage in terms of physical strength.

However, there is another reason why I think people tend to choose one particular gender over another and this is known as "projection". In human psychology, projection is the process of displacing one's feelings onto a different person, animal, or object. The term is most commonly used to describe defensive projection, which means to attribute one's own unacceptable urges to another. For example, if someone continuously bullies and ridicules a peer about their insecurities, the bully might be projecting their own struggle with self-esteem onto the other person. Being the victim of bullying myself while growing up in challenging circumstances following my adoption, I did some searching later in my adulthood in order to understand the causes and the damaging effects of bullying. The concept of projection first emerged in Sigmund Freud's exploration of defence mechanisms. This foundational idea continues to be explored in the literature on modern psychology, including in an article by Bailey and Pico titled "Defense Mechanisms" (updated 2023), and was further refined by his daughter, Anna Freud, in her publication *The Ego and the Mechanisms of Defense* (1936), as well as other prominent figures in psychology. Projection is thought to be an unconscious process that protects the ego of the affected subjects from thoughts and impulses they consider unacceptable. Put simply, by attributing those tendencies and impulses to others, individuals can place themselves above and beyond those urges, without fully recognising it in themselves. This mental process enables them to preserve their self-esteem, making difficult emotions more tolerable. It is easier to attack or witness wrongdoing in another people rather than confront that possibility in one's own behaviour. How a person acts toward the target of projection might reflect how they really feel about themselves. Projection can happen in different scenarios like relationships, parenting, in a workplace, friendships, even in the context of therapy.

Through other online research for this project I also found out that following Freud's concepts, other psychologists, namely Carl Jung and Marie-Louise von Franz, later argued that projection is also used to protect against the fear of the unknown, sometimes to the projector's detriment. Within their framework, people project archetypal ideas onto things they do not understand as part of a natural desire for a more predictable and clearly-patterned world. In the context of choosing a dog's gender, projection might occur when individuals select a male or female dog based on the traits or image they wish to project onto the dog, which in turn reflects certain aspects of their own identity or self-image. For instance, someone might choose a male dog because they associate masculinity with strength and assertiveness, traits they either possess or aspire to embody. Conversely, someone might select a female dog because they perceive femininity as nurturing and gentle, qualities they identify with or want to cultivate. This choice can serve as a way for people to reinforce or express certain aspects of their personality through their pets. As a professional dog trainer and behavioural consultant, I have learnt over the years to consider this important aspect of my clients' personalities in order to gain a better understanding of what training method could better match their pets, or what strategy could be more effective in treating a behavioural issue. People often turn to their pets as a way to cope with or mitigate various psychological and emotional issues, but projection and other psychological tactics are concepts totally alien to our pets; they do not project their insecurities or unresolved issues onto others. Instead, they respond with pure, straightforward emotions; they live in the moment, free from judgment and grudges, and offer us affection without conditions. If humans could adopt even a fraction of this approach by being more present, less judgmental, and offering kindness without expecting something in return, we might find that many of the conflicts and misunderstandings that arise from projection could be diminished. Rather than building up walls of defence or assumptions, we could focus on understanding and connection, much like how pets connect with us.

Let us go back to the other key differences between the two genders. If you ask anyone involved in the pet community for their personal opinion on the differences between male and female pets, their most likely answer would be that males are often more playful, outgoing, and sometimes more stubborn: they may exhibit more dominant behaviours, such as marking territory and being more territorial or protective, but they are also often more affectionate and loyal. Regarding females, such people might say that they are generally more independent, mature, and focused. They are also less likely to exhibit dominant behaviours and may be easier to train. Perhaps the only issue that arises could be the fact that during their heat cycles, un-spayed females can exhibit mood swings and may be less predictable in their behaviour.

By contrast, I would like to propose an intriguing alternative perspective on male dogs and their behaviours, which can indeed be tied to their genetic inheritance and the evolutionary roles they have historically played within pack structures. These traits are not just random but evolved to serve specific functions crucial for the survival and cohesion of a pack. Play, for example, is a critical part of social development in canines, helping them learn boundaries, communication, and social cues. For males, this playfulness can also be a way to assert dominance or to form alliances, which are essential in a pack structure, especially in the context of hunting in groups. Dominance and territoriality are indeed characteristics that are often more pronounced in male dogs – behaviours deeply rooted in their evolutionary past. In the wild, male canines are often responsible for protecting the pack's territory from intruders. Marking territory with urine and displaying dominant behaviours are ways to establish their presence and deter rivals. These behaviours ensure the safety and stability of the pack by maintaining clear boundaries and defending resources. The protectiveness of male dogs is another trait that has been honed through generations of natural selection. In a pack context, males are often at the forefront of defending the group against threats. This protectiveness extends not just to territory but also to members of the pack, including mates, offspring, and other pack members. This behaviour is essential to guarantee the survival of the pack and the continuation of the species.

However, although male dogs can be dominant and protective, they are also known for their loyalty and affection. In a pack, these traits are crucial for maintaining cohesion and cooperation among members. Loyalty to the pack leader and other members ensures that the group functions as a unified whole. This loyalty can translate into strong bonds with human owners, as dogs often see their human family as their pack. Finally, when it comes to cooperation and family dynamics, we ought to bear in mind that in the wild, male dogs play a crucial role in one of the most important cooperative activities; namely, hunting. Their ability to work with other males (and females) in a coordinated manner is vital for the success of the hunt. This cooperation is a key component of pack life, where each member has a role to play. The social behaviours displayed by male dogs, such as communication, teamwork, and leadership, are all part of this cooperative dynamic.

Conversely, if you find yourself more inclined towards choosing a female dog, they are often perceived as more independent and mature compared to males and as easily trainable. Like their male counterparts, these traits have evolved over time to serve specific roles within a pack, such as nurturing, cooperation, and maintaining social cohesion. In the wild, female canines need to be self-sufficient, especially when they are raising pups. This maturity allows them to make decisions (sometimes rather drastic, like sacrificing a pup to increase the chances of survival of the other offsprings) that guarantee their survival and the well-being of their youngsters. Females also tend to be more focused and patient, especially when it comes to tasks related to nurturing and caring for offspring. This is critical in a pack structure, where the survival of the young is paramount for the continuity and propagation of the species. In fact, females are responsible for teaching, protecting, and feeding their pups, roles that require a high level of concentration and dedication. They not only exhibit higher levels of emotional intelligence, which is key to forming strong bonds with their offspring and other pack members, but also demonstrate a high degree of adaptability and problem-solving skills. These traits are essential for managing the challenges of motherhood, such as finding food, protecting pups from predators, and navigating social dynamics within the pack. Their ability to adapt and solve problems ensures they can fulfil their roles effectively, even in changing or challenging environments. To all prospective male dog owners out there – if you are married with children you will know what I am talking about – mothers always seem to have the right solution to any problem.

When it comes to dog training activities, there are also some notable differences between genders. Male dogs can be highly trainable, but they might also be more prone to distraction, especially if they sense a female in heat nearby. They may require more consistent training to curb any tendencies towards dominance or territorial behaviour. Some sporting breeds are also very forgiving if we make mistakes during our training routines, whereas other working types of breeds are less lenient and find it hard to forget their handler's setbacks. By contrast, females are often more eager to please and can be easier to train, particularly in basic obedience.

Their maturity and focus can make them more reliable in training situations. I can cite the case of two golden retrievers, brother and sister Gus and Daisy, who have a completely different attitude towards gun-dog training, Daisy being extremely successful in performing a retrieve and Gus being more easily distracted and always ready to show other males who is boss.

Additionally, there are other aspects to bear in mind when choosing your future dog's gender, one of which relates to the reproductive system. Intact males can be more prone to roaming and aggression, especially if they sense a nearby female in season. Neutering can, of course, reduce these behaviours, but it is important to consider the long-term health implications of neutering. Un-spayed females will go into season, usually twice a year, during which time they may exhibit mood swings, attract male dogs, and require extra care to prevent unwanted pregnancies. Spaying a female dog eliminates these cycles, but comes with its own set of health considerations.

Finally, if we analyse the predisposition towards social interaction of male dogs in comparison to their female counterparts, I can confirm that both male and female dogs are able to excel in social interactions with people, but males might be more consistently outgoing and eager to engage, whilst females might be more selective, showing a deeper bond with their chosen humans. As for socialisation with other dogs, females might generally be easier to manage in social settings due to their typically lower dominance drive and more cooperative nature. However, well-socialised male dogs can also be excellent in group settings, especially if they have been trained and socialised from a young age.

I trust that my insights have helped to clarify the differences between male and female dogs, thus making the decision a bit easier. I have highlighted important aspects of each gender that can guide you in choosing the right companion for your needs and lifestyle, but ultimately, whether you choose a male or female dog, it is all about finding the right fit for your home and family circumstances and what you value most in a pet. Both genders have their unique strengths, and hopefully my explanation has shed light on those main distinctions.

So far I have examined some of the basic aspects to consider when choosing a new puppy like the gender, a suitable breed and breeder, and also the various stages in the developmental process of the canine species. However, a large number of potential or perhaps more inexperienced dog owners are concerned not only about the physical appearance or gender of their future canine companions but also their temperament as a fully grown adult dog. When asked about their ideal pet companion, most people emphasise the importance of a "good" tempered dog, often listing this among the top qualities they seek. But what do they mean by this? The idea of a "good" temperament is inherently subjective and varies depending on the owner's individual expectations and needs. What is considered a good tempered dog for a retired elderly couple living in a flat will differ from the interpretation of a military K-9 corps handler. Thus, when it comes to predicting a puppy's future temperament to meet one's expectations, there are several questions that come to mind, such as: What is considered a "good" temperament in a dog? How much of a puppy's temperament is hereditary? How much influence does the environment have on the puppy's temperament? How accurately can we predict the temperament of an adult dog? To help answer these kinds of questions, ethologists and canine specialists have come up with ways to predict, with surprising accuracy, what a puppy's temperament might be like as an adult.

Temperament Test For Puppies

Over the last few decades, this topic has been the pursuit of numerous experts in veterinary clinical ethology, like Wilsson and Sundgren, Diederich and Giffroy, Van Der Borg, Volhard, Dr. William Campbell, to name just a few. After numerous studies and extensive research, they have developed a series of complicated tests designed to predict not only the puppy's future temperament but also, and most importantly, their natural predisposition or propensity towards training. Indeed, the development of methods to assess a puppy's inherited attitude towards training and temperament has brought about a significant advancement in the selection process for service dogs. By identifying the most suitable candidates early on, ethologists and scientists have enabled organisations to optimise their training programmes, prioritising their training efforts and focusing financial resources on puppies that are considered more likely to succeed in service roles such as guide dogs, emotional support animals, and mobility assistance dogs. In some cases, where these assessments were introduced as pilot-trial, the success rates of dogs undertaking the test to be certified as service dogs rose from 9% to 90% – an astonishing accomplishment.

Of all the various tests available, the Volhard Puppy Aptitude Test (or PAT) and the Campbell Test have become essential tools within the canine community, especially among dog breeders and trainers. They are the most popular and commonly used methods of temperament testing because they are easy to administer, provide quick results in reaching a conclusive assessment, and enable breeders and trainers to place puppies in homes where their temperament and demeanour will be a good fit. This is a positive aspect because it serves to minimise the likelihood of mismatches that could lead to behavioural problems or even rehoming. Temperament tests, in essence, offer a valuable insight into the puppy's future potential and can certainly provide a good indication of the future temperament of a dog, with results that significantly influence how well they fit into your family and lifestyle over the long term. In my experience, however, these tests alone do not necessarily reflect exactly how a puppy will grow up and could be poor predictors of future behaviour because other factors like the environment, the puppy's life experiences, and the socialisation period into adulthood all have an enormous impact during the developmental period of the puppy.

There are certain temperament traits in dogs that are strongly influenced by genetics, particularly those that have been selectively bred into specific breeds to perform particular tasks. These inherited traits have been fine-tuned over multiple generations to ensure dogs excel in roles they were originally bred for, whether this is herding, hunting, guarding, or companionship. For instance, pointers are bred to freeze and point when they pick up the scent of birds, a behaviour that is hardwired into their genetic makeup. Sheepdogs are bred to have strong herding instincts, including the tendency to "eye" and circle livestock. Greyhounds have been bred for their sight-based hunting ability, leading to a natural propensity to chase moving objects. In addition to these breed traits, there are other basic traits found in every dog which are good indicators of how well the dog will adapt to living with humans. The famous dog behaviourist William E Campbell, in his book *Behavior Problems in Dogs* (1975), analysed the main aspects of genetically determined characteristics that were strongly influenced by the selective breeding process perpetuated by our ancestors. This was a deliberate process aimed at enhancing specific inherited traits that made certain breeds more efficient at performing particular tasks. For an in-depth understanding of these traits and how they could influence the choice of a puppy for those seeking a working dog, I have usefully summarised them in the following scheme:

1. Excitability vs. Inhibitability

Excitability:

Definition: An inherited trait where a dog is highly responsive to external stimuli.

Behaviour: Such dogs are often energetic, alert, and quick to react to their environment.

Example: Field trial retrievers are bred for excitability as they need to be attentive to the nuances of hunting, such as tracking the fall of a bird.

Extreme: At the extreme, an excitable dog can become wild and uncontrollable, reacting to everything in its environment without restraint.

Inhibitability:

Definition: The inherited trait of self-control, allowing a dog to react only to specific cues.

Behaviour: Dogs with strong inhibitability can be trained to perform tasks under controlled circumstances, remaining calm and focused until given a command.

Example: Schutzhund German shepherds exemplify this trait, as they need to control their responses until it is time to act, such as in protection or police work.

Extreme: An overly inhibited dog might become withdrawn, rigid, or lethargic, lacking the energy to engage with its surroundings.

Balanced Trait: A dog that balances excitability with inhibitability is poised and assured, reacting appropriately to stimuli without being overly excitable or too passive.

2. Active vs. Passive Defence Reflexes

Active Defence Reflexes:

Definition: An inherited tendency to react to stress or threats actively, often through aggression or assertiveness.

Behaviour: These dogs may bite or attack when they perceive a threat, making them suitable for protection work.

Example: Schutzhund shepherds, selected for their ability to defend and protect, are an example of dogs with active defence reflexes.

Training Consideration: These dogs are trained to react only under specific conditions, balancing their active defence reflex with inhibitability.

Passive Defence Reflexes:

Definition: An inherited tendency to avoid confrontation, displaying more subdued reactions to stress.

Behaviour: Dogs with passive defence reflexes may freeze or retreat when faced with a threat, and are less likely to bite.

Example: Field trial retrievers are bred for passive defence reflexes to ensure they do not harm the game they retrieve.

Training Consideration: These dogs may be easier to manage in non-threatening environments but might require encouragement to engage in certain tasks.

3. Dominant vs. Submissive

Dominant:

Definition: A dog that exhibits leadership tendencies and would naturally assume the role of a pack leader.

Behaviour: Dominance is expressed through behaviours like biting, growling, direct eye contact, and assertive body language (head and tail held high).

Example: Fox terriers, bred to drag foxes from their dens, display dominance and require firm, consistent leadership from their owners.

Challenge: Without proper leadership, dominant dogs can develop maladaptive behaviours such as overprotectiveness, disobedience, and social challenges.

Submissive:

Definition: A dog that readily accepts leadership and follows the lead of its owner or pack leader.

Behaviour: Submissiveness is shown through behaviours like tail wagging, crouching, rolling over, and avoiding direct eye contact.

Example: Spaniels, bred to be submissive hunters, respond well to commands and tend to follow their leader's direction without challenge.

Training Consideration: Submissive dogs generally require a gentler approach and can easily be influenced by a strong, confident owner.

4. Independence vs. Social Attraction

Independence:

Definition: A dog that is self-reliant and less interested in human interaction.

Behaviour: These dogs may prefer to work alone, show little interest in being petted, and are less likely to seek out human company.

Example: The basenji, historically a solitary hunter, exemplifies independence, often operating alone in the field.

Challenge: Independent dogs may require more effort to bond with their owners and might be less responsive to training that relies on social reinforcement.

Social Attraction:

Definition: A dog that is naturally drawn to people and enjoys human company.

Behaviour: Socially attracted dogs are affectionate, enjoy being petted, follow humans around, and are generally eager to be where the action is.

Example: Poodles, known for their strong social attraction, make excellent family pets due to their affectionate and people-oriented nature.

Benefit: These dogs are typically easier to train and bond with as they are motivated by human interaction and approval.

In addition, Elliot Humphrey and Lucien Warner, in their book *Working Dogs* (1934), suggested that two other important inherited characteristics, sound sensitivity and touch sensitivity, play a significant role in determining a dog's behaviour and trainability.

Sound Sensitivity

The sound sensitive dog shows excessive fear, crouching, urinating, or running away when confronted with a loud or sharp sound; they may also overreact to gunshots, shouted commands, and so on. Such negative responses can affect these dogs as they may struggle in environments with frequent loud noises, such as fireworks, hunting or police work, where they are required to remain calm under pressure. In quieter environments or roles where sound sensitivity can be managed, these dogs may thrive, as long as their fear responses are understood and accommodated.

Touch Sensitivity vs. Insensitivity

The touch sensitive dog will be difficult to train with the standard training collar because the correction snap sets off the dog's defensive reflexes (biting, freezing, running away). Conversely, the touch insensitive dog shows little or no response to physical stimuli. Even strong yanks on a training collar might not elicit a response. The touch insensitivity trait was selected for in pit-fighting dogs in order for them to continue fighting despite wounds and injuries. What is commonly called a tough or difficult dog is often a combination of being both dominant and touch insensitive. This dog shows a strong tendency to lead and will be difficult to train. When the owner attempts to assert themselves through a corrective snap on the training collar, the dog does not respond because it cannot feel the collar. To get results, the owner will have to resort to more forceful methods of correction, or use a different stimuli. In one of my case studies, a client with a Staffy Cross that was both dominant and touch insensitive did not respond to traditional correction methods like a training collar, as suggested by the previous dog trainer. The owner, frustrated, found that physical corrections were ineffective and even felt guilty for having to use harsh training methods. I recommended switching to food-based rewards (positive reinforcement) which proved successful. This exemplifies the importance of understanding the dog's inherited traits and adapting training techniques accordingly.

The Campbell Test for puppies alone, consists of a series of simple tests designed to evaluate a few key aspects of a puppy's temperament, such as social attraction, response to handling, willingness to cooperate with a human, and level of independence. It is usually conducted when the puppies are around 7 weeks old, which is considered an ideal age to assess their temperament without too much influence from their environment. Occasionally, I have used the Campbell Test in combination with other tests (PAT) to evaluate different parameters relating to the trainability of the dog. These include social attraction, following, restraint, social dominance, elevation dominance, retrieving, touch sensitivity, sound sensitivity, sight sensitivity, and stability. I find that a broader assessment provides a fuller picture of a puppy's temperament. Before commencing testing, there are some guidelines the handler should acknowledge and strictly adhere to. This is crucial in ensuring the temperament test for puppies is conducted in a controlled and unbiased environment, hence yielding accurate and reliable results. The following are the key aspects to consider:

1. Testing Location

New Location: Conducting the test in an unfamiliar environment guarantees the puppy's responses are genuine and not influenced by prior experiences or comfort with the location. This helps reveal the puppy's natural temperament rather than a response conditioned by familiarity.

Room Spaciousness: It is advisable to carry out the test in a room which is of sufficient size (5-7 square metres) for the puppy to move freely and for the tester to observe their behaviour without interference. It should be free of distractions and other stimuli that might affect the puppy's behaviour.

2. Testing Process

One Puppy at a Time: Testing each puppy individually prevents them from being influenced by the behaviour of their littermates. It allows for a clear and focused assessment of each puppy's individual responses.

No Other Dogs or People Present: The presence of other animals or people could distract the puppy or alter its natural behaviour. The test needs to be about the puppy's interaction with the environment and the handler only.

3. Handler and Scorer Roles

Unknown Handler: The handler in charge of performing the test should be someone the puppy does not know, thus ensuring its responses are not influenced by any previous interactions or familiarity. This helps assess how the puppy reacts to strangers and new situations.

Unbiased Scorer: The handler should be neutral, with no emotional investment in the results. This guarantees that the scoring is objective and free from bias. The scorer's position should allow for a clear view of the puppy's responses without being intrusive, ensuring the puppy is not influenced by their presence.

4. Timing and Condition of Puppies

Before Feeding: Puppies should be tested before they eat to avoid lethargy or distraction due to a full stomach. Hunger can also influence behaviour, but testing before feeding generally ensures the puppy is alert and active.

At Their Liveliest: Testing should be done when puppies are naturally energetic and playful, which is usually mid-morning or after a nap. This means that the puppy's responses are more likely to reflect their true temperament.

Avoid Testing Unwell Puppies: A puppy that is not feeling well might not respond accurately, skewing the test results. It is important to make sure that each puppy is in good health to obtain a fair assessment.

Avoid Testing After Vaccination: Vaccinations can affect a puppy's behaviour, making them more subdued or irritable. Waiting a day or two guarantees that the puppy's temperament is not temporarily altered by the vaccination.

5. Scoring and Observations

First Response Counts: The initial reaction of the puppy is the most genuine and should be the one that is scored. Subsequent reactions may be influenced by the puppy's adaptation to the situation, so the first response is the most telling with regard to their natural temperament.

By following these measures, the handler creates a consistent and unbiased environment that allows for a true assessment of each puppy's temperament. This careful preparation requires some level of knowledge and cooperation from the breeder. If you do not feel confident enough to do it yourself, do not hesitate to seek help from a professional dog trainer or dog behaviourist. The scoring sheet that any prospective dog parent can use to perform the Campbell Test can be found in Appendix B.

Let us now analyse in detail the various elements that make up the more complete version of the Temperament Test and how to interpret the possible outcomes;

1. Social Attraction: This test is used to evaluates the puppy's willingness to interact with people. The handler places the puppy in a room facing the wall and then walks a short distance away from the puppy. They then

kneel and clap their hands softly. This test measures how the puppy responds to a human presence and whether they seek attention or remain indifferent.

Scoring:

1. Comes readily, tail up, jumps, bites at hands.
2. Comes readily, tail up paws, licks at hands.
3. Comes readily, tail up.
4. Comes readily, tail down.
5. Comes hesitantly, tail down.
6. Does not come at all.

2. Following: This test checks the puppy's willingness to follow people and can indicate its predisposition for sociability. The handler places the puppy at the end of a room and then walks away from them, making sure to get the puppy's attention in order to see if they follow. They then assess how the puppy responds to a person moving away.

Scoring:

1. Follows readily, tail up, gets under foot, bites at feet.
2. Follows readily, tail up, gets under foot.
3. Follows readily, tail up.
4. Follows readily, tail down.
5. Follows hesitantly, tail down.
6. Does not follow at all.

3. Restraint: Measures the puppy's response to being held in a vulnerable position. The handler places the puppy on its back on the floor, holds it down with one hand on its chest and assesses how the puppy reacts to being controlled – whether they struggle, remain calm, or show signs of submission.

Scoring:

1. Struggles fiercely, flails, bites.
2. Struggles fiercely, flails.
3. Settles, struggles, settles with eye contact.

4. Slight struggle, then settles.
5. No struggle, tail tucked.
6. No struggle, strains to avoid eye contact.

4. **Social Dominance:** Evaluates how the puppy reacts to gentle pressure or petting. The handler holds the puppy gently around its neck with one hand while stroking backwards along its neck and back for about 30 seconds. The goal is to observe whether the puppy shows dominance by jumping up or whether it remains calm and willing to accept the contact.

   Scoring:
   1. Jumps, paws, bites, growls.
   2. Jumps, paws, licks.
   3. Cuddles up to tester, tries to lick face.
   4. Sits quietly, accepts petting, nudges/licks hands.
   5. Rolls over, no eye contact.
   6. Goes away and stays away.

5. **Elevation Dominance:** This test evaluates how the puppy reacts to being handled and restrained in an unfamiliar position. The handler clasps their hands under the puppy's chest and then lifts the puppy 20 or 30 centimetres off the ground for a period of about 30 seconds. This tests the puppy's reactions to being lifted off the ground.

   Scoring:
   1. Struggle fiercely, bites.
   2. Struggles.
   3. No struggle, relaxed, tail wags.
   4. No struggle, relaxed.
   5. No struggle.
   6. No struggle, frozen, tail/rear legs are tense.

6. **Retrieving:** This test assesses the puppy's willingness to retrieve an object. The handler crouches down beside the puppy and attracts its attention with a crumpled up piece of paper. When the puppy shows

some interest, the handler throws the paper no more than a metre in front of the puppy, encouraging them to retrieve the paper.

Scoring:

1. Chases object, picks it up, and runs away.
2. Chases object stands over it, does not return.
3. Chases object, picks it up, and returns it to the handler
4. Chases object, returns without object to the handler.
5. Starts to chase, loses interest.
6. Does not chase.

7. Touch Sensitivity: This test evaluates the puppy's reaction to slight discomfort or pressure. The handler needs to locate the webbing part of one of the puppy's front paws and press it lightly between their index finger and thumb. The handler then gradually increases pressure while simultaneously counting to ten, stopping immediately when the puppy pulls away or shows signs of discomfort.

Scoring:

1. 9-10 counts before response.
2. 7-8 counts before response.
3. 5-6 counts before response.
4. 3-4 counts before response.
5. 1-2 counts before response.
6. Does not follow at all.

8. Sound Sensitivity: This measures the puppy's response to a loud noise (e.g. clapping or dropping a metal object). The puppy is placed in the centre of the testing area and the handler then asks an assistant stationed at the perimeter to make a sharp noise, such as banging a metal spoon on the bottom of a metal pan or lid.

Scoring:

1. Locates the sound, walks towards it.
2. Locates sound, barks.
3. Locates sound, shows curiosity, walks towards it.

4. Locates the sound.
5. Cringes, backs off, hides.
6. Ignores sound, shows no curiosity.

9. Sight (Chasing) Sensitivity: Assesses the puppy's reaction to a moving object. The puppy is placed in the centre of the room. The handler ties a string around a cloth or a bath towel and jerks it across the floor, 2 feet away from the puppy.

Scoring:

1. Looks, attacks, bites.
2. Looks, barks, tail up.
3. Looks curiously, attempts to investigate.
4. Looks, does not go forward, tail down.
5. Runs away, hides.
6. Ignores, shows no curiosity.

10. Stability: Tests the puppy's reaction to an unusual or surprising object. The handler gently opens an umbrella a couple of metres away from the puppy and places it at the centre of the testing room.

Scoring:

1. Walks forward, tail up, bites.
2. Walks forward, tail up, mouths.
3. Walks forward, attempts to investigate.
4. Look curiously, stays put.
5. Goes away, tail down, hides.
6. Ignores, shows no curiosity.

Interpreting the Results

The puppy's responses to these tests can give you a good idea of their future temperament. After assigning scores (from 1 to 6 or A to F) for each of these tests and comparing them with the results outlined below, you can see how a more comprehensive understanding of the puppy's temperament emerges:

Mostly 1's:

This dog is extremely dominant and has aggressive tendencies. It is quick to bite and is generally considered not good with children or the elderly. When combined with a 1 or 2 in touch sensitivity, will be a difficult dog to train. Not a dog for the inexperienced handler; takes a competent trainer to establish leadership.

Mostly 2's:

This dog is dominant and can be provoked to bite. Responds well to firm, consistent, fair handling in an adult household, and is likely to be a loyal pet once it respects its human leader. Often has bouncy, outgoing temperament: may be too active for elderly people, and too dominant for small children.

Mostly 3's:

This dog accepts human leaders easily. Is the best prospect for the average owner as it adapts well to new situations and is generally good with children and the elderly, although it may be inclined to be active. Makes a good obedience prospect and usually has a common sense approach to life.

Mostly 4's:

This dog is submissive and will adapt to most households. May be slightly less outgoing and active than a dog scoring mostly 3's. Gets along well with children in general and trains well.

Mostly 5's:

This dog is extremely submissive and needs special handling to build confidence and bring it out of its shell. Does not adapt well to change and confusion and needs a highly stable environment. Usually safe around children and bites only when severely stressed. Not a good choice for a beginner as it frightens easily, and takes a long time to get used to new experiences.

Mostly 6's:

This dog is independent. It is not affectionate and may dislike petting and cuddling. It is difficult to establish a relationship with the dog for working or as a pet. Not recommended for children who may force attention on him or her. and is not a beginner's dog.

a) When combined with 1's (especially in restraint), the independent dog is likely to bite under stress.

b) When combined with 5's, the independent dog is likely to hide from people or freeze when approached by a stranger.

With the vast amount of tools and knowledge available today, there is really no excuse for not conducting a thorough research before making the significant decision of choosing a puppy. Given that a dog will be a lifelong companion, integrated into your family and daily life, it is crucial to make an informed choice. To summarise, the temperament tests for puppies are extremely useful tools, but other factors like the environment, socialisation, and training will also play significant roles in shaping their adult personality.

Although the test provides valuable insights, I believe it should be used in conjunction with other observations and considerations when choosing a puppy. If you have an active lifestyle and are looking for a dog that will be able to keep up with you, a more confident and energetic puppy might be a good fit. If your home is calm and you prefer a laid-back companion, a more submissive or less dominant puppy might be ideal. A puppy that is gentle and tolerant will generally integrate well with young children. A puppy with a more balanced, easy-going temperament is usually better for first-time owners, as they tend to be easier to train and manage.

Research on temperament tests has become so relevant nowadays that similar approaches are being applied to test our children. These tests help researchers and psychologists understand the balance between genetic predispositions and environmental influences on a child's behaviour, particularly in cases of behavioural issues connected to temperament. The ongoing Nature vs. Nurture debate is so pertinent to the education of children that it is hoped that by ascertaining the relative influence of genetics (nature) versus the environment (nurture) on human behaviour, some much needed assistance will be provided in creating more effective interventions and support systems for our troubled children.

The reason I put so much emphasis on the importance of performing the temperament test on our puppies is that despite the fact that they are not one hundred percent accurate in predicting an adult's future behaviour, the results of the studies conducted thus far have clearly demonstrated that there is a connection between the genetic heritage of a puppy and the repercussions for their behaviour brought about by the environment and the methods of training used during their upbringing. In this context, I must admit that I feel flattered when I receive compliments from dog owners after successfully addressing their dog's behavioural issues. It is evident that my ability to connect with and understand these dogs on a deeper level plays a significant role in my success. In addition, I think that my personal past experiences, especially those shaped by my own challenges, have given me a unique perspective that allows me to see beyond the surface of the behaviours of the dogs I am rehabilitating and directly to the core issues that drive them. Growing up in an orphanage in the south of Italy in the 1960s, I had a difficult upbringing and my personal experience has led me to reflect on the importance of understanding and addressing behavioural issues with empathy and knowledge, rather than resorting to adverse methods or punishment.

Bringing Your Puppy Home

Your journey towards bringing a new puppy into your life is well underway. If you have followed all the steps highlighted in previous chapters, that is, examined your circumstances before taking the final decision, chosen the right breed that fits your lifestyle, found a reputable breeder, researched temperament tests and are prepared to perform them on your puppy, then you are already halfway through the process. But there is still more to consider as you prepare to bring your new companion home. It is now time to focus on the final steps to ensure your puppy transitions smoothly into its new environment. Preparing both your home and yourself for this new addition is essential for helping your puppy adjust and thrive. This is where the partnership between you and the breeder becomes crucial, as you both play vital roles in making this transition as seamless as possible. Whether you are a first-time dog parent or an experienced one, for the partnership between you and the breeder to work effectively, establishing some key points is crucial. These elements will guarantee a smooth transition for your new puppy and provide peace of mind for both parties. I would list the key points as the following: Good Communication, Cooperation, Availability, Support, Post-Transfer Assistance, and possibly a Return Policy. I will now address each of these in turn.

Good Communication

I believe that establishing a clear and open line of communication with the breeder is crucial, as I see this as one of the major recurrent issues that often strain the relationship between a prospective dog owner and a breeder right from the start. A large number of breeders, due to past negative experiences, are understandably cautious when dealing with new enquiries – they are just being protective of their puppies and are rightly looking for the best homes for them. I think that their caution should be appreciated because, in my opinion, it is a sign of their commitment to the well-being of the dogs. After all, they do not know who is on the other end of the phone and may be hesitant to let one of their puppies go to someone they do not trust. They may have encountered situations where potential clients showed interest but then failed to follow up, or where there were hidden agendas that compromised the breeder's confidence. When making initial contact, be as transparent as possible about your intentions, lifestyle, and experience with dogs. This helps in building trust from the outset. By asking the right questions, showing the breeder you have already done some research and that you are serious about your decision and expectations, the breeder will feel more assured and available to engage in the conversation. It is essential to make sure that both you and the breeder have a mutual understanding of expectations, including providing regular updates, the timeline for picking up the puppy and any other specific care instructions, and questions about vaccinations, house training, feeding, socialisation, and so on. For example, contacting a breeder in advance and asking to have the right of first choice of a puppy puts you in an advantageous position when it comes to selecting the right puppy for you.

Cooperation

There are several measures the breeder could undertake before handing the puppy over for a stress-free and smooth transition to a new home. Working together and cooperating with the breeder to achieve common goals can really make a difference in ensuring the puppy's needs are met before and after the transition. This might include teaching the puppy their name, coordinating basic training practices so that the training can consistently continue in your home to avoid confusing the puppy, or establishing the puppy's dietary preferences early on so that it is not affected by digestive problems when it arrives at a new home.

Availability

Responsible breeders should not have any issue in making themselves available to show prospective clients their homes, the puppy's parents, and the paperwork concerning health screening tests for congenital diseases, showing the puppies when they are ready to be handled (obviously), or answering any questions or concerns you may have, both before and after the puppy comes home. Also, it is crucial to ensure that the breeder is reachable by phone, email, or text, especially in the early days after bringing the puppy home. This is essential for addressing any immediate issues that may arise.

Support

The breeder should provide guidance on everything from feeding schedules to training tips. They should also offer advice on how to handle common issues like separation anxiety or teething. A good breeder often provides written materials, such as a puppy care guide, to help you navigate the early stages of puppy ownership.

Post-Transfer Assistance

A responsible breeder will check in after the puppy has been transferred to your home to see how things are going. They may offer advice if any issues arise during the adjustment period. Some of your initial photos or updates on the puppy would be greatly appreciated by the breeder. Some breeders offer ongoing support throughout the dog's life, providing advice on health, behaviour, and training as your puppy grows.

Return Policy

Most reputable breeders I have dealt with will have a return policy in place in case something goes wrong and you are unable to keep the puppy. This safety net means that the puppy can be returned to a familiar environment rather than being surrendered to a shelter. The return policy should be offered without judgment, recognising that sometimes unforeseen circumstances can make it impossible to keep the puppy.

By focusing on these key points, you and the breeder can work together effectively to facilitate a smooth transition for your puppy. This partnership not only benefits the puppy but also helps create a positive and supportive relationship between you and the breeder, laying the foundation for a successful and fulfilling experience as a new dog owner. I cannot stress enough the important role a breeder plays in ensuring your puppy's transition to your home is as stress-free and as smooth as possible. Over the years I have witnessed a few cases where the relationship broke down dramatically with terrible consequences for all parties involved. After all, when you purchase a puppy from a breeder, you are both entering into a legally-binding contract that can be compared to buying goods, but it is more than a simple monetary transaction. There is, in fact, the implicit understanding that by paying a fee for the puppy, you are also supposed to receive a certain level of service and support and therefore ethical breeders should be invested in the health, happiness, and future of the puppy, and by extension, in the satisfaction of the buyer. There are several steps a reputable and professional breeder should take to prepare a puppy mentally and physically to cope with the drastic experience of transitioning and settling into a new home. I will now discuss these measures, which you can perhaps use as a reference when discussing your expectations with the breeder.

Early Socialisation

A good breeder will have started socialising the puppies at the earliest opportunity. This involves exposing them to various people, sounds, and environments so that they become well-adjusted and confident. Make sure the breeder has begun this process and ask about the specific socialisation techniques used, if any, so that you can consistently carry on the process once you have welcomed the puppy into your own home.

Consistent Routine

Like every dog, puppies also thrive on routine. You should ask the breeder to maintain a consistent feeding, play, and sleep schedule for the puppies.

Most breeders do, but it is better to be certain. This routine can then be continued in your home, providing a sense of stability for the puppy during the transition.

Introduction to Basic Training

As explained in the previous chapter dedicated to training, the first thing a puppy should learn is its name so that it can redirect its attention to you when called. Other basic commands like "Come" and "Sit" are extremely easy to teach as they tend to come naturally to any puppy. Most importantly, some breeders can help with basic crate training or housebreaking, depending on the techniques you intend to use. If the breeder has begun these processes, it will make it easier for you to continue them, easing the puppy's adjustment to your home.

Familiar Scents

Request a blanket or toy that has the scent of the puppy's mother or littermates. This familiar scent can comfort the puppy as they adjust to their new environment. Alternatively, provide the breeder with an item of clothing with your or your chosen family members' scent on it, especially if you have young children at home. It is equally important for the puppy to familiarise themselves beforehand with the scents of their new family.

Health Checks

Ensure the breeder provides a complete health record for the puppy, including vaccinations, deworming, and any other medical treatments. This will allow you to continue necessary care without any gaps. You should also ask the breeder for the results of any genetic tests pertinent to the breed, like eyes, hips, etc.

Gradual Separation

Ask the breeder to start introducing the puppy to short periods of separation from their littermates. This will inevitably happen at some point in its new life with its new family and can help the puppy adjust more easily to being alone in your home, reducing the level of anxiety and making crate training much smoother, especially overnight.

First Vaccinations

As the puppy's immune system is still developing, it is crucial to vaccinate them against the most common and potentially life-threatening diseases such as parvovirus, distemper, adenovirus (hepatitis), and parainfluenza. Later, at the age of 3 months, the rabies vaccine will also need to be administered. These vaccinations build the puppy's immunity and protect it from infections as it begins to explore the world. Typically, there is a two-week waiting period between the first and second vaccinations, during which the puppy should not go outside or interact with unfamiliar animals. To reduce this waiting period and allow your puppy to start socialising and adapting to housebreaking sooner, you can request that the breeder administer the first vaccination when the puppy is around 7 weeks old. This means that by the time the puppy arrives at your home, only one week remains until the second vaccine is due. This adjustment provides a significant advantage in terms of early socialisation, which is vital for a well-adjusted puppy as it can meet other dogs, people, and experience different environments a week sooner, which in turn will positively influence its temperament and development. Being able to go outside earlier will also help with potty training, as the puppy can start learning where to relieve itself in the proper outdoor setting. Finally, a shorter waiting period reduces the stress for both the puppy and the owner. As we all know, puppies are naturally curious, and keeping them indoors for extended periods can be extremely challenging and disruptive.

Dietary Requirements

The breeder can also assist you by switching the puppy's diet to meet your preferences prior to bringing it home. This is particularly important because a sudden change in diet can upset the puppy's digestive system, causing stress and discomfort. If you plan to follow a specific diet, such as the BARF or raw diet, it is crucial to provide the breeder with the food of your choice ahead of time. In this way, the puppy can be gradually weaned onto the raw diet under the breeder's supervision. If you prefer to feed your puppy a high-quality dry food diet, make sure the breeder has the brand you intend to use. This enables the puppy to adjust to the new food slowly, reducing the risk of digestive issues.

Let us now take a look at what steps you can take to ensure your home is ready to welcome your new companion and create a safe and welcoming environment.

Puppy-Proof Your Home

Remove any potential hazards such as electrical cords, small objects that could be swallowed, and toxic plants. Make sure your home is safe for a curious puppy who will be eager to explore and chew on anything it can manage to find around the house (remember that it is at the peak of the teething stage), especially wooden furniture, plastic objects, and items made of leather material.

Create a Comfortable Space

You also need to set up a designated area where the puppy can feel secure. This could be a crate, a playpen, or a cozy corner with a bed and toys. This space will serve as the puppy's safe haven, where it can escape from the attention of children, if any, while it adjusts to its new surroundings.

Create a Toilet Space

Creating a designated toilet space for your puppy is an essential part of successful housebreaking. This helps the puppy learn where it is acceptable to relieve itself, making the process smoother and more consistent for both you and the puppy. I will dedicate a whole chapter to the smoothest and quickest housetraining methods, so for now simply think about the most convenient, accessible, and suitable space in which to start the house-training process. I also recommend purchasing an enzyme-based cleaning spray as indoor accidents will inevitably happen.

Stock Up on Supplies

Make sure you have available all the necessary supplies beforehand, including the food of your choice, water and food bowls (consider buying an elevated set of bowls for a large breed puppy), soft toys, durable chewing toys (Kong rubber toys and deer antlers last forever), the cheapest, simplest, lightest puppy collar and leash, some grooming tools, an old style tick-tock clock (which helps simulate the mother and siblings' heartbeat during sleeping), a hot water bottle (which simulates the warmth of the mother and siblings' bodies), a soft blanket in which you can wrap up the hot water bottle, and finally some organic tasty training treats. Having everything ready will make your tasks easier and the transition for the puppy smoother.

Establish a Routine

Plan a consistent daily routine for feeding, playtime, resting times, and potty breaks. Puppies function like clockwork and thrive on routine, so establishing one early on will help them settle in more quickly, as they will expect to do the same things at the same time. I always recommend planning in advance so that you are able to allocate a period of at least three weeks where you and your family can give undivided attention to the new puppy. Note that this is a crucial period of imprinting, where bonds are strengthened and trusting relationships are forged.

Introduce Family Members Slowly

This is another event that is often overlooked by many new dog parents. If you live with other pets or young children, it is advisable to introduce them to the puppy gradually and in an orderly manner. Each family member should get to spend some time alone with the puppy and become familiar with their character and nature. This will avoid overwhelming the puppy and allow them to form positive associations with their new family members.

Vet Appointments

Although the breeder will have already taken care of the first vet visits for the puppies, it will be necessary to sign up with a veterinary practice of your choice and schedule a vet appointment soon after bringing the puppy home. This guarantees your puppy is healthy and up-to-date on vaccinations, and establishes a relationship with your vet for ongoing care.

Patience and Understanding

Remember that the transition to a new home can be extremely stressful for puppies. They have just been through one of the most traumatic experience in their lives, leaving their mothers and siblings, their familiar environment, and the only human carer they know, and are now being put through the process of environmental adaptation all over again. Be patient and understanding as they adjust, offering plenty of positive reinforcement and comfort.

Sisu

CHAPTER 10

THE JOURNEY BEGINS: BRINGING YOUR NEW DOG HOME

After years of experience through countless training sessions, I have noticed a surprising gap in clear, practical guidance when it comes to welcoming a new puppy into the home. Although social media and online platforms are bursting with advice, the sheer volume of conflicting opinions can often feel overwhelming, leaving new owners unsure where to begin. That is why I have dedicated this entire chapter to this very topic, my aim being to provide you with grounded, trustworthy information and thoughtful options that will allow you to navigate this exciting new chapter with confidence and clarity. Bringing home a new puppy is a completely different ballgame compared to adopting an adult dog, whether from a shelter, family, or friends. The dynamics are just not the same, and I wanted to make sure you receive a clear and simple breakdown of the process. To achieve this, I have split this into two separate sub-chapters, one for puppies and one for adult dogs, so that everything feels manageable and easy to understand. It is one of the services I offer my clients as part of the ongoing support during the puppy search and beyond. The main aim is to provide new dog owners with all the information necessary and the various steps needed to ensure their puppy gets the best possible start in life with their new family. It is all about setting up a strong foundation from the start.

    The first few days and weeks following the arrival of a new puppy at home are undoubtedly the most critical for both the puppy and its human companions. We ought to bear in mind that from the puppy's perspective, this period must feel like navigating uncharted waters. Suddenly, the familiar world that the puppy has known since birth, which included the presence of its mother, siblings, and the familiar environment in which it grew up, are replaced by a completely new habitat filled with unknown humans and brand new sights, smells, and routines. It is a time of significant adjustment for the puppy, who must learn again to trust and bond with its brand new family. From the humans' perspective, whilst it is easy to get swept up in the initial excitement of welcoming a new furry and cute family member, the transition can go in very different directions. Some seasoned dog owners, already in tune with their puppy's needs, navigate this period smoothly and confidently. For others, particularly those who are inexperienced or first-time dog owners, this period can quickly become overwhelming, so much so that on some occasions, I have even seen them doubt their decision to bring a puppy into their homes.

Puppies require constant attention and supervision, training, and most importantly patience as they adjust to their new homes. The initial joy can sometimes give way to stress, as new pet parents face challenges they may not have anticipated, such as house training, the obvious communication barrier, as well as managing the puppy's energy and dealing with the typical "mischievous antics". I hope that in this chapter even the most experienced dog owners might find some new tips or methods that were not part of their previous experience. After all, puppy care has evolved considerably over the past few years with research ongoing, and there may be strategies or insights that can improve even an already solid approach to raising a puppy. To all first-time dog owners, I believe this chapter will enable you acquire all the knowledge you will ever need, so that you do not feel overwhelmed or unprepared for the new arrival. Having a plan and knowing what to expect will help you and your puppy to build a positive relationship from day one. You might experience a few difficulties throughout the process, but the great news is that the physical and mental development of our beloved canine species is a much faster process than it is for their human counterparts. For example, whereas house training a puppy usually takes just a few weeks of consistent effort, potty training a human child can take up to three years. Puppies, due to their natural instincts and fast development, quickly learn to associate a specific area with toileting, especially when trained with a structured routine. By contrast, human children have a much longer and complex developmental process. They need to reach both physical and cognitive milestones, such as bladder control and the ability to communicate their needs, which can vary greatly from child to child. It is not uncommon for children to master potty training around 18 months to 3 years old, and even then, accidents and setbacks are part of the process.

What About Teething?

The puppy teething process typically lasts around 6 months, while in humans, teething extends over several years. Puppies begin teething at about 3 weeks of age when their baby (deciduous) teeth start to emerge. By the time they are around 6 to 8 weeks old, they will have a full set of baby teeth. Between 3 to 4 months, puppies start losing these baby teeth, and by 6 months, most will have their full set of adult teeth. Conversely, the human teething process is much longer and, I may add, much more expensive. Babies begin teething around 6 months old when their primary teeth start to emerge. The full set of baby teeth typically takes about 2 to 3 years to arrive.

Then, around age 6, children begin losing these teeth, and the process of gaining permanent adult teeth continues into their early teens, sometimes even into adulthood when wisdom teeth emerge. Moreover, teething can become an expensive process for children, especially when considering long-term dental care. In addition to regular paediatric dental visits, children may require additional treatments such as orthodontic care, dental hygiene products like toothbrushes, toothpaste, mouthwash, and other hygiene-related products, and dental emergencies like fillings, crowns, or extractions due to accidents or complications during teething. We have also seen that the difficult teenager's rebellious period in puppies will only last a few months, but I remember that my own rebellious period went on way past that. I am extremely optimistic that with the right mindset, preparation, and the practical advice offered in this chapter, whether you are an experienced or first-time dog parent, you can confidently navigate those crucial first few weeks, setting the stage for a lifetime of enjoyable companionship.

Your Puppy's First Journey

Bringing a puppy home for the first time can be a stressful experience for them, especially during the car or train ride. The closed space, car movement, and even the engine sound or the wind noise can trigger alarm bells for a puppy that is not used to travelling. To mitigate potential issues and make the journey as smooth and comfortable as possible, prepare the puppy beforehand and plan ahead by mapping out the route before the journey even begins. If you are planning to travel by car and wish to use a crate or you prefer travelling by train and wish to use a pet carrier, you do not want to wait until the day of your big trip to introduce your puppy to their travel containers. This is the moment when all the communication and preparation work carried out by the breeder will pay off. If the breeder has taken the time to introduce the puppy to travelling in a vehicle, the first car trip to their new home will be a far less stressful affair. The breeder's efforts to make the first car experiences positive and calm will desensitise the puppy to travelling, and the gradual exposure to short car rides will help puppies adjust to the motion of the car, reducing the likelihood of motion sickness. Gradual exposure to a vehicle involves creating positive, non-threatening experiences with the car. You can start by making the vehicle a welcoming and relaxing space. Place a comfortable bed or a blanket in the vehicle, ideally with the scent of the puppy's mother or siblings, put some relaxing classic music on, and have some of the puppy's favourite toys ready to help them feel safe. Stay in the stationary car with the puppy, allowing them to explore the interior at their own pace. It is important not to rush this phase, because it is pretty much about building familiarity without pressure.

With the car parked and the engine off, sit with the puppy inside the vehicle, offering treats and praise to reinforce the idea that the car is a pleasant place to be. Let the puppy jump in and out of the car if they feel more comfortable doing so. Once the puppy seems comfortable and relaxed inside the vehicle, turn the engine on, but keep the vehicle stationary. This introduces the sound and vibration of the car without actually moving. Note that dogs can hear a wider range of frequencies and therefore it is essential to remain very observant of the puppy's body language and behaviour, switching the engine off at the first sign of distress. If everything continues on a positive note, offer the puppy some treats and speak in a calm, soothing voice to associate the engine noise with a positive reinforcement. Once the puppy is accustomed to the sound and feel of the car, it is now time to move the car slightly, for example by rolling a few metres down the driveway. Keep these initial movements brief and gentle and continue to reward the puppy for calm behaviour with praise or treats. If everything goes according to plan, you can begin taking the puppy on short trips, such as driving around the block. Keep the duration of these brief and observe how the puppy reacts. If the puppy remains calm, gradually increase the duration of these trips over time. It is preferable to organise short but frequent driving sessions throughout the day, rather than taking the puppy all of a sudden on a long trip. As the puppy continues to adjust to being in the vehicle, you can extend the length of the car rides even further. Always make sure the puppy is secured in a crate for safety, and when they are fully grown up, you can use a doggy seat belt. To create even more positive experiences, try to associate car rides with fun destinations, like a short visit to the pet shop or to the park, vaccinations permitting, so that the puppy builds a positive association with travel. Hopefully, when the time comes for the puppy to travel with you, they may already be somewhat familiar with car rides, having experienced such trips, or even having been to the vet for their first checkups and vaccinations. If, during these first short trips, the breeder notices that the puppy is sensitive to motion sickness, consult a vet about the best course of action to take. This could include the prescription of calming-aid medications or sedatives to take before the car journey begins. Most puppies will grow out of motion sickness anyway, but it is always better to prevent them from feeling nauseous in the car as this can lead to a long-lasting negative association with car rides as they grow older. The first signs to watch for in puppies suffering from motion sickness include excessive lip licking, whining, drooling, yawning, vomiting, excessive panting, trembling/shaking, and, in extreme cases, peeing and defecating.

Therefore, for your puppy's first car journey, you will need to take with you some of the items you should have already acquired as part of your preparation process for welcoming home your new furry companion. The crate, to start with, should be collapsible for added practicality and large enough for the puppy to stand up and turn around in. It should have a liquid-proof tray at the bottom and be protected by a wee-wee pad in case of any accident. It is always advisable to check the current legislation in place in your country in regard to travelling with pets. In case of a road accident for example, rescuers should be able to access the vehicle without the risk of confronting an unpredictable and traumatised pet. The crate should also be adequately ventilated and equipped with a water container to allow the puppy to remain hydrated throughout the journey. It should also contain a cloth with the scent of the mother or siblings, a soft blanket, or a comfortable bed to allow the puppy to lay down and take a nap. The puppy will also benefit from the presence of some chewy or soft toys. Before the trip, it would be better not to feed the puppy a whole portion of food; instead, take some tasty treats to use as a reward for good behaviour during the journey. Stopping along the motorway or planning to make a quick walk in a park en route would be too risky and never a good idea as the puppy is not yet fully vaccinated, therefore it is advisable to provide some form of exercise before departure to allow the puppy to release their excess energy. Creating a calm and reassuring environment inside the cabin by keeping to a minimum the wind and vehicle engine noise, adopting a relaxed driving style, and perhaps playing some classical music are all factors contributing to a stress-free driving experience. If you travel by train, try to pick a departure time that is off-peak if possible, as the carriages are more likely to be less congested and noisy. For the most sensitive or smaller puppies, you could cover the pet carrier with a soft blanket in order to create a sense of safety and to muffle the often loud noise of the moving train.

Home Sweet Home

Once you have successfully completed the first car trip with your puppy, it is time to introduce them to their new home. This is a crucial step in helping the puppy to settle in and feel comfortable from day one in their new environment. Depending on the duration of the trip and regardless of whether you were able to stop for a wee-wee en route, the first thing to do upon your arrival at home is to take the puppy to the designated toilet space for their first bathroom break. The toilet area needs to be readily accessible and easy to clean, possibly away from the puppy's sleeping quarters. I explain in detail in the next section how to commence and implement the house training routine and the different options available to suit your personal circumstances. For now, let us focus on the key elements to consider to allow the puppy to make the transition into their new home as smooth as possible. Bringing a new puppy home for the very first time is an extremely exciting experience for the whole family, especially if you have children, but it would be advisable to ensure the house is as quiet and calm as possible when you first arrive with the puppy and limit the number of people or other pets around to avoid overwhelming them. This will give the puppy enough time to decompress from the car ride before introducing them to the household and the new environment. For the same reason, I recommend introducing the puppy to one room at a time only, beginning with the designated room where they will initially sleep, eat, play and spend most of their time. This room should already contain their bed, toys, and water bowl. Let the puppy explore the room at their own pace, sniffing and getting familiar with the space, perhaps comforting and encouraging them using a soft tone of voice. It is essential to create a safe space, a quiet area like a crate or a small pen, where the puppy can feel retreat undisturbed if needed. This space will help the puppy feel more grounded and provide them with a sense of comfort similar to their den, especially during the first few days. Once the puppy seems comfortable in this area, slowly introduce them to other parts of the house. Let them explore one room at a time, always keeping it relaxed and positive. If there are multiple family members or other pets, you can now start introducing them to the puppy one at a time, in a calm and gentle manner. Try to avoid overwhelming the puppy with too much attention all at once. Instead, let the puppy approach each person when they feel ready. Remember that this is a big adjustment for them. They may feel a little unsure or nervous during the first few days, so be patient and provide reassurance through gentle touch, calm voices, and positive reinforcement.

As stated previously, the puppy will feel more reassured if they can find continuity in the schedule for the provision of the same primordial necessities they had with their mothers and siblings – food, water, shelter, warmth, safety, playtime, socialisation, toilet routine, and sleep. I cannot emphasise enough the importance of having the main responsible person or the whole family present during the initial period when the puppy first arrives home. This time is crucial for building a strong bond with the puppy, establishing trust, and setting up the foundation for future training and behaviour. Ideally, the primary caretaker, or the entire family, should be fully available and focused on the puppy to enable a smooth transition. The best scenario, in my opinion, would be to take some time off work, plan for the puppy's arrival during a holiday season, or make use of school breaks so that everyone can give the puppy their undivided attention. This is particularly important during the puppy's imprinting period, a vital stage of development where the puppy is highly receptive to learning about their environment, people, and social structure. During this time, puppies form their initial attachments, and by being present, you ensure your puppy begins to recognise the family as their primary source of care, safety, and affection. Whether it is playing, feeding, or training, your presence and participation allow the puppy to learn what to expect from its new life. I appreciate that it is not always possible for everyone to take time off or coordinate perfectly around the arrival of a new puppy, but a holistic approach should encompass the notion of bringing a puppy into the home after thoughtful groundwork well in advance of the time.

In a natural setting, the puppy's mother is constantly present, offering safety, nourishment, and guidance without the need for external obligations like work, holidays, family commitments, and so on. This continuous presence helps the puppy feel secure and supported during its early stages of life. The mother not only feeds and nurtures the puppy but also plays a key role in teaching it important social skills and boundaries, fostering a sense of stability. In a domestic environment, it is almost impossible to replicate the mother's round-the-clock availability, but understanding this natural context helps us see the importance of being present and attentive during those first crucial weeks. The more we can mirror that sense of security and consistency, the better the puppy will adjust. The caregiver's role in this setting is to create a routine and an environment where the puppy feels safe, nurtured, and supported, much like the role of the mother in the wild. This reduces anxiety and builds the foundation for a trusting relationship with their new human family. Moreover, given the puppy's rapid development, especially in the first few months, a little focused effort during this critical period can go a long way toward setting a strong foundation for its future development. By dedicating time and attention to the puppy's initial adjustment, most potential behavioural issues can be prevented, saving owners from the stress that can arise from having an unruly or anxious dog later on. I think we can all agree that a well-planned and supportive environment right from the start can only lead to a more harmonious relationship, helping the puppy grow into a balanced, well-adjusted adult.

Food

At the age of 8 weeks, a puppy will need to eat four times a day in order to receive the right nutrients for their growth and their energy needs. This feeding schedule should be followed until the puppy reaches 16 weeks of age, after which it can be reduced to three meals per day until the age of 6 months. From then on, feeding can be adjusted to once or twice a day, depending on the puppy's size, breed, and dietary requirements. For smaller breeds, which develop more quickly, the transition to fewer meals may happen sooner. Larger or giant breeds, however, may need to stay on a four-meal-a-day schedule for a longer period as their development is slower and they require more nutrients during their growth phase. In general, a medium-sized puppy (Labrador, golden retriever, etc) should gain around 300 grams per week to start with. Keeping a growth chart can be extremely useful in tracking this progress and ensuring the puppy is gaining weight at a healthy rate. Regular monitoring helps you identify any potential health concerns at an early stage and allows you to adjust feeding portions as necessary. If you have any doubts about your puppy's weight or condition, do not hesitate to contact the breeder or do some online research. The general rule for assessing a dog's physical condition is very simple: if you can feel the ribs when gently passing your hand over the ribcage, your dog is most likely in good shape. If the ribs are difficult to feel or you cannot feel them at all, the dog is considered overweight. On the other hand, if the ribs are visible, the dog may be severely underweight, unless it is a breed like a greyhound or whippet, where a leaner frame is part of their natural build. For puppies, however, it is normal and healthy for them to appear a bit chunkier during the growth phase. Puppies need extra nutrients and fat reserves as they develop, so do not be alarmed if your puppy looks a bit chubby. As long as they are getting proper nutrition and exercise, they will naturally become leaner as they grow older. To recap, below is a summary of feeding recommendations:

- 8 weeks to 16 weeks: 4 meals per day.
- 16 weeks to 6 months: 3 meals per day.
- 6 months onwards: 1-2 meals per day (depending on size and breed).

Establishing a consistent feeding schedule is an essential part of a structured routine for a puppy, and plays a significant role in speeding up the housebreaking process. Although a dog's digestive system is similar across breeds, there can be slight individual variations. Thus, it is important to observe how long it takes for your specific puppy breed to relieve itself after eating. By noting this, you can predict more accurately when to take the puppy to the potty area after meals. Moreover, if your puppy is on the BARF diet, they may defecate at more consistent intervals. This is because a dog's stomach acts as a sort of reservoir for raw food – in fact, in an adult dog, the total gastrointestinal transit time is about one to two days on average – and digestion is proportionate to the amount of exercise. This makes potty times more predictable. By contrast, puppies on a kibble diet tend to have more unpredictable digestion and bowel movements. Kibble is partly digested by the time it reaches the stomach and the small intestine and cannot be stored there as efficiently as raw food, making it more difficult to predict exactly when the puppy will need to relieve himself.

To enhance the housebreaking process, you can simply adjust potty breaks based on these observations. Taking your puppy to the potty area consistently at the predicted time after meals will reinforce the housebreaking routine and greatly reduce the chance of accidents happening inside the house. When establishing a feeding routine for your puppy, it is vital to maintain consistency, as this helps puppies adjust quickly and reinforces positive behaviours. I always recommend feeding the first meal immediately after the puppy has relieved themselves. Typically, after waking up at around 7am, you should take your puppy outside for a morning potty routine. Once they have completed their business, serving breakfast becomes a positive reinforcement for both housebreaking and feeding habits. Below is a sample feeding schedule, based on an interval of about 4 to 5 hours between meals:

First meal: Around 7am, after the puppy has had the opportunity to go potty.

Second meal: Around 11am or 12pm, approximately 4-5 hours after the first meal.

Third meal: Around 3pm or 4pm.

Fourth meal: Around 7pm or 8pm.

Puppies thrive on routine, and they will soon anticipate their meals at the set times. When transitioning from 4 meals to 3, it is essential to do so gradually. You can arrange this by slowly bringing the second and third meals closer together, eventually combining them into one more substantial meal. At the same time, it is necessary to adjust portion sizes to ensure they are getting enough food. As for how much food to feed them, it is important to know that puppies require a daily amount of food that correspond to about 5% to 6% of their ideal body weight. For adult dogs, the daily intake is typically around 2% to 3% of their ideal body weight, but this can vary according to the breed, activity level, and type of diet.

Now that the feeding routine is in place, you can organise the puppy's daily activities according to the meal times in order to establish a consistent, well-structured routine that can be adjusted to your personal circumstances or those of your family if you have children. This routine helps the puppy adjust and thrive while blending smoothly into your family's schedule. On the following page you can find an example of a daily chart that the owner and I worked out together to reflect her personal circumstances, this includes the direct involvement of the children in the puppy's daily schedule during socialisation and training times.

Sample Daily Chart: Feeding & Potty Training Schedule

Time	Activity	Custom Tailoring
7:00 AM	Wake up & first outing to potty area	Works well for families with children and their school schedules.
7:15 AM	First meal (breakfast)	Feed after potty for positive reinforcement.
7:30 AM	Playtime/short walk and socialisation	Before work or school starts, families can interact with the puppy.
8:00 AM	Potty break (after playtime)	Quick and easy potty time after playtime.
9:00 AM	Nap time	Ideal time if you're heading out to work or school-run; gives the puppy some downtime.
11:00 AM	Potty break (after waking up)	Quick potty time immediately after waking up.
11:15 AM	Second meal (lunch)	Schedule fits well with lunch breaks for those working from home.
12:00 PM	Socialisation, light training, or mental stimulation	Small training sessions or puzzle toys to stimulate and mentally engage the puppy.
1:00 PM	Potty break (after physical activity)	Quick potty time immediately after training and physical activity.
1:15 PM	Nap time	Encourages resting during the afternoon.
3:00 AM	Potty break (after waking up)	Quick potty time immediately after waking up.
3:15 PM	Third meal (afternoon snack)	Schedule fits well with children returning from school.
3:30 PM	Playtime/socialisation	After-school fun for children or family members to bond with the puppy.
4:15 PM	Potty break (after playtime)	Ensures no accidents after play.
4:30 PM	Rest period/Nap time	Allows the puppy to rest while children do homework and the household winds down.
6:30 PM	Potty break	Prepare for the evening meal.
7:30 PM	Fourth meal (dinner)	Routine meal to prepare for bedtime wind-down.
7:45 PM	Potty break	Reinforces potty training before bedtime.
8:00 PM	Family bonding/quiet playtime	Relaxing time with family members or winding down for the evening.
9:30 PM	Potty break	Ensures the puppy is ready for bed.
10:00 PM	Bedtime	Establish a calm routine to help the puppy sleep through the night.

In this particular example, potty breaks were scheduled to follow the puppy's naps and playtime requirements, but you can add a further potty break outing immediately after the main meals, according to the type of diet chosen for your puppy. Note that puppies have smaller and weaker bladders at this age; they are simply unable to hold the pee for longer period of time and therefore need to relieve themselves more frequently. If we consider the above schedule as an example, as the puppy was growing, we gradually reduced the number of meals from 4 to 3 per day, then to 2, while adjusting portion sizes to reflect the growing rate of the puppy. If you would like to use the same timing schedule, feel free to adjust the chart to fit your puppy's specific needs and your schedule.

House Training

Now, let us explore the most effective methods for establishing a consistent and efficient housebreaking routine, ensuring the process is smooth and stress-free for both you and your puppy. First and foremost, it is important to understand that, in a natural setting, a puppy instinctively perceives as its den, the space immediately in the proximity of the area where he sleeps, eats, or interacts with his family. Everything beyond that space is considered the "outdoors". Similarly, when we bring a new puppy into our expansive homes, the puppy does not grasp the concept that areas like the living room or bedroom are still part of the house. As a result, it may feel free to relieve itself in those spaces without recognising them as part of its indoor environment.

Another key consideration to keep in mind is that both puppies and adult dogs instinctively prefer to relieve themselves away from their dens. This behaviour is deeply rooted in their evolutionary history. Leaving faeces and urine near their living area would not only be unsanitary, increasing the risk of spreading diseases such as heart-worms, parvovirus, leptospirosis, and intestinal parasites, but the scent could also attract predators with, as you can imagine, more serious consequences. Consequently, dogs instinctively tend to move away from their den to relieve themselves, while puppies start displaying the same behaviour as soon as they are able to crawl. When they reach sexual maturity, male dogs will then use urine and faeces as a way to mark their territory, further solidifying this instinctive behaviour. Similarly, before going through the housetraining process, puppies living in human households will adopt exactly this same behaviour, and with a bit of observation, you can learn to recognise the signs that indicate they need to go potty, making it possible to train them to relieve themselves in dedicated areas of the house.

The behavioural pattern associated with this activity follows the same ritual. You may observe the puppy moving away from their current play or resting area and start the circling motion while sniffing the ground; additionally, you may observe the area around the anus starting to dilate. These are all clear indicators that it is time to take them immediately outside or to their designated potty area. By paying close attention to these cues, you can establish a consistent routine that aligns with their natural instincts, making housebreaking a much smoother and stress-free experience. Accidents are inevitable, especially during the early days of housebreaking. The way we deal with these accidents, however, can have long lasting consequences for the puppy's future behaviour. Dogs live entirely in the present moment, so if you catch your puppy relieving itself on your brand new carpet, even a few seconds after the act, it is already too late for a correction to be effective. Scolding the puppy in an untimely manner or, even worse, rubbing their nose in it (in this case they might even think you want them to eat their own faeces), will likely confuse them further; in their mind they are not doing anything wrong except answering the call of nature. Instead of associating your reprimand with the act of relieving itself indoors, the puppy may think that what upset you was the sight of the urine or faeces. As a result, they might adopt different strategies to avoid getting into trouble next time it happens, such as relieving themselves in hidden areas or even eating the faeces to eliminate the evidence (a behavioural issue known as coprophagy). Moreover, there is no point in trying to engage in complicated dissertations to explain to the puppy that what they did was unacceptable, they simply don't speak your language and more likely do not understand a word you are saying. This is why it is crucial to either catch them in the act and correct the behaviour with the use of the negative marker (the lower growling warning sound), or just let it go and resign yourself to cleaning it up.

If you happen to catch your puppy in the middle of relieving themselves, it is important to remain calm and maintain a neutral demeanour. Avoid scolding or reacting negatively, as this will only confuse them. Instead, gently pick them up and take them outside or to their designated toileting spot, allowing them to finish their business in the appropriate place. This reinforces the idea of where they should be going without creating fear or anxiety around the process. Because the smell of urine or faeces can attract the puppy back to the same spot, you will need to clean up the soiled area by using enzymatic cleaners to eliminate any scent left over at the crime scene. The enzymatic cleanser needs time to work effectively, breaking down the odour-causing molecules. To use it properly, spray the solution over the soiled area and allow it to sit for at least 15 minutes. This gives the enzymes enough time to "eat away" at the molecules responsible for the smell. Afterwards, you can proceed to clean and rinse the area with your regular cleaning products, ensuring the spot is fully sanitised and odour-free.

Based on this premise, we can now delve into the three fundamental methods you can choose for housebreaking your puppy: crate training, paper or wee-wee pad training, and the outdoor-only method. Each of these approaches comes with its own advantages and challenges, and the best choice will depend on your personal circumstances, lifestyle, availability in terms of time, and the ability to maintain consistency throughout the process. I will now explore each method in detail.

Crate Training Method

Crate training is perhaps the most commonly used method for housebreaking puppies, particularly for people living in cities without easy access to outdoor spaces. It is based on the principle that dogs instinctively avoid soiling their sleeping area, and therefore it encourages the puppy to hold its bladder until it is taken outside. The crate should be large enough for the puppy to stand up, turn around, and lie down comfortably, but not so big that they feel they can soil one side and still rest comfortably on the other. Puppies have a natural inclination not to eliminate where they rest, so keeping the space just right helps reinforce this behaviour. Most crates on the market nowadays are collapsible, making them highly practical for both housetraining and for transporting the puppy safely and securely on car journeys. They are also provided with a washable plastic or metal tray at the bottom for easy cleaning in case of accidents. This makes it easier to maintain hygiene while ensuring the puppy remains comfortable.

I recommend using a VetBed or similar bedding material in the crate. The VetBed is machine washable and is designed to retain warmth while allowing any urine to filter through, keeping the surface dry and comfortable for the puppy. Some crates also come with a practical cover that can create a cozy and enclosed environment, mimicking the natural dens that dogs seek for shelter and security in the wild. This added cover provides a sense of privacy and safety, making the puppy feel more comfortable and at ease, especially during rest periods or moments of overstimulation. It can also calm the puppy during stressful situations by blocking out excess light or distractions, encouraging them to relax and settle down. Finally, if you are planning to fly long distances with your dog, it may be wiser to invest in an airline-approved container rather than a standard crate. These containers are specifically designed to meet airline regulations, ensuring the safety and comfort of your pet during travel. They are built to be extremely sturdy, durable enough to last a lifetime, and can even be forklifted if needed, making them a more practical long-term solution for frequent travellers.

The first step in the crate training method is to allow the puppy to familiarise itself with the crate. It should be perceived as a resting spot, a safe haven where they can sleep, relax, or retreat when they need time alone from the children for example. I advise placing the crate in a calm area of your home, where the puppy can see and hear the family but will not feel overwhelmed by their activities. You can feed the puppy inside the crate, place some of their favourite toys there, and even have playtime around and inside the crate. This creates positive associations with the crate and encourages the puppy to use it voluntarily, as though it is their own personal retreat rather than a place of isolation or confinement from the family.

As a general rule, puppies need to urinate immediately after waking up and after drinking, eating, playing, and after a training session. The method is simple, keep the puppy inside the crate during nap times or when they need to be left unsupervised and take them out regularly following the daily routine set out at the beginning. To help your puppy maintain a consistent potty routine, begin by taking them to their designated potty area, whether indoors or outdoors, every hour. After three days, increase the interval between potty breaks by 15 minutes, meaning you would take the puppy out every hour and 15 minutes. After another three days, extend it to 1.5 hours, and continue adjusting gradually. It is essential to monitor your puppy's progress and, if you notice any setbacks, return to the previous interval to avoid accidents. The goal is to help the puppy effectively develop bladder control over time, but it is crucial to never exceed a three-hour gap between potty breaks, especially for young puppies.

Additionally, when taking the puppy out to relieve themselves, I use a cue word like "wee-wee" while they are urinating. Repeating this consistently helps the puppy associate the word with the action, allowing them to eventually pee on command. This technique makes housebreaking more efficient and structured; however, puppies, especially those on a kibble diet, need to relieve themselves more frequently. Before we proceed, I would like to briefly highlight the key difference between the BARF diet and conventional dry-food (kibble) diet when it comes to housebreaking. Because kibble is a dry food, puppies on this diet require significantly more water intake throughout the day. As water should always be readily available, this results in more frequent and sometimes unpredictable urination, which can make housebreaking a bit more challenging. On the other hand, puppies on a BARF (raw) diet consume food that contains a substantial amount of moisture. This reduces their need to drink additional water, meaning they will urinate less frequently. Consequently, housebreaking can be a bit easier as the puppy's hydration is naturally regulated by their food intake.

When it comes to defecating, it is essential to observe and calculate how long it takes for your puppy to digest their meals so you can schedule potty breaks accordingly. Puppies generally have fairly predictable digestive systems, but this timing can vary depending on the type of diet, the breed, and individual differences. For puppies on a kibble diet, digestion may be faster, meaning they may need to relieve themselves soon after meals, typically within 30 minutes to an hour. By contrast, puppies on a BARF diet may take longer to process their food as raw diets are more nutrient-dense and less processed. Monitoring their routine for a few days will give you a good sense of when your puppy is likely to need to go, enabling you to pre-empt accidents and reinforce their housebreaking progress. Scheduling outings right after meals is one of the best ways to maintain consistency and reduce the likelihood of accidents indoors.

One final consideration for the overnight schedule is that whilst some puppies often adapt rapidly to holding their bladder through the night, other younger puppies may still need a midnight potty break – they are all different individuals with different needs. To accommodate this, I recommend initially adjusting the daily schedule to include a late-night outing at around midnight and then a first morning potty break at 5 a.m. Gradually extend the interval between these breaks by increasing the morning time by 15 minutes every three days. For example, shift the morning break to 5:15 a.m. after three days, then to 5:30 a.m., and so on until you reach a wake-up time of around 7:30 a.m., depending on your personal schedule.

On a lighter note, I once had a funny experience with a young female Labrador puppy. The owner was thrilled to report that the puppy was housetrained overnight in just a few days, an impressive feat I thought! However, her excitement turned to surprise when she later discovered, through a baby monitor, that the puppy had been eating her own faeces, a condition known as coprophagy. It turns out the puppy was cleaning up after herself in a rather unexpected way! I will address and provide valuable insights on coprophagy and other behavioural issues in a dedicated chapter as it is indeed one of those common themes among clients seeking professional consultation. I hope that by shedding light on the causes, potential solutions, and preventive measures for behaviours like coprophagy I will be able to offer help and support to pet owners affected by this rather fastidious issue.

Paper or Wee-Wee Pad Training

When using this method, the puppy is trained to relieve itself on a designated spot inside the house, usually using old newspapers or the wee-wee pads. The latter have the advantage of benefitting from a waterproof layer underneath the absorbent one, which is more hygienic overall. It is a practical solution for people with limited access to outdoor spaces, those who live in high-rise buildings, or those who cannot take the puppy outside frequently. It is a method based on the concept that once the puppy consistently uses the pads, we can gradually move them towards the door to eventually transition to outdoor potty areas. Like every other method, there are pros and cons to consider before deciding on paper or wee-wee pad training. In favour of this method, I would highlight the convenience, especially for those living in apartments or areas where outdoor access is limited or during bad weather, the safety, as it allows young or unvaccinated puppies to relieve themselves in a clean, safe environment indoors before they are fully ready to go outside, and the flexibility for those who are not always available to take the puppy outside regularly. Against this method I would like to emphasise the fact that some puppies may become overly reliant on indoor pads and struggle to adjust to outdoor bathroom routines later on, sometimes for the rest of their lives. I have seen this happening countless times, especially in smaller pets or toy breeds who are so used to doing their business indoors they become unable to relieve themselves outdoors, even in the park. In these situations I often rely on the crate method, based on the principle that dogs do not like to do their business in the area where they sleep.

I recall a particularly memorable case involving a beautiful black and tan dachshund who, at 2 years old, was still toileting indoors, much to the owner's frustration. For three consecutive days, I took him along with me and my team everywhere, even on our three daily scheduled walks with our other regular group of dogs, trying to let him spend as much time as possible outside, yet he stubbornly refused to produce a single drop of pee. At home, to maintain consistency and has a last resort, I fed him and kept him in the crate whenever he was not being supervised, but still no success. Then, on the third day, during a walk in Kensington Gardens, he finally relieved himself, and from that moment on, the issue was finally resolved.

In yet another instance, for those who remember my appearance on the BBC's Celebrity Dog School in support of the charity Children in Need, they might recall a similar situation with the celebrity client I was paired with, the late Miss Dora Bryan. Her dog George, a Tibetan terrier, had developed the unsavoury habit of peeing both outdoors and indoors. In fact, Dora had even placed a real tree log on top of some old newspaper in the kitchen so George could relieve himself as if he was in the park! These cases highlight how entrenched indoor toileting habits can become in some dogs and the amount of patience and consistent training that is required to resolve such behaviours – sometimes people just don't have the mental strength to be consistent and simply give up. Other cons associated with this method, besides the potential delayed transition to the outdoor areas, are the lack of a dedicated indoor area for the puppy to relieve themselves, and the mess created by the faeces and urine if not cleared up in a timely manner. For this method to be highly effective, I usually recommend covering a larger than necessary area with several wee-wee pads and gradually reducing the size of the area as the puppy becomes more reliable. In addition, always associate a cue word with the action of peeing and profusely reward the puppy for using the correct area. Because dogs have a strong instinct to return to the same spot to relieve themselves, I recommend wetting the new wee-wee pad with a small amount of urine from the old pad. This familiar scent will help guide the puppy to view the new pad as the designated potty area. Encourage the puppy to sniff the pad, reinforcing the connection between the scent and the appropriate place to relieve themselves by using the cue words of your choice, like "Go Potty" or "Wee Wee". After a few days of gradually reducing the number of wee-wee pads, the puppy should begin to reliably relieve themselves on a single pad. Once this habit is established, you can start moving the pad closer to the door, reinforcing the connection between going to the potty and the outdoor area. Thereafter, place a pad scented with the puppy's urine just outside the door to start with and progressively further away from the door and to the street. This process enables the puppy to associate outdoor potty areas with their familiar scent. With consistent cues and positive reinforcement, the puppy will ideally begin to relieve themselves outdoors reliably, and even on command, within the timeframe of a week or so.

The Outdoor-Only Method

The Outdoor-Only Method is my favourite because it is both efficient and straightforward for the puppy to learn. This approach not only speeds up the housebreaking process but also strengthens the bond between the puppy and the owners as it requires frequent and direct interaction. The methodology for this type of training holistically taps into the dog's natural instinct to relieve themselves away from their den, a behaviour inherited from their evolutionary past. It is also environmentally friendly as fewer wee-wee pads and newspapers are wasted. The Outdoor-Only Method simply consists of taking the puppy outside following a structured daily schedule based on feeding times and specific key moments in the puppy's daily routine. These moments include immediately after waking up from a night's sleep or a nap, after drinking water, after the main meals, following playtime, and during or right after training sessions, during which the puppy might have drunk some water after receiving reward treats. By consistently taking the puppy outdoor during these crucial moments, but most importantly "at the right time", you are reinforcing the habit of going potty outside and making it easier for the puppy to associate the outdoors with their toilet needs. In addition, by taking the puppy out regularly, you create opportunities for positive reinforcement and giving your puppies what they crave most, undivided attention, making the method highly effective and rewarding for both you and the puppy. Another advantage of focusing solely on outdoor potty training is that there is much less chance of accidents inside the house.

Regardless of the method used, my advice is to always establish a clear association between the act of relieving themselves and a specific cue word. This training can prove invaluable in various situations, such as when you are in a hurry, dealing with bad weather, or preparing for a long journey on public transport or a car trip. By using the cue word consistently, you can prompt your puppy to relieve themselves on command, making daily routines and travel far more convenient.

On the negative side, there are other issues to consider when using this method, like the time commitment required. In fact, owners need to be available to take the puppy out frequently, which can be challenging for those with busy schedules. This is why I recommend taking some time off work or postponing other commitments and allocating at least two weeks of your time to share this crucial period of development and imprinting with your puppy. Bad weather, such as rain or cold, could also make this method less appealing for both the puppy and the owner, who might dislike the idea of having to go outside regularly. This method can be also impractical for those living in apartments, high rise buildings, or places without easy access to outdoor areas. There could be also be potential delays in learning if the method is not adhered to consistently, as the puppy may take longer to learn or have accidents indoors.

As you can see, each method has its pros and cons, and choosing the right one depends exclusively on your lifestyle, your living arrangement, and most importantly your ability to maintain a consistent training schedule. It is essential in my opinion to select a method that realistically aligns with your personal circumstances and environment, ensuring both you and your puppy can follow through successfully. As always with dogs, consistency is key to establishing good habits and a stress-free housebreaking process, but other elements are equally important.

Sleeping Arrangements

In the preceding sections I talked about how to manage and deal with the initial steps such as the first journey home, house training, daily routines, and feeding schedules. I now come to another extremely important topic that frequently arises during preparations for welcoming a new puppy: how to prepare for and manage the puppy's first night at home. The first night a puppy arrives at their new home is undoubtedly a pivotal and emotionally charged time, both for the puppy and the new owners. As with any young creature experiencing a major life change, the adjustment can be overwhelming. My personal experiences growing up in a children's home first and later moving in with my adopted family allow me to sympathise deeply with the feelings of sudden separation and change that any living being must go through, especially at such a young age. If, for the puppy, it marks the first time away from its mother, siblings, and the familiar surroundings with which they had just begun to bond, then for the new owners, the first night is a chance to set the tone for the puppy's adjustment and help them feel safe and comfortable in their new environment. While it is true that some may assume that a puppy will "just adapt" naturally, it is important to acknowledge that this transition can be both stressful and confusing for the puppy. I have witnessed firsthand how this abrupt change has negatively impacted a puppy's development, causing anxiety, fear and behavioural issues because it was not handled properly.

There are some precautionary steps we can take to make the transition easier for the puppy and these involve recreating the environment the puppy was accustomed to. The first thing we need to do is to create a safe, cozy space, a den-like environment where the puppy feels comfortable and reassured. This could be a crate or a comfortable dog bed placed in a playpen. When they sleep, puppies are used to the warmth of their siblings and mother's bodies; therefore, to mimic the warmth and comfort of their previous environment, we can wrap up the warm water bottle I recommended you purchase in a soft blanket and also place some soft toys inside the crate. To further simulate the comforting presence of the mother and siblings, I suggest placing an old-fashioned tick-tock clock or a metronome near or on top of the crate as this mimics the rhythmic heartbeat the puppy is used to feeling while it is sleeping. I find that this soothing sound helps calm the puppy down, reducing anxiety during those first few nights in the new home. If possible, bring home a blanket or toy covered with the scent of the puppy's mother or siblings, as familiar scents can also provide comfort and reduce the sense of isolation.

Before placing the puppy in the crate at bedtime, ensure the puppy has expended excess energy, has had a chance to relieve themselves, and that the house is quiet. Any ongoing activity in the home can stimulate the puppy's curiosity and desire to be involved, making it harder for them to settle down and rest. A calm, quiet environment will signal to the puppy that it is time to sleep. Before I forget, during the first few days of acclimatisation, it is also vital to avoid overwhelming the puppy with too much stimulation throughout the day. Introducing them to too many new people at once, or allowing them to explore multiple rooms in the house too soon, can overload their senses and keep them in an alert state. This heightened excitement can make it harder for them to settle down and rest when it is time for sleep. By gradually introducing new experiences in a controlled manner and giving them time to process their new surroundings at their own pace, the puppy will feel reassured and it will put them in a more relaxed state of mind.

I cannot emphasise enough the need to stick consistently to the planned daily routine as any variation can keep them in an alert state. Puppies thrive on routines, as it helps them feel safe, grounded and provides structure and stability. It also contributes to discharging the exuberant amount of energy typical of this period in their development. When deciding where to place the crate, you have a few options. One approach is to put the crate in the room where you spend most of your time, like the kitchen or the living room, so that the puppy feels it is an active member of your "pack" and settles more easily. Hopefully, if the puppy becomes accustomed to sleeping and being alone for a few hours during the day, it will more readily accept being alone at night. The other option is to have an additional crate in your bedroom to provide the puppy with your comforting presence during those first crucial nights. You can then gradually move the bedroom crate closer to the door, and after a few nights, transition the puppy to the main crate located in the daytime room. This gentle progression helps the puppy adapt to sleeping independently while still feeling secure.

It is common for puppies to cry during the night, especially when they are first separated from their family. Puppies are social creatures and are not used to being alone. Whilst it can be tempting to rush in and comfort them every time they vocalise their discontent, it is essential to strike a balance. You do not want to reinforce whining, but you also don't want to leave the puppy feeling completely abandoned. A gentle whisper or talking in a soft tone of voice can offer reassurance that they are not alone in this new, strange environment without creating dependency. Over-dependency on human pack members is a recurring issue that frequently arises during my consultations, even more so in the last few years in the aftermath of the COVID-19 pandemic. In normal circumstances, it is expected that a puppy or a dog will experience a mild level of stress when separated from the owners and this should not be considered a matter of concern; however, in some cases the stress reaction is so intense that it can be diagnosed as a behaviour problem. The behavioural diagnosis that emerges is known as "Separation Anxiety" – a condition in which a puppy or dog finds the isolation from the rest of the group extremely stressful and discomforting, typically manifesting through behaviours such as excessive whining, barking, howling, or destructive actions like chewing furniture or personal items. I imagine that separation anxiety has always been an issue for some dogs; it most likely occurred during the transition from working dogs to companion pets and was probably inadvertently created by well-meaning owners who allowed their pets to become overly dependent on them. There is also evidence that some dogs may be predisposed to this condition due to inherited traits from their parents.

The advent of the COVID-19 pandemic, however, with its lockdowns that forced people to spent more time at home, has exacerbated the problem even further. During this period, dogs who were living a perfectly balanced life became used to the constant companionship of their human parents, making it harder for them to adjust when their owners returned to work or resumed their normal routines. Ultimately, whether the condition arises as a consequence of owners inadvertently fostering over-dependence or is magnified by unique circumstances like the pandemic, the root cause typically lies in an imbalance in how the dog is trained to handle time alone. My advice in this regard is to strike a balance between the time the dog is allowed to spend with their human pack and the time spent alone in isolation. By consistently practising this, we can help our puppies to develop the resilience needed to handle separation without becoming overly anxious.

To convey in a clear and effective way how the issue can develop, I often describe the concept of separation anxiety as the amount of time a dog can handle being away from the pack being inversely proportional to the time spent constantly around humans. In other words, the more time dogs are allowed around humans, the less time they will be able to cope when being alone. For dog owners currently facing the challenges of separation anxiety in its full intensity, I highly recommend reading the dedicated chapter on behavioural issues, their causes, and their solutions. For the moment, I will focus on the essential steps you need to take to help puppies to build confidence and learn how to be more relaxed when left alone. The sense of independence and self-reliance can and must be built gradually by leaving the puppies on their own for an increasing period of time during the day, though never for intervals longer than three or four hours. When speaking with some first time pet owners, I have noticed that people often find it flattering when their dog follows them everywhere in the house, but this can lead to an unhealthy attachment if not managed properly. To recap, below are some of the key strategies you can employ to manage the puppy's first few nights and help establish a peaceful sleeping routine.

- Create a Comfortable Sleeping Space

Make sure your puppy's crate or designated sleeping area is warm, cozy, and feels safe. You can use soft bedding, such as a VetBed, and perhaps consider covering the crate with a blanket to mimic a den-like environment. For puppies missing the presence of their mother and littermates during the night, placing a ticking clock or a metronome nearby can simulate the comforting sound of the heartbeat of the family pack.

- Tire Them Out Before Bed

Make sure the puppy has had sufficient physical and mental stimulation before bedtime. Engage in a play session, a short walk, or some light training to burn off excess energy. Also ensure the puppy has relieved themselves before being put to bed to avoid them waking up due to discomfort.

- Gradually Introduce Crate Training at Night

For puppies struggling to be alone, initially placing the crate in your bedroom can help. You can gradually move it farther away as the puppy gets more comfortable with the idea of sleeping separately. This phased approach can reduce the anxiety associated with separation at night.

- Minimise Stimulation at Bedtime

Before bed, dim the lights and lower any noise in the house. Puppies can be easily stimulated by activity, and a quiet, calm environment helps them transition to sleep mode. Avoid giving them excessive attention immediately before bed, as this could make them more anxious when it is time to settle down.

- Respond to Nighttime Whining Wisely

When puppies whine or cry during the night, it is crucial to assess whether they need a bathroom break or are simply seeking attention. If you suspect they need to go outside, take them out quietly and calmly, avoiding any interaction that might signal playtime. Over time, this should decrease as they learn to settle down on their own.

- Stick to a Consistent Night Routine

Consistency is crucial. Keep a regular bedtime, and follow the same process each night so that the puppy becomes familiar with the routine. Gradually, the puppy will learn that night is for sleeping and not for playtime or attention-seeking behaviour.

- Prepare for Night-time Breaks

Young puppies may not yet have full bladder control and may need to go outside once or twice during the night. Plan for a final bathroom break before bed and a consistent early-morning potty routine to help establish bladder control. I suggest implementing this process by following a specific routine which consists of taking the puppy out to relieve themselves as late as possible before bedtime, say at midnight, and set up the alarm clock as early as possible in the morning, let's assume at 5am. Once the puppy has relieved itself, you can go back to sleep and resume the usual daily routine at 7am. You will need to maintain this schedule for a couple of days or so and then gradually start increasing the sleeping time by moving the bedtime schedule forward to 11:45pm and setting the alarm clock later at 5:15am. Follow the schedule for another two or three days and then move the bedtime forward by another 15 minutes to 11:30pm and wake up the puppy at 5:30am, and so on. Continue this gradual adjustment, shifting the times by 15-minute intervals every few days, while always observing the puppy's behaviour and bladder control until you reach your preferred bedtime schedule, which could be bedtime at 10:30pm and wake-up call at 7am. Over the years I have successfully followed this routine while training several puppies on behalf of some of our clients and find it an excellent tool for helping them not only to develop bladder control but also for easing them into a consistent and uninterrupted sleeping schedule. Over the span of a couple of weeks, the puppy should be able to hold their bladder for longer stretches, allowing you to sleep through the night. If setbacks happen, as they often do with young puppies, calmly returning to the previous step in the process can help them regain confidence and avoid frustration for both you and your puppy.

Basic Training Routines

During the first few days after your puppy's arrival, give them time to get used to their new environment by following the key steps outlined in previous chapters. This initial period allows your puppy to adjust to their surroundings, routines, and the new family dynamic. Once you observe that the puppy has settled in and that they have adapted to their new environment, such as eating, sleeping, and relieving themselves according to a schedule, then you know that the daily routine is comfortably established and that it is time to start an early training programme. This step is extremely important because it prepares your puppy for future outdoor experiences after they have completed their vaccinations. In the past, it was customary to keep puppies indoors until they had received the full course of vaccinations, which usually took around two weeks. Whilst this approach protected them from potential diseases, it had significant drawbacks. Young puppies, who are full of energy and curiosity, were kept inside during a critical period of their development. This often led to frustration for both the puppy and the owners. Additionally, delaying outdoor exposure also slowed the socialisation process, as puppies missed out on early interactions with other dogs and new environments. In some cases, it even complicated the housetraining process. Fortunately, modern veterinary practices have evolved, and today the first vaccination can be given as early as 7 weeks of age. This means that the puppy only needs to stay indoors for about a week before they are allowed to explore outdoor spaces like parks. We must take advantage of this and use this indoor period effectively to teach the puppy the first basic commands, which will be vital once they are ready to venture into the outdoor world.

Holistically speaking, I think it is unrealistic and unfair to expect a puppy to respond to commands like the recall in a park full of distractions. If they have never been properly trained to respond and have not been taught these commands in a familiar, controlled environment, we cannot expect them to perform well in a busy and stimulating place, like a park full of new scents, dogs, people and other distractions. Instead, teaching basic commands such as "Come", "Sit", "Heel", and "Leave It" early on will set your puppy up for success during their first outings. This ensures they are well-prepared and confident when facing the prospect of exploring the park environment for the first time, and will set the foundation for positive outdoor experiences in the future. In addition, it will foster better behaviour and a stronger bond with you, making them more likely to trust and follow your instructions when outside. Most of the commands we teach our dogs are simply adaptations of their inherited prey drive instincts. These instincts, which have been honed over centuries, originally served practical purposes such as herding, guarding, and protecting, aiding our ancestors in their daily lives. In a natural context, puppies do not fully engage with their prey drive until they are mentally and physically mature, typically when they join adult dogs in hunting activities. Because of this, teaching complex commands to a very young puppy is often ineffective (although some working breeds would certainly prove me wrong); they simply aren't ready to grasp or perform at that level. However, there are certain basic commands that a young puppy can learn quickly and effectively, such as "Come", "Sit", "Heel", and "Leave It". These simpler commands are well within a puppy's capability and provide a solid foundation for managing their behaviour during their first outings. Although a puppy might not be ready to perform more complex tasks, mastering these basic commands early on is crucial, and it teaches the puppy the process of learning. It genuinely serves to build structure and communication between the owner and the puppy, setting the stage for more advanced training later, while keeping the puppy safe and manageable during early socialisation and exploration outdoors.

If you are in the position where you are forced to wait two weeks between the first and second inoculation, and direct interaction with other dogs is not advised until their vaccinations are complete, you can still expose your puppy to new environments by allowing them to observe the outside world from a safe distance (e.g. through a window or from your arms). You can also invite pet owners with vaccinated, calm adult dogs into your home for supervised interactions if possible, thus giving the puppy a gentle introduction to canine social behaviour. I encourage you to refer to Chapter 5 for a comprehensive evaluation of the best methods for teaching your puppy the basic essential commands. However, there are a few final considerations I must address to make certain our puppies are fully prepared to handle various every-day life situations, particularly if you live in an urban environment. These include introducing the puppy to grooming sessions and visits to the vet, navigating public transportation, and acclimating them to the myriad noises and stimuli that come with city life. Preparing your puppies early on, so that they can confidently face these experiences without stress and anxiety, will make them more resilient and adaptable to novelty situations as they grow.

Grooming Sessions

Who can fail to appreciate that warm, comforting feeling when caressing the fluffy coat of some of the most adorable dog breeds? The soft touch of their fur has a special appeal, often evoking a sense of calm and joy, making these breeds even more irresistible. From the tiny Pomeranian, through various mid-sized poodle mixes, all the way to the large Saint Bernard and Leonberger at the other end of the spectrum, there are plenty of fluffy, long-coated breeds to choose from. Each breed offers its own unique charm and aesthetic appeal, but it is essential to remember that these fluffy coats come with grooming responsibilities and care requirements that vary in intensity depending on the chosen breed.

When it comes to choosing a canine companion, most people and especially children find themselves more attracted to breeds which exhibit physical features that make them look less threatening towards humans, such as big and rounded head shapes, big eyes, floppy ears, short muzzles, and definitely soft and fluffy fur. Undoubtedly, the texture of a dog's fur is often one of the key reasons people are drawn to a particular breed and studies have shown that physical interactions with pets displaying such characteristics triggers certain hormonal responses in humans, such as the release of oxytocin, which is associated with feelings of affection and bonding. This highly appreciated trait in dogs, however, did not evolve for the sake of beauty or human preference. Rather, a dog's coat serves the functional purpose of protecting them from the elements. In our modern societies, where dogs live alongside humans in heated and air-conditioned homes, they no longer rely on their coats for protection in the same way they did years ago. Nevertheless, in countries susceptible to extreme climate conditions, some long or double coated breeds have become very popular and fashionable. These dogs are often required to adapt to environments that do not always suit the natural structure of their coats. Regular grooming sessions therefore become an essential daily requirement to preserve the dog's health and comfort throughout changing seasons and varying weather conditions. In addition, grooming is crucial for the prevention of common issues such as matting, grass seeds, overheating, skin irritations, and dermatitis.

That said, grooming, in my opinion, should be viewed from a more holistic perspective as it serves a deeper purpose that goes beyond the mere function of ensuring the hygiene and coat maintenance of the animal. Across the animal kingdom, including our human species, grooming is a widespread activity and it has been discovered that it indeed has profound social implications. Ethologists have revealed that grooming plays a crucial role in the bonding process between members of the pack in wolves and feral dogs and it can certainly take on the same function when dogs live with their human companions, helping to foster trust and cooperation and ultimately strengthening their relationship. During grooming, the threshold for aggressive behaviour is reduced to a minimum, regardless of age, gender, or social ranking within the group: physical touch and sharing are encouraged and the invasion of personal space is highly tolerated, all of which contributes to the reinforcement of social bonds.

Another striking behavioural characteristic of grooming that I have observed when cuddling up and stroking my little Chihuahua is the fact that he can become so relaxed that he can quite literally fall asleep, and this is peculiar to all those other species which, in a natural context, devote substantial amounts of time to performing this activity. This seems to reflect the fact that social grooming has a number of other physiological effects that include reducing the heart rate and lowering behavioural indices of stress. In evolutionary terms, whilst most dogs are inherently comfortable with tolerating grooming behaviours such as licking, scratching, rubbing against an object to satisfy their itch, biting their skin, and so on, not all puppies are genetically predisposed to easily tolerating the more invasive grooming practices that humans often employ. These routines, such as the use of slicker brushes, hot and noisy dryers, medicated or unsuitable shampoos, and nail trimming, can sometimes be stressful for dogs. Therefore, if you are planning to get a long-coated breed or one of those breeds whose coats are prone to matting and knotting, you need to introduce grooming activities early on in your puppy's life.

As part of their daily routines, puppies should be brushed regularly, perhaps using treats in association with the use of positive reinforcement techniques, learn to be handled by strangers (the groomers) without showing signs of anxiety and stress, and allow professionals like groomers and veterinarians to examine all parts of their body, like paws, ears, anal glands, and mouth. Because hair dryers and blasters are commonly used in all major grooming parlours, it is advisable to gradually introduce the puppy to the noise produced by the engine, perhaps with some cotton balls placed in their ears to muffle the sound to start with. Dogs possess a far more sensitive range of hearing, enabling them to pick up sounds that lie beyond the frequencies humans can perceive. In nature, this heightened sensitivity allows them to detect subtle noises, such as distant sounds or ultrasonic frequencies, which play a crucial role in their awareness of their environment. Lower or higher frequencies produced by the electric motors of these appliances are well within the broader hearing spectrum of dogs. They may be inaudible to us humans, but are easily detected by the more advanced auditory system of our canine companions.

You can test your puppy's tolerance to the frequencies produced by the electric motors of hair dryers and blasters by turning on a kitchen appliance or the hoover and observing their reaction. If they react badly, fear not, because anxious puppies can fortunately be made less sensitive to certain noises through the use of *desensitisation*. This method involves gradually exposing the puppy to the sound in a controlled and positive environment, starting at a low volume and slowly increasing the intensity over time. By pairing these experiences with positive reinforcement, such as treats or praise, the puppy learns to associate the sound with something pleasant, ultimately reducing their anxiety and helping them remain calm in the face of unsettling noises they will inevitably experience at the dog parlour. I highly recommend organising a few mock visits to the dog parlour with your puppy so they become accustomed to the bustling and noisy environment they will encounter when it is their turn to be groomed. Parlours often have large windows where you and your puppy can observe the groomers at work, allowing the puppy to familiarise themselves with the setting. Meeting and greeting the groomer in a friendly, relaxed manner can also be highly beneficial for the puppy. As always, positive reinforcement is key – by associating the grooming environment with a pleasant experience, your puppy will be better prepared and more confident when the time comes for their actual grooming session.

Veterinary Visits

The same principle applies to vet appointments. A puppy or young dog will inevitably need to visit the veterinary clinic during their developmental period, whether to fully complete their vaccination course or for any unexpected issue. I have encountered cases where dogs have ingested all sorts of dangerous items such as fishing hooks, pieces of tennis balls, plastics, face masks, underwear, or socks. Given that vaccinations involve needles and some level of discomfort, it is natural for puppies to develop a reluctance to return after their first visit. I recommend using the same gradual and positive approach as for grooming sessions by slowly exposing the puppy to the vet environment. This creates a more positive association with the clinic, making future visits less stressful for you both. As mentioned previously, it is always advisable to gradually accustom your puppy to being handled by different people so that vet visits will be less stressful. Take your puppy to the veterinarian practice of your choice, just for a friendly visit (without any medical procedures) to start with, as this will enable them to get used to the new environment. Let them explore the surroundings and meet the veterinary nurses and staff; they will be more than happy to make the first visits the most memorable experience for your puppy through the use of treats, verbal praise, and positive reinforcement. If your dog is suffering from anxiety and experiencing stress when visiting the vet, I encourage you to refer to the chapter dedicated to behavioural issues in dogs. In that section, you will find valuable insights into how to identify signs of anxiety and stress, along with holistic methods for addressing and resolving these issues effectively.

Exposure to Noise and Other Urban Stimuli

City environments present a unique set of challenges for puppies. The constant stream of unfamiliar sounds of traffic, construction, sirens, and the bustle of crowded streets can easily overwhelm a young dog if not introduced thoughtfully. It is essential to expose your puppy to these urban stimuli in a gradual, controlled manner, always rewarding calm and confident behaviour. This early imprinting prevents fear or anxiety from developing later in life. If you live in a busy city and plan to use public transport, early desensitisation is also crucial. Introduce your puppy to buses, trams, or underground trains with short, positive outings, making sure they feel secure at every stage.

A key element in preparing a puppy for travel on public transport is gradual exposure to the unfamiliar noises, crowded environments, and sense of motion they will experience while in transit. This process can begin simply by walking near a busy train or underground station without the pressure of actually boarding. Encouraging the young dog to calmly observe the new environment, interact with people, and experience the surrounding activity while using praise, treats, and reassurance can go a long way to creating positive associations. These early exposures build confidence and lay a solid foundation for stress-free travel experiences later on, when it really matters. I have seen firsthand how crucial this approach can be in shaping the future behaviour of a puppy.

One case that stands out is that of Brady, a gorgeous Yellow Labrador Retriever who came to me with a very specific issue. During our daily walks in the park, Brady was a picture of composure, extremely playful, happy, relaxed, and social. But the moment we stepped out of his front door and encountered street noise, it became a different story. Just getting to the car was a struggle. Brady's issue was not simply a dislike of loud sounds; it had developed into a full-blown phobia of traffic. Helping him required several weeks of work, combining desensitisation, counter-conditioning, and carefully structured training. We took it slowly, step by step, ensuring each experience was manageable and ended on a positive note. With patience and consistency, I managed to achieve our goal and expectations for Brady as he eventually overcame his fear and transitioned from a troubled pet to a confident and adaptable companion, a transformation that made all the effort deeply rewarding.

In the spirit of holistic guidance in raising a confident and dependable puppy, I believe that taking the time to patiently and positively guide your puppy through new experiences is one of the greatest gifts you can offer. By doing so, you are equipping them with the tools to thrive in an urban environment, enabling them to grow into a well-adjusted, resilient, and confident adult dog who can accompany you with ease through the ever-changing rhythm of city life.

BRINGING HOME A RESCUE OR ADULT DOG

Welcoming an adult dog or rescue into your life is a beautiful act of compassion, and one that comes with its own unique set of challenges and considerations. Unlike puppies, adult dogs often arrive with a bit of history. They may have already experienced love, loss, neglect, or confusion, and that emotional baggage, whether visible or not, can shape their early days in your home. It is during this delicate time that your patience, empathy, and reassurance will mean the world to them. Whereas puppies are blank slates, eager to learn and adult themselves to your world, adult dogs come with several habits, good or bad, that are already in place. Moreover, despite their best efforts, rescue centres sometimes simply do not have the full background story of the dog. I recall one particular case where a kind-hearted lady decided to adopt a dog from a well-known rescue centre in Battersea Park in London. This young female dog, however, had been so profoundly traumatised that her behaviour was extremely erratic and unpredictable. She would lunge at anything that moved – other dogs, people, even children and wildlife. The new owner reached out to me for guidance, and while I worked with them, it became clear that this was beyond typical behaviour modification. After a few sessions, I saw how much the lady was struggling; her emotional strength had drained and the situation was taking a toll on both of them. It broke my heart, but I ultimately advised her to return the dog to the shelter, knowing that sometimes, despite all our love and effort, we have to acknowledge when a situation is too much for both parties. The decision was painful, but it was compassionately made with the dog's best interests at heart.

In cases like this one, most probably the previous owners have withheld or even altered information in the hope of ensuring the dog would be accepted into care. This is not an uncommon situation, and it does not mean the dog is problematic, it simply means there are unknowns that need to be addressed before considering rehoming. It is vital to approach these situations with an open heart and a flexible mindset. That said, whether you decide to rescue a dog from a shelter or from a household through family and friends, it is crucial to take a close look at your personal circumstances, especially if you have children in the household. Bringing a rescue dog into a family is a big decision and should be made with careful thought and planning. So, what should you look for?

Temperament and Energy Levels

The first step is to schedule multiple visits to the rescue centre or the family's home, allowing you to observe how the dog interacts with you in its own familiar environment. Pay attention to signs of shyness, eagerness, curiosity, anxiety, or calmness. Unlike puppies, whose personalities are still developing, adult dogs often give you a much clearer sense of who they are just by spending time with them. Dogs do not hide their true selves; during interactions like walks, playtime (whether it is too rough or overly dominant), or simply hanging out, their traits will shine through. You will quickly see their temperament in action, allowing you to make a more informed decision as to whether they are a good fit for your home. It is essential to choose a dog whose energy levels and temperament align with your lifestyle and family circumstances. This ensures you will be better prepared to meet their needs and create a harmonious relationship right from the start. In the meantime, you can prepare your home to welcome your new dog. Setting up a quiet, comfortable space for your new companion is essential. Prepare a bed, water, and a few toys in a designated area where they can feel secure. Limit their access to the rest of the house at first, using baby gates or closed doors to prevent them from being overwhelmed and avoid letting them chew on things that could be tempting or unsafe.

Previous Training and Behavioural Patterns

A large number of rescue dogs already come with basic obedience skills in place, and some may have had prior training in a previous home. However, others may need a bit of help unlearning certain behaviours or rebuilding trust. Pay close attention to cues like leash manners, house training, and how they respond to commands, or sometimes their lack of response. These observations will give you a clearer picture of the areas where they might need extra help and support. If you have the chance to speak with the dog's previous owners, do not hesitate to ask them to demonstrate the commands that the dog already knows, the tone of voice they used, and the training methods they employed. This can offer valuable insight into their past training and help you continue their learning journey smoothly. That said, the most important thing during the early stages is to build trust. Use positive reinforcement, treats, praise, and a calm, encouraging voice to reward any good behaviour. Focus on bonding first before jumping into obedience training. Many rescue dogs may be sensitive to harsh tones or corrections, so be gentle and patient as they adjust to their new family. When introducing your dog to family members, do so one at a time in a calm, controlled manner. If you have other pets, begin introductions with brief, neutral-space interactions, such as on a walk, before bringing them indoors. Always watch for signs of stress or anxiety, like panting, pacing, or freezing, and back off if needed to avoid overwhelming them.

Adaptability and Social Tolerance

Adult dogs may take a little longer to adjust to a new routine or home. Unlike puppies, who seem to adapt almost seamlessly, older dogs often need a bit more patience, gentle guidance, and consistency. It is vital to pay attention to how they react to other members of your family, other dogs, strangers, noises, and being left alone, especially in those early weeks of adjustment. It is also imperative to establish a steady routine and clear boundaries from the start, signalling that you are the main decision maker and leading the household in a fair and consistent manner. When they sense fair, confident leadership, they will feel more secure and eager to adapt, following your lead as they settle into their new life with you. The honeymoon period can last anywhere from a few days to a few weeks, during which you may notice your dog's personality evolve as they settle into their new routine. This is perfectly normal. During this time, offer calm leadership, empathy, and understanding. Celebrate small victories like the first tail wag, a cozy nap on the couch, or when they come to you on command. These moments are milestones in building a lasting, loving bond.

Health and Physical Condition

Adult dogs often come with a known health history, which can actually make things more predictable and manageable. Take note of their physical condition, including their weight, coat, movement, and dental health. Whilst dogs coming from shelters are usually checked by in-house vets, it is still a good idea to arrange a thorough check-up with your own vet to confirm that everything is in order. This will give you peace of mind and address any potential health concerns early on, setting your new companion up for a happy, healthy life in their new home.

As you can probably tell by now, welcoming a new dog into your family is not a one-size-fits-all experience. On the one hand, puppies require more structure, more frequent training sessions, and lots of early socialisation, but they do not come with set habits and behavioural traits. On the other, adult dogs can offer more immediate companionship and emotional depth, especially when given a second chance in a loving home. By following these steps, you will set the stage for a peaceful transition and help your new dog feel safe, loved, and secure in their new home. Every dog is unique, but with a bit of patience and a lot of heart, you can build a strong foundation for a joyful future together.

Rex

CHAPTER 11

THE HOLISTIC APPROACH TO BEHAVIOURAL ISSUES AND PHOBIAS

The holistic approach to addressing most of the behavioural issues and phobias we might find in our domesticated pets is built upon the concept of treating the dog in its entirety. It involves taking into consideration their physical, emotional, and psychological well-being, rather than focusing too narrowly on treating the specific problematic behaviour alone. This method does not seek solely to eliminate the symptoms but it also aims to identify and address the underlying causes of the behaviour, highlighting the relationship between mental and physical well-being. In the context of understanding dog behaviour, a holistic approach therefore considers the environment, the dog's emotional state, the predisposition of the breed, the overall health condition, diet, physical exercise, and social interactions as parts of a whole and connected system.

Before I address the causes and propose possible remedies for treating the most common behavioural issues reported by dog owners when they seek professional advice, it is important to pause for a moment and reflect on the meaning of the word "behaviour" itself. What do we actually mean when we use this term? Loosely speaking, behaviour is the word used to describe how someone or something acts. It is what a person or an animal does either to make something happen, make something change, or to keep things the same as they are, so as to gain access to whatever is necessary to satisfy the basic needs. Behaviour is the response of an organism to events that are happening or it perceives might happen. These events can occur internally in the body of a person or an animal, like thoughts (yes, experts say that dogs are self-aware and can think), pain, and inner feelings, or they can occur externally, as a reaction to stimuli they find in the environment and that includes other animals or people. For any dog owner or professional trainer or behaviourist, observing and diagnosing the behaviour is probably the easy part. It is the understanding of why some dogs do what they do that is much more complicated.

During the course of my training sessions or behavioural consultations with my clients, I frequently put a substantial emphasis on the notion that when we observe any behaviour in our dogs, good or bad, they are simply trying to tell us something that is very important to them, and because they cannot communicate using our own language, they turn to behaviour as a form of expression that is so undisguised and blunt it transcends words; we just need the right tools to translate and understand it. In other words, a dog's behaviour is their way of communicating needs or desires in response to a given environment, an emotional feeling, an underlying health issue, or the lack of fulfilment of their natural instincts.

Behaviour, however, does not originate as a deliberate and well-thought strategy for controlling a stimulus. Initially, all behaviours are probably just a reflex, a response following a particular anatomical or physiological reaction. An example of reflex behaviour is when we instinctively put our arm and hand up to shield our eyes from the sun or a bright light source. This action occurs without conscious thought, as the body responds automatically to protect the eyes from potential harm. Reflex behaviours like this are fast and involuntary responses to external stimuli that guarantee our safety. Similarly, dogs exhibit reflex behaviours, such as flinching when they hear a loud sound or pulling their paw back when they step on something sharp. Behaviours that prolong the life of an animal and increase its chance of reproducing are favoured by the process of natural selection; over time, a particularly advantageous behaviour spreads throughout a species. Moreover, the predisposition of an organism to display a certain behaviour is innate, otherwise the responses generated would not be subjected to natural selection and evolution. For the organism to apply them successfully, reinforcement and/or maturation is required. Behaviour is, consequently, the outcome of the combination of our dog's innate dispositions and environmental factors.

Some behaviours require little conditioning from the environment for the animal to display it, while other behaviours require more. These characteristics clearly indicate that certain undesirable behaviours in dogs are often inadvertently reinforced by a lack of understanding and/or flaws in the way owners communicate with their dogs. When we fail to recognise or misinterpret the reasons behind our pets' actions, we may unintentionally encourage behaviours that we find undesirable. I often compare the language of dogs to that of our children. Both communicate in a raw, unfiltered manner, free from the constraints and etiquette that govern social conventions. They express their needs, emotions, and desires with an uninhibited straightforwardness that is basic yet extremely effective. There is no pretence in their communication; whether they are seeking attention, expressing discomfort, or signalling joy, their language is direct and instinctual. Just as children will cry, laugh, or reach out without hesitation or shame, dogs will bark, wag their tails, or nudge for attention. The simplicity of this form of communication, which is totally independent of societal norms, is the fundamental key to successfully connecting with our dogs and understanding their behaviour.

Just today, while I was listening to a fascinating radio programme about animal communication, the guest speaker said something that made me reflect on how human communication is shaped by cultural learning and social expectations. He commented that when an adult walks through a room full of people, he or she will use words like "excuse me" to communicate to the crowd their intention to cross the room with an awareness of personal space, courtesy, and the desire to avoid conflict. This example perfectly highlights the distinction between human communication, which is often shaped by social etiquette and norms, and the more direct, instinct-driven communication we observe in animals and young children. This level of communication requires cognitive awareness of both one's own actions and their impact on others. By contrast, young children, like dogs, operate with less regard for these learnt social conventions. A child may push through a crowd without saying anything, simply because they have not yet fully internalised the social rules that adults follow. Similarly, dogs do not adhere to the same social norms as humans. They navigate spaces based on instinct, without considering the impact on those around them, whether that means stepping on toes or bumping into people. This example perfectly illustrates that if we want to truly understand and communicate with our dogs in a holistic way, we must simplify our communication and bring it down to its original basic form.

Dogs rely heavily on body language, facial expressions, a different pitch or tone of voice, and other simple cues, which are immediate and raw compared to the layered complexity of human conversation. By scaling down our communication and focusing instead on clear, direct signals like our posture, tone of voice, and gestures, we create a language that our dogs are more likely to understand intuitively. To have a better idea of what I mean by scaling down, I invite you to watch an extremely interesting movie called *Quest for Fire* (1981) by the brilliant French film director, screenwriter, and producer Jean-Jacques Annaud. He is best known for directing *The Name of the Rose* (1986), *The Lover* (1992), *Seven Years in Tibet* (1997), and the striking *Wolf Totem* (2015), among several other successful movies. *Quest for Fire* is especially fascinating because it really takes you back to prehistoric times and offers a glimpse into the origins of language and communication among our ancestors. Not a single word is spoken; rather, communication is basic and raw, composed of sounds, gestures, and body postures. Let me clarify – I am not suggesting that we should revert to the ways in which our ancestors communicated, but if we want to connect effectively with our pets, we should not expect them to grasp the full complexity of human language. Instead, we should make an effort to learn and communicate in a way that aligns with how dogs naturally understand the world, which has changed little since ancient times.

Sometimes when interacting with our dogs, a grunt or a growl goes a long way.

Going back to the analysis and the function of a behaviour, we can say that it can be used to externalise feelings or emotions that are extremely simple and whose meanings are very clear for us to understand. For example, if a person is jumping up and down with excitement, we assume that that person is really happy; similarly, if we see someone crying, we think that it is because they must be extremely sad. But there are circumstances when certain needs, feelings, or emotions are kept inside for such a long time that they escalate and heighten to a point where people find it almost impossible to convey them through speech, and so instead they express them through an explosion of emotions, usually in a physical form, or by screaming, crying and even turning to aggression. I believe that to be also true in our dogs, except that these externalisations – some trainers refer to them as a dog's "State of Mind" – can manifest in different ways due to their inability to verbally communicate with their human companions. Regardless, whether verbal (barking, hauling, growling, etc.) or non-verbal (body language, tail position, piloerection, etc.), in moments of heightened anxiety, fear, or discomfort, the ability of our dogs to process information and communicate effectively is severely undermined and sometimes the only way for them to relay their state of mind to us is to display a certain behaviour. For dogs, each behaviour serves a purpose, such as to satisfy their needs, attract the attention of the owner or another dog, gain access to an item or activity, get away from something unpleasant, or experience a sensorial stimulation. The latter is described as the physical and emotional experience that occurs when the brain interprets signals from sensory receptors in the body, such as sound, touch, taste, sight, and smell, as observed when our dogs seem to go wild when running on the sand.

Before I delve deeper into analysing the core issues surrounding problematic behaviours in dogs, I would like to emphasise the importance of two key aspects regarding the display of certain behaviours. The first is that the interpretation of a dog's behaviour is often subjective and highly influenced by the owner's personal perspective, cultural background, and expectations. What one person might find acceptable or even attractive in a dog's actions, another might see as problematic or undesirable. A popular saying within the dog community says, "One person's behavioural nightmare is another's perfect pet." A Border Collie that chases and snaps at joggers may also excel as a working herding dog. A dog that barks at night could be a valuable deterrent to intruders, or a serious annoyance to a sleep-deprived neighbour. For instance, a dog jumping up to greet someone might be viewed by one owner as an enthusiastic display of affection, while another owner might find it rude or disruptive. I attribute much of this to cultural perspective. Being Italian myself, it is deeply ingrained in our culture to greet everyone, whether familiar or unfamiliar, by embracing and kissing each other's cheeks, an act that involves an utter and complete invasion of one's personal space. This physical closeness, however, is considered a natural expression of warmth and connection in most Mediterranean cultures. By contrast, I found out very quickly when I moved to England that this form of greeting is typically reserved for close friends and family members, while strangers or acquaintances are met with a more formal and distantly cold handshake. The differences in the custom of greetings are just one example of how culture shapes our attitude towards matters like personal space and physical touch, and how this attitude is projected onto our pets. Ultimately, if we truly want to resolve these issues, we must also consider the dog's needs, instincts, and motivations. After all, behaviour is a two-way street, and successful solutions lie in meeting somewhere in the middle.

The other important aspect to consider is the differentiation between what is an inherited or an acquired behaviour in dogs. Inherited behaviours are those that are genetically programmed and passed down through generations. Some of these behaviours are purely instinctual, such as rolling on dead animal corpses or onto animals' excrement, howling when left in solitary confinement, or even digging in the garden. All these actions are remnants of survival tactics from their wild ancestors and served distinctive purposes, such as camouflaging their scent in preparation for hunting, communicating with other members of the pack across distances, or creating a safe shelter. Whilst these instincts may no longer serve the same purpose as dogs have adapted to and enjoy living comfortably in our modern domestic setting, they nonetheless remain deeply ingrained in their behavioural repertoire, often manifesting in ways that perplex or frustrate their human companions. Some other inherited behaviours, however, are tied to a dog's breed and instincts, such as herding in Border Collies, hunting on sight in Greyhounds, or retrieving in Labradors and Golden Retrievers. These behaviours were ingrained in our dogs and passed down through generations through a process of selective breeding conducted by our ancestors, and were aimed at enhancing specific traits that served practical purposes. For these reasons, they are more resistant to change or suppressing entirely, as they are deeply rooted in the dog's genetic makeup and instinctual drives. For example, I have occasionally been asked if I could train Golden Retrievers and Labradors to stop jumping into water or muddy puddles, or to train a Border Collie to refrain from herding other dogs during our regular walks in the park.

One inherited trait I find particularly fascinating and which we can still find in some of our pets concerns one of the most popular breeds, the black Labrador retriever, and its ability to dive underwater. This breed originated from the Labrador Territory (hence the name), which is an area situated northwest of the island of Newfoundland. Curiously, there is also another breed from Newfoundland called, logically enough, the Newfoundland. Long before the establishment of European colonialists in the Canadian territory, many Spanish, French, Portuguese, and English fishermen were operating with their fishing vessels in these regions off the Atlantic coast, presumably bringing their dogs with them. These various breeds commingled on the huge but isolated island, creating a canine race that became known as the St. John's dog, after the capital of Newfoundland. They originally came in different sizes, ranging from the smaller Labrador retriever we are familiar with today to the majestic Newfoundland. These were then brought back to England and bred with British hunting dogs to create what became known as the Labrador retriever. The forefather of today's Labrador retrievers were well-known for their infatuation with water and their unique skills at operating in it as they hauled nets and long lines. They also dived for cod that had slipped off the hook, and even retrieved fishermen's hats blown into the water by the wind. Fishermen reportedly preferred the shorthaired dogs over their longer-coated siblings, as the ice did not accumulate on their water-resistant coats (the same reason why the original Saint Bernard had a short coat). These dogs were mainly black in colour, with a thick tail that acted like a rudder to help them steer in water. Newfoundland's fishermen were justifiably proud of their dogs and were not shy about showcasing their dogs' impressive skills. In fact, when their ships packed with salted cod crossed the ocean, they would dock in the port of Poole in Dorset on the southern English coast. Once there, they encouraged their clever dogs to perform for gathered crowds by retrieving objects tossed into the water. These dogs were more than just companions, they were essential partners in the fishermen's daily work, and were renowned for their strength, endurance, and remarkable ability to swim in harsh, icy waters.

For lovers of the famous liquor Brandy, I once read the amusing anecdote of a dog named "Brandy", a St. John's dog imported by the 5th Duke of Buccleuch and his brother, Lord John Scott. During one trip across the Atlantic, Brandy jumped into the rough waters to retrieve the cap of one of the fishermen. He swam for almost two hours in the icy Atlantic waters before crew members managed to rescue him and get him back on board. Exhausted but resilient, Brandy was finally revived after he was given several doses of an unnamed liquor that the fishermen carried on board, and legend has it that the liquor was indeed named after Brandy in his honour.

By contrast, acquired behaviours are learnt through the dog's life experiences and their exposure to the environment. These behaviours are shaped by the dog's interactions with humans, other animals, and their surroundings. Dogs may learn to beg for food at the table or they can become fearful of certain stimuli through reinforcement or repeated exposure. I cannot stress enough the notion that to effectively address and approach the most common behavioural issues in a holistic and informed way, it is fundamental to understand both the subjective nature of the behaviour and the distinction between inherited and acquired behaviours.

The key point is that dogs themselves do not inherently classify their behaviours as "good" or "bad"; they are simply driven by their instincts in response to changes in the environment, or to satisfy their needs. When planning a proper and effective therapeutic intervention to address complex behavioural issues, there are various approaches and methods to choose from. Each option should be carefully considered and based on the specific needs of the dog as well as those of the owners, the nature of the behaviour, and on the desired outcome.

Animal behaviour therapy is both a science and an art, and over the years, it's become quite a trendy profession. These days, it's not uncommon to hear titles like "behaviourist," "dog listener," or "canine consultant" being used by people from all sorts of backgrounds. While some practitioners have a solid academic or veterinary foundation, many come into the field through personal passion, hands-on experience, or as a lifestyle career. I'll be honest, I'm one of those who didn't arrive here through the traditional academic route. I don't hold a degree in animal behaviour. What I do have, however, is decades of real-world experience working with dogs and their people, day in and day out. Over time, this has given me a deep, practical understanding of canine behaviour that books alone can't teach. I've helped hundreds of dogs and owners find harmony together, using kind, effective, and evidence-based methods. That said, I always encourage dog owners to be discerning when choosing someone to help with behavioural issues. Since this field isn't strictly regulated and qualifications can vary widely, your best bet is to look for someone with a solid track record, trusted recommendations, and ideally, referrals from your vet. If that person also brings compassion, patience, and practical experience to the table, whether or not they have letters after their name, you're in good hands. In contrast to established fields such as cardiology, dentistry, or even mechanical engineering, where protocols are well-defined and widely standardised, the discipline of animal behaviour therapy is characterised by a broad heterogeneity of methodologies and theoretical underpinnings. This diversity reflects both the evolving nature of this relatively new field and the unique challenges associated with assessing and modifying a behaviour in non-verbal subjects like dogs. The empirical studies that can allow scientists to rigorously compare the efficacy of one behavioural intervention against another (e.g., method X versus method Y) still remain rather limited. Consequently, most cases are evaluated using intra-subject comparisons, wherein the effectiveness of a given treatment is measured by observing reductions in the frequency, the intensity, or the duration of the targeted behaviour relative to pre-intervention baselines. Although there is growing consensus among practitioners regarding the need for more systematic, evidence-based research into behavioural diagnosis (like the Ethogram) and methodologies, such efforts are frequently constrained by the complex, multifactorial, and interactive nature of animal behaviour problems. Each case is shaped by a constellation of variables, including genetics, developmental history, environmental context, and the quality of human-animal interactions, rendering controlled comparisons inherently difficult.

When compared to the old-fashioned approach or the more conventional rehabilitation treatment strategies, which usually tend to focus on either correcting the unwanted behaviour through aversive techniques, avoiding the trigger that causes the problem, or the implementation of training regimens alone, a holistic approach involves delving deeper into the dog's life experiences, environment, and health to uncover and understand the underlying cause of the issue. In my experience I find that phobias and behavioural problems often arise from factors such as past trauma, poor socialisation, anxiety, dietary requirements or even physical discomfort due to underlying medical conditions. In essence, the holistic approach seeks to answer questions like: What are the most common behavioural issues? What are the reasons behind these behaviours? What is it that our dogs are trying to communicate? How can we address these issues in a holistic and compassionate way? I hope the following pages will not only answer your questions but also provide valuable insights to help you better understand and address any challenges with your dog. Let's get started!

To answer the aforementioned questions, I firstly need to refer to the branch of science that studies the behaviour of species namely, ethology. Derived from the Greek words Ethos, meaning "character", and Logia, meaning "the study of", ethology focuses on understanding how and why animals behave in certain ways, particularly in their natural environments. Ethologists employ scientific methods to observe and analyse how animals interact with each other, their surroundings, and other species in order to understand the evolutionary, genetic, and environmental factors that shape their behaviours. When it comes to understanding the behaviour of our domesticated dog, most ethologists focus their research on observations of the dog's closest relative, the grey wolf, with whom they share 99.8% of their DNA. In this regard, the role of ethology is vital because it provides a scientific framework for understanding and recording the behaviours of these animals in their natural setting. By observing and identifying these natural behaviours, we can better distinguish between what is considered a typical behaviour for an animal versus behaviours that are abnormal or induced by external factors like stress, the domestication process, or human influence.

With respect to our domesticated dogs, typical behaviours are those that are consistent with the natural instincts and normal actions of the canine species, as seen in its natural environment. If you observe your dog's normal behaviour carefully, you might notice that they will consistently display the same behaviour according to the context and environment with which they are interacting. During social interaction, your dog will exhibit behaviours like tail wagging, play bowing, barking, play chasing, or sniffing as part of their communication with other dogs and humans. When you take your dog to the park for their regular exercise routine, you will certainly notice the emergence of the hunting or prey drive behaviour in the form of chasing, stalking, or retrieving, which are common in most dog breeds as part of their hunting instincts. When you cuddle on the couch watching television you might observe grooming activities like licking, which is not just for hygiene purposes but also for social bonding. What about territorial marking? Urinating to mark territory is typical for both male and female dogs as part of their instinctive behaviour. Digging is also a typical behaviour that allows dogs either to cool off, bury something, or explore. There are other perfectly natural behaviours, however, that are considered gross or abnormal by dog owners, like rolling in fox excrement or dead animals, licking female's dog urine or another dog's genitals, eating other animal's excrement like horse faeces or bird droppings, or marking the owner's bed or resting place. All these aforementioned behaviours are perfectly normal and serve different purposes, which I will discuss in the following pages.

Atypical behaviours, on the other hand, are actions that deviate from what is considered normal or expected for the canine species. These can be signs of stress, anxiety, illness, or behavioural issues. For example, whilst some barking is normal, excessive vocalisation in the form of barking or howling can indicate anxiety, boredom, or frustration. Compulsive behaviours or repetitive actions like tail-chasing, excessive licking, or pacing can be signs of anxiety or neurological issues. Aggression in dogs can also be considered normal in certain situations, such as defensive or territorial aggression, or in the display of intentions, but unprovoked full physical aggression with the intention of harming humans or other dogs is atypical and requires intervention. Other atypical behaviours could include self-mutilation or resource guarding.

Ethologists employ an extremely valuable tool when documenting and observing animal behaviours, namely the Ethogram. This provides a comprehensive list of behaviours along with the systematic description of an animal's behavioural repertoire that is typical of that species. Because a well compiled ethogram can include a wide range of crucial information about a dog's behaviour, such as the social context, the dog's body posture, facial expressions and any released vocalisations, indications of the initiators of the actions as well as the recipients, it provides a standardised catalogue of behaviours, allowing all professionals involved in the care, training, or treatment of dogs, such as veterinarians, trainers, and behaviourists, to share a common language. In the airline industry and other specialised fields for example, the importance of communication is often a matter of life and death and has therefore been standardised and coded to ensure clarity and uniformity across different professionals. This creates a common language that can be universally understood, minimising the risk of miscommunication. For example, pilots, air traffic controllers, and ground staff use specific terminology and protocols, such as the NATO phonetic alphabet and predefined phrases, to communicate effectively, regardless of language barriers. This approach is crucial for safety and efficiency, as everyone involved shares the same understanding of key terms and instructions. An ethogram serves a similar purpose in the study and treatment of dogs. By using this structured list of typical canine behaviours, everyone can accurately describe, interpret, and address a dog's actions, ensuring consistency in understanding and improving the effectiveness of interventions. Sometimes it is difficult for dog owners to describe the behaviour accurately; for this reason, I also recommend using video footage to gain a clearer understanding and accurately record the events leading up to, during, and after the behaviour in question. This visual documentation provides valuable insights, allowing professionals to assess the behaviour in context and identify triggers or patterns that may not be immediately apparent. By reviewing the footage, it becomes easier to track progress, refine intervention strategies, and ensure the chosen treatment is effectively addressing the behaviour. This method can be particularly useful for complex cases where subtle cues or environmental factors play a significant role.

A typical Canine Ethogram (selected behaviours) should include the following:

Social Interaction Behaviours

Play bow: The dog lowers its front legs while keeping the rear end raised, often wagging the tail. This signals the intent to play and invites other dogs or humans to engage in playful interaction.

Dominance display: The dog stands tall, sometimes placing a paw or head over another dog, with the ears forward and tail raised. This indicates an attempt to assert dominance.

Submission (active or passive): In active submission, the dog may lower its body, wag its tail, lick another dog or human, and exhibit appeasement gestures. In passive submission, the dog rolls onto its back, exposing its belly, often with its tail tucked and ears back.

Mounting: A dog mounts another dog, object, or person, which is often associated with dominance or excitement. It can be a social rather than sexual behaviour.

Vocalisations

Barking: Can vary in pitch and intensity depending on the situation. Barking can signal alertness (high-pitched, repeated barks), excitement (rapid, short barks), or frustration (loud, continuous barking).

Growling: A low, guttural sound often used as a warning or threat, indicating that the dog is feeling defensive, aggressive, or uncomfortable.

Whining: High-pitched, soft vocalisation that can indicate distress, pain, or a desire for attention.

Feeding and Hunting Behaviours

Sniffing the ground: The dog uses its highly developed sense of smell to detect scents on the ground, often related to food or territory marking by other animals.

Stalking: The dog crouches low, moving slowly and deliberately towards a target (e.g. a toy or another animal). This behaviour is a remnant of the hunting instincts in certain breeds.

Chewing: The dog gnaws on bones, toys, or other objects. Chewing satisfies a dog's natural urge to use its teeth and jaws, and may also be a form of stress relief.

Rest and Sleep Behaviours

Circling before lying down: The dog may circle several times before settling down. This behaviour is thought to be a leftover instinct from wild ancestors preparing a sleeping area.

Sleeping positions:

1) Curled up: The dog lies in a tight ball with its nose tucked under its tail, a position that conserves warmth.

2) Sprawled out: The dog lies on its side with legs extended, indicating relaxation and comfort.

Body Posture and Movement

Tail wagging: Different tail positions and movements indicate various emotional states:

1) Fast, loose wag: Excitement or happiness.

2) Stiff wag: Caution or uncertainty.

3) Tail tucked: Fear, submission, or anxiety.

4) Ears back: The dog pulls its ears flat against its head, which can indicate fear, submission, or stress.

5) Hackles raised: The fur along the dog's back stands up, often indicating fear, excitement, or aggression.

Aggressive Behaviours

Baring teeth: The dog displays its teeth in a warning sign of aggression or defensiveness. This may accompany a growl.

Snarling: A combination of growling and baring teeth, signalling that the dog is ready to attack or defend itself.

Biting: An actual aggressive behaviour where the dog closes its jaws around another animal, person, or object.

Exploratory Behaviours

Sniffing (air or ground): The dog uses its sense of smell to gather information about the environment, other animals, or humans.

Digging: The dog uses its paws to scratch or dig at the ground, bedding, or objects. This may be related to nesting behaviour or signify an attempt to uncover something.

Stress or Anxiety Behaviours

Pacing: The dog walks back and forth in a repetitive pattern, often indicating nervousness or anxiety.

Lip licking: The dog repeatedly licks its lips, a common signal of stress, discomfort, or appeasement.

Yawning: Dogs often yawn when they are stressed or feeling tense, a behaviour that can help calm them.

Shaking off: Similar to when a dog shakes off water, this action is often a way for the dog to release stress or tension after an uncomfortable or intense situation.

Elimination Behaviours

Urine marking: The dog lifts its leg (males or females) and releases a small amount of urine on vertical surfaces, which serves as a territorial marker.

Kicking dirt after elimination: The dog uses its hind legs to kick up dirt or grass after defecating or urinating, spreading its scent.

Lastly, I would like to emphasise that the ethogram can be effectively used in conjunction with the Canine Behavioural Questionnaire (CBQ) to further diagnose the issue. Whilst the ethogram provides a detailed catalogue of observable behaviours, the questionnaire offers insights into the dog's environment, history, and specific circumstances surrounding the behaviour. Together, these tools give a more comprehensive understanding of the underlying causes, allowing for a more accurate diagnosis and tailored intervention plan. Combining both approaches will guarantee that no detail is overlooked in the process of addressing and resolving the behavioural issue. By standardising the way behavioural concerns are reported and evaluated, the CBQ provides a clearer picture of the underlying causes of a dog's behaviour and guides the development of an effective and tailored behaviour modification plan. An example of a typical CBQ can be found in Appendix A.

When I first began my career as a professional dog trainer, after earning my qualifications from the British Institute for Professional Dog Trainers, the majority of my clients sought guidance on how to teach their dogs the most basic commands. Behavioural problems were relatively limited and often stemmed from a lack of understanding of the canine nature, issues related to miscommunication with pets, or neglecting a dog's basic needs for exercise, mental stimulation, and social interaction. However, in recent years, I have noticed a radical shift in this trend. Today, I can see an ever growing focus on addressing a broader range of unwanted behavioural issues, and much less emphasis on basic obedience training. I am uncertain whether this significant increase is due to genetic factors, the challenges posed by modern environments, or human-driven changes. Regardless of the causes, it is crucial that we work to identify the underlying reasons for these behaviours and apply a holistic approach in addressing them.

Based on recent statistical research and surveys conducted among pet owners and veterinarians in the most developed countries, the most common behavioural problems in dogs can be identified, in no particular order, as follows:

- Aggression
- Separation Anxiety
- Jumping Up on People and Other Dogs
- Fear and Phobias
- Leash Reactivity and Pulling
- Coprophagy
- Excessive Barking
- Destructive Chewing
- Hyperactivity or Over-Excitement

- Mounting and Humping
- Resource Guarding

    These behavioural issues are a major contributory factor to the growing number of dogs being re-homed or relinquished to shelters each year. When dog owners struggle to manage problematic behaviours such as aggression, separation anxiety, or excessive barking, it can lead to frustration and a feeling of helplessness; but let's be honest, most behavioural problems in dogs don't just appear out of thin air. In many cases, they're shaped (often unintentionally) by us humans, our habits, our lifestyles, and the environment we create for our dogs. Sure, some issues are rooted in genetics or medical conditions, but the bulk of the "problem behaviours" I come across start at the other end of the lead. The good news? We've come a long way in understanding how dogs think, feel, and relate to the world around them. Thanks to the explosion of research into canine behaviour, and a growing number of vets who take behavioural health seriously, we're now better equipped than ever to tackle these issues with empathy and the help of science. Still, the stats tell a sobering story. In the UK, around 10% of dogs are re-homed at some point during their lives, often because of behaviour problems. That's somewhere between 500,000 and 700,000 dogs out of a total population of about 8 million. It's a reminder that as much as we love our dogs, when communication breaks down, relationships can too. That said, the man-dog relationship is more secure and longer lasting than the institution of marriage, which has an only 50% 'survival' rate in many Western countries. Despite, or perhaps because of, their misbehaviours, dogs evoke remarkable loyalty from their people! the human-dog bond is still one of the most resilient partnerships around, so maybe your dog chewing the sofa isn't grounds for divorce after all! Joking aside, what makes this relationship so special is the loyalty on both sides. And it's this very loyalty that gives us the foundation to work through behavioural hiccups, big or small, and come out the other side with an even stronger connection.

    In the following sections, I present a detailed analysis of the potential causes underpinning these behavioural issues and provide practical strategies aimed at achieving long-term resolution. Some of the problems listed have already been explored in earlier chapters, and I encourage you to revisit those sections for a deeper understanding and step-by-step guidance on how to address them effectively.

AGGRESSION

Several recent studies have shown that aggression is one of the leading reasons as to why domestic dogs are relinquished to shelters or euthanised (e.g. Powdrill-Wells, Taylor & Melfi, 2021). In particular, these studies found that aggression towards humans or other animals accounted for a significant percentage of all the surrendering cases. Regrettably, most dogs with a history of biting or serious episodes of aggression face a higher risk of euthanasia, as the resources shelters have to rehabilitate them are often extremely limited. Over the years, I have been involved in the rehabilitation of several rescued dogs, some with successful outcomes while others, I am afraid to say, proved too complex or high-risk for the average owner to handle, making surrender a heartbreaking but sometimes unavoidable decision. There are no quick fixes as the process of rehabilitating an aggressive pet requires a lot of time, patience, and consistent effort. Even when a dog is considered fully rehabilitated, there remains a lingering sense of caution, a small voice in the back of one's mind reminding you to always remain vigilant. Aggressive behaviour can lead not only to serious legal complications, including potential lawsuits, but also poses a direct risk of harm to both humans and other animals. This is why it is crucial to take proactive steps in preventing such behaviour from developing, starting as early as puppyhood.

Within the canine species, aggression is a natural and rather functional behaviour, serving various purposes that contribute to survival and the continuation of the species. It is not inherently negative but rather a means of communication, protection, and resource management. For instance, a mother dog may exhibit maternal aggression, fiercely protecting her puppies from perceived threats to guarantee their survival. Resource guarding is another instinctual behaviour, where a dog defends food, toys, or other valued possessions to secure vital resources. Similarly, territorial aggression arises when a dog perceives its home, back garden, or even a car as its domain, instinctively working to keep intruders at bay. Dogs may also display protective aggression, defending their owners or familiar individuals from perceived dangers. By contrast, pain-related aggression occurs when a dog experiencing discomfort reacts defensively to avoid further pain, often lashing out if touched or moved. In domesticated dogs, aggression is considered a rather complex behaviour that is often influenced by different factors like genetics, the environment, training, and socialisation.

In my experience as a behavioural consultant, the aggression I regularly observe in pet dogs often stems from fear, resource guarding, frustration, or learnt behaviours that are mostly influenced by human interaction. Whilst most professionals in our field agree that aggression can be a natural response in certain situations, it becomes problematic when it is excessive, unpredictable, or directed inappropriately towards humans, other pets, or unfamiliar stimuli like joggers, bicycle, and cars. There is a clear distinction between the aggressive behaviour of our domesticated dogs and that of their canine counterparts in the wild. In fact, the aggression we observe in a natural setting is primarily functional. It is used for survival, hunting purposes, establishing a social hierarchy, or defending the territory from rival groups. Furthermore, it must be said that aggressive behaviour within a natural context is rarely excessive or unnecessary. The very nature of pack structures dictate the use of aggression as a form of expression and communication among its members. Disputes are often settled through body language, displays of dominance, or submission rather than outright fights. Aggression within a stable pack is usually controlled and rarely escalates to serious injury. This is a strategic survival instinct because, if we think carefully about it, a pack cannot afford to lose any valuable member over internal disputes, especially when cooperation is essential for hunting, protection, and overall survival. Instead, most conflicts are resolved through ritualised displays, body language, and submission signals, ensuring the group's stability while maintaining a social hierarchy.

The holistic approach to aggression in domesticated pets acknowledges that a large number of behavioural issues arise from a disconnection between our pets' natural instincts and the artificial environments in which they live. This approach emphasises understanding, prevention, and rehabilitation rather than simply treating aggression as a standalone problem. Our pets are social animals and, like their counterparts living in the wild, are born with ingrained communication methods, body language, and conflict-resolution strategies. Before I delve further into this topic, I would like to point out that there is a distinction to be made between aggression and reactivity. These two behaviours in our domesticated dogs are closely connected, but are two completely different matters that are often misinterpreted and, if poorly managed or left unaddressed, can result in a natural occurrence like reactivity easily escalating into aggression.

Reactivity often stems from fear, frustration, or over-arousal, leading to exaggerated responses such as barking, lunging, or growling. When these behaviours are repeatedly reinforced or mismanaged by owners, they can develop into true aggression where, contrary to their natural instincts, the dog actively seeks to confront or eliminate a perceived threat.

Let me give an example of how an owner's reaction can unintentionally reinforce leash reactivity, which is an issue I witnessed on a daily basis when walking with my dog here in London. A common misunderstanding among dog owners concerns how they react to their pet's reactivity when on the leash. For instance, when encountering another dog while walking on the street, an anxious owner might instinctively tense up, tighten the leash, or pull their dog back. This unintended pressure on the leash and the altered emotional state of the owner signals to the dog that there is indeed something to be concerned about, reinforcing their reactive behaviour, whether it be barking, lunging, or displaying aggression towards the other dog and growling.

To make matters worse, some owners then try to soothe their dog by petting or speaking in a reassuring tone, which the dog interprets as praise for their reaction rather than a cue to remain calm. Funnily enough, when I ask whether the owner experiences the same behaviour when the dog is off the leash during a walk in the park, the answer I get is mostly negative. In fact, when dogs are on a leash, their natural fight-or-flight response is restricted as they cannot choose to flee from a perceived threat. As a result, some dogs resort to a reactive behaviour as an alternative to submission or escape, using displays such as barking, lunging, or growling to create distance and regain a sense of control over the situation. The ideal response in this situation would be for the owner to lead by example, and by that I mean staying relaxed, keeping a loose leash, and confidently moving forward without hesitation. Previous leash training is essential, as it gives the owner the confidence that their dog will follow their lead in any situation. This is the true purpose of training – it strengthens the bond between owner and dog while reassuring the dog that the situation is always under control. By projecting calm energy and confident body language, the owner helps the dog feel secure, reassuring them that leadership is in place and that there will not be any issue during the casual encounter on the street. This sense of trust allows the dog to relax, ultimately reducing reactive tendencies over time.

So, what would be the best and most appropriate strategy to break this vicious cycle? The correct approach depends on the severity of the aggressive behaviour (if the reactivity has already escalated into aggression) and also on the dog's threshold for reactivity. If the issue has only recently begun to manifest, especially in younger dogs, it is typically easier and quicker to resolve. Conversely, if the behaviour has been reinforced over months or even years, modifying it will require more time and effort. Nevertheless, there is always hope, regardless of the severity, as any dog can reconnect with its natural instincts when guided through the right training and rehabilitation process. I always recommend counter-conditioning and positive reinforcement as alternatives to the more common trends that promote avoidance-based methods, such as crossing the street or avoiding all dog encounters altogether. Moreover, rather than reacting emotionally or using corrective measures like shouting or applying tension on the leash, which will only escalate the issue further, owners should focus on a gradual desensitisation in a controlled manner. This involves rewarding calm behaviour when the dog notices a trigger, maintaining enough physical distance from the trigger to reduce the intensity, and eventually introducing alternative behaviours such as making eye contact with the owner on cue ("Watch Me"), asking the dog to assume the sit position, or walking calmly with the subject in the heel position. At this stage, the primary objective is to stimulate the dog to build new associations, learning that staying calm leads to rewards, while exerting reactivity does not. I cannot stress enough the importance of implementing this first stage. As much time should be taken as necessary to ensure the dog is fully prepared for the more critical second phase of the rehabilitation process. Rushing through this phase can lead to setbacks, so patience and consistency are keys.

The second phase is more challenging but crucial for helping the dog generalise what they have learnt in a controlled environment and transfer it to real-life situations. This involves arranging a structured introduction with a familiar, well-mannered dog in a planned scenario, such as meeting a friend with their dog on a walk. Initially, the reactive dog may exhibit the usual barking and lunging, but it is essential for both owners to remain calm and patient, as dogs will often mirror their handlers' energy. I might add that true calmness cannot be faked, as dogs have an extraordinary ability to detect anxiety through facial expression, scent, and body language. To project a relaxed demeanour, owners can redirect their own anxious energy by humming a light-hearted tune or engaging in friendly conversation while allowing the dogs to go through the natural greeting ritual of sniffing each other in a relaxed manner. This approach will definitely help a reactive dog gradually build confidence and self-control around other dogs. Over time, by repeating these steps in different settings, the dog will learn to fully trust the handler and to manage their reactivity in a more controlled and predictable way, so that eventually the behaviour will extinguish itself organically. Finally, I encourage regular, controlled interactions with other dogs rather than resorting to avoidance. Denying dogs the opportunity to socialise only perpetuates the problem, reinforcing unwanted behaviour until it escalates beyond control. True progress comes from gradual, positive exposure, allowing the dog to build confidence and develop appropriate social skills.

Moving forward, the other most likely causes of aggression in our domesticated dogs can be summarised as follows:

Fear-Based Aggression

This type of aggression is typically rooted in the dog's negative past experiences, in a lack of socialisation during the developmental period known as imprinting, or in the presence of other environmental stressors. It can be observed in those dogs that feel threatened or are cornered and consequently, as a self-defence mechanism, resort to reacting aggressively to protect themselves. Essentially, the display of fear-based aggression is used to communicate that the dog does not want to engage in any sort of interaction with whatever stimulus is triggering the behaviour (a human or another animal) and that it can only feel safe if a certain distance is kept at all times. If the message is ignored and the distance is not created, a dog might feel trapped and the behaviour might escalate to aggression. Some dogs may inherit a more nervous or reactive temperament, making them more prone to fear-based responses, but in the majority of cases this type of aggression is largely influenced by human management, past experiences, and environmental restrictions.

If we compare our dogs to their counterparts living in the wild, the latter have a wider range of coping mechanisms for dealing with fear, significantly reducing the need for aggression. Firstly, unlike our domesticated dogs that are often confined by leashes, fences, or human-controlled spaces, wild canines have the option to flee from perceived threats rather than being forced into confrontation; we have all heard of the flight-or-fight theory. Wild canines are also naturally cautious by nature and will prefer to avoid rather than confront a perceived dangerous stimulus whenever possible. The other big difference is that whilst wild canids grow-up adapting to the huge variety of stimuli they find in the natural environment, making them less prone to fear-driven reactions, domesticated dogs are often exposed to other unnatural human-made stimuli and can be easily startled by everyday noises or unfamiliar objects if they have not been exposed to them during the imprinting phase of their development. That is why it is of the utmost importance to gradually expose our young puppies to every possible scenario they are likely to encounter later in life as fully grown adults, and this particularly applies to those pets living in big cities. Finally, a crucial yet unfortunate factor to consider when analysing this issue is the significant role of human intervention in causing fear-based aggression. Abuse, neglect, harsh training methods, unpredictable or inconsistent handling, and even a single traumatic event, such as a slap or scold given to a puppy, can all leave a negative and lasting impact on the dog's personality and their ability to cope with what they perceive as challenging situations. These adverse experiences can shape a dog's perception of the human species and the world in general, reinforcing fear-driven responses that ultimately will manifest as aggression.

The behavioural therapy and treatment of this type of aggression should focus on addressing the root cause rather than just the symptoms. It requires an enormous amount of patience, consistency, and a carefully structured treatment plan and approach that focuses primarily on rebuilding the dog's confidence with the objective of transforming their emotional response to the perceived threats. As I explained previously, in a reactive dog, the use of training, desensitisation, counter-conditioning, and positive reinforcement are always preferable to other aversive and punishment-based techniques. When dealing with a fearful dog, punitive measures, such as scolding or applying physical correction through heavy-handling, the use of pinch, or a shock collar are never the solution and should be excluded altogether in any treatment plan. Indeed, the use of punitive techniques can actually have the opposite effect and contribute to an increase in fear and anxiety; it may even inhibit the dog's behaviour in your presence and teach them not to exhibit warning signals, so that the dog then bites without warning in the future. For instance, if you punish or reprimand your dog for growling or barking at another pet during an encounter, perhaps because you feel embarrassed, you risk suppressing an essential form of communication. Growling is a warning, a way for dogs to express discomfort or stress. If you teach your dog that growling leads to punishment, they may stop giving warnings altogether and go straight to a bite when they feel threatened. The correct approach to effectively rehabilitate a fearful and aggressive dog follows the same principles I described earlier.

I have already mentioned training as being one of the crucial elements of the rehabilitation process, as it strengthens the bond between dog and owner, fostering trust and clear communication regardless of the circumstances. A well-structured training routine reinforces the owner's role as a calm, confident leader, providing the dog with a sense of security and consequently reducing reactive behaviours. Moreover, by conducting it in a familiar and controlled environment, training allows the dog to learn in a balanced, stress-free state of mind, rather than reacting to perceived threats, such as an unfamiliar dog on the street, with fear or aggression. Through positive reinforcement and structured exercises, the dog develops impulse control, confidence, and the ability to follow the handler's directions. Moreover, in potentially reactive situations, the dog should not be allowed to take the initiative and consequently make decisions on its own, simply because it will follow its inherent instincts which do not always go hand in hand with the behavioural etiquettes and norms dictated by our society. Without clear guidance, the dog may resort to using the inherited fight-or-flight behaviour, which can have undesirable consequences. Effective training means that rather than reacting out of fear or uncertainty, the dog learns to look to its owner for direction, fostering a calmer and more controlled response. To make it easier to understand and apply the correct methodology, I will now break it down into several clear and practical steps.

Identify and Manage the Triggers

First and foremost, before taking any action it is essential to observe and identify what triggers the behaviour and determine when and why the dog becomes aggressive. An extremely valuable tool in this process is video recording, which allows for the creation of an ethogram which, as described earlier, is a detailed behavioural analysis documenting the dog's actions before, during, and after an aggressive episode. By reviewing the footage, we can closely examine the dog's body language and posture, including all those subtle cues that might slip through the visual-only observational process, such as ear and tail position, piloerection, lip licking, paw lifting, shaking, snarling, or other stress signals. The benefit of this in-depth examination is that it provides crucial insights into the dog's emotional state, and this will further illuminate the causes and how to tailor an effective training and rehabilitation plan. It also helps determine whether the dog is exhibiting true aggression or simply reactivity, as the two require different approaches to rehabilitation.

On this topic, aggression vs reactivity, I would like to refer to a case study I encountered during the rehabilitation of a client's Labrador retriever, which highlights the practical implications of research into interspecies emotional communication via chemo-signals. The dog in question had developed a habit of chasing joggers, but the owner noted a particularly unusual pattern: the dog did not react to all joggers, only to some. This inconsistency prompted me to recall the study by Dr. Biagio D'Aniello on "Interspecies Emotion Transfer via Chemo-signals" (2018), which demonstrated that dogs can detect and respond to human emotional states, such as fear or happiness, through scent alone. In the study, dogs exposed to sweat samples collected from humans experiencing fear (watching a scary movie) displayed increased stress behaviours and elevated heart rates, suggesting they were not only detecting fear-related chemo-signals, but were also emotionally influenced by them. Conversely, dogs exposed to sweat samples collected from humans experiencing happiness were much more relaxed and willing to interact. In fact, the heart rate data in the control and happy conditions were significantly lower than in the fear condition. The findings of this study ultimately suggest that interspecies emotional communication is facilitated by chemo-signals.

Applying this insight to the case, I hypothesised that the Labrador may have been reacting specifically to joggers who were themselves fearful at the sight of the dog. Fear-induced chemo-signals, likely emitted unconsciously by these individuals, could have triggered a defensive or reactive response in the dog. This would explain why the chasing behaviour appeared selective rather than indiscriminate.

This case underlines the importance of considering not just the dog's behaviour, but also the emotional states of the humans they interact with, even at a distance. Our little Chihuahua, for example, can smell the presence of his human and dog friends from hundreds of metres away (depending also on the wind direction) and enthusiastically runs ahead to meet them. D'Aniello's study thus reinforces the idea that effective behaviour modification, particularly in cases of reactivity or aggression, must take into account the subtle cues dogs pick up from their environment, including those we may not be consciously aware of.

Once we have established a clear picture of the situation and know with certainty what actually triggers the dog's aggressive behaviour, we can gradually commence exposing the dog to that particular trigger, but we do that from a safe distance to start with, to ensure the trigger remains well below the dog's reactivity threshold. After a period of initial controlled exposure, we can enter the second stage of the rehabilitation process which consists of using desensitisation and counter-conditioning techniques to reverse the dog's state of mind at the sight of the trigger, shifting it from fear and anxiety to a state of neutrality or even positive association. It is important at this stage to avoid all those overwhelming situations that might contribute to reinforcing the state of fear in the dog's mind. Gradual exposure, at a pace the dog can handle, enables progress to be made without triggering setbacks or increasing the dog's level of stress. In the aforementioned case of the jogger-chasing Labrador, we developed a targeted rehabilitation plan that incorporated both counter-conditioning and controlled exposure. Understanding that the dog may have been reacting specifically to joggers emitting fear-related chemo-signals, our goal was to change the emotional association the dog had with joggers in general, especially those who moved quickly and displayed subtle signs of tension or unease. To do this, we enlisted the help of several dog-loving volunteers who were comfortable around dogs and willing to take part in structured training sessions. These individuals would jog past the dog at a manageable distance, then gradually begin to stop and offer high-value treats to the Labrador, always using calm, non-threatening body language.

Over time, the dog began to associate joggers with positive outcomes rather than potential threat or arousal. The reactive behaviour decreased significantly as the dog's emotional response shifted from suspicion or excitement to relaxed anticipation in expectation of the tasty treats. This case not only demonstrates the practical application of research into interspecies emotional transfer, but also the power of desensitisation paired with positive reinforcement. By creating a safe and positive encounters with joggers, we holistically helped the dog reframe a previously triggering context without the need for punishment or avoidance.

Desensitisation and Counter-conditioning

As I explained previously, desensitisation is the gradual and systematic process whereby a dog is exposed to the trigger at a controlled intensity until it no longer provokes an emotional response. In my opinion, this is a highly effective and humane behaviour modification technique, especially when compared to other methods like flooding, which is very much like throwing a child into a pool to teach them to swim. Flooding forces the dog into an overwhelming exposure to triggering stimuli, and most of the time this technique often increases the fear and stress towards the trigger. By contrast, desensitisation allows the dog to build confidence at its own pace, leading to more lasting and positive behavioural changes. The intensity of the stimulus can be managed and controlled in different ways depending on the nature of the stimulus. The first step is to manage the distance from the trigger, beginning from far away and gradually getting closer and closer.

If a dog is afraid of loud noises such as fireworks, a gradual desensitisation process can help them learn to cope. By slowly increasing the volume of pre-recorded sounds of fireworks, played through home speakers (going from low to high), the dog can become accustomed to the noise in a controlled and non-threatening environment. Over time, this method enables the dog to build resilience, reducing the fear and anxiety normally associated with all other loud sounds, like the back-firing noise of a vehicle. If the stimulus is a moving object (such as a scooter or a bicycle), you will need to adjust the speed at which it moves, gradually working from slow to fast.

Counter-conditioning, on the other hand, is a behavioural modification method in which the trigger that creates the negative emotional response is paired with something known and favourable in order to create an opposite and more positive emotional response in the dog. We can use whatever form of reward is the most positive in your dog's mind: tasty food treats are commonly used to create a positive emotional state in greedy breeds like Labradors and Golden retrievers, or, if your dog is particularly playful and likes to work for fun, toys and games can be used to create a positive emotional response.

For instance, if your dog is frightened when a motorcycle passes by (the motorcycle being the trigger that provokes the negative emotional response), you can gradually change the dog's emotional response by associating the trigger with something positive. Starting with approaching a stationary motorcycle and giving your dog a very tasty treat and further progressing by delivering the treat when the engine is fired up until he remains neutral each time a motorcycle passes by. You will also find it extremely helpful to ask your dog to perform an alternative behaviour like sitting or lying down while delivering the tasty treats. I could mention countless examples where I have successfully used these techniques to modify a dog's emotional state of mind, regardless of the stimulus. Nevertheless, I find that a more effective strategy is to combine desensitisation with counter-conditioning because the use of either desensitisation or counter-conditioning alone is often not sufficient for an effective and long lasting result. In fact, by pairing the two techniques, I feel

I can better control the intensity of the dog's reaction to the trigger with a more careful exposure to ensure the subject is not frightened, while at the same time making the exposure a much more pleasant experience by adding the counter-conditioning technique. In my experience, this holistic approach is far more effective in reshaping the dog's emotional responses and, furthermore, promotes long-term behavioural change.

Small Dog Syndrome

Because we are examining reactivity and aggression in our domesticated dogs, a notable phenomenon worth discussing is the so-called "Small Dog Syndrome". The common belief is that this behaviour arises primarily from how small dogs are treated by their human caregivers rather than being an inherent trait of small breeds. However, I would argue that the root cause of the issue runs much deeper than we might think in the dog's psyche and is directly related to the evolutionary process of the canine species under the influence of human selection. Domestication was not simply about taming wild animals but also about selectively breeding them for specific traits, whether for hunting, herding, guarding, and later merely for companionship. During this process, whilst certain instincts, such as the prey drive and social hierarchy, remained largely unchanged, human intervention has drastically altered one crucial factor: the dog's size. Whilst a dog's natural instincts, such as prey drive, social rituals, play, and other interactions, remain largely intact, the extreme size variations introduced through domestication and selective breeding have significantly impacted how exceptionally small or large dogs perceive and interact with their canine counterparts.

Unlike their wild relatives of the Canidae species such as wolves, foxes, coyotes, and jackals, which maintain a relatively consistent range of sizes, domesticated dogs now exist at opposite extremes, from tiny toy breeds like Chihuahuas and Pomeranians to giant breeds like the San Bernard, Irish Wolfhound, or the Great Dane. We can imagine how this size disparity can have profound repercussions on the behaviour of the smaller breeds. A small dog, when faced with a much larger animal, may instinctively compensate through heightened vigilance, defensive aggression, or assertive posturing; behaviours often mistaken for stubbornness or overconfidence.

To put this into perspective, imagine lying on the ground and looking up at a Labrador or golden retriever. I am sure that from that vantage point, they would certainly appear enormous to you too. Now, consider how small dogs like the Chihuahua or Pomeranian perceive a German shepherd or a Great Dane. Their world is often dominated by towering figures, which naturally influences their reactions. The same happens in the human species. Although some of us are generally accustomed to height differences, others may still experience a sense of awe or intimidation when standing next to an exceptionally tall person, such as a basketball player for instance. In the same way, small dogs live in a world where everything is oversized, and their behaviour reflects this reality. Understanding this context allows us to see Small Dog Syndrome not simply as the result of indulgent human behaviour but as a complex interplay between instinct, perception, and the artificial size variations introduced through selective breeding. These artificially created extremes influence a dog's confidence, social approach, and overall perception of the world, shaping their interactions with both humans and other dogs.

Build Confidence Through Positive Reinforcement

The next step in the treatment of fear-based aggression is to use the positive reinforcement technique so that the dog will associate previously fearful situations with positive experiences. This approach enables the dog to gradually reshape their emotional response to a particular trigger so that they exhibit a more positive demeanour. Positive reinforcement techniques can be used effectively to reward calm behaviour when the dog encounters a trigger, and again to reward the dog after performing an alternative behaviour, such as "Watch Me" (eye contact) or walking in a heel position to redirect the focus away from the trigger. It is crucial to avoid punishing fear-based aggression, even though the instinctive reaction, often driven by embarrassment or the fear of being judged by other dog owners, may be to correct the behaviour harshly. Punishment only heightens the dog's anxiety, reinforcing their fear and ultimately exacerbating the issue rather than resolving it. Instead, a calm, patient, and positive approach is essential to building confidence and reducing reactivity over time.

Establish Consistent Leadership and a Predictable Routine

As discussed in previous chapters, creating a structured environment with clear leadership based on trust and fairness and a predictable daily routine is fundamental in helping a fearful dog feel secure. Dogs thrive on consistency, and when they understand what to expect each day, they experience less stress and uncertainty. Simple routines such as regular feeding times, designated walk schedules, and consistent training sessions can provide the stability they need to feel safe. A dog that perceives its owner as a calm and confident leader is less likely to feel the need to take control of situations through reactive behaviour. Leadership, in the holistic sense, does not mean dominance but rather offering guidance and reassurance. When a dog knows that its owner is in control, it can relax instead of feeling it must handle every encounter on its own. For example, if an owner remains composed during a stressful situation, such as an encounter with another dog or a stranger, the fearful dog is more likely to follow suit. It is also important to bear in mind that our domesticated dogs are highly sensitive to human emotions and body language. If an owner reacts with tension, frustration, or fear, the dog will likely mirror these emotions, reinforcing anxious behaviour. Thus, maintaining a calm and relaxed demeanour is essential. If a dog senses that its owner is unfazed by a situation, it will gradually learn that there is no real threat and begin to adjust its own response accordingly.

Engaging in structured activities throughout the day is an excellent way to help a fearful dog build confidence and redirect its focus in a productive manner. Depending on the breed, some effective confidence-boosting activities may include Obedience Training, which consists of teaching basic commands (such as "Sit", "Stay", and "Heel"). These activities not only improve behaviour but also reinforce the dog's trust in its owner. It helps the dog understand that looking to its handler for direction is always rewarding and beneficial. Additionally, the more time a dog spends engaged in purposeful training, the less opportunity they have to enter states of heightened arousal or overstimulation. Regular training provides both mental structure and emotional balance, which are essential for building confidence, especially in dogs that are anxious, insecure, or overly excitable.

Scent Work: some highly energetic working breeds (Jack Russell, cocker spaniels, Labrador retrievers, etc), who possess a naturally elevated physical and mental activity level, require increased stimulation, structure, and outlets for movement and engagement. For those breeds, scent work exercises allow them to use their natural foraging instincts, enabling them to build confidence by accomplishing tasks on their own terms. This is particularly helpful for fearful dogs, as it provides mental stimulation without direct confrontation with triggers.

Agility Training: introducing agility exercises, even at a basic level, encourages dogs to problem-solve, follow cues, and build self-assurance through physical challenges. Successfully completing obstacles allows fearful dogs to gain confidence in their abilities and surroundings. By combining structured leadership, emotional control, and engaging confidence-building activities, fearful dogs can gradually overcome their anxieties and develop a more balanced and calm state of mind.

Use Proper Handling Techniques

One common mistake I frequently observe is the improper use of collars and leashes. Owners often unknowingly create excessive tension by wrapping the leash around their hands, which not only restricts movement but also increases the risk of injury for both the handler and the dog. This practice is particularly dangerous when dealing with large or strong dogs, as a sudden pull can easily cause a loss of balance or even a fall. Moreover, constant leash tension can heighten a dog's stress levels and make them feel trapped, which may escalate reactive behaviour. Instead of keeping the leash tight, it is better to maintain a relaxed grip and allow for some slack, enabling the dog to move more naturally and confidently. A properly fitted collar should be snug enough to stay in place but loose enough to allow two fingers to slip comfortably between the collar and the dog's neck. This guarantees security without restricting movement or causing discomfort. Pinch collars and metal prong collars, while sometimes still used for training purposes by old-fashioned dog trainers, are generally inadvisable as they can cause pain, physical injuries, and even psychological distress. Repeated pressure from these devices can lead to soft tissue damage, skin irritation, and increased anxiety or fear-based aggression.

For better control without causing discomfort, consider using well-fitted management tools such as a Front-Clip Harness which has a chest connector loop that gently redirects the dog's movement without putting pressure on the neck, making it a great option for dogs that tend to pull. Alternatively, the Head Halter is designed to guide the dog's head in the desired direction, providing additional control while minimising strain on the owner's hands and arms. As you can see, selecting the right equipment and handling the leash properly can make a significant difference in reducing stress and improving the overall walking experience for both dog and owner. A word of advice on remote-controlled correction devices like electric collars, vibrating collars, citronella spray collars, and compressed air "burst" cans – which are sometimes marketed as quick fixes for the correction of unwanted behaviours – these devices can be risky for the average dog owner to use without professional supervision. If the correction is given at the wrong time or used too frequently, it can confuse or frighten the dog, making the problem worse and often doing more harm than good. In some cases, these tools can create fear, anxiety, or even aggression, especially if the dog does not understand why it is being corrected.

Another issue I find recurs often is dependency. In the long term, the over reliance on these devices give some owners a false sense of control as they find that their dog only listens when they are wearing the equipment. This undermines the goal of building trust, communication, and voluntary compliance, with no lasting behavioural change. Whilst such tools may have a place in professional hands, particularly when applying operant conditioning principles (e.g. the removal or addition of a stimulus to reduce unwanted behaviour), they must be used with clear protocols, timing precision, and a deep understanding of canine behaviour. Without proper technique and context, these devices risk masking symptoms rather than resolving the root cause of the behaviour.

For most pet owners, the safest and most effective approach involves positive reinforcement, clear communication, and building trust with the dog. If you are facing a persistent behavioural issue, consult a qualified trainer before considering any form of aversive device.

Case Study: When the Tool Becomes the Problem

A client once contacted me for help with her adolescent border collie named Max, who had developed a habit of bolting towards other dogs while off-lead at the park. Frustrated and overwhelmed, she had resorted to using a remote-controlled vibrating collar she purchased online. The idea was to use the vibration as a warning signal to stop Max mid-run. Unfortunately, without a clear training plan or guidance on timing, Max began to associate the vibration with the presence of other dogs, rather than his own behaviour. Over time, he grew anxious and tense whenever he saw another dog, even if he was on the lead and not misbehaving. His reactivity escalated, and he started barking and lunging, behaviours he had not previously displayed. By the time I was called in, Max had already lost all his confidence and had become wary not only of other dogs but also of his owner's cues. We patiently worked together to phase out the use of the device and instead implemented a counter-conditioning protocol: Max learnt that the appearance of other dogs only predicted good things, like tasty treats, positive interaction with the owner, or fun and playtime, with no aversion involved. Within a few weeks, Max's anxiety decreased and his focus on the owner improved dramatically.

By contrast, I once worked on a case involving a highly-driven German shepherd who had developed a deeply ingrained habit of chasing towards cars, joggers, even cyclists. The dog had been through multiple trainers in the USA and was at risk of being re-homed as the situation had become too stressful for the owners to handle. After extensive foundational work using positive reinforcement, structured obedience training, and impulse control games, the owners still found it difficult to get rid of the remote collar (the dependency effect I mentioned previously), and so I agreed to work with the device, but only under strict conditions. The goal was not punishment, it was simply used at the lowest perceptible level to interrupt fixation and refocus the dog on us before the chase began (remember the 8 stages of the Prey Drive Instinct?). Every correction was immediately followed by a reinforced alternative behaviour (like eye contact or a recall) and the dog's body language was monitored carefully throughout.

Because I had a deep understanding of timing, threshold, and the dog's emotional states, the use of the collar never caused distress. Over time, the dog began to respond to verbal cues alone, and the collar was phased out entirely. These contrasting cases illustrate a vital point: the effectiveness of any tool lies not in the tool itself, but in the skill, timing, and empathy of the handler. Whilst remote devices can serve a purpose in rare cases, they are never a substitute for a well-structured training plan based on trust, communication, and understanding.

Address Underlying Medical Issues

Last but not least, fear-based aggression can sometimes stem from underlying medical conditions such as chronic pain, thyroid imbalances, or neurological disorders. Because dogs cannot verbally express discomfort, their distress often manifests through changes in behaviour, including increased reactivity or aggression. Given that pain and illness can have a profound impact on a dog's emotional state, a thorough veterinary examination is crucial to rule out any medical issues before implementing a behavioural training plan.

In severe cases where anxiety is extreme and significantly hinders progress, a veterinarian or veterinary behaviourist may recommend short-term medication to help manage stress levels. When combined with structured training and behaviour modification, anxiety-reducing medications can enhance the dog's ability to learn and form positive associations. However, medication should always be viewed as a temporary aid rather than a primary solution, with the ultimate goal being to equip the dog with coping strategies that promote long-term emotional stability.

I truly believe that with the right holistic approach, fear-based aggression can be successfully managed and improved. The key is to build trust, provide positive experiences, and guide the dog towards feeling safe in different environments. By addressing the root cause rather than just the symptoms, owners can allow their dogs to develop confidence and self-control, leading to a calmer, more balanced pet.

Territorial Aggression

For our domesticated dogs, the display of territorial aggression and reactivity to protect other members of the pack are often a natural and instinctive part of their behavioural repertoire. These behaviours, such as barking at strangers or patrolling the perimeter of the home, are rooted in their evolutionary history as protectors of their pack and environment. Whilst any dog may exhibit reactivity and territorial aggression tendencies, certain breeds have been specifically developed and selected for their guarding and watchful traits, making them more predisposed to such responses. Breeds like German Shepherds, Rottweilers, Dobermans, and Mastiffs, for example, were traditionally used for guarding properties, herding, or personal protection. As a result of this process of selection occurring over a period of centuries, these dogs may be naturally inclined to be more vigilant and reactive to unfamiliar people approaching their human companions, or animals entering what they perceive as their territory or domain. However, if they are not properly managed through consistent training and, more importantly, early socialisation and exposure in modern domestic settings, these natural instincts can escalate into a full display of aggression that can be extremely problematic and difficult to eradicate. Left unchecked, territorial aggression can not only strain the relationship between the dogs and their human companions, but can also pose challenges within broader society and their relationships with other dogs. As is often the case in these situations, it is crucial to distinguish between an appropriate territorial alert, such as barking briefly when someone approaches the home, and an excessive, inappropriate aggressive response. Recognising this difference is essential for addressing the behaviour ethically, effectively, and working toward its permanent eradication from the dog's behavioural repertoire.

There are several effective tools available for addressing territorial aggression in dogs. Among the most impactful, I recommend implementing consistent training routines, early socialisation and exposure, and behavioural modification techniques such as desensitisation and counter-conditioning.

In my opinion, dog training is one of the most powerful tools for managing territorial aggression in dogs, as it serves to reshape the dog's understanding of its environment, contributes to reducing anxiety, and reinforces the use of alternative and non-aggressive behaviours. Dog training lays the foundation for communication, structure, and impulse control, allowing the dog to understand what is expected in various situations. Let me explain how and why it works and, more specifically, how to put into practice some training techniques:

Training Builds Predictability and Structure

Dogs thrive on routine and structure – they are creatures of habit who feel safest when their environment is predictable. Much like clockwork, they find comfort in knowing when they will be fed, walked, or engaged. Consistent training establishes a clear set of rules and boundaries upon which the dog learns to rely. When a dog knows what to expect and how to behave in various situations, it feels less compelled to take control of the environment through territorial displays.

Training Replaces Reactive Behaviour with Controlled Responses

As discussed previously, aggression often stems from the dog's instinctive reaction to a perceived threat. Because this response is deeply rooted in their natural behavioural repertoire, shaped by both evolution and selective breeding, it can be extremely challenging to eliminate. Rather than attempting to suppress this behaviour altogether, I often encourage dog owners to redirect it through structured, learned cues, such as teaching commands like "Speak and "Quiet". It is vital to recognise that asking our dogs not to behave in ways we have historically bred them to behave, such as guarding, is both unrealistic and unfair. Instead, I prefer to acknowledge and be grateful for them using their instinct by reinforcing it in a controlled way. For instance, I praise a dog for alerting me to something unusual with a few barks and then gently cue them to settle with "Quiet" or "Shush". Holistically speaking, I think that this method not only respects the dog's nature but also builds trust and communication, reinforcing that the human is in control and appreciative of the dog's efforts without allowing the behaviour to escalate unnecessarily. Other highly useful cues I recommend are asking the dog to go to their "Place" when someone knocks at the door, staying calm and sitting instead of barking or lunging at the postman or the delivery man, and making eye contact for guidance. Over time, the dog will understand that calm behaviour is more rewarding than aggression.

Training Reinforces the Owner's Role as Leader

A dog displaying territorial aggression is often unsure whether it needs to "take charge" of a situation. Training plays a crucial role in helping the dog understand that leadership and decision-making are the owner's sole responsibility. When a dog learns to trust and defer to the owner's consistent guidance, the pressure to defend or control territory is significantly reduced and they do not feel the same pressure to guard or control space.

In many cases, owners unknowingly place their dog in a leadership role, whether through a lack of experience, distraction, or inconsistency in maintaining boundaries and expectations. However, being a leader is a demanding role that requires vigilance, confidence, and constant decision-making. For a dog, this can be a source of stress and most dogs are actually relieved to relinquish that responsibility once they recognise their owner as a capable and dependable leader. This shift not only strengthens the human-dog bond but also promotes a calmer and more secure state of mind for the dog. After all, in the canine world, leadership is about the well-being and preservation of the pack – dogs work for the good of the group. If that role is not filled, the dog will instinctively step up, because they think someone has to. But when they see that you are calm, controlled, and in charge, they can finally just be dogs.

Training Helps Reduce Anxiety

The aggressive behaviours we see in our domesticated dogs often come from underlying fear or insecurity, especially around things or situations they were not properly exposed to during the imprinting phase of their development. This early window is crucial for shaping how they respond to the world later on.

The good news is that regular training sessions, especially when based on positive reinforcement, can turn things around by facilitating the processes of desensitisation and counter-conditioning. By creating positive emotional associations with potentially triggering situations, such as a stranger approaching the house or the sound of the doorbell, we enable the dog to feel more confident and less reactive. Over time, they start to see those once-scary things as no big deal.

Let's put all of this into practice with a real-life example. Imagine a dog that barks and lunges every time a delivery driver comes to the door. This is a common scenario most dog owners are all too familiar with, and is triggered by a mix of territorial instinct, excitement, and maybe even a bit of fear. Instead of trying to suppress the barking entirely, we can channel it into something more structured and manageable. The first step is to teach the dog a "Speak" command, giving them permission to bark when prompted. Once they have mastered that, we introduce a "Quiet" or "Shush" command so that they learn when it is time to stop. This gives the dog clear guidance and helps shift the behaviour from reactive to responsive.

Next, we train the dog to go to a specific "Place" like a mat placed a few metres away from the door. Each time the doorbell rings, we guide the dog to the mat and reward them with treats and praise for staying calm. Over time, they start to associate the sound of the bell not with chaos, but with a chance to earn rewards for maintaining a relaxed behaviour.

To take this a step further, we can add some counter-conditioning. When the delivery person appears, we continue to praise and reward the dog for staying calm. If the delivery person is willing, they can even toss the dog a treat (safely, of course). This helps transform the emotional response from "Stranger danger!" to "Hey, this person brings snacks!" With repetition and consistency, the dog learns a whole new routine, one that replaces anxiety and aggression with calm anticipation and positive outcomes.

If rules or training are applied sporadically or inconsistently, the dog becomes confused and unsure about what is expected. In the long run, this uncertainty fuels the dog's reactivity, reinforcing the very territorial behaviour you are trying to extinguish. Conversely, training creates clarity, reinforces trust, and equips the dog with better alternatives to aggressive behaviour. It is not solely about obedience, it is about creating emotional stability and a shared language between dog and human.

Possessive Aggression

Also known as resource guarding, possessive aggression occurs when a dog reacts defensively, growling, snapping, or even biting to protect something they consider valuable. This could be food, toys, a favourite resting spot, or even a person. Whilst at first glance it may seem like stubbornness or dominance, this behaviour often stems from insecurity, fear of losing access to a resource, or past experiences where the dog had to compete for essentials like food or comfort. Signs of resource guarding can range from subtle body language displays like freezing, stiffening, and giving a hard stare to more obvious displays such as growling, lunging, and even biting. Understanding these signals early on, perhaps through the use of an ethogram or videos, is crucial to prevent further escalation.

Although ethologists view possessive aggressive behaviour as a natural and even necessary behaviour for survival in the wild, in a domestic environment it is considered problematic, especially when directed towards people or other pets. In a natural context, dogs instinctively protect what they perceive as valuable, but in our modern household setting, this behaviour can lead to conflict, stress, and even injury if not properly addressed. I have witnessed firsthand how unexpected and intense possessive aggression can be. One particularly memorable case involved a little dachshund who became fiercely protective of an old-style telephone receiver that sat on a side table next to the sofa. It sounds amusing at first; after all, a dog guarding a telephone is not something you hear about every day, but I can assure you that the situation was anything but light-hearted. In fact, whenever the lady of the house sat on the sofa, the dog would lie beside her, keeping a close eye on the receiver. If her husband tried to approach the phone, the dachshund would immediately lunge and growl, sometimes even attempting to bite. The attachment was not really about the telephone itself, it was about the proximity to his favourite person and the perceived threat of someone else invading that shared space or indeed "resource".

I find that this kind of possessive behaviour can be confusing for some pet owners, especially when the object in question seems random or insignificant. But for the dog, it represents something highly valuable, whether it is access to a person, a space, or simply a familiar item that brings comfort or status. These scenarios highlight just how nuanced and emotionally charged resource guarding can be for dogs, who are still driven by their inherited instincts. This is why it is so important to approach each case with a holistic perspective in order to understand first how the behaviour originated and then plan a consistent training regimen using proper behaviour modification techniques. My advice, however, is to prevent rather than cure. Possessive aggression, resource guarding, and other behavioural issues can be avoided altogether or mitigated by starting earlier in the developmental stages when the dog is still a puppy. Teaching young dogs that human interaction around their food, toys, or other valued items leads to positive experiences is crucial to fostering trust and reducing the likelihood of aggressive guarding later on. Every dog is different, and although a puppy or young dog may have never shown any signs of reactivity around food, toys, or other resources, it is still essential to assess their tolerance, especially in households with young children. Puppies can be unpredictable as they grow and develop, and behaviours can shift over time depending on experiences, maturity, and environment. For that reason, I always recommend gently testing a puppy's comfort level around food and valued items in a calm, measured manner. This allows pet owners to identify any early signs of possessiveness and address them through positive reinforcement before they escalate and become problematic.

From experience, I find that this becomes even more important in homes with children. Kids are naturally curious and may not understand boundaries, making it vital to ensure that the puppy is comfortable with gentle handling during meals and play. Just as importantly, children should also be taught how to respectfully interact with the dog, especially when it is eating, chewing, or playing with a favourite toy. Let us take as an example a case scenario when a puppy is eating; you can start testing by calmly approaching the puppy while speaking softly and gently petting them. Try occasionally dropping high-value treats into their bowl, something even more desirable than what they are eating. This approach creates a positive association with your presence near their food.

Once the puppy becomes comfortable with this, you can gradually build up to gently restraining them and briefly removing the bowl. Immediately praise them and return the bowl, reinforcing the idea that they do not need to fear losing their resources. This teaches them that human involvement does not equal loss, it means having more good things. A similar approach can be used with toys. While your puppy is chewing or playing, approach them calmly and offer a treat in exchange for the toy. Then return the toy after a few seconds. Practising this regularly teaches the puppy that surrendering an object does not mean they lose it forever, and that good things come from cooperation. Training plays a crucial role in preventing resource guarding, particularly when it starts early in a dog's life. Teaching a puppy or young dog to sit and wait calmly before accessing food, toys, or other valued items is an effective way to build impulse control and reinforces the idea that the human controls the resources, not the dog. This not only prevents the development of possessive behaviours but also establishes a healthy structure in the dog's routine. When a dog learns that calm behaviour and patience result in access to what they want, it naturally reduces anxiety and the urge to guard. Over time, with consistency and the use of positive reinforcement, these simple exercises, such as waiting for a release cue before eating or calmly giving up a toy when asked, can create a dog that feels secure, trusts their owner, and does not feel the need to defend their possessions.

If you have missed the opportunity to prepare a puppy or young dog in these crucial early stages, or have adopted a rescue dog and are unsure how they will respond in situations involving resources, do not worry, there is still plenty you can do. Whilst early intervention is ideal, resource guarding can still be effectively managed and improved at any stage of a dog's life with the right holistic approach. By implementing a structured behaviour modification plan, which includes a consistent training regime, desensitisation, counter-conditioning, and most importantly clear communication, you can help your dog feel safe and secure around valued items. The key is to work at the dog's pace, avoid triggering defensive responses, and use training and positive reinforcement to build new associations with people approaching their food, toys, or resting spots.

For the successful treatment and long-term resolution of resource guarding, the first step is to teach your dog to accept your approach and give up any objects on command. The goal is to help the dog understand that relinquishing possession of an object will result in an even more appealing reward, one that outweighs the value of the item they are guarding. Before diving into the treatment plan, it is important to note that training is critical. You must first establish control over your dog's behaviour and ensure they are well-trained in basic obedience commands. If your dog cannot reliably sit, stay, come when called, or allow you to approach calmly when not in possession of a valued item, the chances of successfully addressing possessive behaviour are significantly reduced. These foundational obedience skills are not just helpful, they are vital for creating a structured environment in which more advanced training can take place. Without them, it becomes extremely difficult to communicate expectations or redirect your dog's behaviour effectively. Therefore, if you feel your dog needs more time or support to strengthen these basic commands, I strongly recommend starting there. I can assure you that a solid foundation in obedience will make the process of resolving resource guarding much more manageable and far more successful in the long term.

The basic commands to reinforce when preparing to address resource guarding are "Come, "Sit", and "Stay". Detailed step-by-step instructions for teaching these foundational cues can be found in earlier chapters. Mastery of these commands creates a reliable communication system between you and your dog, which is crucial before progressing to more complex behaviour modification exercises. Additionally, it is essential to work on the speed at which you pace your own approach. Dogs usually become tense or reactive simply because their owners move too quickly or lean over them in a way that feels confrontational. Practising calm, confident, and non-threatening body language when approaching your dog, especially around food or toys, will create a sense of trust and reduce the likelihood of triggering possessive behaviour.

The next step consists of introducing commands specifically designed to address resource guarding: "Give" and "Drop It". At this stage you will need to start by practising with low-value objects that your dog is less likely to guard (e.g. an old toy or a less favourite chew bone). Encourage your dog to pick up the item, or gently place it and hold it in his mouth then give the "Give" or "Drop It" command while offering a more highly prized treat or toy in exchange. However, even if your pet learns to drop or give on cue, this will not prevent them from stealing, therefore it might also be possible to train your dog to "Leave" items and not pick them up again if you can effectively supervise this. The key here is to consistently reinforce the notion that relinquishing the object results in something better. Over time, you can begin to use higher-value objects, like their favourite toy or a rawhide, but only once the dog has mastered giving up the low-value items. You can then gradually increase the challenge, always rewarding the dog with treats that are more desirable than the object they are relinquishing. Always maintain a positive and playful environment throughout your training sessions. Your dog should feel safe, engaged, and happy. When the atmosphere is encouraging rather than stressful, learning becomes much more effective, and your bond will strengthen as a result. As mentioned before, the aim during these sessions is to create a strong association in your dog's mind: giving up possession equals something better. To facilitate this, you will need to be patient and consistent in your training. With each successful exchange, reinforce that you are the provider and that giving up an item to you will always result in a positive outcome.

Finally, the key to long-term success in treating these behavioural issues is maintaining consistency. Training does not end after the first few sessions; it requires ongoing practice and supervision. Incorporate the "Give" and "Drop It" exercises into daily routines, even in relation to other contexts and other objects. The more opportunities your dog has to practise giving up items for a higher-value reward, the more reliable this behaviour will become. Moreover, in the initial stages, it would be advisable to closely supervise your pet in order to prevent incidents of guarding. If your dog is left unsupervised and has access to valuable resources, they may fall back into their old habits. Above all, be patient; overcoming resource guarding is a gradual process. With time, your dog will learn that they do not need to protect their possessions, and that sharing and cooperating with you leads to better outcomes.

In more serious cases of possessive behaviour, the intervention procedure may need to be adjusted slightly to guarantee both safety and effectiveness. When a dog has already picked up or taken possession of what it considers to be a high-value object, it is critical that the owner avoids any direct confrontation. Instead, the first step is to calmly retrieve a highly valued food reward, something the dog finds especially enticing and very difficult to resist. From a safe distance of about five to six metres, the owner should then call the dog using a cheerful tone of voice, showing them the reward clearly to capture their attention. Hopefully at this point the dog will voluntarily drop the item in order to get the treat or, if the training has been effective, will do it on cue following the command "Give" or "Drop it". If that happens, the owner will need to move away from the item, and gently continue to back up while simultaneously issuing a second cue, such as "Come" followed by the command "Sit". This sequence is repeated two or three times, reinforcing the dog's decision to disengage with the object.

The key here is patience and timing. The food reward is not given immediately. Instead, it is withheld until the dog is at least five to eight metres away from the object, ideally lured into another room entirely if possible. Once the dog has reliably disengaged, is calmly sitting, and has been guided away, it can be praised, offered the reward, and gently held by the collar (only if this is already part of a positive and familiar handling routine). At that point, the dog should be calmly escorted to a separate space, either outside or into another room with the door closed. Only then should the owner return to retrieve the item. Crucially, during these first few stages, the exchange should never take place directly in front of the dog and the object they were guarding. Doing so risks reinforcing the idea that people approaching the object constitute a threat. If at any point during this process the dog exhibits signs of aggression, such as growling, lip lifting, snapping, lunging, or biting, the owner should immediately disengage and leave the area. Under no circumstances should they attempt to physically take the item from the dog as that would turn into a highly dangerous situation. Once the dog begins to voluntarily give up the object without confrontation, the owner can then move forward to the next critical phase: reinforcing the desired behaviour and maintaining consistency over time. This stage is essential as it ensures that the new, more appropriate response becomes the dog's default behaviour, ultimately leading to a long-term and sustainable solution.

Pain-Induced Aggression

Pain, discomfort, or undetectable injuries are one of the most overlooked yet powerful motivators of aggressive behaviour in dogs. Unlike humans, dogs cannot articulate when something hurts. As a result, they often rely on body language, avoidance behaviour and, in more serious cases, defensive aggression to communicate their discomfort. This type of aggression typically stems from a desire to protect themselves from further pain and should never be mistaken for bad behaviour or disobedience. It is not a sign of a bad temperament, but rather a clear communication from the dog to say: *"Please don't touch me, I hurt"*. What may look like "bad behaviour" could actually be a symptom of an underlying medical condition. Do not attempt to discipline or correct the dog in moments of pain-induced aggression. This could increase their fear and worsen the situation, potentially leading to more intense or frequent outbursts. Firstly, it is crucial to recognise some of the signs that may indicate something is not quite right or is uncharacteristic of a normally calm and friendly dog. Some of the signs to watch out for include:

Growling or snapping when touched in specific areas.

Avoidance behaviours (hiding, flinching, or cowering).

Changes in posture (stiff movements, limping, or difficulty lying down or getting up).

Sudden sensitivity during grooming or when putting on a collar or harness.

Guarding behaviour over a particular body part (e.g. licking or shielding it).

Dogs may also show less obvious signs such as reduced playfulness, a reluctance to jump or climb stairs, or a change in appetite or sleep patterns.

A review of several clinical cases involving dogs referred for aggression revealed that the most common underlying causes of pain in dogs were hip dysplasia, chronic otitis (ear infection), dental pain, neurological problems, skin injury, and osteoarthritis of the elbow. These findings highlight that orthopaedic issues, especially hip dysplasia, are among the most frequent sources of pain-induced aggression. Dogs suffering from joint degeneration often lash out, not out of dominance or fear but because movement and touch cause them significant pain. It is therefore crucial to determine whether sudden changes in a dog's behaviour may be linked to some sort of physical discomfort.

If your dog suddenly displays signs of aggression, especially if these are out of character or seem to be triggered by touch or movement, I strongly recommend scheduling a visit with your veterinarian as your first course of action. Pain-induced aggression can often go unnoticed because dogs are incredibly stoic and instinctively hide their discomfort. A thorough veterinary examination, including diagnostic tests such as X-rays, blood tests, or in-depth neurological assessments, can identify whether your dog is suffering from any of the illnesses mentioned above. Identifying and addressing the physical source of discomfort is essential before beginning any behavioural training or modification plan. It is literally impossible to train away discomfort and pain and trying to do so may make things worse. Only once medical issues have been ruled out or are being treated can a tailored behavioural intervention plan be safely and effectively put in place.

In my experience, addressing the underlying physical causes often leads to a complete or near-complete reversal of the aggressive behaviour. When the source of pain is removed, the dog no longer feels the need to defend itself, and their temperament often returns to normal without the need for extensive behavioural retraining. Nevertheless, depending on how long the behaviour has been present and whether it has become a conditioned response, some dogs may require a combination of pain management medications together with physical therapy, a change in their diet with the addition of supplements, even a gentle reintroduction to handling through a process of desensitisation. Unfortunately, in complex cases the intervention of a veterinary behaviourist is often required. As always, an holistic approach is best suited in these types of situations and compassion, consistency, and patience are key during the recovery process. I cannot stress enough the importance of avoiding sudden movements or situations that may startle the dog; instead, reinforce calm behaviour with positive rewards.

Frustration-Induced Aggression

Also called redirected aggression, this type of behaviour occurs when a dog becomes highly aroused due to excitement, frustration, or overstimulation, and is unable to reach the original target of that arousal. As a result, the dog turns and directs its aggressive response towards a different, often unintended, target nearby. A common example that I notice when passing by a property with my own dog involves two dogs running along a fence, barking at a me or other passersby. When they are unable to access the dog or person on the other side, the arousal may escalate to a point where the dogs turn on each other with growls and sometimes even start to fight. I can recall an instance of frustration-induced aggression from a case I worked on involving Archie and Freddy, two spirited young terriers living under the same roof. Whenever the doorbell rang, both dogs would bolt towards the front door in a frenzy, barking, growling, and jostling to be the first to greet the mysterious guest. The excitement and anticipation created such a high state of arousal that it often escalated into full-blown fights between the two, right there in the hallway.

This wasn't at all about dominance or dislike, it a case of was frustration boiling over. The inability to immediately access the stimulus (in this case, the visitor) created tension, and that tension had to go somewhere. Sadly, it was redirected onto each other. In order to manage the situation, we had to take some preventive measures. I recommended the use of crates or baby gates to physically separate them whenever a visitor was expected. This allowed them to calm down individually without feeding off each other's energy. In addition, I advised the owners to work on desensitisation to the sound of the doorbell and to introduce alternative behaviours, like going to their mats or sitting calmly on cue for example, paired with positive reinforcement. Over time, with consistency and a bit of management, Archie and Freddy were able to handle the once-chaotic doorbell scenario with much more composure. If you have more than one dog in the household and you notice rising tension in moments of excitement, such as when visitors arrive, food is being prepared, or play gets too intense, consider these as red flags. You ought to watch for early signs of frustration and step in with the appropriate management tools before escalation. Physical barriers, clear routines, and calm reinforcement of alternative behaviours can make all the difference. Prevention really is better (and safer) than cure when it comes to inter-dog conflict.

Another frequent scenario I often notice in the park is when two dogs are already engaged in a conflict and a human attempts to intervene. In a heightened state of arousal, one of the dogs may inadvertently redirect its aggression onto the person stepping in, often leading to injury. You might have been directly involved or witnessed situations where redirected aggression occurred during a regular walk. A dog on a lead may become overly stimulated, perhaps by another dog, a person, or animal, and if it is unable to approach or react to the source, it may turn around and nip at the handler holding the leash. It is vital to remember that redirected aggression always happens when the dog is in a heightened state of arousal. The longer the arousal persists, the more likely it is that redirection will occur. Moreover, redirection tends to occur more frequently in dogs that are naturally more intense, high-energy, or excitable by nature. These are the dogs that often seem to be "on alert", highly responsive to environmental stimuli, and extremely quick to react. Whilst this temperament is often appreciated and a sign of intelligence and enthusiasm, it also means that these dogs can escalate into a state of arousal more rapidly, and once there, are more likely to redirect their frustration or excitement onto a nearby person or animal. If you are the proud owner of breeds like Terriers, Border Collies, or Shepherds and are confronted with similar issues, you will need to ensure that your dog's physical, mental, and emotional needs are being consistently met.

One of the most effective ways to reduce the likelihood of redirected aggression is to make sure that the dog is provided with adequate daily exercise, consistent training, and meaningful environmental enrichment, as these go a long way towards helping them feel calm and fulfilled. A well-exercised, mentally stimulated dog is far less likely to leap into a reactive state simply because it has an outlet for that energy and arousal. Put simply, a tired dog is a content dog. When a dog is relaxed, satisfied, and confident in its environment, it is significantly less prone to the kind of over-arousal that leads to redirected aggression. The only practical advice I can give in this situation is simply that you will have work with your dog to change its emotional state and stop the behaviour from occurring.

Social Aggression

Social aggression in dogs is often considered a normal, species-typical behaviour. Its purpose is not rooted in malice, but rather in communication and conflict resolution within a hierarchically structured group. In a natural or semi-natural pack setting, social aggression helps establish and maintain order, set boundaries, and prevent constant confrontations by reinforcing roles and expectations among group members.

Rather than being purely negative or harmful, these displays, such as growling, snapping, or body blocking, are often mere ritualised forms of communication. They serve to solve disputes and reduce actual physical conflict. In fact, most canine social aggression occurs in brief episodes and is resolved quickly, helping to preserve the cohesion and functionality of the pack. As mentioned in previous chapters, escalation into physical confrontation or outright fighting is not only unnecessary in most cases, it is actually *counterproductive* and potentially damaging to the whole group. In the wild, an injured pack member becomes a liability. A limping or weakened dog cannot contribute effectively to hunting, defending territory, or helping raise the young. In short, they lower the pack's overall efficiency. That is why canine species have evolved intricate social cues and conflict-resolution behaviours to avoid real injury whenever possible. Their survival depends on cooperation and balance within the group. Canines work for the benefit of the whole pack, not for individual gain, unlike humans, I may add! That said, it is crucial to distinguish between the natural context in which dogs have honed their social skills over thousands of years of evolution and the human domestic context where these interactions are often misinterpreted. In the wild, dogs use these skills to maintain balance and order within the pack, resolving conflicts without escalating into full-blown violence. This hierarchy and the ability to navigate social tension is essential for the survival of the group. Yet, in a domestic environment, these same behaviours can easily be misunderstood by humans who may see them as signs of aggression or unfairness, particularly when dealing with a young puppy. What might be a normal social exchange in the canine world could seem harsh or frightening to us, especially when we are not aware of the nuances in their communication. This misunderstanding can lead to confusion, frustration, and unnecessary intervention, which may inadvertently disrupt the dog's natural development and learning process.

When humans bring a new puppy into a home where there is already an adult dog, the older dog (especially if a male) may initially display behaviours such as avoidance, growling, snarling, or even attacking the puppy. These actions are a natural way for the older dog to establish its social status and communicate boundaries to the newcomer. In the wild, these behaviours are essential for maintaining the structure and balance within the pack. The older dog is not necessarily being aggressive or malicious, it is simply asserting its place in the hierarchy. Nevertheless, humans often misunderstand this process and rush to protect the puppy by interrupting the older dog's actions. By doing so, they inadvertently confer on the puppy a status it has not earned. Repeatedly intervening can lead to further confusion, as the older dog may become more frustrated and the puppy might not learn important social cues. In some cases, this can escalate into a full-blown confrontation with severe consequences and even injuries. Instead of interfering, it is better to let the dogs work out their differences naturally while supervising them. This allows the older dog to establish its role and the puppy to learn proper behaviour. Of course, the interactions should never get violent or dangerous, but a certain level of discipline from the older dog is often necessary for long-term harmony. If things do escalate, the humans can step in to ensure safety, but it is important to let the dogs establish their own dynamic as much as possible. Although I have established that these behaviours may be functional in a canine social group, issues can arise when they are directed toward humans or when they occur in domestic environments where the human household has failed to establish clear rules, boundaries, or leadership. In such cases, what is "normal" in a canine context can become problematic in a human one, especially if it goes unchecked or is misinterpreted for a long period of time.

Another possible cause of intra-specific aggression in multi-dog households is castration. When a male dog is castrated, he loses the influence of the male hormone testosterone, which is the primary hormone responsible for most of the social behaviours we associate with male dogs, including, of course, dominant behaviours and sexual drive. This hormonal shift can alter the way the dog is perceived by other dogs in the household. In fact, without the scent of male testosterone, a neutered male dog might smell more similar to a female dog, which can be confusing to the other dog, especially if they have been used to the distinct scent of a male dog. In some cases, this can result in what appears to be sexual behaviours being misinterpreted as dominance challenges. For instance, a male dog might try to mount a neutered dog or become overly aggressive, confusing mating behaviours with dominance displays. In these situations, the dog that was castrated may also experience changes in its own behaviour, feeling less assertive or possibly more submissive, which could be misinterpreted by other dogs as a sign of weakness, leading to increased tension or aggression. Similarly, an un-castrated dog may respond with heightened aggression as a means of establishing or maintaining dominance over a dog that no longer exhibits traditional masculine traits.

In my experience, I find that the key to addressing this issue lies in understanding that these behaviours are often related to hormonal changes rather than natural aggression. It is essential to manage these social dynamics carefully and, if necessary, seek professional help from a dog behaviourist to ensure both dogs are comfortable and the pack's hierarchy remains balanced. Holistically speaking, understanding the role of social aggression from a dog's perspective allows us to approach the behaviour with more empathy and clarity. With proper training, structure, and clear communication from the humans involved, most socially motivated aggression can be managed or even prevented altogether. Intra-specific aggression can also occur outside the household when a dog becomes aggressive towards unfamiliar dogs. This type of aggression can be triggered by various factors and can manifest in different ways, from growling and barking to full-blown fights. Some of the common causes of this are as follows:

Past Negative Experiences

If a dog has had a traumatic experience with other dogs in the past, such as being attacked or bullied, it may develop fear-based aggression towards other dogs. The dog may perceive any dog it encounters as a potential threat, leading to defensive or aggressive behaviour. This type of aggression is often accompanied by signs of anxiety or fear like cowering, raised hackles, or a stiff body posture.

Lack of Socialisation

Dogs that have not been properly socialised during the critical period of puppyhood (usually between 3 and 14 weeks of age) are more likely to display aggression towards other dogs later in life. Puppies who miss out on positive experiences with other dogs during this time may grow up fearful, unsure, or overly reactive when meeting new dogs. Similarly, adult dogs who have not had positive interactions with dogs outside of their immediate circle may struggle to behave appropriately when meeting unfamiliar dogs, often resorting to aggression as a coping mechanism.

Predatory Instincts

Some breeds, particularly those with a strong prey drive, may exhibit aggressive behaviour towards other dogs due to their instinct to chase and capture prey. This can lead to frustration-based aggression, especially if the dog feels the need to chase the other dog but is unable to do so. Certain breeds, such as terriers and herding dogs, have stronger prey drives and may show aggressive tendencies if they feel triggered by fast-moving or smaller dogs.

Neutering and Hormonal Changes

Although neutering or spaying is typically a responsible decision for controlling the pet population and preventing certain health problems, it can sometimes have unintended behavioural effects. In some dogs, neutering can alter their hormonal balance, which can contribute to aggression. Male dogs, in particular, may experience changes in aggression towards other dogs, especially if they were neutered later in life. These hormonal changes can affect their ability to regulate their interactions with other dogs, potentially leading to heightened territorial behaviour or dominance displays.

Territorial Behaviour

Dogs are naturally territorial animals, and can become aggressive when they feel their territory is being invaded by unfamiliar dogs. Whether it is their home, a specific spot on a walk, or even the car, some dogs will defend what they perceive as "their" space. This territorial aggression can escalate when the dog perceives a threat from another dog, even if the other dog is just passing by or has no intention of starting a confrontation.

Resource Guarding

Similar to resource guarding in the household (with food, toys, or beds), dogs can also display resource guarding behaviours in public. For instance, if a dog feels it has something valuable (such as a favourite toy or an item it considers precious), it may become aggressive towards other dogs that approach it. This could happen when dogs are out on a walk and encounter another dog near a favourite spot, such as a park or a street corner.

As with other types of aggression, intra-specific aggression towards stranger dogs is a complex issue, but with patience, proper management, and training, most dogs can learn to coexist peacefully with others. The key is understanding the underlying causes, ensuring your dog is adequately socialised, and providing consistent training to manage and redirect aggressive behaviour. Resolving intra-specific aggression takes time. Each dog is different, and the process can vary depending on their individual temperament, past experiences, and the severity of the aggression. Consistency, patience, and positive reinforcement will eventually enable the dogs learn to coexist peacefully. The steps I recommend for treating this kind of behaviour are largely similar to the ones mentioned in previous paragraphs and can be summarised in the following key points:

1. Manage the Exposure

If your dog shows aggression towards unfamiliar dogs, you will need to manage their exposure to situations where aggression might occur. This could involve:

- Avoiding off-leash areas where interactions with unfamiliar dogs are inevitable.

- Walking your dog during quieter times of day to reduce encounters with other dogs.

- Keeping your dog on a leash and using a proper harness to maintain control during walks.

2. Gradual Desensitisation and Counter-Conditioning

To reduce aggression, you can gradually desensitise your dog to the presence of other dogs through a process called counter-conditioning:

Start at a distance: Begin by allowing your dog to observe other dogs from a safe distance, where they do not react aggressively. Reward calm behaviour with treats or praise.

Gradual approach: Over time, slowly reduce the distance between your dog and other dogs while keeping them calm and relaxed. Reward your dog for maintaining composure.

Positive associations: Pair the presence of other dogs with positive experiences, like treats, toys, or praise, so that your dog begins to associate other dogs with good things.

3. Teach "Leave It" or other focus Commands

Training your dog to respond to a "Leave It" or "Watch Me" command can help redirect their attention when they start to get fixated on other dogs. With consistent training, your dog will learn to ignore the other dog and focus on you instead.

4. Work on Socialisation

If your dog is not properly socialised, gradually expose them to well-behaved, calm dogs in controlled environments. This will help your dog learn appropriate social behaviour and reduce their fear or aggression towards other dogs. Puppy classes or controlled meet-ups with a trusted dog can assist in this process.

5. Exercise and Mental Stimulation

An under-exercised or bored dog is more likely to be reactive. Make sure your dog is getting enough physical exercise and mental stimulation through play, training, and enrichment activities. A tired dog is less likely to become overly aroused by the presence of other dogs.

6. Consult a Professional

If your dog's aggression is persistent or severe, you will need to seek help from a professional dog trainer or behaviourist. They can assess the situation and design a personalised training plan to address the aggression, taking into account your dog's history, breed, and temperament.

7. Consider Medical Evaluation

Finally, if the aggression is sudden or has increased in intensity, it is worth consulting a veterinarian to rule out any underlying health issues, such as pain or hormonal imbalances, which might be contributing to the aggressive behaviour.

Predatory Aggression

Predatory aggression is a behaviour embedded in a dog's natural hunting instincts; it is not rooted in fear, anxiety, or territorial defence. As mentioned in the chapter dedicated to the prey drive, predatory aggression is a sequence of hardwired behaviours that exist in all dogs to varying degrees, depending largely on breed-specific traits and individual predispositions. Nevertheless, one of the most common misconceptions held by dog owners is the belief that any behaviour resulting in harm must be categorised as aggression. Whilst understandable, this notion is both inaccurate and potentially dangerous when it comes to behaviour assessment and intervention planning. In canine behaviour, predatory behaviour and aggressive behaviour differ not only in their purpose but also in motivation and presentation. Although both may result in injury, the motivations, triggers, and emotional states behind them are fundamentally different. If we carefully observe dogs performing either actions, we can clearly see that predatory behaviour brings the dog closer to its target, whereas aggressive behaviour serves the purpose of creating distance from what the dog perceives as threat or conflict.

Understanding this distinction is vital for addressing the behaviour appropriately and ensuring the safety of all involved. Aggression is driven by emotion, usually fear, insecurity, frustration, pain, or territorial instincts.

It often involves creating distance or asserting control in a situation perceived as threatening or challenging. Predatory aggression behaviour, by contrast, is silent, emotionally flat, and incredibly focused. You typically won't see the warning signs you would expect in other type of displays of aggression: no growling, no barking, no hackles, and no defensive posturing. It is swift, efficient, and almost mechanical in nature. The display of the Prey Drive sequence is so beautiful to watch that I like to describe it as poetry in motion.

Before attempting to modify or redirect predatory aggressive behaviour, it is important to accept that the prey drive is a normal and natural behaviour in dogs. It must not be classified as a bad behaviour, nor does it mean that the dog is dangerous in a general sense, dogs are just born with it and even if they are regularly fed as pets, they cannot resist their natural instinct if the opportunity arises. Unfortunately, in today's domestic environment, an unchecked prey drive can present significant challenges, especially in households with the presence of small pets (cats, rabbits, ferrets, etc.), small children, or in circumstances where a dog has access to livestock or wildlife or can enjoy the freedom of frequent off-leash outings. Another salient point is that understanding your dog's breed tendencies can help anticipate and prevent issues. Sighthounds, terriers, herding breeds, and, to a certain extent, some working dogs are especially prone to chasing or stalking movements. Because their prey drive sequence may be more intact and embedded, it can be more difficult to interrupt. Having established that a dog's predatory tendencies are part of its natural instinctual repertoire, management becomes not just helpful but essential, especially when we choose to share our homes, parks, and neighbourhoods with these animals in the context of our modern, human-centred society.

Unlike their wild ancestors who needed to rely on the full predatory sequence for survival, our domesticated dogs now live in a world where chasing, grabbing, and biting are not only unnecessary, as they can rely on a consistent and scheduled diet, but can also pose serious ethical, legal, and safety concerns. The sight of a squirrel in the park, a cat or a fox crossing the street, or a child riding on a bicycle are all potential triggers for the dog whose high prey drive lies just beneath the surface. For this reason, it is the full responsibility of any pet owner to recognise that although predation is not considered aggression, it can still result in injury or distress to other animals (or people) if not effectively managed and controlled. I could mention numerous cases over the years of dogs with an exceptionally strong prey drive instinct, either in the context of the dog walking activities of my company or during training sessions aimed at managing and controlling this behaviour; bear in mind, however, that our dogs did not choose this world, we brought them into it. Managing predatory aggression is not about suppressing a dog's natural instincts; rather, it is about developing strategies and safeguards tailored to the individual dog's triggers, breed tendencies, and level of responsiveness.

Let us take the case of Trudy, a spirited little fox terrier, as an example. True to her breed's heritage, Trudy possessed an incredibly strong prey drive. Once she picked up the scent of a squirrel in the park, it was as if a switch had flipped in her brain: she would be gone in a flash, tearing through underbrush with single-minded stamina and determination. These moments were not just unpredictable; they were dangerous. On one occasion, she teamed up with Ferus, a beautiful Irish Setter, and together they disappeared for about an hour in the stunning grounds of Kensington Gardens, following the invisible trail of their chosen quarry. Being out of sight for an extensive period of time, I did not know what they had been up to or where they had been; they would not respond to their names, or even to the rustling of a treat pouch. This was the moment when the owner and I decided it was time to intervene. Trudy's behaviour became such a regular occurrence that she earned the affectionate nickname "Trudini" after the legendary magician Houdini who was known for his dramatic escapes. Managing Trudy's behaviour became an exercise in both understanding and patience. It was not that she was "bad" or "stubborn", in fact her behaviour was not about disobedience at all. It was driven by her instinct. She was not chasing squirrels to annoy anyone, she was chasing squirrels because it is what her brain and body were designed to do. The solution came not in punishment, but in a strategic combination of training and management.

At the very beginning of the training plan, Trudy was no longer allowed off-leash in unenclosed areas, and I began working on the recall training with the aid of a long-line in distraction-free environments, using a multitude of scrumptious and tasty treats. At the same time, I asked her owner to introduce high-intensity games like flirt pole chases and scent tracking in the house and in the garden to channel her natural drives in ways that were both safe and satisfying. I then paired the voice recall "Come" with three hoots of a gun-dog training whistle followed by a treat reward, still using the long line which I subsequently let loose on the ground. Over a short period of time, Trudy's behaviour improved enormously, not because her instincts subsided dramatically, but because they were finally being acknowledged and redirected in a productive way (towards chasing something we could control, her favourite rubber ball). The nickname Trudini stuck, but now it is used fondly, not out of frustration. This is one example of how I dealt with our little fox terrier, but the same holistic approach can be applied to other similar breeds.

The first step when it comes to managing this behaviour is often the simplest: do not let the dog be in a situation where they are more likely to fail if given the opportunity to follow their prey drive instinct. The second step is to establish and consistently implement a solid foundation of training, as this can be highly effective in managing predatory instincts. Commands like "Leave It", given to the dog at the stalking phase and before the chasing phase of the prey drive sequence, will interrupt the focus on a potential prey object. The use of a strong and reliable recall command like "Come" represents an essential cue when trying to prevent a chase. Other commands like "Watch Me" or "Look" are extremely helpful when it comes to disrupting stalking and fixation and re-engaging the dog's brain. Furthermore, impulse control exercises such as "Stay, "Wait, "Place", and "Go To Your Mat" should be taught first in low-distraction environments and then gradually generalised to other contexts and real-life situations. We should not underestimate the importance of providing our highly prey-driven dogs with appropriate outlets.

Dogs with a high prey drive need to do something with their instinctual high energy levels. That "something" should be safe, structured, and satisfying for the dog. Flirt poles and tug games (with rules) can mimic chase and grab under a controlled environment. They can also be used to reinforce the basic obedience commands previously described. Some of the most active breeds can benefit from the introduction of scent work and tracking exercises in order to channel their intense focus. The use of puzzle toys and food-dispensing games are also a very good outlet through which to satisfy a dog's mental stimulation needs. One point must be clear though, management and training go hand in hand. Whilst management helps prevent unwanted behaviour, training builds the skills necessary to change it. Most people rush through the training process because they successfully notice progress in the behaviour of their dog, but if the dog is not yet fully trained or cannot reliably disengage from the prey drive sequence, I would recommend avoiding any exposure to triggers. In fact, each time a dog has the opportunity to rehearse predatory behaviour, the neural pathway strengthens, making the behaviour harder to extinguish in the future. I am a strong advocate of using play and games to integrate training commands while interacting with my own dogs or those trusted in my care.

The holistic nature of activities like playing, as observed in wild animals, reveals it to be a natural tool for learning and development in young puppies. In wolves, foxes, and wild canids, play is not merely a recreational activity; it serves an essential role in practising hunting sequences, refining motor skills, and establishing social dynamics. By mirroring this organic form of learning, we allow our domesticated dogs to absorb commands and behavioural expectations in a way that feels intuitive to them. When training is embedded in play, dogs remain more engaged, more relaxed, and more likely to retain what they learn. It becomes a shared experience rooted in instinct, rather than a top-down exercise in control. Playful learning strengthens the human-canine bond, promoting an emotional balance, and provides a positive outlet for energy, especially when directed at fulfilling core drives like the predatory sequence. It is, in many ways, the bridge between the primal and the domestic.

There are numerous games I can think of which tap directly into the dog's natural drives, especially its predatory instincts. For a more in-depth description of the prey drive sequence, I invite you to refer to the dedicated chapter. What follows here is a detailed description of some of these games:

Orienting & Eye Stalking: Focus-Based Games

In the wild, the predatory sequence starts by orienting to movement, sound, or scent and seeking. This is quickly followed by a fixed gaze, the "eye" phase, which precedes stalking. Herding breeds, like Border Collies and Australian shepherds, often hover around this part of the sequence. They are wired to detect, track, and control movement, but rarely make contact.

Watch Me Game: Teaching your dog to fixate on your face, rather than on a moving target, is an excellent way to redirect the "eye" phase. Begin with a treat held near your eyes and mark the moment your dog locks on with a cue like "Yes!" or a click followed by a reward. This builds a reliable focus and detachment from external distractions.

Targeting: This involves teaching them to touch a target (your hand) with their nose or paw to create an interactive routine that channels the dog's drive to lock onto something you can control. You can even use moving targets, like a stick for example, to make this game more dynamic.

Tracking and Nose Work: Laying scent trails in the garden or using beginner-level scent work kits readily available online allows the dog to hone their orienting skills in a way that requires focus and mental effort, not physical confrontation.

Stalking & Chasing: Movement-Based Games

The chase is perhaps the most exhilarating and stimulating part of the predatory sequence for most dogs. The chasing phase and the thrill exerted by the movement of a prey is extremely difficult to override once triggered, so it is better to incorporate this drive into structured play.

Flirt Pole Work: This toy is essentially a long stick with a rope and a lure attached at the end of it. It mimics the erratic movement of the prey. It is excellent for working on impulse control. Ask your dog to "Wait" before allowing them to "Take it". Always end the game with a "Drop It" or "Out" command to reinforce control.

Recall-Chase Combo: Allow your dog to begin chasing a toy or person, then call them back mid-chase using an excited tone and high-value reward. You can use a long-line to help with the recall. This reinforces impulse control and helps to establish a solid recall, even under situations of high arousal.

Controlled Fetch: Fetch can either be a chaotic free-for-all or a well-structured outlet for prey drive. Introduce pauses, cues for release, and end the session with calm behaviour to prevent things from spiralling out of control.

Grab & Bite: Tug Games with Rules

Dogs who live for the "grab" moment can find deep satisfaction in tug games. When done with rules, tug can be one of the safest and most engaging outlets for bite-related instincts.

Tug with Release Cue: Establish clear start and stop cues. "Take It" means go, while "Drop It" ends the round. When the dog releases, mark the moment and either reward them with food or re-engage in play.

Spring Poles or Rope Anchors: For strong, high-drive dogs, you can create a fixed rope setup that allows them to tug independently. This can reduce the risk of accidental injury to the human while still offering an outlet for intense grab behaviours.

Tug as a Reinforcer: Use tug to reward obedience behaviours such as recall, heel, or a perfect stay. This elevates the value of training and integrates the prey drive constructively in highly-driven breeds like Malinois and German shepherds.

Dissect & Consume: Puzzle Solving & Chewing

The final stages of the predatory sequence, dissecting and consuming the prey, are often overlooked but are an equally vital part of the behaviour, especially for dogs who love to destroy things. Giving them appropriate outlets can prevent destructive chewing around the house.

Food-Stuffed Toys: Use Kongs, Toppls, or similar toys filled with wet food, peanut butter, or frozen broth. These satisfy the "dissect and consume" urges while providing mental stimulation for the dog.

Shreddable Boxes: I have heard from some pet owners that supervised cardboard destruction can be a safe way for their dogs to act out the tearing phase. Being extremely house proud, I don't particularly like to recommend this activity, but for those who do, hiding a few small treats inside the cardboard can add to the excitement.

Snuffle Mats and Scatter Feeding: From time to time you can also encourage your dog's natural foraging behaviour by hiding kibble in a snuffle mat or tossing it across the lawn. This slows feeding and satisfies the dog's need to search and "uncover" food.

Mixed Sequences & Integrated Training

Many games naturally incorporate multiple elements of the predatory sequence. These mixed exercises allow your dog to engage fully in a structured, enriching activity.

Scent Work Courses: These setups can include a scent trail (orient), tracking behaviour (stalk), and locating a reward (consume). This taps into the full spectrum of natural hunting behaviours.

Hide-and-Seek: Which household with children has never indulged in a game of Hide-and-Seek with their pet? Whether hiding yourself or your dog's favourite toy, this game activates multiple layers of the sequence and reinforces a strong recall.

Agility & Obstacle Courses: With tunnels to stalk through, hurdles to chase over, and scent targets to orient toward, these courses stimulate both the body and the brain.

I am fully aware that I have devoted considerable space to this topic, but if I may offer a final and heartfelt thought on this often misunderstood aspect of canine behaviour, it would be this: understanding and honouring our dog's predatory sequence is not an indulgence, it is a necessity. When dogs are denied appropriate, structured outlets for their deep-rooted instincts, frustration inevitably builds up, often surfacing in destructive or even dangerous ways. By offering targeted games that align with your dog's individual predatory strengths, you are not simply meeting a biological need, you are building trust, improving obedience, and fostering emotional wellbeing. Whether you share your life with a high-drive terrier or a laid-back retriever, every dog benefits from being allowed to express their inner predator safely, joyfully, and with your thoughtful guidance.

Separation Anxiety

Separation anxiety is a condition that can significantly affect a dog's emotional well-being, often manifesting as an intense attachment to their human family members. Dogs suffering from separation anxiety experience considerable distress when separated from their owners, exhibiting behaviours such as excessive barking, whining, or howling, as well as destructive tendencies like chewing furniture, scratching doors, or even soiling the house. These dogs typically have a strong need to stay close to their owners, following them around the house from room to room, and often show reluctance to spend time alone or outdoors. The anxiety can start long before the owners leave, often triggered by simple cues like dressing up for work or picking up a coat or keys. Before I proceed any further, I need to make a distinction between separation anxiety and another related but fundamentally different condition known as containment phobia. Although the symptoms may sometimes appear similar, such as destruction, vocalisation, or attempts to escape, they stem from different underlying causes and therefore require different approaches to treatment.

Separation anxiety is rooted in the emotional bond a dog forms with their human companions. Dogs suffering from this condition experience intense stress when left alone, not simply because they are by themselves, but because they are specifically without their person. These dogs often shadow their owners throughout the house, struggle to settle when left alone, and may display frantic behaviour as soon as departure cues are noticed. The anxiety is triggered by the absence of the human, and the dog's behaviour is directed at seeking reunion or coping with the distress of that absence.

By contrast, containment phobia refers to a dog's fear or aversion to being confined in a small space, such as a crate, a pen, or even a closed room, regardless of whether the owner is present. In this case, the distress is caused not by the feeling of separation, but by the sensation of being trapped or restricted in a small environment. Dogs with containment phobia may panic when enclosed, even if their human is nearby. The behaviour may stem from a history of being locked up for long periods, traumatic experiences during confinement, or a lack of early positive exposure to being in a confined space. This distinction is crucial. Treating a dog for separation anxiety by confining them to a crate, for example, may worsen symptoms if the dog is actually suffering from containment phobia. Similarly, treating a dog for containment issues when their true distress stems from being left alone will fail to address the root cause of their anxiety.

In some cases, a dog may experience both conditions simultaneously, adding a further layer of complexity to the rehabilitation plan. Understanding whether your dog is reacting to being alone, being confined, or both is the first essential step towards crafting an effective behavioural intervention. One key indicator that a dog is suffering from containment phobia, as opposed to separation anxiety, is the specific objective which becomes the focus of their distress. Whilst dogs with separation anxiety tend to display anxious behaviours that are more generalised or directed towards the area from where their owner departed, dogs with containment phobia often concentrate their escape efforts on points of perceived exit. You might notice intense scratching, biting, or pawing at doors, door handles, windows, baby gates, or vents, essentially any part of the enclosure that represents a potential way out. In some cases, dogs may injure themselves in their frantic attempts to escape, breaking teeth or nails, or rubbing raw patches on their paws or muzzles. The panic is not about being alone per se, but about feeling trapped or confined within a space they perceive as restrictive or inescapable.

When owners leave, the symptoms of separation anxiety become apparent. Alongside the vocalisations and destructive behaviours, the dog may exhibit physical signs of distress, such as restlessness, shaking, excessive salivation, or even refusing to eat. In some cases, the anxiety is triggered by specific departures, such as when the owner leaves for work, whilst in other situations it can occur after the owner has already returned home and is preparing to leave again. The reunion after a separation often sees the dog overexcited and aroused, unable to calm down from the heightened emotions.

Notably, not all dogs with separation anxiety crave constant physical contact. Some might prefer solitude during certain times, but the condition itself is not necessarily about a need for constant attention. It can also arise from traumatic experiences that happen when the dog is left alone, such as during storms, fireworks, or other frightening events. Dogs who experience both separation anxiety and a fear of loud noises or storms require a more tailored treatment plan that addresses both issues and which includes desensitisation and counter-conditioning.

The key to preventing separation anxiety begins early, especially with puppies. Teaching them to spend time alone, whether in a crate or designated area, helps them feel comfortable with short periods of separation. This early training teaches them that being alone does not result in negative experiences, allowing them to handle longer separations more calmly in the future. However, if a dog is already showing signs of separation anxiety, whether they are a rescued or a re-homed pet, it is crucial to approach the condition with patience, understanding, and the right combination of behavioural interventions and training. Fortunately, with patience, consistency, and the right approach, it is possible to help even the most anxious dog to build the confidence and mental balance required to stay calm during absences. I have laid out several focal points for the foundation of a comprehensive behavioural modification plan below.

1. Establish a Predictable Routine

One of the cornerstones of reducing anxiety is creating a calm, structured environment. Dogs thrive on predictability, and anxious dogs in particular benefit from knowing what to expect. Begin by structuring your day around regular times for feeding, play, walks, training, and rest. This clear division between interactive periods and downtime enables the dog to understand that solitude is normal and not something to fear. Align solo play and rest periods with your usual departure times to build comfort during those hours.

2. Environmental Enrichment: Meeting the Dog's Needs

When you are present, ensure your dog receives adequate physical and mental stimulation. This includes regular walks, engaging play sessions, obedience training, and time for cuddling and connection. Fulfilled dogs are better equipped to relax when alone. Before scheduled periods of inattention, offer your dog novel toys, chew items, or food-dispensing puzzles. These not only redirect their focus but also provide them with a sense of comfort and satisfaction.

3. Create a Consistent Reward Protocol

For dogs suffering from separation anxiety, your attention is the most valued resource. This represents both a challenge and an opportunity. Begin by identifying what behaviours you want to reinforce, such as calmness, independence, and settled postures, and which you need to ignore, such as following, whining, or attention-seeking.

Start by teaching the dog to lie down calmly or stay on a mat, rewarding them only when they are relaxed. If your dog demands attention, resist the urge to engage. Wait until they offer the desired behaviour, then reward them calmly. Over time, increase the duration of calmness required before giving attention. The goal is to teach the dog that independence, not clinginess, earns rewards.

4. Train the "Settle Down" Cue

Teaching your dog to settle down on command is invaluable. Begin by luring your dog onto a mat or designated resting spot and reward quiet behaviour. Use your preferred training method, whether this is clicker training, head halter guidance, or food luring. Gradually extend the amount of time your dog must remain settled before receiving praise or treats. Avoid casual petting or interaction during this phase: let the dog clearly understand that calm, quiet behaviour is the key to receiving attention.

5. Designate a Relaxation Area

Design a safe, cozy space for your dog, such as a bed, crate, or mat, where they can learn to rest peacefully. This area should be associated with positive, calming experiences: gentle classical music, the familiar scent of one item of clothing, their favourite toys, or feeding routines. Begin by guiding the dog to this spot during routine training or after exercise. Initially, use food or play as a lure, and only release the dog when they are calm. Over time, this space should become the dog's own refuge, a familiar place where they feel safe and secure in your absence.

6. Reinforce Obedience Through Everyday Routines

Incorporate basic training into your daily interactions using a "nothing in life is free" approach. Ask your dog to perform simple commands like "Sit" or "Stay" before receiving anything they want, be it meals, walks, or access to the outdoors. This practice fosters impulse control and builds a foundation of respectful behaviour that will benefit your dog in moments of stress or change.

One of the most counterproductive responses to separation anxiety is punishment or overly emotional greetings upon return. If your dog has been anxious during your absence, perhaps leading to destruction, house soiling, or excessive vocalisation, it is essential to understand that these behaviours are not acts of spite or misbehaviour, but expressions of your dog's emotional distress. Scolding your dog after the damage has occurred will not help. In fact, it will likely make things worse. From your dog's perspective, your return is already a highly charged moment: if it is followed by anger or punishment, it only deepens the anxiety associated with your departures and homecomings. Worse, it teaches the dog that your return is unpredictable and unsafe, amplifying the fear of being left alone. Similarly, excited greetings can be just as problematic. They may seem affectionate, but they reinforce the idea that your absence is a big event, something worth worrying about. To help your dog normalise separations, you need to make your departures and arrivals as emotionally neutral as possible. Upon returning home, you need to ignore your dog until they have fully settled down. This may take five to fifteen minutes, especially in the early stages of training. Wait until your dog is calm, perhaps lying down, quiet, or casually exploring the house, before gently initiating interaction. In time, your dog will learn that staying relaxed is the fastest way to receive your attention, and your comings and goings will no longer be a source of emotional upheaval. Besides training, which should be always used in conjunction with any treatment plan, there are other strategies that can be adopted to desensitise an anxious dog.

Dogs are also remarkably observant creatures. As time passes, they begin to recognise a series of behaviours that reliably precede your departures, such as grabbing your keys, putting on shoes, collecting your bag, or even something as subtle as brushing your teeth or closing a particular door. These pre-departure cues become strongly associated with the emotional upheaval of being left alone and, as a result, can trigger anxiety before you have even stepped out of the door.

As part of the desensitisation process and to ease this anticipatory anxiety, you can begin by altering how your dog perceives these cues. The aim is to break the emotional association between these actions and your absence. One effective strategy is to perform these departure routines without actually leaving. Pick up your keys and walk to the door, but then sit down on the couch. Put on your shoes and jacket, then make a cup of tea. Do this repeatedly throughout the day, but never pair these actions with an actual departure. Just as important is to watch your dog's body language. Initially, they may become alert or even anxious. Nevertheless, with calm and consistent repetition, they will gradually learn that these cues no longer predict anything significant. You are teaching your dog that keys do not always mean goodbye, and sometimes they mean nothing at all. Limit these desensitisation exercises to three or four repetitions per day, ensuring your dog has fully relaxed before repeating the routine. If done correctly, the dog will gradually habituate to these formerly anxiety-inducing cues. When the cues become neutral, your actual departures are less likely to cause distress. This kind of pre-departure desensitisation is a small but powerful component of a successful treatment plan. It empowers you to shift your dog's emotional response from panic to peace, just one cue at a time.

In the more severe cases of separation anxiety I have encountered, I have collaborated closely with veterinary professionals as I find that drug therapy can offer valuable support, particularly in the early phases of a structured behaviour modification programme. When used thoughtfully and under veterinary supervision, medication can ease the dog's emotional intensity, making it more receptive to the learning process that lies at the heart of long-term recovery. However, medication alone is not a cure. Whilst tranquillisers may sedate a dog and reduce the likelihood of destruction simply by dulling their physical responses, they do not address the underlying emotional distress. Moreover, sedation without emotional relief can be detrimental, as the dog remains anxious but lacks the ability to act out, effectively trapping them in their discomfort. Antidepressant medications such as fluoxetine and clomipramine are the most commonly prescribed drugs for separation anxiety in dogs. These work by altering the brain's chemical balance, making it easier for the dog to process stress and learn new coping mechanisms. When used correctly and under veterinary supervision, they can dramatically reduce anxiety and facilitate learning during retraining efforts. In more complex cases, these drugs may be used in combination with other anti-anxiety medications to better manage symptoms. Additionally, pheromone therapy, such as diffusers or sprays containing dog-appeasing pheromones, may create a calmer environment in both your presence and absence. These can be useful adjuncts to the overall management plan, especially for sensitive or highly reactive dogs. That said, I would like to reiterate that the cornerstone of treatment remains behavioural retraining. Following a holistic approach, the ultimate goal is to enable the dog to develop emotional resilience, independence, and the ability to tolerate being alone. No medication can replace the consistent, thoughtful work required to reshape your dog's emotional responses.

Jumping Up

Jumping up is one of those unwanted behaviours frequently mentioned during my training sessions, as dog owners often find it particularly challenging to control and manage. Adopting a holistic approach to understanding the behaviour of our domesticated pets should encourage us to look beyond the surface and consider deeper influences; specifically, the reasons why every dog has this behaviour embedded in their DNA and how human cultural and social norms have shaped our expectations and interactions with our dogs.

Jumping up serves a very specific evolutionary purpose rooted in survival and the procurement of food. In a natural or wild context, young canines often jump up to lick the faces and tap the chins of adult pack members returning from a hunt. This gesture is a way of soliciting regurgitated food from the adults and is both appeasing and practical as it contributes to strengthening the social bonds between pack members. The behaviour is instinctual and begins early in life in tandem with the weaning phase, with puppies engaging in this ritual long before any formal training takes place. As puppies grow and begin to take part in the hunting or foraging process themselves, they no longer need to rely on adults for food in the same way. Nevertheless, the behaviour of jumping up often remains and evolves into a social greeting ritual. It becomes a way for dogs to reconnect with familiar pack members, reaffirm social bonds, and express excitement and affection. When dogs jump up on humans in an attempt to reach and lick their faces, they are essentially performing the same ingrained social ritual, we just happen to be standing high up rather than down to their level. To the dog, this action is a friendly and natural greeting, a gesture meant to elicit attention, affection, or even a resource. It is not about dominance, spite, or defiance, but a deeply rooted behaviour shaped by evolutionary biology and social communication. This understanding is crucial when addressing jumping as a behavioural issue. Rather than labelling the behaviour as simply "bad" or "naughty" we can acknowledge that it has a functional origin. From there, our goal becomes one of redirecting the behaviour in a way that aligns with human expectations without suppressing the dog's natural desire to connect. By teaching dogs an alternative, incompatible behaviour, like sitting calmly to greet for example, we give them a clear, achievable way to meet their social needs in a human environment. In this way, we create mutual understanding so that the dog still gets the connection they seek and the human receives a polite and manageable interaction.

Furthermore, what might be seen as a behavioural problem in one context could be tolerated, or even welcomed, in another. Let me explain – we cannot ignore the fact that the way we greet one another as humans varies greatly across cultures, and this naturally affects how we interpret a dog's attempt to greet us. For instance, in Mediterranean cultures (where I am from), greetings between people often involve close body contact, embraces, and even cheek-kissing. In this context, a dog jumping up to say hello may feel like a natural extension of that warmth and physicality. In such cultures, the behaviour is more readily excused or even encouraged, and is viewed as a sign of affection and connection.

Conversely, cultures with more formal social boundaries, where personal space is valued and physical greetings are more restrained, often view the same behaviour as disruptive or impolite. In Japan for example, greetings reflect a deep cultural emphasis on respect and social hierarchy. Rather than physical touch, the norm is the bow, which varies in depth and duration depending on the level of formality and relationship. Although handshakes are becoming more common in international settings, they are often performed with both hands and a slight bow as a sign of politeness. Similarly, in India, a traditional and respectful greeting is the "Namaste", where both palms are pressed together in front of the chest with a slight bow of the head. This gesture means "I bow to the divine in you" and is used widely, especially in more formal or spiritual contexts. Physical contact like handshakes may occur, especially in urban areas, but many prefer the non-contact approach out of respect for personal and cultural boundaries. In these environments, a jumping dog may trigger discomfort or concern, especially when guests or small children are involved. Understanding this dynamic is essential for effective training. It allows us to be more compassionate and consistent in our response while tailoring our approach to reflect both the dog's nature and the owner's environment. In doing so, we shift from simply correcting behaviour to fostering communication and mutual understanding with our beloved pets.

Similarly, differences in eye contact, vocal expression, and the use of physical gestures between cultures can significantly affect not only how dogs are trained but also how they interpret human communication. We

Italians, for instance, are notorious for our animated and expressive use of hand gestures, vocal tone, and close physical presence. Although this can enhance emotional connections, it may also overwhelm more sensitive dogs or be misinterpreted by them depending on their previous experiences or individual temperament. By contrast, some cultures value more restrained, formal interactions where communication is quieter, more distant, and physical touch is minimal. These differences are not lost on dogs. In fact, dogs are incredibly adaptable creatures who constantly read and respond to human cues. However, their reactions, whether an averted gaze, lowered posture, or enthusiastic jumping, can easily be misunderstood if we are not attuned to canine body language within the broader context of both species-specific and culturally influenced behaviour. For example, in some cultures, direct eye contact is seen as a sign of respect and engagement, whilst in others (and in canine communication) it can be a challenge or even a threat. A dog that looks away is often displaying polite deference, but to an untrained human eye this might be misread as guilt or disobedience. Understanding these cross-cultural nuances not only helps trainers communicate more clearly and empathetically with dogs, but also empowers dog owners to interpret their pets' behaviour through the lenses of context, compassion, and mutual respect, which I like to refer to as the holistic way.

Correcting jumping up involves a clear, consistent approach that respects the dog's natural instincts while reshaping the behaviour into something more appropriate. Other strategies that can be employed to correct this behaviour include ignoring the dog that jumps up for attention or greetings, or, less ideally, the use of punishment. Whilst ignoring can be an extremely effective method, especially when combined with rewarding calm, grounded behaviour, the use of punishment should be strongly discouraged. In fact, punishing a dog for jumping up can cause more harm than good. It may suppress the behaviour momentarily but does not address the underlying emotional motivation, such as excitement, anxiety, or the desire for social interaction. Worse, it can damage the human-dog bond, create confusion, and potentially lead to fear-based behaviours or even aggression. Furthermore, punishing the behaviour is often an inconsistent and unreliable strategy. Not every person the dog encounters, be it a visitor at home, a passerby on the street, or a stranger at the park, is inclined (or able) to punish the dog for jumping up. Inconsistency in how the behaviour is addressed only creates confusion for the dog, making it harder for them to learn what is appropriate and what is not. Dogs thrive on clarity and consistency. If one person rewards jumping up with attention, another scolds the behaviour, and someone else simply ignores it, the dog receives mixed signals. As a result, the jumping up may persist, or it can even escalate, because the dog does not understand what outcome to expect or which behaviour is being reinforced.

Thus, the focus should always be on guiding the dog towards more appropriate behaviours like sitting politely or keeping four paws on the ground and rewarding those consistently, so that the dog learns what is expected in a positive, clear, and confidence-building way. If you have decided that the best strategy is to ignore the behaviour, you should not talk, touch, or even look at your dog (even eye contact is a form of communication) when they jump up. You should turn your back or step away calmly. Bear in mind that any attention (even saying "No!") can serve to reinforce the behaviour. You can instead reward any acceptable alternative behaviour offered by the dog. As soon as all four paws are on the ground, mark it with a cue like "Yes!" or click (if using clicker training), then immediately offer attention, praise, or a treat. As always, consistency is the key; everyone in the household (and visitors) must follow the same rule. It is vital to avoid confusing the dog with mixed messages (e.g. tolerating jumping when you are in a good mood but scolding it later) – this will confound the dog and ultimately delay learning.

Another good strategy is to set up short training sessions where someone enters the room or home, keeping the dog on a lead if necessary to prevent rehearsal of jumping, and ask your dog to sit before the person approaches. If your dog jumps, the person turns and walks away. Try again after a few seconds. For some extremely excitable dogs, it might help to scatter a few treats on the ground as someone enters to redirect their focus and keep them grounded. Alternatively, you can toss a toy they love to redirect their energy and excitement into an appropriate outlet. Generally, calm behaviour should be encouraged, praised, and reinforced, even outside of greeting contexts. Dogs learn faster when calm behaviours consistently lead to good outcomes. As mentioned earlier, the one thing you do not want to do is to punish the dog. Unfortunately, in the early stages of my dog training career, I learnt the damaging effects of punishment firsthand. This was the method I was taught by my trainers at the time, and I followed it with the intention of correcting unwanted behaviour. However, I gradually began to realise the profound negative impact it had, not just on the dogs, but on the overall relationship between my dog and me. Punishment can create fear, confusion, and anxiety. Instead of teaching a dog what not to do, it often teaches them to fear the consequences of their actions without offering clear guidance on what they should do instead. When harsh methods or punishment are used, the dog will respond to your verbal cues, not because it understands or is willing to cooperate, but out of fear. Thus, the dog's motivation shifts from a desire to please and understand their handler to a reaction driven by fear of the consequences. This approach can be confusing for the dog, as it does not offer a clear understanding of what they should do instead. In my experience, positive reinforcement and patience are far more effective in the long run. Once I had shifted my approach to focus on rewarding desired behaviours and preventing unwanted ones through redirection, I noticed a profound improvement not just in the dog's behaviour but also in their emotional well-being. In conclusion, do not knee your dog in the chest or push them away harshly, and do not shout or scold during jumping; it often backfires by feeding the attention-seeking motive.

Fears and Phobias

The terms "fear" and "phobia" are often used interchangeably when discussing canine behaviour, but they refer to very distinct experiences that require different approaches to treatment. Fear is considered a normal and adaptive response to perceived threats. It is an inherent survival mechanism and most dogs will experience fear at some point in their lives. For example, a dog may show fear when confronted with a loud noise, unfamiliar situation, or a new person. Fear triggers the fight-or-flight response and is often short-lived, subsiding once the threat is removed or resolved. Phobias on the other hand are extreme and irrational fears that cause the dogs to experience a persistent and prolonged distress. They go beyond typical fear responses and are often triggered by specific events (like thunderstorms, fireworks, or certain triggers present in the environment). Unlike normal fear, phobias do not subside once the trigger is removed, and they can escalate over time if left unaddressed. A behavioural assessment can be extremely useful in ascertaining whether the issue is a normal fear response or a case of phobia, and is carried out by observing the dog's behaviour in relation to the trigger.

Before I explore the various strategies and treatment plans used to deal with fears and phobias, I need to reiterate that dogs and humans communicate in fundamentally different ways. For dogs, the emotional context behind our words carries far more weight than the words themselves. They are highly attuned to our tone of voice, body language, and situational patterns. I find that a large number of owners, although acting out with the best of intentions, unknowingly reinforce their dog's fear by pairing comforting phrases like "it's okay" or "good boy" with stressful experiences, such as nail clipping, veterinary visits, or thunderstorms. Over time, dogs begin to associate those well-meaning words with the feeling of discomfort, thus creating a learnt link between the phrase and the fear-inducing event. In effect, the reassurance becomes a predictor of something unpleasant (as seen in the Pavlovian experiment), which can worsen the dog's anxiety and even cause fearful responses before the actual trigger appears. For instance, a dog shows signs of stress (panting, trembling, pacing) when facing a trigger. The owner, with good intentions, then says "it's okay" in a soothing tone of voice. The stressful event (e.g. the groomer holding a nail clipper, a vet holding a syringe, or a thunderstorm) follows.

You can see how the phrase "it's okay" gradually becomes a predictor of something unpleasant. The dog reacts with fear even earlier next time, because the cue itself has become part of the fear chain. In the same way, dog owners can unintentionally reinforce phobias by rewarding fearful behaviours. In fact, petting or using a reassuring and appeasing tone of voice during a fearful reaction (like trembling, cowering, or hiding) can accidentally reinforce that response. When we repeat words or actions (such as grabbing the leash or getting the car keys) before a scary event, we condition the dog to anticipate anxiety.

Another factor that can create a phobic experience is overexposure. Pushing a dog into overwhelming situations too quickly can backfire, heightening sensitivity instead of building resilience. Just as not everyone learns to swim by being thrown into deep water, dogs do not overcome their fears through forced exposure to the trigger. On the contrary, this type of behavioural modification technique, known as flooding, can make the problem worse, intensifying the dog's emotional response and leading to avoidance, shutdown, or even aggression.

Finally, it is all too easy to fall into a vicious cycle where the owner's emotional state in the presence of a trigger directly influences the dog's behaviour. Dogs are incredibly perceptive creatures: they are often more attuned to our emotions than we are ourselves. They read our body language and are sensitive to our tone of voice, posture, even our breathing. If the owner becomes tense, nervous, or overly concerned during thunderstorms, vet visits, or fireworks, the dog will often interpret that tension as confirmation that something is indeed wrong and will act accordingly. In essence, dogs mirror our emotional states. Therefore, if you are calm and confident, your dog is more likely to feel safe. Conversely, if you are anxious or uneasy, your dog is likely to reflect that back, amplifying their fear response. This creates a feedback loop where the dog becomes more fearful, the owner becomes more worried, and the cycle continues.

The first step toward breaking this loop is self-awareness. Owners need to learn how to manage their own emotional responses and lead by example before they can expect their dog to remain calm. Practicing neutrality, calm breathing, and positive body language during stressful moments can make a significant difference in how the dog perceives the situation. If you are already caught in this loop there are other tactics you can adopt to break these habits and make your dog feel more comfortable. For instance, you can assume a more neutral and confident form of body language and, at the same time, avoid using overly emotional phrases of reassurance. Eventually, your confidence will help the dog feel more secure. Another good practice is to change the association of the trigger by pairing the feared event (or the cue for it) with high-value rewards, even before the dog gets anxious. If the dog has learnt to associate the phrase "it's okay" with a fearful event, you can change its association by using it during a fun game or while giving a treat so that it shifts the emotional tone. For minor signs of anxiety or fear-induced situations, it is advisable to avoid fussing. Calmly carry on through the experience by maintaining a neutral behaviour and reward only calm, relaxed states.

So far, we have established that fear is a normal, adaptive behaviour, especially in the wild, where it plays a vital role in helping dogs assess risks and to survive dangerous situations. In the domestic environment where we feel safe and secure, that instinct in our dogs remains, serving as a protective mechanism that alerts dogs to perceived threats in their surroundings. If you have raised a confident and well-balanced dog, rest assured that it will be able to cope with most fearful situations appropriately. A healthy fear response, when kept in check, is not only considered a natural event but can also be beneficial. It helps the dog navigate the world with a sense of caution and self-preservation, a bit like raising our children.

The real challenge, however, lies in addressing unexpected or abnormal events. Just because a dog is generally confident does not mean that it is immune to developing anxiety or phobias if exposed to trauma, overstimulation, or poorly handled fear-inducing experiences. It is imperative to intervene early, with calm and thoughtful strategies, to prevent normal fear responses from escalating into chronic fear or full-blown phobias. A treatment plan for managing fear includes the use of a technique known as desensitisation, which I have already discussed in previous chapters. To recap, it involves gradually exposing the dog to the feared stimulus at a low intensity and rewarding calm behaviour to help them build tolerance of the stimulus. For example, if your dog is afraid of the noise emitted by the vacuum cleaner, you might start by placing the vacuum cleaner near them without turning it on, praising and rewarding calm behaviour, and gradually moving towards running the vacuum cleaner. I am a big supporter of using desensitisation paired with counter-conditioning. This involves changing the dog's emotional response to the feared stimulus. You could pair the fearful situation (e.g. the vacuum cleaner) with something positive like treats or play, helping the dog associate the fear-inducing stimulus with something pleasurable.

In the early stages of a treatment plan you can also create a safe space like a crate or designated room, where the dog can retreat during stressful situations and feel secure if it needs to. Training sessions that reinforce basic commands and build up a dog's confidence through positive reinforcement can also help them to manage fearful situations more effectively. As far as the treatment of phobias is concerned, desensitisation and counter-conditioning are equally effective techniques and are probably the first point of reference. However, because phobias are by definition far more intense than fear, the desensitisation process often takes longer and requires more patience from all those involved in the therapeutic treatment. For example, for a dog with a fear of thunderstorms, desensitisation could involve playing recordings of thunder at a very low volume initially and pairing it with rewards until the dog learns to associate the sound with positive experiences. In severe cases of phobia, especially when the dog's quality of life is significantly impacted, medication may be necessary. Medications like fluoxetine or clomipramine (SSRI or TCA classes) may be prescribed by a vet to reduce anxiety and facilitate the effectiveness of the behavioural modification process.

Lastly, providing a safe space for the dog during triggering events, like a thunderstorm for example, is key. This may involve creating a safe space similar to a den, where the dog feels secure. It is also important to acknowledge that some fearful responses are hardwired into a dog's genetic code. Just as certain breeds have been selected for traits like guarding, herding, or retrieving, temperamental traits, such as sensitivity to noise or neophobia (fear of new things), can also be inherited. In fact, it is not unusual nowadays to come across Labradors or golden retrievers, breeds historically associated with gun dogs, who are frightened by the sound of gunshots. Whilst their working ancestors may have been selectively bred for steadiness and confidence in noisy environments, not all modern individuals retain those traits. Many of these breeds now come from lines bred more for companionship than field work, and their sensitivity to sound may not have been filtered out genetically.

When a dog experiences a fearful event, it typically responds by following its inherent instincts; most notably, the urge to *escape from danger* or *escape to* seek *safety*. If you find yourself in such a situation – for example, walking your dog in the park when a sudden noise like a car backfiring startles them and they bolt - it is important to remain calm and take immediate, thoughtful action. If the dog runs off (*escape to safety*), leave something familiar at the location where you last saw them, such as the leash or their blanket (if you happen to carry one with you), a worn item of your clothing, or their favourite toy. These scent cues can serve as a beacon of comfort, helping the dog find their way back if they attempt to return. I have personally experienced this instinctual response with our own little Chihuahua. After a fearful encounter with a hyper-energetic dog during a walk, he managed to slip away (*escape from danger*) and run all the way back home. Though the situation was distressing at the time, what stood out was his ability to navigate familiar territory and seek the safety of his own environment. In fact, when we run back home to check his whereabouts, we found him sitting calmly on our doormat waiting for us, shaken but unharmed.

I remember another particular case that perfectly illustrates the power of fear responses and also the value of scent in a dog's world. One of our married couple clients had taken their Labrador to a fireworks display while holidaying in the South of France. They were watching the show from the comfort of their convertible car when, at the very first explosion, the dog panicked and leapt from the vehicle, overcome by the fight-or-flight instinct. Within seconds, he had vanished into the night. Understandably distraught, the owners immediately began searching for the frightened dog but after a few hours they called me in the middle of the night asking for help. I advised them to return to the site and leave the dog's blanket, which carried the familiar scent of the dog, at the location where the car had been parked, and then continue the search. Sure enough, several hours later, once the fireworks had ended and the environment felt safe again, they returned to find their dog curled up on the blanket, waiting for them. This experience highlights not only how strong and instinctive fear reactions can be but also the deep role that scent and routine play in a dog's ability to find safety. In overwhelming moments, dogs often seek the last place they felt secure, and scent can act as a powerful homing beacon. It also reinforces the importance of avoiding overwhelming environments, especially for sound-sensitive dogs, and having a safety plan in place during events like fireworks or thunderstorms. Something as simple as a familiar scent object can help guide a frightened dog back to security.

On another occasion, Frida, one of our Australian shepherds was out for a walk in the beautiful open spaces of Kensington Gardens when a cannon shot rang out across the park, part of a traditional gun salute to mark the Queen's birthday. The sudden and unexpected noise startled her so intensely that she bolted across the park and on to an extremely busy road, narrowly avoiding traffic, and disappeared from my sight. Although I was worried and devastated, what happened next was remarkable. She somehow managed to navigate her way home entirely on her own, which was located a few kilometres away from the park. Despite the fear, disorientation, and chaos, she returned to the place she associated with safety and comfort. This story, like many others, reminds me that fear can override training, reason, and even deep bonds of trust in the heat of the moment. Yet, it also shows how incredibly attuned dogs are to their environment, their memory, and their internal compass. Although this event had a happy ending, it could have turned out very differently. It thus serves as a powerful reminder that even well-trained, confident dogs can succumb to overwhelming fear, and that sound desensitisation, awareness of local events, and secure leash practices (I still see people walking their dogs off the leash on busy streets) are all crucial, especially in urban environments where loud or unexpected noises are more likely.

Leash Reactivity and Pulling

Pulling on the leash is another issue commonly reported during my training sessions. From an evolutionary perspective, one of the main reasons dogs pull on the leash is simply that dogs and humans are built to move differently and, most importantly, at a different pace. Dogs are naturally inclined to walk at a faster, more exploratory pace. Their movement is driven by instinct, curiosity, and sensory input, especially scent. Their evolutionary role as hunters and scavengers meant they needed to cover ground efficiently, often zig-zagging to follow scent trails or respond to environmental stimuli. Humans, on the other hand, adopt a more deliberate and slower walking pace, shaped by different evolutionary needs. Moreover, in modern times, the gap has widened even more, as people often walk while distracted by phones, engaging in conversations, or multitasking, which slows the pace further and breaks the rhythm of the walk from the dog's point of view. This natural mismatch in walking styles often leads to tension, literally, on the leash. For dogs, pulling is not just an indication of impatience, it is merely an attempt to reconnect with the world at their own natural speed and style. From a behavioural perspective, it is essential to remember that dogs, like all animals, repeat behaviours that work. Every behaviour has a function and serves a purpose in enabling the dog to achieve a desired outcome. If pulling on the leash consistently results in getting closer to something the dog wants, whether that is an enticing smell, another dog, a favourite park, or even just forward movement, then, from the dog's point of view, pulling is a successful strategy. With each subsequent outing the behaviour will reinforce itself, hence the dog will be eager to repeat the behaviour ever more efficiently to achieve the perceived positive outcome.

    This is why many dogs continue to pull, despite repeated corrections or attempts to manage it. The behaviour is being unintentionally reinforced by the outcome. The leash tightens, the dog continues to move forward, and that forward motion reinforces the pulling. Furthermore, when we tighten the leash and pull backward, the dog's natural response is to pull forward, not out of defiance but due to an automatic, reflexive reaction called the opposition reflex. This is a survival mechanism deeply embedded in the nervous system. It helps animals (and humans) maintain balance and resist being moved against their will. Think of it this way; if I push you backward unexpectedly, your body instinctively applies a counter force of equal intensity to prevent falling and to stay upright. Dogs do the same. When they feel the backward pressure coming from the collar or the harness, their body compensates by leaning forward and pulling harder. The more we pull back, the more the dog pushes forward. It becomes more like a tug-of-war exercise, and the dog thinks that is just how walking on a leash works. The use of a harness can actually reinforce pulling behaviour, as it makes the act of pulling more efficient and comfortable for the dog. Think of sled dogs, who wear specially designed harnesses that distribute pressure across their chest and shoulders, allowing them to pull heavy loads with ease. Whilst harnesses can be helpful in specific situations, such as for dogs with respiratory issues or for safety in the car, they are not always ideal for leash training, especially if your goal is to reduce pulling. In fact, for dogs that are already inclined to pull, a standard harness may inadvertently encourage and reward that behaviour by giving them the physical leverage to do so more effectively.

This is why traditional "jerk and pull" methods used in an attempt to control or manage pulling on the leash often backfire, especially if used in connection with choke chains and prong collars, which is how I was taught to deal with this issue in the old days. They not only reinforce the unwanted behaviour but also create tension, discomfort, and in some cases, emotional frustration or, even worse, leash reactivity. Instead of trying to control with force, the more effective approach is to remove the reward that follows pulling and teach the dog that only calm, loose-leash walking leads to forward motion.

This is where the A-B-C method can help us understand and resolve leash pulling by breaking down the behavioural sequence.

A stands for Antecedent: What happens immediately before the behaviour?

B stands for Behaviour: What does the dog actually do?

C stands for Consequence: What happens immediately after the behaviour?

Let us walk through a common example - imagine you are walking on the street and your dog starts pulling toward another dog.

A = Your dog sees another dog ahead.

B = Your dog pulls hard on the leash.

C = You (intentionally or unintentionally) move closer to the other dog.

In this case, the action of pulling brings your dog closer to something it desires; namely, an expected social interaction with another dog or just excitement. Hence, the behaviour is rewarded by the outcome, making it more likely to be repeated in the future. You can see that from the dog's point of view, this is simply logical: "I pull = I get closer = pulling works".

This behaviour must not be confused with leash reactivity or fear. In fact, if the dog did not want to approach the other dog, their behaviour might look completely different; you might notice freezing, backing away, barking, or lunging in an attempt to create distance. These behaviours serve a different function, such as asking for space or communicating unease and discomfort at the sight of the other dog, and require a different approach.

To modify this behaviour and raise a dog that does not pull on the leash, please refer to the previous chapter dedicated to implementing the various leash walking training techniques. However, one principle must be emphasised, prevention is always more effective than correction. Teaching good habits from the very beginning, before pulling becomes an ingrained pattern, saves both time and frustration later on. Puppies or newly adopted dogs benefit immensely from being shown what is expected in a calm, structured way before they have had the chance to rehearse and reinforce the pulling behaviour. Dogs, as creatures of habit, are shaped by the routines we allow or unintentionally reward. If we consistently permit pulling, even if it is just to reach the park gate or greet a friendly dog, we are teaching them that pulling is an acceptable way to navigate the world. Changing this habit later requires unlearning, which is always more difficult than shaping the right behaviour from the start.

We can apply the previously mentioned ABC method to teach your dog to walk nicely on the lead. If you have re-homed or rescued a dog from a shelter, this method provides a simple yet effective framework for understanding and shaping your dog's behaviour while walking on the leash. The first step consists of marking and rewarding a slack in the leash and you can start indoors, in a low-distraction environment, or in your garden if you have one. Clip the leash on and stand still. Your dog will react with excitement to the sight of the leash in expectation of a nice walk. It is important to ignore the unwanted behaviour and patiently wait until the desired behaviour casually occurs. The moment you notice even the slightest slack in the leash, meaning your dog is not pulling, mark the moment with a cheerful "Yes!" or click (if you use the clicker training method) and quickly deliver a treat. You can place the treat in their mouth or drop it at your feet to encourage them to stay close. Then take one or two steps forward and repeat the process. In this case the ABC method consists of:

A (Antecedent) = The dog is on a leash, and you are holding treats.

B (Behaviour) = The dog stays close enough for the leash to remain loose.

C (Consequence) = Delicious treats and happy, encouraging praise.

This is a very simple but equally effective approach to start with.

The second step involves using luring to help build and shape the desired behaviour. In the early stages, luring is a helpful tool that can be used to guide the dog into the correct position. Take several small treats in your hand, close your fingers around them, and hold your hand at your left-hand side, right at nose level. The goal is to have the dog literally "magnetised" to your hand and standing in the starting "Heel" position. As long as the dog stays with you and the leash remains loose, reward every 2-3 seconds with a tiny treat to start with and then build up the time until the dog is able to focus on you uninterrupted. You can then start moving slowly and deliberately, only a few steps at a time, following a random pattern. In this scenario, the ABC method works as follows:

A = The leash is clipped on and your treat hand is visible.

B = The dog follows the treat hand, walking at your side with a loose leash.

C = The dog receives a small treat and is praised with warmth and enthusiasm.

This approach builds positive associations with staying near you and, over time, your dog will learn that walking close and keeping the leash loose pays off, without ever needing to pull. Once you have mastered leash control in a familiar and distraction-free environment, it is time to transfer everything you have both learnt outside to a real-life case scenario. To implement a training routine that teaches your dog how to walk on the leash appropriately, I invite you again to refer back to the chapter dedicated to basic dog training and commands.

Coprophagy

Also known as coprophagia, this is a behaviour described as the act of eating faeces and is quite a common concern among pet owners, particularly in puppies and young dogs. Usually it does not require any sort of particular intervention, as it often resolves itself when the dog reaches a stage of maturity, when consistent supervision and a good nutrition regimen is in place, but it can become a concern if the behaviour is persistent or reappears in adulthood. Coprophagia in adult dogs can arise for different reasons, like the administration of poorly digestible diets, underfeeding, the presence of parasites, or digestive enzyme issues. Also, any medical problem that leads to a decrease in absorption of nutrients may prompt a gastrointestinal upset or cause an increase in the appeal of the dog's stool, leading to increased hunger and stool-eating. In these cases, a veterinary check is strongly recommended to exclude any potential underlying medical issues. Ultimately, understanding the causes and contributing factors underpinning coprophagia can help prevent it from becoming a long-term habit. The behaviour has a strong instinctive basis, as mother dogs eat their puppies' stools to keep the den clean and free from harmful bacteria and parasites, as well as to avoid attracting predators to the scent. This survival-driven behaviour can sometimes linger in some dogs, particularly females, especially if reinforced by lack of attention and a poor diet.

I recall a striking case involving two female Labradors, Kim and Maya, a mother and her daughter, whose owner reported a persistent case of coprophagia. One morning, I observed the behaviour firsthand: as the mother defecated, the daughter stood right behind her, waiting to immediately consume the stool. When it was the daughter's turn, the mother did exactly the same. This mutual behaviour likely stemmed from instinctual pack habits and early learning in addition to a poor diet. Remarkably, a simple dietary change from kibble to raw food resolved the issue within days, as the stools no longer contained undigested nutrients that made them appealing. Unfortunately, a few months later, the dogs were sent to a boarding facility where they were fed kibble again, and not surprisingly, the behaviour resurfaced. That was the proof I needed to confirm that a poor diet is indeed one of the factors contributing to this behaviour.

As for puppies, they may eat faeces as part of their natural development. During the transition from milk to solid food, this behaviour can contribute to populating their gut with beneficial bacteria essential for the digestion and absorption of nutrients. While for many people coprophagy, the act of eating faeces, is understandably unpleasant (if not downright revolting) to witness, it does have a biological purpose, particularly during a dog's early development. As mentioned previously, this behaviour often resolves naturally with the right combination of balanced nutrition, good hygiene, and consistent supervision. Interestingly, humans have stumbled upon a similarly curious practice, albeit in the realm of medicine rather than behaviour. In the United States, there are medical treatments available to patients that are suffering from severe gut dysbiosis or malabsorption syndromes in which healthy bacteria are extracted from a donor's stool and then introduced into the patient's digestive system, a procedure known as faecal microbiota transplantation (FMT). While the method might sound unconventional, it has shown promising results in restoring gut health and normal function. So while dogs might not be thinking about microbiomes or intestinal flora when they engage in this behaviour, it's a fascinating reminder that nature has its own way of recycling nutrients, and that sometimes, the solutions to health problems come from places we'd least expect.

We should also bear in mind that puppies explore the world with their mouths. When left unsupervised, they may investigate, play with, or ingest any new object they find, including faeces, simply out of curiosity, boredom, or as part of their scavenging instincts. Puppies also observe and imitate. A lactating female will clean and ingest her pups' faeces as part of natural nest hygiene, which causes some puppies to mimic this behaviour if they see their mother or even littermates doing the same.

Lastly, it is worth noting that if a puppy receives a significant reaction, whether positive or negative, after eating stool, the behaviour may be unintentionally reinforced. From the dog's perspective, attention is attention, and a strong emotional response from the owner can inadvertently encourage the puppy to repeat the behaviour in the future. It is also vital to address one of the most harmful myths that still circulates in some circles;

the outdated technique of rubbing a dog's nose in their faeces. Not only is this method ineffective and inhumane, but it also completely disregards how dogs learn. Punishment delivered after the act has no connection for the dog, as they are incapable of associating the punishment with something that happened even moments earlier. Instead of discouraging the behaviour, this approach only creates confusion, stress, and can erode the trust between the dog and the owner. Worse still, such a gesture could even be misinterpreted by the dog as an expectation or prompt, essentially suggesting that stool has a purpose or relevance, potentially reinforcing the very habit the owner wishes to eliminate. Clear, consistent supervision, a calm response, and an understanding of the reasons behind the behaviour are always more effective than any form of punishment. Please refer to the chapter dedicated to house training a puppy for a more in-depth explanation on how to prevent this issue from arising in the first place.

Another viable explanation for this behaviour, often overlooked by trainers and behaviourists, is that there may be a physiological motive underpinning coprophagia. Because dogs have far fewer taste buds than humans, they rely heavily on their extraordinary sense of smell to determine whether what they scavenge is edible. Most modern canine and human diets are based on processed foods, which may pass through the digestive system without being fully broken down or absorbed. As a result, faeces can still contain undigested or partially digested nutrients, making them appealing to a dog's nose. From a physiological standpoint, what we consider waste may still register to a dog as a viable food source.

For the management and the long-term resolution of this behaviour, I believe that the best possible approach is prevention. This can be achieved by implementing simple but thoughtful changes in the dog's daily routines and lifestyle choices. For adult dogs who are already experiencing this issue, this might include improving the quality of the dog's diet, ensuring they are mentally and physically stimulated, closely supervising them during toileting routines, and avoiding unintentionally reinforcing the behaviour through excessive attention. If you are dealing with a young dog or a puppy, it is sufficient to stick with a consistent daily schedule so that you can anticipate when they need to relieve themselves after their main meal. In addition, supervise them closely during toilet time, clean up promptly after they have relieved themselves to remove temptation, and make sure they are eating a nutritious, balanced, and digestible diet. A switch to a fresh or raw diet has, in some cases, resulted in an almost immediate improvement, particularly when the original diet left stools rich in undigested matter. Mental stimulation and regular positive interactions also go a long way towards reducing boredom-driven behaviours: if the dog is busy with some engaging activity, it will be less inclined to search for stools to eat. In some persistent cases, or when coprophagia reappears in adulthood, it is always worth consulting a veterinarian to rule out possible medical causes such as parasites or malabsorption issues. Patience, consistency, and an understanding of what motivates the behaviour are crucial. With the proper support and the right environment, most dogs will outgrow coprophagia, especially when, in accordance with the holistic approach, their needs are being met and their world is structured in a way that promotes healthy and species-appropriate behaviours.

Excessive Barking

Excessive barking is one of the most common concerns raised by dog owners and often causes many dogs to be relinquished or re-homed. But before we can address it effectively, we must understand its roots, not only from a behavioural perspective but also from an evolutionary one. Humans have selectively bred dogs for thousands of years to perform specific tasks, a large number of which required the use of vocalisation. Breeds that were specifically developed for guarding, herding, or alerting roles were intentionally selected for their tendency to bark. In fact, barking is one of the traits that most distinguishes dogs from their wild ancestors. Wolves rarely bark as it is deemed extremely counterproductive; it can disrupt hunting and interfere with the daily functions of the pack. Conversely, dogs, particularly those living in close proximity to humans, use barking as a key method of communication. If we think about it, it was considered very useful for early humans to have a dog that barked at approaching predators or strangers. The dog became a living alarm system, a protective companion who could sense and respond to environmental changes before the humans could even notice them. In many ways, barking was considered a valuable trait, a sought-after desirable signal, and not a nuisance. That instinct has not vanished just because we have moved into suburban homes and modern city life. Dogs still bark to alert us of perceived threats or as a reaction to fearful experiences, to communicate boredom or stress, or to demand attention. What we unfairly call "excessive barking" is often just a mismatch between what the dog was bred to do and the environment we now expect them to live in. Nonetheless, when barking becomes excessive, it often indicates an unmet need or a misunderstanding between the dog and the owner.

In my opinion, rather than viewing barking as a nuisance, it is more helpful to interpret it as a message: the dog is trying to tell us something. Some dogs bark out of boredom or loneliness, particularly if they are left alone for long periods of time with little or nothing to do. Others bark in response to external stimuli such as passersby, other dogs, or sudden noises. In some cases, barking becomes a form of attention-seeking behaviour, especially if the dog has learnt that barking reliably results in interaction from the owner, even if that interaction is negative. There is also a category of barking that stems from anxiety. Dogs suffering from separation anxiety, for example, may bark or howl (a type of vocalisation used to recall the pack) continuously when left alone, often accompanied by other signs of distress such as pacing, destruction, or elimination in the house. Understanding the function of the barking and ascertaining whether it is a behavioural issue that can be dealt with through training, or an issue arising as a consequence of a dog's emotional state of mind, is crucial in order to address it effectively. Every behaviour has a consequence that either reinforces or discourages it. If barking leads to a desired outcome for the dog, whether it is the appearance of the owner, a door being opened, or simply a successful attempt at attention seeking, then the behaviour is likely to be repeated. Holistically speaking, it is important to take a step back and ask ourselves, "What purpose is the barking serving for my dog?" before deciding how to intervene.

In cases where excessive barking is the result of a dog following its natural instincts, instincts carefully selected by humans over multiple generations, we can intervene effectively with a strategic plan based purely on the implementation of a consistent training regimen. The goal here is not to suppress the barking altogether but to manage and subsequently redirect it in a way that fits our modern lifestyles, which often require a quieter, more controlled environment. To manage excessive barking, I usually recommend teaching our dogs to bark on command and then stop the barking action on cue. It is a practical and effective method which the dog perceives as fun and a bond-strengthening exercise. Furthermore, by teaching your dog the "Speak" and "Quiet" commands, you give them an outlet for their instinct to bark, while also having control over when and how much they bark.

The first step in this process is teaching your dog to "Speak". To do this, you will want to encourage the dog to bark naturally. This is easiest when the dog is already stimulated by something, like the sound of the doorbell, a knock on the door, or the sound of a squeaky toy. When your dog barks, immediately say the command "Speak" in an enthusiastic tone of voice, and as soon as the dog responds to your command, reward them profusely with praise and their favourite treat. Even if the dog's barking is not perfectly timed with the cue at first, reward the effort anyway. Over time, the dog will begin to associate the word "Speak" with the action of barking, and they will learn to bark on command. Once the "Speak" command is established, you can begin introducing the "Quiet" or "Shush" command. After your dog barks a few times on cue, abruptly say the command "Quiet" or "Shush" in a more assertive tone of voice. This will cause the dog to suddenly stop barking as you have introduced something different from the usual cue word "Speak". The moment the dog stops barking, whether briefly or for a longer period of time, reward them with praise and a treat. As your dog becomes more proficient with the "Quiet" command, you can begin to increase the duration of silence required before offering a reward. Start with just a few seconds of quiet, then gradually extend the time as your dog gets better at controlling their barking. This teaches your dog that calm behaviour is what brings the reward. The key here is consistency and timing, only reward the dog when they stop barking, reinforcing the concept that silence is the desired behaviour. In addition to these two commands, it can be helpful to add a release cue, a phrase like "Okay" or "All Done". This lets your dog know that the training session has concluded and they can resume normal activity. The release cue helps the dog understand when the exercise is over, providing clarity and structure to the training process and an easy transition to real-life situations. In essence, by teaching your dog both the "Speak" and "Quiet" commands, as well as the release commands, you not only allow them to express their natural instinct to bark but also gain control over when that behaviour is appropriate. Over time, your dog will learn that barking is acceptable only in certain situations, and that the behaviour should be brief and properly cued by the owner. Make sure the dog acknowledges that calm behaviour will always be rewarded.

This method, grounded in positive reinforcement, allows dogs to fulfil their natural instincts without disturbing the peace of the household and, most importantly, that of its neighbours. On the other hand, if the excessive barking is caused by an altered state of mind, the behaviour is a symptom of a deeper emotional issue that needs to be addressed with patience and a tailored behaviour modification plan. I remember working with a family who had recently adopted a two-year-old mixed breed dog named Buster. He had settled into his new home with enthusiasm, but within days the neighbours began complaining about his barking whenever the family left the house. They insisted he was fine during the day, as he had access to the garden as well as to plenty of toys and mind-game devices, but the barking and howling would start within minutes of their departure and continue in intervals for hours. We decided to install a baby monitor and pretend to leave the house. Together with the whole family we observed Buster on video while standing a few metres away from the property and the real issue became clear. Buster was not barking out of boredom as he had plenty of entertainment at his disposal, he was barking from a place of distress, as the absence of the family took priority over anything else. He would run from window to door, occasionally howling, then sit silently staring at the door and begin barking again. This was a classic case of separation-related anxiety, not simply nuisance barking. We came up with a solution that required a layered approach. Firstly, we reduced the amount of time he was left alone using a combination of a dog-walking service and rearrangement of his daily schedule. We then introduced a predictable daily routine that helped Buster feel secure, with enrichment activities like scent work and puzzle feeders to redirect his mental energy. We also changed how departures were handled – no dramatic goodbyes or emotional returns – and taught him to settle on a mat using a reward-based method. Gradually, Buster began to build tolerance towards being alone for short periods, supported by calm exits and a background soundscape in the form of classical music that blocked any external noise triggers. Perhaps one of the most powerful shifts came from the owners themselves. Initially, they were anxious and tense each time they had to leave the house, worrying about complaints and feeling frustrated by Buster's anxious behaviour. However, as their understanding of the issue grew, their energy also changed. They moved from reacting emotionally to Buster's unhappiness to observing his behaviour from an analytical perspective, and Buster responded in the same way. Within a few weeks, the barking had diminished significantly, and with continued work, it faded almost completely.

This case highlights that barking is not the problem itself, it is merely the symptom. It must be perceived as a form of canine expression, and as conscious pet parents, it is our job to listen, understand the cause, and help the dog find healthier ways to cope. The completely wrong way to approach excessive barking is by resorting to punishment, often out of frustration or embarrassment, especially when the dog's behaviour is drawing attention from neighbours or others around you. Feeling overwhelmed if your dog's barking becomes disruptive is understandable, but punishing the dog in response to their natural instincts can only exacerbate the issue. Punishment-based methods, such as yelling, spraying the dog with water, or using aversive devices like citronella spray or shock collars, do not address the root cause of the behaviour. Instead, they often create confusion, anxiety, and fear in the dog. This can undermine the bond of trust between you, making it more difficult to resolve the problem in the long term. Moreover, punitive methods can lead to other unwanted behaviours, such as increased anxiety, aggression, or further barking, particularly when the dog is unable to understand why they are being punished. Such punishment does not teach the dog what to do; it only tells them what not to do. This is where positive reinforcement (i.e. teaching the dog what behaviour you want to see) is far more effective and long lasting. By focusing on rewarding quiet behaviour and providing structure, you allow your dog to learn that calmness leads to positive outcomes, which is a far more sustainable solution than trying to suppress the barking through fear or discomfort.

<u>Destructive Chewing</u>

Although not always listed among the most frequent behavioural complaints from dog owners, I do come across this issue on occasion during my training sessions. Whether it's shredded cushions, gnawed furniture, or a chewed-up remote control or designer sunglasses, this behaviour can be frustrating, costly, and pose a potential health risks for the dog. But before considering corrective measures or aversive responses as our first reaction upon finding the mischief, it is essential to investigate the underlying causes driving the behaviour, and how a holistic approach that evaluates the dog's environment, emotional state, routine, and unmet needs can not only treat the behaviour, but help to prevent it in the first place.

The first step to take in order to effectively address destructive chewing, consist of carrying out a behavioural anamnesis, that is a detailed history and analysis of the dog's behaviour, routine, and environment. For this purpose you can refer to the Behavioural Questionnaire found at the end of these pages. The important questions we should ask ought to include:

- **The dog's age and breed**: Is the dog teething (puppies) or from a breed with high oral drive who are predisposed to carry things in their mouth (e.g., retrievers, terriers)?
- **When does the chewing occur?** Only when left alone, during the night, or after a walk?
- **What is being chewed?** Objects with your scent, items from one room only, or random household items?
- **How is the dog exercised, mentally and physically?**
- **Has there been a recent change?** New schedule, home, pet, or family member?

Destructive chewing in my experience is rarely a standalone issue. In fact it can indicate the presence of other underlying problems such as:

- Boredom and under-stimulation
- Teething (in puppies)
- Separation anxiety or stress
- Lack of boundaries or consistent structure
- Learned behaviour reinforced by attention

A holistic approach therefore considers important factors like the dog's emotional state, environment, instincts, nutrition, routine, and last but not least the communication with humans. When these aspects are overlooked or inadequately addressed, dogs may resort to chewing as a self-soothing behaviour, a coping mechanism to alleviate the negative effects of accumulated stress or frustration. Notably, the act of chewing stimulates the release of endorphins in the canine brain, promoting a calming effect and reinforcing the behaviour as a form of emotional regulation. So, what can we do to prevent this issue in the first place and ensure it is addressed appropriately if it arises? The answer lies within the questions we asked previously above. By examining the root causes, such as; *Why is the dog chewing? What need is being unmet? What environmental or emotional factors are at play?* we are able to shift our focus from symptom correction to effective prevention. When we provide appropriate outlets for chewing, consistent structure, enrichment, emotional balance, and healthy communication, we not only treat the behaviour but promote long-term behavioural wellness. To summarise here are the key points:

1. Meet the dog's Physical and Mental Needs.

A tired dog is a much calmer and mentally balanced dog. Destructive chewing often signals an excess of unreleased energy.

- *Physical Exercise*: Include age-appropriate as well as breed-appropriate activities (e.g., off-lead running, structured walks, scent games).
- *Mental Stimulation*: Use puzzle feeders, sniffing games, hide-and-seek, basic training sessions, or controlled enrichment like food-dispensing toys to stimulate your dog's brain.

Another useful tip would be to make sure to satisfying your dog's **prey drive instinct** through structured games (like flirt pole sessions, "find it" games, or controlled tug). These activities can help redirect chewing into healthier outlets.

2. Proper Enrichment and Chew Outlets.

In the wild, chewing is a natural canine need, it doesn't only help to relieve negative feelings such frustration and stress, but it also engages the dog's jaw and brain.

- Provide safe chews like antlers, yak milk chews, natural rubber toys, or frozen KONGs filled with nutritious treats.
- Don't leave all the toys around and all at the same time. Rotate the toys regularly in order to maintain novelty.
- For teething puppies, offer them either frozen carrot sticks or cloths soaked in chamomile tea and frozen.

3. Implement Structured Routine and Alone-Time Training.

As previously stated, dogs thrive on routine. The lack of predictability can often lead to anxiety and consequently to chewing as a self-soothing behaviour.

- Establish consistent times for meals, walks, play, and rest.
- It is crucial to teach our dog to feel safe by being alone gradually, especially during the first few months during imprinting. Use desensitisation and counter-conditioning if the chewing is linked to separation anxiety. If that is the cause, you will need to practice short, positive departures using a cue word and build up duration slowly (please refer to the dedicated paragraph).

4. Create Safe Spaces and Implement Management.

If your dog needs to be left alone unsupervised, you will need to put in place measures in order to manage the environment so that you can prevent damage and instead reinforce success.

- Use crate training methods as explained in the dedicated chapter (when introduced positively) or limit the dog's access to certain areas with baby gates.
- Dog-proof your home: remove access to dangerous or valuable items when you're not around.
- Provide an inviting "chew zone" with engaging toys and calming background music or diffusers, like **Adaptil Pheromone Diffusers**, **valerian**, **CBD** (vet approved), or **calming herbs which** may help particularly those more anxious chewers.

5. Training and Communication

Many dogs chew destructively simply because they don't understand boundaries through no fault of their own. Teaching through positive reinforcement builds trust and clarity. For example:

- Reinforce calm behaviour, especially when your dog is chewing the right object.
- Interrupt (not punish!) undesirable chewing with a calm redirection: offer an alternative chew and then praise profusely.
- Teach cues like **"Leave it"**, **"Go to bed"**, and **"Settle down"**.

Most importantly, avoid punishment. Scolding a dog after the chewing has occurred is unfair and utterly ineffective. As we know, dogs live in the present moment and are unable to make meaningful associations between a punishment and an action that took place even minutes earlier. As a result, reprimanding them after the fact does not teach them what they did wrong, it only creates fear, confusion, and emotional insecurity, which may, in turn, worsen the problem. A more constructive approach is to redirect the behaviour proactively and address the underlying needs driving it.

When it comes to choosing appropriate items for dogs to chew on, I often recommend natural options such as deer antlers or raw bones. These satisfy the dog's instinctive need to gnaw while offering long-lasting engagement. However, it's worth noting that some veterinarians advise against their use due to the potential risk of dental fractures—since these items are harder than the enamel of a dog's teeth, they could, in theory, cause a tooth to crack. Personally, I have never witnessed this in any of the dogs in our care, but if this is a concern for you, there are plenty of alternative chew products available. Many of these are made of durable rubber or other synthetic materials that are gentler on the teeth and designed to be safely broken down and digested if swallowed in small pieces. My own introduction to deer antlers came by chance many years ago while walking dogs in Richmond Park. During the rutting season, the resident stags would sometimes lose antlers after fierce mating battles. On one occasion, a Labrador Retriever found a shed antler and proudly carried it back to the vehicle. He was so content chewing on it during the drive home that I decided to leave it in the van. It became a shared treasure—each dog, in turn, taking great satisfaction in chewing it during our daily outings. Since then, I've kept antlers as a staple in our toolkit for enrichment and stress relief.

In conclusion, destructive chewing is not simply a nuisance, it is often a symptom of unfulfilled emotional, physical, or psychological needs. Over the years, I've worked with many dogs whose chewing habits told a deeper story often directly connected to unmet needs, unspent energy, or unspoken stress. A holistic approach has consistently helped me uncover these hidden causes. It allowed me to look beyond the behaviour itself and address directly the underlying causes, whether they stemmed from boredom, stress, lack of appropriate outlets, or unmet instinctual drives. By simply taking steps towards enriching the dog's environment, providing suitable chew items, maintaining a balanced routine, and building strong human-canine communication, we can not only treat the problem effectively but also prevent it from developing in the first place. Most importantly, we must avoid punishment, which only serves to increase confusion or anxiety.

Hyperactivity and Over-Excitement

Some dogs seem to operate in a perpetual "always on the go" mode, even when their physical exercise needs are consistently met. Behaviours such as jumping on guests, pacing around the house, barking excessively, or spinning with excitement at the slightest trigger, can be especially challenging for owners with a naturally lower energy level. While high energy levels are expected and natural in certain breeds or during the developmental stages (like adolescence) of a young dog, true *hyperactivity* or *over-excitement* can indicate deeper behavioural imbalances that deserve attention, and certainly not an aversive approach.

In my experience, hyperactivity in dogs is often misunderstood. Many owners interpret it as simply part of the dog's personality or assume the dog is just too" spoiled." However, what is often labeled as hyperactivity may actually stem from a combination of deeper, interconnected factors which I can highlight as:

- Insufficient physical and mental stimulation.

- Lack of clear boundaries or inconsistent training.

- Emotional dysregulation in the form of anxiety, frustration, or an inability to self-soothe.

- Reinforcement of arousal-based behaviours (e.g., unintentionally rewarding jumping or barking)

- Overstimulation in the home (in the presence of hyperactive children for example or because of disrupted rest cycles during the dog's daily routine).

Furthermore, in some cases the dog may not be truly hyperactive at all but rather untrained, under-exercised, or chronically in a state of over-arousal. Recognising the difference between these important aspects is key to choosing the right intervention following a holistic approach. Another important factor to consider is the main difference between what is described as Energy and Dysregulation.

All dogs possess a natural reserve of energy that, if analysed in a more primitive context, would be directed toward essential survival tasks such as hunting, foraging, guarding, or exploring. However, when this energy lacks a productive outlet in a modern domestic setting, it can easily become misdirected or excessive. True hyperactivity often reveals itself through signs such as impulsiveness, poor focus, and difficulty settling, even after adequate physical exercise. These dogs may genuinely struggle to relax and are frequently mislabelled as "naughty," "stubborn," or "uncontrollable," when in fact they are simply overwhelmed.

Over-excitement on the other hand, often referred to as emotional dysregulation, tends to be situational and context-dependent. Unlike generalised hyperactivity, this behaviour usually arises in specific scenarios, such as when guests arrive, during playtime, or while out on walks. In these moments, the dog becomes overwhelmed by arousal or stimulation and struggles to maintain self-control. Rather than being disobedient, these dogs simply lack the skills to regulate their emotional responses. What they need is guidance in learning how to pause, reset, and eventually "switch off" when the situation requires it.

Finally, let's not forget that, although dogs have adapted remarkably well to our modern lifestyle, their primal instincts and the energy levels once essential for survival and work remain very much alive. When these inherent drives aren't acknowledged or properly fulfilled, behavioural issues like hyperactivity are likely to emerge as a result. As with many other behavioural issues, a holistic approach for the treatment of hyperactivity and over-arousal isn't about "suppressing" the behaviour but rather understanding the *cause*, and subsequently creating the right *conditions* for a permanent change of the behaviour. As with many other behavioural rehabilitation plans that contemplate the holistic approach, those dog owners affected by this issue should adhere to a consistent set of guiding principles, namely:

1. Assess the Dog as a Whole entity.

Carry out a behavioural anamnesis, perhaps using again the Behavioural Questionnaire, which should ask questions like:

- The dog's daily routine: Is the dog under- or over-stimulated?

- Nutrition: Is the the type of diet fuelling erratic energy (BARF diet or kibbles)?

- Rest: Does the dog get enough calm downtime away from children and other stimuli?

- Breed traits: Are you working with a natural high-drive dog (e.g., a working line Border Collie or Malinois)?

- Social learning: What behaviours has the dog been inadvertently reinforced for?

2. Provide Structured Outlets for Excess Energy

- Physical exercise should be *appropriate* for the type of breed, temperament, age etc., not just aimless running or constant ball throwing, which can actually ramp up arousal.
- Mental stimulation (scent work, puzzles, obedience training) is often more effective than physical exercise in tiring an excitable dog.
- Satisfy innate needs: For example, a terrier might benefit from digging games, a retriever from fetch and carry tasks and so on.

3. Teach Calmness

Sometimes dogs literally need to *learn* to calm themselves down. Techniques to achieve this may include:

- training the dog for commands like" Settle" on a mat or a designated resting place.
- Capturing and rewarding calm behaviour and balanced state of mind.
- Establish structured routines with rest periods built in, similar to the table provided in previous chapter (puppy's daily routine).
- Practising exercises that encourage neutrality during greetings and transitions (e.g., getting ready for walks).

4. Calm the Environment

A chaotic, noisy home with unpredictable stimulation (TV, children, direct views to the outdoors through open windows, or constant interaction) can keep a dog in a state of chronic alertness. Designate calm zones and limit access to overstimulating spaces when needed.

5. Use Relationship-Based Training

I always recommend to try and avoid harsh corrections, they often increase frustration or even fear and phobias, making hyperactive behaviour worse. Instead do the following:

- Build focus and impulse control through reward-based training ("Watch me" command).

- Avoid overexcitement during greetings or playing sessions.
- Consistently reinforce calm choices when spontaneously offered by the dog.

According to the training principles outlined in the previous chapters, including the four quadrants of operant conditioning and classical conditioning techniques, let us now explore how to address hyperactivity and over-excitement in practical terms. Despair not: even the most excitable dogs can learn the art of relaxation. Like any other skill, calmness must be taught, practiced, and reinforced. Below are simple yet powerful exercises designed to help dogs transition from a state of arousal to one of calm. These routines can be incorporated into daily life and are especially helpful when used proactively, for example, before a walk, during overstimulating play, or in anticipation of known triggers like guests arriving.

1. "Go to Mat" or "Settle Down" Training

The purpose of this exercise is to build an association between a physical space and relaxation.

How to do it:

- Choose a mat or bed and place it in a quiet area designated for resting.
- Lure with treats or cue the dog to lie down on the mat.
- Reward timely each calm postures (lying on one hip, resting head, sighing) spontaneously offered by the dog.
- Say a calm phrase like "settle down" or "go/on your mat" and toss treats occasionally while the dog remains calm.
- Practise this daily, gradually increasing the duration.
- Increase the amount of time using the partial reinforcement schedules techniques.

One word of advice if I may, and that is to avoid using excited or high pitched tone of voice or too much praise. Remember, the goal is *calm*, not celebration.

2. Sniff-and-Search Game (Scent Scattering)

The purpose of this exercise is to activate the dog's natural seeking system, which promotes a calmer and more focused demeanour as well as mental satisfaction.

How to do it:

- Choose a quite place either in the garden or indoors, casually scatter small treats or bits of food on the ground.

- Encourage your dog to *sniff and search* for the treats quietly.

- Be patient and allow them to explore at their own pace, possibly refraining from adding any commands, a part from a cue word of your choice like "find it" for example to signal to the dog the beginning of the action.

This option works very well because the activity of sniffing in itself, helps to lower the dog's heart rate and blood pressure. It is grounding and calming, the opposite of arousal-based games like fetch.

3. Slow Pattern Games (e.g., "1-2-3 Treat Game")

This game that most of my clients, especially children, find very amusing, contributes to redirect the dog's focus on us and also reinforces a sense of predictability when dogs come across an overstimulating environment.

How to do it:

- Take your dog to a quite or familiar environment and stand still while keeping your dog on leash.

- Calmly say "One... two... three" and then feed a treat.

- Repeat the pattern using a soft, rhythmic tone of voice.

- Practise at home first for a few times, then try it outside when distractions appear. You will be surprised by your dog's reaction.

As a variation for this exercise, you can use the same structure but present the reward when the dog looks at you or lies down.

4. Implement Passive Calming Sessions with Chews or Licking Mats

This will encourage your dog's inherent and natural behaviours like licking and chewing for example, activities that soothe the nervous system by the release of the endorphin type hormones.

How to do it:

- Offer a long-lasting chew (e.g., deer antler, safe bone, a Kong toy stuffed with peanut butter or a favourite treat.

- Provide this in a calm environment with soft lighting and soothing music.

- Leave the dog to it so that he can engage *independently*, without interaction with others.

One very important thing to mention in this case is that it would be preferable not to use chews to distract from anxiety (e.g., during fireworks). The goal is to create positive associations with peaceful moments, not to suppress fear.

5. *Create a Breathing Space with The "Pause and Watch" Technique*

This holistically based method helps to interrupt the dog's overstimulation by inviting stillness and mindfulness.

How to do it:

- When your dog is starting to become overstimulated (e.g., before a walk, at the park gate), stop and ask them to "wait." As simple as that.

- Take a deep breath yourself and recompose your thoughts.

- Wait silently for your dog to make eye contact or offer a desirable behaviour like sit, then reward calmly.

- Practise this exercise daily in short but frequent repetitions, until your dog begins to offer calm behaviours automatically in anticipation.

By implementing some or even a combination of these methods consistently and integrating them into your dogs' daily routine, will teach them that calmness is not only possible, but desirable and extremely rewarding. We need to remember that our dogs don't come pre-programmed with an 'on-off switch', it's something we need to teach and nurture over time possibly starting since puppyhood. Just like children learn how to soothe themselves through bedtime routines or quiet time, dogs too need structured experiences that reinforce calmness, relaxation, and stillness. As someone who has worked with hundreds of dogs over the years, I've seen first-hand how much calmer and more balanced a dog becomes when their lifestyle, training, and emotional world are aligned. Hyperactivity isn't something we need to "correct", it's rather something that we need to understand, and then gently reshape.

Mounting and Humping

Mounting or humping is a natural canine behaviour that often causes confusion, and on occasion, a fair amount of embarrassment for some dog owners. However, in adolescent dogs, both males and females, the surge in sexual hormones can significantly influence behaviour, often manifesting indeed as mounting or humping. Let's face it, teenage dogs aren't that different from teenage humans, I do remember going through the same phase myself as a teenager: all hormones and very little common sense. The difference though is that your dog might decide to hump a guest's leg rather than slamming the bedroom door and blast loud music. Either way, it's a phase that calls for patience, an opportunity to establish clear boundaries, and a healthy sense of humour. A recent study, (Fusi J, Veronesi MC, Prandi A, Probo M, Faustini M, Peric T.), investigating hormonal changes during puberty in dogs sheds light on this phenomenon. Instead of relying on blood samples, which are impractical for long-term monitoring, researchers measured concentrations of testosterone (T), 17β-estradiol (E2), and progesterone (P4) in the dog's hair and nails, two biological materials that can reflect hormonal accumulation over a longer period of time in comparison to the traditional blood tests. The study involved five male and five female dogs and found a marked increase (twofold) in testosterone levels in males just before puberty. In females, estradiol rose significantly during puberty, followed by a notable increase in progesterone afterwards. This research highlights how hormonal fluctuations, especially around the pubertal period, can help explain the rise in sexually motivated behaviours such as mounting. Under normal circumstances therefore, it's perfectly natural for adolescent dogs to exhibit mounting or humping behaviour associated with the hormonal surge of sexual arousal. However, when this behaviour becomes persistent, sometimes even obsessive, it is usually less about reproduction and more about something else entirely. In fact, more often than not, excessive mounting is linked to social tension within the family group or pack of dogs, overexcitement, stress relief, or simply a lack of impulse control in some of our more mischievous, over-the-top characters. Just like teenage humans might fidget, pace, or act out, dogs too can channel their internal chaos into awkward (and occasionally theatrical) displays. At the time of writing, I'm in the process of training Sisu, the Leonberger puppy featured in one of the photographs in this book. Now 10 months old, he's just started to display this behaviour rather obsessively, likely triggered by the hormonal rollercoaster typical of adolescence. I've been managing it with a kind but consistent approach, setting clear boundaries and calmly interrupting the behaviour when necessary. No major dramas, just steady guidance and redirection, exactly what growing giants like him need to learn at this stage: a bit of self-control.

Let's now take a moment to highlight the other motivations, beyond sexual, that can drive this behaviour and, if left unchecked, potentially escalate into a more persistent or problematic pattern.

Excitement or overstimulation: Many dogs have the tendency to mount when they are overly aroused during play or social interactions.

Stress or anxiety: Sometimes mounting can serve as a displacement behaviour, something dogs do to self-soothe when they feel conflicted or uncertain.

Attention-seeking: If a dog learns that mounting gets a big reaction from people, even if it's negative attention, they may repeat the behaviour.

Social tension: In interactions with other dogs, mounting can sometimes be a way of establishing hierarchy or testing social relationships.

Habitual or compulsive tendencies: If reinforced over time, it can become a habit or even a compulsive behaviour, especially in dogs that struggle to regulate their emotional states.

So, What Can We Do to Prevent or Manage It?

As with most behavioural challenges, the solution lies in observation, understanding, and providing the dog with appropriate outlets and guidance. Here's how I approach it from a holistic behaviour and wellness standpoint:

- Rule Out Medical Causes

Before assuming the excessive act of mounting is purely a behavioural issue, it's essential to rule out any possible underlying medical factors. Urinary tract infections, skin irritation, hormonal imbalances, or even neurological issues can all contribute to the consolidation of the behaviour. A consultation with a vet is the first step if the behaviour is either new, persistent, or increasing in frequency.

- Assess the Context

Remember when I mentioned the use of an Ethogram to assess the behaviour more precisely? In this situation an Ethogram could be very helpful in establishing the possible causes of the behaviour. We should ask ourselves questions like: When does the behaviour usually occur? Is it during exciting moments, in new environments, or when the dog is left alone? It would be very useful to keep a journal to identify patterns. Often, you'll find that mounting is linked to periods of heightened arousal, lack of stimulation, or social stress.

- Provide Physical and Mental Outlets

Boredom and excess energy are major contributing factors to the insurgence of mounting behaviour. I can assure you that a well-structured daily routine that includes both physical exercise (e.g., structured walks, fetch, swimming etc.) and mental stimulation (e.g., scent games, puzzle feeders, training drills) can reduce unwanted behaviours significantly. We ought to bear in mind that a tired dog is not just one who has had a run in the park, but one that is mentally and emotionally satisfied because he has been given the opportunity to use his brain and body in balance.

- Redirect the Behaviour

Forgive me if I might sound repetitive at times but Redirection often works better than Punishment. Rather than scolding your dog, calmly interrupt the mounting and redirect him to a more appropriate behaviour like offering him a chew toy, initiate a training cue like *"Sit"* or *"Go to your bed"*, or engage them in a calming activity. With consistency, dogs can learn new, more acceptable coping strategies as an alternative to mounting excessively.

- Teach Calmness and Impulse Control

Try to incorporate relaxation sessions into your daily routine. Exercises like the "Settle on a Mat", "Wait", or simply reinforcing moments of stillness can go a long way especially in those inherently hyper active breeds. In my own work, I've found that teaching dogs to relax is as important, if not more, than teaching them to "work" or obey commands.

- Avoid Reinforcing the Behaviour

Sometimes, without realising it, we tend to reinforce mounting by laughing perhaps out of embarrassment, reacting loudly, or trying to physically remove the dog in a firm and dramatic way, all of which can be both exciting and/or rewarding to an already aroused dog. Try to remain calm, quiet, and redirect firmly but gently.

Let's not forget that dogs are emotional beings who communicate and cope in ways that are often misunderstood by humans. As we have seen, mounting isn't necessarily a sign of dominance or disobedience, it's rather used as a form of communication, a coping mechanism, or a natural response to arousal. By treating it with curiosity rather than frustration, we can create an environment in which our dogs feel more balanced and understood, just another reminder that behaviour is never random; it's information waiting to be translated.

On a less serious note, if you happen to witness, or be the unwilling target of, a mounting episode, try to see the funny side. I remember one particular occasion that turned into a lesson in humility and humour. I had been invited to participate in the glamorous reopening of the iconic Asprey store on Bruton Street in Mayfair, London. The event was designed to reflect quintessential British elegance: white and purple-themed uniforms, a chauffeur-driven Rolls Royce in matching livery, and a staged street scene to impress the media and guests. My role? To add an extra touch of sophistication, handling two immaculate Standard Poodles, perfectly groomed and ready to charm the audience and the media present for the occasion. As celebrities began to arrive, I found myself near the red carpet area just as Sir Elton John stepped out of his car. A known animal lover, he kindly asked for a photo with the dogs, which I was delighted to facilitate. Cameras clicked, the crowd admired the scene... and then the giggling started. I turned around, puzzled by the growing laughter, only to discover that the two Poodles were enthusiastically humping each other right in front of the paparazzi. The timing couldn't have been worse, or better, depending on your perspective. The dogs had unintentionally stolen the spotlight, and the photo made the front page of the tabloids the next day. In situations like these we need to try to see the funny side, because sometimes, that is all we can do. So, keep your cool, have a quiet chuckle, and redirect. With consistency (and a good sense of humour), your dog will move past this phase, and you'll gain a story that's hard to top at dinner parties.

Resource Guarding

As previously discussed in the chapter addressing aggression and fear, the issue of resource guarding warrants careful attention. For a more detailed analysis, I invite you to revisit that section. In summary, however, it is important to emphasise that resource guarding can be effectively addressed through the holistic framework outlined in this book, supported by the wealth of evidence-based behavioural science available to us today. Ultimately, by fostering understanding, patience, and a commitment to kind, ethical training practices, we can guide our dogs toward greater emotional balance and cooperative behaviour. It is my hope that the insights shared throughout these pages will not only help you navigate behavioural challenges, but also deepen the bond between you and your dog, a bond built on trust, respect, and mutual growth.

In this final chapter, dedicated to some of the most commonly reported causes of behavioural issues in our pets, I would like to take a step back and try, just for a moment, to put myself in our modern pet's shoes. Rather than focusing solely on the animal's behaviour, let us ask ourselves: what might we be doing wrong on our side? What human habits, assumptions, or expectations might be contributing to the development of these issues? One particularly relevant concern, one I encounter almost daily in my work, is our growing tendency to attribute human emotions, thoughts, and motivations to our pets. This phenomenon is known as **anthropomorphism**.

Anthropomorphism

The term *anthropomorphism* comes from the Greek *anthropos* (human) and *morphe* (form), and it refers to the act of attributing human characteristics, intentions, or emotions to non-human beings or objects. While this might seem a harmless practice, or even endearing, when applied to our pets, it can seriously impact our ability to understand and respond appropriately to their true needs and behaviours. This tendency isn't new. Even Charles Darwin, in 1872, observed how people naturally described animals in human-like terms. And it's not limited to pets. We see it in how we relate to natural forces, fictional characters, and even machines like humanoid robots. In each case, there's a human inclination to seek familiarity by projecting (again the concept of projection) our own traits onto something "other." We must recognise however, that when it comes to our pet animals, this projection can create both a sense of closeness and also a barrier to true understanding their behaviour and needs. For example, interpreting a dog's bark as a request to play, or a cat's meow in front of the fridge as a polite demand for food, may seem reasonable. But such interpretations can oversimplify complex behaviours and lead to confusion or even conflict. Consider a dog that shows the whites of its eyes, commonly referred to as "whale eye", while lying still as a child hugs it tightly. A well-meaning parent might interpret this as tolerance or affection, when in fact, the dog is displaying a clear sign of discomfort or stress. Misreading this signal could lead to a bite, not because the dog is unpredictable, but because its subtle warnings were ignored in the first place.

During the research for my book, I found out that one of the reasons humans so easily fall into anthropomorphism is deeply rooted in neuroscience. Studies show that animals and humans share brain structures involved in emotion processing, such as areas within the limbic system and cortical regions. This overlap makes it tempting for humans to interpret animal expressions and behaviours through a human lens, especially when facial expressions appear similar. However, different species use different regions of the face to express emotion, which can easily lead to misinterpretation. What may look like sadness or guilt in a dog, for example, might instead be a form of appeasement or stress. Research by Urquiza-Haas and Kotrschal revealed that observing distress in animals activates the same neural regions in the human brain as when witnessing human suffering, specifically the medial prefrontal cortex, inferior frontal gyrus (IFG), and anterior insula (a region of the brain deep in the cerebral cortex). In fact, some people experience stronger emotional responses to animal suffering than to human suffering. This emotional resonance is at the core of human empathy and explains why we're often quick to ascribe human-like emotions to animals, especially when they display behaviours or facial cues that resemble our own. There is also a deep social dimension to anthropomorphism. As gregarious beings ourselves, we're drawn to relationships and social bonds, and animals, particularly dogs, fulfil many of these psychological and emotional needs. Dogs, due to their long-standing co-evolution with humans, often occupy a privileged space in our social world. Many people don't just see their dogs as pets, but as family members, emotionally entwined with the household.

This deep emotional connection can lead us to assign human characteristics to dogs as a way to fulfil unmet social or emotional needs. As noted by Díaz-Videla, anthropomorphism can be driven by factors such as a desire for control, feelings of loneliness, the pursuit of social connection, and emotional dependence on non-human companions. In a modern world where human relationships can feel fragmented or stressful, dogs offer a stable, nonjudgmental presence, and this can reinforce our tendency to see them not just as animals, but as almost-human confidants.

It is quite plausible o assume that Anthropomorphism often stems from that deep emotional bond we tend to form with our pet companions as well as from our very human desire to feel understood and connected with them. But if we truly want to nurture that bond and promote our dog's welfare, we must meet them on their terms, not ours. That means learning to read their cues, acknowledging the species-specific drivers behind their behaviour, and respecting the differences in how they process the world. I truly believe that when we do that, we don't diminish the relationship, we deepen it, with empathy grounded in understanding rather than assumption. With these premises in mind, let's delve deeper into the subject in order to understand the process.

Anthropomorphism begins with process of projection, which we have already discussed before. For instance, if we see a dog acting in a certain way, hesitating at the door, hiding under a table, barking at another dog, we are inclined to interpret these behaviours using our own emotional vocabulary. A dog hiding after a scolding is labeled as "guilty." A clingy dog is seen as being "jealous" when a new pet arrives. A dog who doesn't want to come inside is described as "stubborn" or "defiant." In reality, dogs do not feel or express emotions in the same complex, layered ways that humans do. Their behaviour is shaped by their inherited instinct, process of conditioning, and past experiences, not moral judgments or strategic emotional manipulation, that we humans excel in devising.

During a training session for example, a devoted dog owner once told me with genuine conviction that her dog understood the concept of time, specifically, that she would return home from work at 6pm. Each morning, she would point at the large wall clock in the kitchen and tell her dog, "I'll be back when the little hand is on the six." According to her, the dog would obediently sit by the clock and wait, and at 6pm, she would always be there to greet her joyfully at the door. While I find this story heartwarming, it speaks volumes about the emotional bond between humans and their dogs, and it is also a prime example of anthropomorphism. Dogs do not understand clock time (you could be gone for minutes or hours) or numerical representations. However, while they don't interpret the ticking hands of a clock the way we do, dogs *do* have an internal sense of time, one shaped by routine, sensory cues, and biology. At the heart of this ability lies their ***circadian rhythm,*** the internal clock that governs daily patterns of sleep, wakefulness, hunger, and activity. Much like in humans, this rhythm provides dogs with structure and predictability, allowing them to anticipate daily events such as walks, meals, and rest. Beyond this biological rhythm, dogs also rely heavily on their **sensory perceptions,** particularly smell and environmental changes. For example, a dog may begin to anticipate mealtime not because it's 6:00 p.m., but because hunger cues align with habitual feeding times. Likewise, many dogs appear to "know" when their owners are due home. This isn't magic, some scientists believe it's linked to ***olfactory cues***, such as the fading intensity of their owner's scent over time, which helps dogs estimate the duration of their absence. If a dog regularly sees patterns such as the light changing, traffic noise increasing, or smells and sounds that coincide with the owner's return, she may indeed wait at the door at roughly the same time each day. But this is not evidence of an understanding of time in the human sense. Projecting complex cognitive abilities like time-telling onto our dogs, while rooted in genuine feelings of affection, risks distorting our perception of how they truly experience the world. In doing so, we might overlook the more subtle but equally impressive ways in which dogs adapt to our schedules and form deep emotional attachments, certainly without needing to read a clock. Projecting complex cognitive abilities like time-telling onto our dogs, while rooted in genuine feelings of affection, risks distorting our perception of how they truly experience the world. In doing so, we might overlook the more subtle but equally impressive ways in which dogs adapt to our schedules and form deep emotional attachments, certainly without needing to read a clock.

To summarise, the most common consequences of anthropomorphism can be described as follows:

- ***Miscommunication***: When we assume dogs understand language or intentions like humans do, we set them up for failure. Commands are issued like polite requests rather than clear cues, leading to confusion and inconsistent behaviour.

- ***Reinforcing Unwanted Behaviour***: A puppy or a young dog jumping up on a guest may be interpreted as "excited to see you" and rewarded with affection, unintentionally reinforcing a habit that later becomes problematic.

- ***Emotional Mislabeling***: Describing a reactive dog as "protective" or "loyal" may downplay the need for training and support, delaying behavioural intervention and putting the dog (and others) at risk.

- ***Misdirected Discipline***: A classic example is the "guilty look." A dog lowers its head or avoids eye contact after doing something the owner disapproves of. This is often mistaken for remorse, but in fact, it is just a dog's calming signal, a response to the owner's body language or tone of voice, not an admission of wrongdoing.

- ***Inappropriate Humanisation***: Treating dogs like children, dressing them up, carrying them everywhere instead of walking, or pampering them excessively, can deprive them of natural behaviours like social interaction with other dogs and people, sniffing, and problem-solving skills. In extreme cases, this can even lead to anxiety or behavioural regression as I have noticed many times during my training sessions.

In conclusion, Anthropomorphism is an increasingly common tendency in human-animal relationships, particularly in the context of companion animals. While it may stem from empathy and affection, this tendency can have unintended negative consequences on animal welfare. It is essential to remember that although pets may exhibit behaviours or expressions that resemble human emotions, they are not human, and interpreting them as such can lead to misunderstandings, inappropriate care, or misguided training approaches. At the same time, it is important to acknowledge that anthropomorphism may, in part, be the natural by-product of the deep evolutionary relationship between humans and dogs. After thousands of years of cohabitation, mutual reliance, and emotional bonding, it is understandable that we might perceive them as "almost human." However, it is precisely this closeness that requires us to be even more vigilant and respectful of their true nature, not by human standards, but through a clear understanding of their species-specific needs and ways of communicating. Moreover, our companion animals have species-specific biological, emotional, and behavioural needs that differ not only from those of humans but also among themselves, varying by species, breed, age, physiological state, and individual characteristics. Recognising the fundamental differences in their anatomy, physiology, and behaviour allows us to meet those needs more effectively and ethically.

Ultimately, true respect and care for our animal companions come not from imagining them as human, but from understanding and honouring their nature as animals. This awareness forms the basis of a more responsible, informed, and compassionate relationship, one that enhances both the animal's well-being and the human-animal bond.

And so, as we come to the end of these pages, my hope is that you walk away not just with tools and techniques, but with a deeper sense of connection to the incredible creature at your side. Training, when done with empathy and understanding, is not about control, it is about communication. It is about learning to listen just as much as it is to guide our faithful companions. Through the holistic approach, we are not just shaping behaviour, we are building a bond rooted in trust, respect, and mutual growth.

This book, for me, is more than a guide, it is essentially a thank you, a tribute to the dogs that, over a career spanning more than 30 years, have walked beside me, challenged me, taught me, and loved me unconditionally. It is a way of giving back to a species that has given me so much, helping me to fulfil my dreams and, in the process, shaping me into a better version of myself. If this work offers even a small piece of that gift to others, then it has done its job.

Thank you for accompanying me on this journey. If you've found value in these pages or wish to share your own experiences, I warmly invite you to connect with me. You can find more information, updates, and resources at www.vipetslondon.com, or feel free to reach out directly, I always enjoy hearing from fellow dog lovers and passionate trainers.

REFERENCES

Chapter 1

Dugatkin, L.A. (2018). The silver fox domestication experiment. *Evolution: Education and Outreach,* 11(16) . https://doi.org/10.1186/s12052-018-0090-x

Hart, B.L., Hart, L.A., Thigpen, A.P., & Willits, N.H. (2014). Long-term health effects of neutering dogs: comparison of Labrador Retrievers with Golden Retrievers. *PLoS One, 9*(7), e102241. https://doi.org/10.1371/journal.pone.0102241

Hoffman, J.M., Creevy, K.E., & Promislow, D.E.L. (2013) Reproductive capability is associated with lifespan and cause of death in companion dogs. *PLoS One,* 8(4), e61082. https://doi.org/10.1371/journal.pone.0061082

Mery, F. (1970). *The life, history, and magic of the dog.* Madison Square Press/Grosset & Dunlap, New York.

Stoyanov, G.S., Matev, B.K., Valchanov, P., Sapundzhiev, N., & Young, J.R. (2018). The human vomeronasal (Jacobson's) organ: a short review of current conceptions, with an English translation of Potiquet's original text. *Cureus,* 10(5), e2643. https://doi.org/10.7759/cureus.2643

Wang, X., Pipes, L., Trut L.N., Herbeck, Y., Vladimirova, A.V., Gulevich, R.G, Kharlamova, A.V., Johnson, J.L., Acland, G.M., Kukekova, A.V., & Clark, A.G. (2018). Genomic responses to selection for tame/aggressive behaviors in the silver fox (*Vulpes vulpes*). *Proc Natl Acad Sci USA, 115*(41),10398-10403. https://doi.org/10.1073/pnas.1800889115

Zink, M.C. et al. (2014). Evaluation of the risk and age of onset of cancer and behavioral disorders in gonadectomized Vizslas. *Journal of the American Veterinary Medical Association,* 244, 309–319.

Chapter 2

Basaev, A., & De Vital, W. (Directors). (2017). *Red dog* [Film]. Good Dog Enterprises; Woss Group Film Productions.

Krause, H., Ganslosser, U., & Hohlfeld, N.M. (2023). Dog training, keeping and selection around 1300, using the example of Albertus Magnus and Petrus de Crescentiis. *Animals (Basel),* 13(23), 3698. https://doi.org/10.3390/ani13233698

Mech, D. (1970). *The wolf: ecology and behaviour of an endangered species.* The Natural History Press, New York.

Spielberg, S. (Director). (2011). *War horse* [Film]. DreamWorks Pictures; Reliance Entertainment; Amblin Entertainment; The Kennedy/Marshall Company.

UNESCO (2024). *The social impact of sport: unlocking the potential of sport to drive social transformations.* Paris, UNESCO.

Wisdom, J.P., Saedi, G.A., & Green, C.A. (2009). Another breed of "service" animals: STARS study findings about pet ownership and recovery from serious mental illness. *American Journal of Orthopsychiatry,* 79(3), 430-6. https://doi.org/10.1037/a0016812

Xenophon. ([4th Century BE]). *Cynegeticus (on hunting).* Translated by E. C. Marchant & G. W. Bowersock. Harvard University Press.

Chapter 3

Pavlov, I. (1927). *Conditioned reflexes: an investigation of the physiological activity of the cerebral cortex.* Oxford Univ.

Pavlov, I. (1928). *Lectures on conditioned reflexes: twenty-five years of objective study of the higher nervous activity (behaviour) of animals.* (W. H. Gantt, Trans.). Liverwright Publishing Corporation. https://doi.org/10.1037/11081-000

Roach, J. (Director). (2000). *Meet the parents* [Film]. TriBeCa Productions; Nancy Tenenbaum Productions.

Vieira de Castro, A.C., Fuchs, D., Munhoz Morello, G., Pastur, S., de

Sousa, L., & Olsson, A.S. (2020). Does training method matter? Evidence for the negative impact of aversive-based methods on companion dog welfare. *PLoS One*, 15(12), e022502.
https://doi.org/10.1371/journal.pone.0225023

(Domjan, 2003) Michael P. Domjan Title: The Principles of Learning and Behavior, Loose-Leaf Version Contributor: James W. Grau Edition: 7, revised Publisher: Cengage Learning, 2016
ISBN: 1337275247, 9781337275248

Chapter 4

Healy, K., McNally, L., Ruxton, G.D., Cooper, N., & Jackson, A.L. (2013). Metabolic rate and body size are linked with perception of temporal information. *Animal Behaviour*, 86(4), 685-696.
https://doi.org/10.1016/j.anbehav.2013.06.018

Högstedt, G. (1983). Adaptation unto death: function of fear screams. *The American Naturalist*, 121(4), 562-570. University of Chicago Press.
http://www.jstor.org/stable/2460982

Office of National Statistics. (2023). *Deaths by dog attack in the UK 2019 to 2023 including all context of death.* Available from:
https://www.ons.gov.uk/aboutus/transparencyandgovernance/freedomofinformationfoi/deathsbydogattackintheuk2019to2023includingallcontextofdeath

Chapter 5

Office of National Statistics. (2024). *Families and households in the UK 2023.* Available from:
https://www.ons.gov.uk/peoplepopulationandcommunity/birthsdeathsandmarriages/families/bulletins/familiesandhouseholds/2023

Ramnerö, J., Molander, O., Lindner, P., & Carlbring, P. (2019). What can be learned about gambling from a learning perspective? A narrative review. *Nordic Psychology*, 71(4), 303–322
. https://doi.org/10.1080/19012276.2019.1616320

Chapter 6

Galvany-López, P., Martí-Vilar, M., Hidalgo-Fuentes, S., & Cabedo-Peris, J. (2024). The impact of dog-assisted therapy among children and adolescents with autism spectrum disorder: a systematic review. *Children (Basel),* 11(12), 1499.
https://doi.org/10.3390/children11121499

Seyfarth, R., & Cheney, D. (1990). The assessment by vervet monkeys of their own and another species' alarm calls. *Animal Behaviour*, 40(4), 754-764. https://doi.org/10.1016/S0003-3472(05)80704-3

Smith, S., Dell, C.A., Claypool, T., Chalmers D., & Khalid A. (2023). Case report: A community case study of the human-animal bond in animal-assisted therapy: the experiences of psychiatric prisoners with therapy dogs. *Front. Psychiatry*, 14, 1219305.
https://doi.org/10.3389/fpsyt.2023.1219305

Zenithson, Y.N., Pierce, B.J., Otto, C.M., Buechner-Maxwell, V.A., Siracusa, C., & Were, S.R. (2014). The effect of dog–human interaction on cortisol and behavior in registered animal-assisted activity dogs. *Applied Animal Behaviour Science*, 159, 69-81.
https://doi.org/10.1016/j.applanim.2014.07.009

Chapter 7

Bálint, A., Andics, A., Gácsi, M., Gábor, A., Czeibert, K., Luce, C. M., Miklósi, A., & Kröger, R.H.H. (2020). Dogs can sense weak thermal radiation. *Scientific Reports*, 10(1), Article 3736.
https://doi.org/10.1038/s41598-020-60439-y

Billinghurst, I. (1993). *Give your dog a bone. The practical commonsense way to feed dogs for a long healthy life.* Warrigal Publishing Co.

Kiełbik, P., & Witkowska-Piłaszewicz, O. (2024). The relationship between canine behavioral disorders and gut microbiome and future therapeutic perspectives. *Animals (Basel),* 14(14), 2048.
 https://doi.org/10.3390/ani14142048

Linnell, J. D. C., & Cretois, B. (2018). Research for AGRI Committee – The revival of wolves and other large predators and its impact farmers and their livelihood in rural regions of Europe. European Parliament, Policy Department for Structural and Cohesion Policies, Brussels. https://www.europarl.europa.eu/thinktank/en/document/IPOL_STU(2018)617488

Lombardo, M. P. (2012). On the evolution of sport. *Evolutionary Psychology*, 10(1), 1-28. https://doi.org/10.1177/147470491201000101

Moxon, R., Freeman, S.L., Payne, R., Godfrey-Hunt, J., Corr, S., & England, G.C.W. (2023). A prospective cohort study investigating the impact of neutering bitches prepubertally or post-pubertally on physical development. *Animals (Basel)*, 9, 1431
. https://doi.org/10.3390/ani13091431

National Geographic. (n.d.). *Wolves of Yellowstone*. National Geographic. Education. https://education.nationalgeographic.org/resource/wolves-yellowstone/

News in Health (NIH). (2018, February). *The power of pets. Health benefits of human-animal interactions.*
https://newsinhealth.nih.gov/2018/02/power-pets

Ninomiya, H., Akiyama, E., Simazaki, K., Oguri, A., Jitsumuto, M., & Fukuyama, T. (2011). Functional anatomy of the footpad vasculature of dogs: scanning electron microscopy of vascular corrosion casts. *Veterinary Dermatology*, 22(6, 475-81. https://doi.org/10.1111/j.1365-3164.2011.00976.x

Chapter 8

Ennik, I., Liinamo, A.-E., Leighton, E., & van Arendonk, J. (2006). Suitability for field service in 4 breeds of guide dogs. *Journal of Veterinary Behavior: Clinical Applications and Research*, 1(2), 67-74. https://doi.org/10.1016/j.jveb.2006.06.004

Georgevsky, D., Carrasco, J.J., Valenzuela, M., & McGreevy, P. D. (2014). Domestic dog skull diversity across breeds, breed groupings and genetic clusters. *Journal of Veterinary Behavior*, 9(5). https://doi.org/10.1016/j.jveb.2014.04.007

Thelwell, E. L. R. (2019). Paws for thought: A controlled study investigating the benefits of interacting with a house-trained dog on university students' mood and anxiety. *Animals (Basel),* 9(10), 846. https://doi.org/10.3390/ani9100846

Chapter 9

Bailey, R., & Pico, J. (2023, 22 May). Defense mechanisms. StatPearls [Internet], NOH Library of Medicine. Available from: https://www.ncbi.nlm.nih.gov/books/NBK559106/

Birkhead, T., & Schulze-Hagen, K. (2024). A new foundation for the study of bird behaviour: Konrad Lorenz's 'Kumpan' paper of 1935. *Journal of Ornithology*, 165 (1), 5-14. https://doi.org/10.1007/s10336-023-02105-4

Campbell, W. E. (1975). *Behavior problems in dogs.* American Veterinary Publications

Dietz, L., Arnold, A.-M. K., Goerlich-Jansson, V. C., & Vinke, C. M. (2018). The importance of early life experiences for the development of behavioural disorders in domestic dogs. *Behaviour*, 155(2-3), 83-114. https://doi.org/10.1163/1568539X-00003486

Freud, A. (1936). The ego and the mechanisms of defense. In *The Writings of Anna Freud* (vol. 2, pp. 3-191). New York, NY: International Universities Press.

Humphrey, E., & Warner, L. (1934*). Working dogs: An attempt to produce a strain of German shepherds which combines working ability and beauty of conformation.* John Hopkins Press.

More, T. (1516). *Utopia.* Penguin Books.

Chapter 11

Annaud, J-J. (Director). (1981). *The quest for fire* [Film]. International Cinema Corporation; Ciné Trail; Belstar Productions; Stephán Films; Gruskoff Film Players Ltd.

D'Aniello B., Semin G. R., Alterisio A., Aria M., & Scandurra A. (2018). Interspecies transmission of emotional information via chemo-signals: from humans to dogs (*Canis lupus familiaris*). *Animal Cognition,* 21, 67-

78. https://doi.org/10.1007/s10071-017-1139-x

Fusi J, Veronesi MC, Prandi A, Probo M, Faustini M, Peric T. Peripubertal Testosterone, 17β-Estradiol and Progesterone Concentrations in Hair and Nails in Dobermann Dogs. Animals (Basel). 2023 Jul 7;13(13):2241. doi: 10.3390/ani13132241. PMID: 37444039; PMCID: PMC10339877.

[Paul E.S., Mendl M.T. Animal emotion: Descriptive and prescriptive definitions and their implications for a comparative perspective. Appl. Anim. Behav. Sci. 2018;205:202–209. doi: 10.1016/j.applanim.2018.01.008.]

Powdrill-Wells, N., Taylor, S., & Melfi V. (2021). Reducing dog relinquishment to rescue centres due to behaviour problems: Identifying cases to target with an advice intervention at the point of relinquishment request. *Animals,* 11(10), 2766. https://doi.org/10.3390/ani11102766

[Urquiza-Haas E.G., Kotrschal K. The mind behind anthropomorphic thinking: Attribution of mental states to other species. Anim. Behav. 2015;109:167–176. doi: 10.1016/j.anbehav.2015.08.011.]

[Videla M. El antropomorfismo en la relación humano-perro de compañía: ¿Recurso o indicador de patología? In: Díaz Videla M., Olarte A., editors. Antrozoología. Potencial Recurso de Intervención Clínica. Editorial de la Universidad de Flores; Buenos Aires, Argentina: 2017. pp. 49–64]

APPENDIX A

Canine Behavioural Questionnaire (Example)

CANINE BEHAVIOR CONSULTATION QUESTIONNAIRE

GENERAL INFORMATION	
Name:	Date of consultation:
Address:	Postal (zip) code:
	Email:
Phone: Home: ( ) Business: ( )	Fax: ( )
For referred cases: Veterinarian's name & clinic:	Clinic phone:
Clinic address:	
How did you hear about our service?	

PET INFORMATION			
Pet's name:			Date of birth:
Weight:	Sex: M/F	Neutered: Y/N	Age neutered:
Any change after neutering?			
Breed:	Color:		Age obtained:
Where did you obtain this pet?		Breeder (if applicable):	
Describe previous home/homes (if known):			
For what purpose was your pet obtained?			
Behavior of parents or littermates (if known):			
Briefly describe your dog's personality (e.g., quiet, confident, excitable, unruly, bold, stubborn, etc.)			

THE HOME ENVIRONMENT	
Type of food:	How often is your pet fed?
When fed?	Type of treat(s)?
How often do you give treats?	When do you give treats?
List any supplements:	
List all other pets, including species, breed, age, and sex:	
Describe how your pets get along with each other:	
List each family member living in the home (include sex and age of children):	
Describe briefly how your pet gets along with each family member including any problems:	

Anxiety/fear:

Noise sensitivity Y/N If yes, describe:

Phobic/excessive fear/panic Y/N If yes, describe:

Shyness/timidity (non-aggressive), e.g., ears back, cowering, tail tucked, shaking, retreating, hiding, etc. Y/N

If yes, describe any situations not discussed previously where your dog is fearful or overly anxious:

How long after exposure to these events is finished does your dog settle down (i.e., back to normal)?

Additional problems or comments:

DEPARTURE BEHAVIOR SCREENING		
When you go out is your dog confined or crated? Y/N If yes, indicate if crated or what areas are restricted:		
How long is the dog left alone on the average day?		
At what time of the day is your dog left alone?		
How does your dog react when you prepare to leave?		
Has your dog ever been left at a kennel, veterinary office, or with a friend/relative?		
If yes, describe your dog's reaction:		
Is the dog ever alone outdoors? Y/N	How often?	How long (average)?
Where is the dog left when outdoors?		
How does your dog react to being left alone outdoors?		
Does your dog exhibit any behavior problems when you leave it alone? Y/N		
If No, proceed to Reactivity below	**If Yes, please continue to answer the following questions**	
Describe your dog's behavior when left alone at home (list problems and how long after departure they occur):		
Does the behavior differ depending on length of time or time of day left alone?		
How does your dog react at the time of departure (as the last person prepares to leave)?		
Does the behavior differ depending on who is the last to leave?		
What is the dog's reaction at homecomings?		
Have you ever left the dog alone in the car? Y/N If yes, how does it react?		

REACTIVITY – indicate how your dog reacts to each of the following (check all that apply)						
Familiar dogs on property:	Calm ☐	Excited ☐	Ambivalent ☐	Fearful ☐	Friendly ☐	Aggressive ☐
Familiar dogs off property:	Calm ☐	Excited ☐	Ambivalent ☐	Fearful ☐	Friendly ☐	Aggressive ☐
New dogs on property:	Calm ☐	Excited ☐	Ambivalent ☐	Fearful ☐	Friendly ☐	Aggressive ☐
New dogs off property:	Calm ☐	Excited ☐	Ambivalent ☐	Fearful ☐	Friendly ☐	Aggressive ☐
Strangers outside on property:	Calm ☐	Excited ☐	Ambivalent ☐	Fearful ☐	Friendly ☐	Aggressive ☐
Strangers off property:	Calm ☐	Excited ☐	Ambivalent ☐	Fearful ☐	Friendly ☐	Aggressive ☐
Strangers arriving indoors:	Calm ☐	Excited ☐	Ambivalent ☐	Fearful ☐	Friendly ☐	Aggressive ☐
Car rides:	Calm ☐	Excited ☐	Ambivalent ☐	Fearful ☐	Friendly ☐	Aggressive ☐
Thunderstorms/fireworks:	Calm ☐	Excited ☐	Ambivalent ☐	Fearful ☐	Friendly ☐	Aggressive ☐
Other loud noises (e.g., shouting):	Calm ☐	Excited ☐	Ambivalent ☐	Fearful ☐	Friendly ☐	Aggressive ☐

HOUSETRAINING SCREEN

Where is your dog's primary location for elimination?	
On average, how many times a day does your dog a) urinate _____ b) defecate _____	
Is your dog completely housetrained? Y/N	
If Yes, please proceed to Medical Screen	**If No, please continue to answer the following questions**
Does your dog ever eliminate outdoors? Y/N	Do you accompany your dog to its elimination site? Y/N

What is *your dog's* favored location outdoors?
What is *your* preferred location for your dog to eliminate?
What do you do after your dog eliminates in the correct location?
What do you do when you catch your dog soiling in an incorrect location?
Does your dog signal to eliminate? Y/N If yes, describe:
About how often does your dog housesoil?
When is the dog most likely to housesoil?
Does your dog soil in the home by urinating, defecating indoors or both? (circle one)
What are the most likely locations for indoor elimination?
Does your dog housesoil when family members are at home? Y/N If yes, describe:
Does your dog housesoil while you are watching? Y/N If yes, describe:
What do you do when you find urine or stool in the improper location?
Does your dog urine mark? Y/N If yes, describe:

Does your dog ever eliminate in a location where he/she has been sleeping? Y/N	Does your dog ever leak/dribble urine? Y/N
Do you ever confine your dog to a crate? Y/N If yes, does your dog ever eliminate in the crate? Y/N	
Uncontrollable urination when excited? Y/N	Uncontrollable urination when frightened? Y/N
Does urine leak while your dog is a) sleeping? ☐ b) walking? ☐ c) approached by owners? ☐ d) approached by stranger? ☐	

MEDICAL SCREEN

Appetite: Normal ☐   Voracious ☐   Decreased ☐   Picky ☐   Increased ☐   Eats fast ☐

Does your pet have any arthritis or other painful conditions? Y/N If yes, describe:

Have you noticed any deficits in your pet's senses? Y/N If yes, describe:

Does your pet drink or urinate excessively? Y/N If yes, describe:

Stools: Normal ☐   Constipation ☐   Less frequent ☐   More frequent ☐   Soft/diarrhea ☐
Urine: Normal ☐   Infrequent ☐   More frequent ☐   More volume ☐

Does your pet have normal eating and bowel movements? Y/N If no, describe:

Does your pet have any other medical problems? Y/N If yes, describe:

Is your pet presently on any medication? Y/N If yes, describe (include name, dosage, duration):

Has your pet had any laboratory tests (blood, urine, X-rays, etc.)? Y/N If yes, indicate any abnormal findings:

If this is a referred case, please have your veterinarian complete the medical section of this questionnaire

AGGRESSION SCREEN				
Has your pet ever displayed any:	Threatening displays? Y/N	Growling? Y/N	Bite attempts? Y/N	Bites? Y/N
When was the most recent attempt to bite or threaten?				
If yes, has this problem been entirely resolved? Y/N				
Situations causing aggression				
Petting/handling/restraint: growled ☐	attempted to bite ☐	bitten ☐	no aggression ☐	
If yes, describe:				
Eating food or treats: growled ☐	attempted to bite ☐	bitten ☐	no aggression ☐	
If yes, describe:				
Chewing toys/stolen objects: growled ☐	attempted to bite ☐	bitten ☐	no aggression ☐	
If yes, describe:				
Waking up: growled ☐	attempted to bite ☐	bitten ☐	no aggression ☐	
If yes, describe:				
If there have been no signs of aggression (growl, bite attempts, biting) or if it has been entirely resolved, then proceed to next page				
Is aggression the primary reason for today's visit? Y/N				
What is the potential for injury: a) none/preventable ☐	b) minimal ☐	c) moderate ☐	d) severe ☐	
Is the problem serious enough that you will be unable to keep your pet if it is not improved? Y/N				
Is your dog ever aggressive to members of the immediate family? Y/N If yes, who?				
Describe:				
Is your dog ever aggressive to visitors to your home? Y/N Were the people known, strangers, or both? (circle one) Describe:				
Is your dog aggressive to people when off property? Y/N Were the people known, strangers, or both? (circle one) Describe:				
Is there a particular person or type (age, sex, uniforms) that your dog is most likely to threaten or bite?				
Is there a particular location or situation where aggression is most likely to occur?				
Has your dog ever bitten hard enough to break skin or cause injury? Y/N If yes, describe:				
Describe situations where your dog barks, threatens, or growls, but does not bite:				
Does your dog ever display aggression to other animals? Y/N If yes, what animals?				
Describe aggression:				
When your dog threatens or attempts to bite, how do you handle the situation and what is the dog's reaction?				
After your dog has bitten how do you handle the situation and what is the dog's reaction?				
How would you describe your dog's attitude at the time of the aggression? (bold, protective, outgoing, fearful, etc.)				
How would you describe your dog's expression and postures at the time of aggression? (cowering, ears back, tail tucked, hackles raised, retreating, hiding)				

REINFORCER ASSESSMENT

What is your dog's favorite reward?

If you could give your dog ANY food as a reward, what would be the favorite? List the top five:

Other than food, what rewards (e.g., toy, affection) would be most enticing to your dog? List the top five:

DAILY ACTIVITIES AND ROUTINE

Type of exercise/play:

Who exercises/plays?

How often/how long?

Favorite game(s):	Favorite toy(s):

Where is your dog's favored sleeping spot?

Where does the dog sleep at night?

Have you ever used a crate for confinement? Y/N If yes, describe crate and location

Describe the dog's reaction to being crated?

Do you still use a crate? Y/N If no, when and why did you stop?

Briefly describe the usual daily schedule for the family:

TRAINING

Has this pet had obedience training? Y/N ☐ Class ☐ Private instructor ☐ I trained my pet at home

Describe training classes your dog has had (including trainer's name if applicable):

Type of training collar used	Dog's response	Success (rate 1–5; 1 = poor, 5 = good)
None, trained off leash		
Neck collar Y/N If yes, indicate type:		
Remote collar Y/N If yes, indicate type, i.e., shock, citronella, etc.		
Head halter Y/N If yes, indicate type:		
Body harness Y/N If yes, indicate type:		

How would you describe the training? Reward-based ☐ Assertive/domineering ☐ Aversive/mostly corrections ☐ Other: ☐

Briefly describe the training techniques:

What training was most successful?

What training was least successful?

Describe your dog's learning ability:

Is there any ongoing training? Y/N If yes, describe:

List family member(s) with most control:

List family member(s) with least control:

PRINCIPAL COMPLAINT
What is the primary problem? (aggressive, destructive, housesoiling, barking, etc.):
How would you describe the severity of this problem? (circle one)   Mild   Moderate   Severe
Have you considered euthanasia? Y/N Comment:
Please answer all of the following unless they have been entirely covered in another section
When did the problem begin?
What age was your pet when this problem started?
What do you think caused the problem?
Describe the problem, beginning with the most recent incident:
Describe previous incidents:
Describe the first incident:
How often does the problem occur?
Has there been a recent change in frequency or severity? Y/N If yes, describe:
Describe any changes in the home or the pet's health when the problem first started:
What has been done so far to try and correct the problem?
What has been the dog's response?
List any techniques that have been at all successful:
List any techniques that have made the problem worse:
List any drugs (include dosage) tried so far, and the dog's response to medication:
List any other dietary treatments, supplements, or remedies and the dog's response:

For each of the following use a scale of 1 (poor) to 5 (excellent) to indicate how your dog responds			
1. Sit:	Sit-stay 1 minute:	Sit-stay 5 minutes:	Sit-stay 10 minutes:
2. Down:	Down-stay 1 minute:	Down-stay 5 minutes:	Down-stay 10 minutes:
3. Come (indoors):	Come (in yard):	Come (in park):	
4. Heel – with no distractions:		Heel – with distractions:	
5. Give/drop:			
Does your dog know any tricks? Y/N List/explain:			
Can you get your dog to settle on command? Y/N If yes, describe:			

PUNISHMENT

Have you ever used any of the following for punishment or training?		
1. Physical punishment:	Y/N	Dog's reaction:
2. Noise punishment (shaker can/siren):	Y/N	Dog's reaction:
3. Ultrasonic:	Y/N	Dog's reaction:
4. Water sprayer:	Y/N	Dog's reaction:
5. Verbal reprimands:	Y/N	Dog's reaction:
6. Physical handling: Muzzle grasp:	Y/N	Dog's reaction:
Pinning:	Y/N	Dog's reaction:
7. Time-out:	Y/N	Dog's reaction:
8. Booby traps/repellants:	Y/N	Dog's reaction:
What punishment is most effective?		
Does any punishment make the problem worse? Y/N If yes, describe:		
Has punishment ever led to threatening behavior or aggression? Y/N Explain:		
Does your dog respond differently to punishment from different family members? Y/N If yes, describe:		

HANDLING

How does the dog react to the following types of handling?	
Nail trimming?	Ear cleaning?
Brushing?	Bathing?
Rubbing belly?	Patting head?
Grabbing collar?	Being lifted?
Rolling over?	Teeth brushing?
Giving pills?	Giving liquid medications?
Hugging/kissing?	

| **MISCELLANEOUS** |||
(please answer any of the following that have not been previously discussed)		
Disobedient:		
Jumps up (owners) Y/N	Jumps up (strangers) Y/N	Won't come when called Y/N
Nips/grabs with mouth Y/N	Only listens when feels like it Y/N	Pushy/demanding Y/N
On furniture where not allowed Y/N	In rooms where not permitted Y/N	
Exploratory: Normal ☐ Infrequent ☐ Increased ☐ Excessive ☐		
Activity: Normal ☐ Lazy/inactive ☐ Restless/won't settle ☐ Highly active ☐ Overactive ☐		
Sleep: Normal ☐ Increased ☐ Less frequent ☐ Restless sleep ☐ Night waking ☐		
Stool eating: Y/N If yes, own stools ☐ other dogs ☐ cats ☐ other:		
Garbage raiding: Y/N Food stealing: Y/N Eats non-food items (pica) Y/N Licks objects Y/N		
If yes to any of above, describe:		
Destructive: Chewing Y/N Digging Y/N Other:		
If yes, describe:		
Grooming: Normal grooming Y/N Excessive grooming/licking Y/N Self-injurious Y/N		
If there is abnormal grooming, describe:		
Repetitive/compulsive/unusual activity: Tail chasing ☐ Sucking ☐ Star gazing ☐ Fly chasing ☐ Light chasing ☐ Staring ☐ Other:		
If yes to any of above, describe:		
Chasing Y/N If yes, describe:		
Hunting/predation Y/N If yes, describe:		
Sexual habits: Masturbation Y/N Mounting Y/N Roaming/running away Y/N		
Describe any undesirable sexual habits:		
Vocalization: Barking Y/N Howling Y/N Whining Y/N		
If yes, describe:		

APPENDIX B

Campbell Test Scoring Sheet

Puppy (color, sex) _____ Litter _____ Date _____

TEST	PURPOSE	SCORE	#	√
Social Attraction: Place the puppy in test area. From a few feet away, the tester coaxes the pup to her/him by clapping hands gently and kneeling down. Tester must coax in a direction away from the point where it entered the testing area.	Degree of social attraction, confidence or dependence.	Came readily, tail up, jumped, bit at hands	1	
		Came readily, tail up, pawed, licked at hands	2	
		Came readily, tail up.	3	
		Came readily, tail down.	4	
		Came hesitantly, tail down.	5	
		Did not come at all	6	
Following: The tester stands up and slowly walks away encouraging the pup to follow by lightly clapping hands and using verbal encouragement. Make sure the pup sees you walk away.	Degree of following attraction. Not following indicates independence.	Followed readily, tail up, got underfoot, bit at feet	1	
		Followed readily, tail up, got underfoot	2	
		Followed readily, tail up.	3	
		Followed readily, tail down.	4	
		Followed hesitantly, tail down.	5	
		No following, or went away.	6	
Restraint: Crouch down and gently roll the pup on his back and hold it with one hand for a full 30 seconds. Do not use too much pressure. The object is not to keep it on tis back but to test its response to being placed in that position.	Degree of dominant or submissive tendency. How it accepts stress when socially and/or physically dominated.	Struggled fiercely, flailed, bit.	1	
		Struggled fiercely, flailed.	2	
		Settled, struggled, settled with some eye contact.	3	
		Struggled. Then settled.	4	
		No struggle.	5	
		No struggle, straining to avoid eye contact.	6	
Social Dominance: Let pup stand up or sit and gently stroke him from the head to back while you crouch beside him. See if he will lick your face, an indication of a forgiving nature. Continue stroking until a recognizable behavior is established.	Degree of acceptance of social dominance pup may try to dominate by jumping and nipping or it is independent and walks away.	Jumped, pawed, bit, growled	1	
		Jumped, pawed.	2	
		Cuddles up to tester and tries to lick face.	3	
		Squirmed, licked at hands.	4	
		Rolled over, licked at hands.	5	
		Went away and stayed away.	6	
Elevation Dominance: Bend over and cradle the pup under its belly, fingers interlaced, palms up and elevate just off the ground. Hold it there for 30 seconds.	Degree of accepting dominance while in position of no control.	Struggled fiercely, bit, growled	1	
		Struggled fiercely,	2	
		No struggle, relaxed.	3	
		Struggled, settled, licked.	4	
		Rolled over, licked at hands.	5	
		No struggle, froze.	6	
Retrieving: Crouch beside pup and attract its attention with crumpled up paper ball. When the pup shows interest and is watching, toss the object 1 to 2 meters in front of pup.	Degree of willingness to work with a human. High correlation between ability to retrieve and successful guide dogs, obedience dogs, field trial dogs.	Chases object, picks up object and runs away.	1	
		Chases object, stands over object, does not return.	2	
		Chases object and returns with object to tester.	3	
		Chases object and returns without object.	4	
		Starts to chase object, loses interest	5	
		Does not chase object.	6	

ABOUT THE AUTHOR

Gianni Valesini is a canine behaviour specialist with over three decades of hands-on experience working with dogs and their owners. Originally from southern Italy, Gianni's journey into the world of dogs began not from a place of confidence, but from a childhood encounter that sparked both fear and fascination. That encounter eventually grew into a lifelong passion and profession. After moving to London in the mid-1990s with his beloved Dobermann, Reni, Gianni co-founded V.I.Pets, one of the first premium dog walking and training services in Central London. Over the years, he has worked with hundreds of dogs, rescue cases, puppies, working lines, and misunderstood family pets, applying a practical, empathetic, and science-informed approach. His style blends classical learning theory with real-world insight, offering a training method that is both effective and humane. Whether he's helping a reactive terrier settle into apartment life or guiding a young Labrador through their first recall, Gianni believes that good training is about building a language of trust between humans and dogs. This book is a culmination of his experience, philosophy, and deep respect for the emotional lives of dogs.

  vipetslondon

www.vipets-london.com

NOTES

www.ingramcontent.com/pod-product-compliance
Ingram Content Group UK Ltd.
Pitfield, Milton Keynes, MK11 3LW, UK
UKHW051841041025
463504UK00007B/41/J